ANARCHY OR CHAOS

OLE BIRK LAURSEN

Anarchy or Chaos

M. P. T. Acharya and the Indian Struggle for Freedom

OXFORD
UNIVERSITY PRESS

Oxford University Press is a department of the
University of Oxford. It furthers the University's objective
of excellence in research, scholarship, and education
by publishing worldwide.

Oxford   New York

Auckland   Cape Town   Dar es Salaam   Hong Kong   Karachi
Kuala Lumpur   Madrid   Melbourne   Mexico City   Nairobi
New Delhi   Shanghai   Taipei   Toronto

With offices in

Argentina   Austria   Brazil   Chile   Czech Republic   France   Greece
Guatemala   Hungary   Italy   Japan   Poland   Portugal   Singapore
South Korea   Switzerland   Thailand   Turkey   Ukraine   Vietnam

Oxford is a registered trade mark of Oxford University Press
in the UK and certain other countries.

Published in the United States of America by
Oxford University Press
198 Madison Avenue, New York, NY 10016

Copyright © Ole Birk Laursen 2023

All rights reserved. No part of this publication may be reproduced,
stored in a retrieval system, or transmitted, in any form or by any means,
without the prior permission in writing of Oxford University Press,
or as expressly permitted by law, by license, or under terms agreed with
the appropriate reproduction rights organization. Inquiries concerning
reproduction outside the scope of the above should be sent to the
Rights Department, Oxford University Press, at the address above.

You must not circulate this work in any other form
and you must impose this same condition on any acquirer.

Library of Congress Cataloging-in-Publication Data is available
Ole Birk Laursen.
Anarchy or Chaos: M. P. T. Acharya and the Indian Struggle
for Freedom.
ISBN: 9780197752159

Printed in Great Britain by Bell and Bain Ltd, Glasgow

CONTENTS

Acknowledgments	vii
Note on Text and Translation	xi
List of Abbreviations	xiii
List of Illustrations	xv
Introduction	1

PART I
NATIONALISM, EXILE, AND WAR, 1906–19

1. Nationalism in the British Empire	27
2. Exile in Europe	37
3. The Ghadar Period	51
4. War against the British Empire	57
5. International Socialism and World Peace	71

PART II
REVOLUTION AND COMMUNISM, 1919–22

6. Revolution in Russia	87
7. The Indian Communist Party	101
8. Anti-Communist Activities	115

PART III
ANTICOLONIALISM, ANARCHISM, AND ANTI-MILITARISM, 1922–34

9. Anticolonialism and Anarchism in Weimar Berlin	125

CONTENTS

10. Anti-Imperialism and Anti-Militarism   143
11. Ultra-Leftists and Outsiders   157

PART IV
ESCAPE AND RETURN TO INDIA, 1934–45

12. Escape from Europe   171
13. Return to India   185

PART V
FREEDOM, VIOLENCE, AND ANARCHY, 1945–54

14. Towards Freedom   199
15. Violent Independence   213
16. Anarchy   223

Epilogue: Afterlife of an Indian Revolutionary   239

Notes   247
Published Works by M. P. T. Acharya   297
Bibliography   313
Index   329

ACKNOWLEDGEMENTS

This book has preoccupied my life for almost ten years, during which time I have relied heavily on many friends and colleagues for intellectual debates, emotional support, or just simple questions, not least the many scholars and archivists across the world whom I have never met but only corresponded with. In many ways, my thinking about M. P. T. Acharya started in 2008 when I joined the AHRC-funded collaborative project 'Making Britain: South Asian Visions of Home and Abroad, 1870–1940', led by my PhD supervisor Susheila Nasta as well as Elleke Boehmer and Ruvani Ranasinha. I am thankful not only to them, but also to Rehana Ahmed, Sumita Mukherjee, and Florian Stadtler, with whom I worked closely on the project. I also learned a lot from Rozina Visram and Lyn Innes in those days. A special thanks also to my PhD supervisor David Johnson, whose advice, feedback, and comments I have continued to depend on. At the Open University, Alex Tickell has always generously offered help and assistance. Constance Bantman's support and advice has inspired and helped me in so many ways for which I am ever grateful. The book would not have happened without Frederik Byrn Køhlert, whose friendship and intellectual conversations for more than twenty years have carried me through difficult times. A special thanks also to Lisa Caviglia, who patiently listened to my stories and read my work.

I am thankful to the Carlsberg Foundation for awarding me a postdoctoral research fellowship at the University of Copenhagen, which allowed me to undertake initial research, as well as the help and encouragement of Ravinder Kaur. A short-term fellowship from the

ACKNOWLEDGEMENTS

Danish Institute in Rome allowed me time to write, and a visiting research fellowship from the Fondation Maison des Sciences de l'Homme (FMSH) found a home at the Centre d'histoire de l'Asie contemporaine (CHAC) at Université Paris 1—Sorbonne, where Christina Wu, Sara Legrandjacques, and Quentin Gasteuil helped me think through ideas. I benefitted greatly from a research fellowship at the International Institute for Asian Studies (IIAS) in Leiden, where staff and colleagues Philippe Peycam, Lisa Caviglia, Rocco Cestola, Joppan George, Zoë Goodman, Ben Linder, and Christian de Pee offered friendship and intellectual conversations. At the Leibniz-Zentrum Moderner Orient, Berlin (ZMO), I was lucky to have the guidance and help of Heike Liebau and archivist Alisher Karabaev.

I am indebted to many friends and scholars who, in various ways, have offered comments or clarifications, including Matthew S. Adams, Saptadeepa Banerjee, Nirode K. Barooah, Dave Berry, Jesús Cháirez-Garza, Stuart Christie, Alan de Siqueira Coutinho, Oliver Crawford, Vadim Damier, Andrew Davies, Smaran Dayal, Marie-Genevieve Dezes, Pragya Dhital, Anatoly Dubovik, Marianne Enckell, Danny Evans, Martyn Everett, Maria Framke, Michael Gilligan, Tom Goyens, Robert Graham, Ramachandra Guha, Tim Harper, Laura Galián, K. Ullas Karanth, Ruth Kinna, Robert Kramm, Julia Lange, Stephen Legg, Carl Levy, Jonathan Loar, Stephen Mackinnon, Kama Maclean, Gregor May, Natalia Mikaberidze, Fredrik Petersson, Maia Ramnath, Barry Pateman, Gautam Pemmaraju, Dominique Petit, Shaun Pitt, Bhavya Ramakrishnan, Maria Ridda, Hartmut Rübner, Sukhraj Singh, Uwe Sonnenberg, David Struthers, Lydia Syson, Hikaru Tanaka, Vineet Thakur, Sarthak Tomar, Asya Vigdorchik, Shawn Wilbur, Liz Willis, Jim Yeoman, Kenyon Zimmer, and Andrew Zonneveld.

The project has required extensive research in archives across the world, many of which I have not been able to visit in person and therefore relied on archivists and staff on site. I am particularly grateful to the staff at Arbetarrörelsens Arkiv och Bibliotek; Biblioteca y archivo de sociología y economía; British Library, London; Cambridge South Asian Archive; Center for International Research on Anarchism, Japan; Centre International de Recherches sur l'Anarchisme, Lausanne; David M. Rubenstein Rare Book & Manuscript Library,

viii

ACKNOWLEDGEMENTS

Duke University; Houghton Library, Harvard University; Institut Français d'Histoire Sociale, Archives nationales, Paris; International Institute of Social History, Amsterdam; Leibniz-Zentrum Moderner Orient, Berlin; Library of Congress, Washington D.C.; Mitchell Library, Glasgow; Mundaneum Archives, Mons; National Archives, Kew; National Archives of India, New Delhi; National Archives and Records Administration, College Park, Maryland; Politisches Archiv des Auswärtigen Amts, Berlin; Russian State Archive for Social and Political History, Moscow; Sabarmati Ashram Preservation and Memorial Trust, Ahmedabad; Joseph A. Labadie Collection, Special Collections Library, University of Michigan, Ann Arbor; Stockholm City Archive, Stockholm; Swedish National Archives, Stockholm; Tamil Nadu Archives, Chennai; and Walter P. Reuther Archive, Archives of Labor and Urban Affairs, Wayne State University, Detroit.

Although we only met in person a few weeks before submitting the manuscript, I have benefited greatly from numerous email exchanges with Lina Bernstein over the years. Lina also put me in contact with Sophie Seifalian who kindly shared and gave permission to use photos of Acharya and Nachman.

I am grateful to Michael Dwyer at Hurst & Co. for taking a chance on this project and to Alice Clarke and Mei Jayne Yew for invaluable editorial guidance. I am also grateful to the anonymous reviewers who provided helpful comments along the way.

Lastly, I am grateful to my parents for always supporting me.

NOTE ON TEXT AND TRANSLATION

In historiography and historical primary sources, Acharya's name is variously given as Mandayam Parthasarathy Bhayankaram Acharya, M. P. B. T. Acharya, or M. P. Tirumalachari. However, in a letter to the Office of the Secretary of State for India, Director of Passport Department, London, England, 8 January 1926, he stated his name as: 'Mandayam Prativadi-Bhayankaram Tirumalacharya, Madras, India, always signing for brevity's sake as follows: M. P. T. Acharya'. Hence, I have used this as standard throughout. In his writings, Acharya published under the names 'Mr. Bhayankar', 'Acharya', 'M. A.', 'M. Acharya', 'M. P. T. Acharya', 'P. T. Acharya', and the pseudonym 'Marco Polo', but for ease of understanding I have used Acharya throughout. In the List of Works, I have used the original author name, e.g., Marco Polo. In other cases, where names and spellings vary in sources and historiography, I have made a judgment on most common usage, e.g., Hem Day (not Marcel Dieu), E. Armand (not Ernest-Lucien Juin), and Lotvala (not Lotwalla). For Japanese and Chinese names, I have followed standard conventions, i.e., for Takamure Itsue, Takamure is the surname. Acharya's writings were often reprinted or published simultaneously in various periodicals and in different languages, but wherever an English version exists, this is used for reference. All translations are my own, unless otherwise stated. The names of countries and cities reflect usage and spelling conventions appropriate to the period under discussion, but current names are listed in brackets after first mention, e.g., Bombay (now Mumbai) and Constantinople (now Istanbul).

LIST OF ABBREVIATIONS

AA	Auswärtiges Amts
AITUC	All-India Trade Union Congress
ARA	American Relief Administration
BLC	British Llano Circle
CAPE	Council for Action and Propaganda in the East
CNT-FAI	Confederación Nacional del Trabajo/Federación Anarquista Ibérica
Comintern	Communist International
CPI	Communist Party of India
CRIA	Commission for International Anarchist Relations
CUP	Committee of Union and Progress
DCI	British Department of Criminal Intelligence
DSC	Dutch-Scandinavian Committee
ECCI	Executive Committee of the Communist International
GPU	Russian State Political Directorate
HAA	Hindusthan Association of America
HACE	Hindusthan Association of Central Europe
HAPC	Hindusthan Association of the Pacific Coast
IAC	International Antimilitarist Commission
IAMB	International Anti-Militarist Bureau against War and Reaction
ICP	Indian Communist Party
IHRS	Indian Home Rule Society
IIC	Indian Independence Committee
IIS	Indian Institute of Sociology

LIST OF ABBREVIATIONS

INC	Indian National Congress
INK	Indiska Nationalkommittén
INP	Indian Nationalist Party
INSIB	Indian News Service and Information Bureau
IRA	Indian Revolutionary Association
IRACC	Indian Revolutionaries Abroad Commemoration Committee
IWMA	International Working Men's Association
IWW	Industrial Workers of the World
JAF	Japanese Anarchist Federation
KAPD	Kommunistische Arbeiter-Partei Deutschlands
KPD	Kommunistische Partei Deutschlands
LACO	League Against Colonial Oppression
LAI	League Against Imperialism
LSI	Libertarian Socialist Institute
NEP	New Economic Policy
NfO	Nachrichtenstelle für den Orient
NKID	People's Commissariat for Foreign Affairs
PAICRC	Provisional All-India Central Revolutionary Committee
SAC	Sveriges Arbetares Centralorganisation
Sovinterprop	Soviet International Propaganda
SPRI	Secrétariat Provisoire aux Relations Internationales
WRI	War Resisters' International
YHA	Young Hindusthan Association

LIST OF ILLUSTRATIONS

Every effort has been made to contact all copyright holders. The publisher will be pleased to amend in future editions any errors or omissions brought to its attention.

1. Lower Secondary Examination Diploma, Hindu High School, Triplicane, 16 April 1902. *Old German Files, 1909–21, 8000–1396, M1085, North American Records Administration.*

2. M. P. T. Acharya, United States, *c.* 1914. *Old German Files, 1909–21, 8000–1396, M1085, North American Records Administration.*

3. Virendranath Chattopadhyaya, Stockholm, 28 February 1919. *SE / SSA / Överståthållarämbetet för polisärenden 4 / Utlänningsavdelningen / E III a vol. 7, no. 1985, Stockholm City Archive.*

4. A group of delegates arrive in Petrograd for the Second Congress of the Communist International, Petrograd and Moscow, 19 July–8 August 1920. An official greets the French communists Marcel Cachin and Louis-Oscar Frossard, flanked by Karl Radek on the left and Grigori Zinoviev on the right. Behind Radek, looking at the camera, is M. P. T. Acharya. *Boris Souvarine Collection at the Graduate Institute, Geneva.*

5. Delegates leaving the Smolny, Petrograd, for the formal opening session of the Second Congress of the Communist International, 19 July 1920. Acharya can be seen at the bottom left-hand corner. *Boris Souvarine Collection at the Graduate Institute, Geneva.*

6. Opening session of the Second Congress of the Communist

LIST OF ILLUSTRATIONS

International, Tauride Palace, Petrograd, 19 July 1920. Indian delegates sitting second section from the bottom of the photograph, third row of desks. From the aisle and left to right: Abani Mukherji, M. P. T. Acharya, Evelyn Trent, M. N. Roy, Mohamed Shafique. *Russian State Archive of Socio-political History (RGASPI), 389/1/19.*

7. After the opening session at the Tauride Palace, the delegates marched to the Square of the Victims of the Revolution, Petrograd, 19 July 1920. Acharya can be seen in the lower left-hand corner. *Boris Souvarine Collection at the Graduate Institute, Geneva.*

8. Procession to the Square of the Victims of the Revolution, Petrograd, 19 July 1920. *Boris Souvarine Collection at the Graduate Institute, Geneva.*

9. M. P. T. Acharya, wedding photograph, 1922. *Courtesy of Sophie Seifalian and Lina Bernstein.*

10. Magda Nachman, wedding photograph, 1922. *Courtesy of Sophie Seifalian and Lina Bernstein.*

11. IWMA founding meeting, Berlin, 25 December 1922–2 January 1923. Back row, left to right: Hermann Ritter; Theo Schuster; Armando Borghi; Edvin Lindstam; Johan Gerhard van Zelm; Theo Dissel. Middle row, left to right: Orlando Ángel; Augustin Souchy; Alexander Schapiro; Rudolf Rocker; Alibrando Giovannetti; Bernard Lansink Jr. Front row, left to right: Frans Severin; Virgilia d'Andrea Borghi; Diego Abad de Santillan. *A Wertheim, International Institute of Social History, Amsterdam.*

12. Mandayam Acharya, residence permit, Berlin, 12 May 1925. *Courtesy of Politisches Archiv des Auswärtigen Amts, Berlin, Germany, RZ 207/78315.*

13. M. Acharya, IAMB membership card, 20 August 1929. *Archief IAMV, International Institute of Social History, Amsterdam.*

14. Hindusthan Association of Central Europe, Berlin, protest meeting against Gandhi's arrest, 6 May 1930. Saumyendranath Tagore is speaking, Acharya is sitting on the floor in the back, and to the right is Jaya Surya Naidu. *Bild 102-09732, Bundesarchiv, Berlin.*

xvi

LIST OF ILLUSTRATIONS

15. M. P. T. Acharya, Bombay, *c.* 1935. *Courtesy of Sophie Seifalian and Lina Bernstein.*

16. Close-up of M. P. T. Acharya, Bombay, *c.* 1935. *Courtesy of Sophie Seifalian and Lina Bernstein.*

17. M. P. T. Acharya, Bombay, 13 September 1935. Back of the photo reads: 'Myself on a hot night on my bed. Before me on the table an AEG electric fan'. *Courtesy of Sophie Seifalian and Lina Bernstein.*

18. M. P. T. Acharya, *c.* 1935. *Courtesy of Sophie Seifalian and Lina Bernstein.*

19. Magda Nachman outside their home at 56 Ridge Road, Bombay, *c.* 1937. *Courtesy of Sophie Seifalian and Lina Bernstein.*

20. Institute of Foreign Languages, Bombay, 13 April 1951. Nachman exhibition, the day after her death. Acharya with the back to the camera. *Free Press Bulletin (14 February 1951). Author's own collection.*

M. P. T. Acharya, *c.* 1950s. *Courtesy of Mar y Sol Gracia Graells, Victor Garcia Papers, B.A.S.E., Montady, Spain.*

INTRODUCTION

'Let them call me an anarchist.'

In November 1922, the Indian revolutionary M. P. T. Acharya fled Russia with his new wife, the Russian artist Magda Nachman, and shortly thereafter arrived in Berlin on a Russian passport. He had spent the last three and a half years in Russia, Afghanistan, and Central Asia, associating with proto-nationalists, pan-Islamists, *Muhajirs*, communists, Bolsheviks, and anarchists, all as part of the struggle for Indian freedom from British rule. As a delegate of the Indian Revolutionary Association (IRA), a revolutionary body he had formed with Abdur Rabb in Kabul in late 1919, he had attended the Second Congress of the Communist International in July 1920, and he was one of the founding members of the exiled Indian Communist Party (ICP) in Tashkent in October 1920. However, shortly after the formation of the ICP, Acharya fell out with the domineering M. N. Roy, who had captivated Vladimir Lenin at the Second Congress, and he was subsequently expelled from the party in December 1920. Having become critical of the Bolshevik regime and the ICP and now associating with anarchists, Acharya was no longer tolerated in Moscow and, in November 1922, he and Nachman managed to escape to Germany. In Berlin, perhaps not knowing where else to go, Acharya and Nachman returned to Leibnizstrasse 42, where he had briefly lived during the First World War, in the Charlottenburg district, home to many Indians in the interwar period.

From the safety of Berlin, Acharya wrote to Igor Reisner, the secretary to Yakov Suritz, first Russian ambassador to Afghanistan, who had accompanied him to Kabul in the autumn of 1919, and explained his hurried flight from Russia. According to Acharya, now considered a counter-revolutionary, the Russian State Political Directorate (GPU) had issued a warrant for his arrest and directed border guards not to let him pass. Miraculously, he said, he managed to escape. In turn, Acharya accused the Bolsheviks of repressing true revolutionaries such as the anarchists with whom he was now aligned. In fact, he wrote defiantly to Reisner: 'let them call me an anarchist'.[1] In Berlin, he intended to work with his old friend Virendranath Chattopadhyaya, known as 'Chatto', to expose the brutalities of the Bolshevik regime, unless they stopped persecuting dissenting revolutionaries and expelled Roy from the ICP. This did not happen, of course, and in the following years, as Acharya aligned himself with the anarchists, he campaigned vigorously against Roy and the Bolsheviks. Throughout the next three decades, based in Berlin and Bombay, Acharya would become India's most prominent anarchist activist and theoretician, charting new territories in Indian anticolonial thought. Acharya's flight from Russia and his letter to Reisner illustrate several key issues and questions that are central to understanding the multifarious and complex nature of his trajectory through the underbelly of global political events: nationalism, anticolonialism, exile, war, revolution, communism, anarchism, pacifism, freedom, and independence. These issues preoccupy this intellectual biography of Acharya, which accounts for the complex and entangled histories of anticolonialism and anarchism through a detailed exploration of his actions, wanderings, thoughts, and connections with key actors of the time.

Nationalism, exile, and war

By the time Acharya arrived in Berlin in 1922, he had a long track record of revolutionary activities. Born in Triplicane, Madras, in India in 1887, Acharya belonged to a particular generation for whom, as Tim Harper puts it, 'it seemed that never before had the future been so open to imaginative possibilities' and who, in response to colonial repression, 'focused their gaze on more distant, worldly horizons'.[2] In the early twentieth century, Acharya had been involved in nationalist activities in India, editing the nationalist paper *India* in Madras and Pondicherry in 1907 to 1908, before having to flee India to evade

INTRODUCTION

arrest by the British authorities. In November 1908, he arrived in Marseille, proceeding immediately to Paris and then on to London, where he lodged at the notorious India House, then under the leadership of Vinayak Damodar Savarkar and his right-hand man V. V. S. Aiyar. Leaving London in August 1909 on an ill-fated mission to support the Rifs against the Spanish invaders in Morocco, this venture was quickly abandoned and brought Acharya to Lisbon before he landed in Paris, where he worked with Madame Cama, Lala Har Dayal, Chatto, and S. R. Rana, as well as with Egyptian nationalists and Russian revolutionaries in exile. All of them became central figures to Acharya's life throughout the next years and decades. In November 1910, Acharya first visited Berlin, working as a tea salesman, before he moved to Munich and then to Constantinople in 1911 to collaborate with Young Turks in the Committee of Union and Progress (CUP). Acharya was a well-known Indian revolutionary by that time and the British intelligence service watched him closely. In the summer of 1912, however, he escaped the watchful eyes of the British and left for New York City. During his two-year sojourn in the US, he associated with Ghadarites, exiled Irish revolutionaries, and anarchists, before his old friend Chatto beckoned him to Berlin shortly after the outbreak of the First World War.

Exploring Acharya's early years in India, his initiation into nationalist politics, and journey into exile opens a window onto the Indian nationalist movement of the early twentieth century. It allows for a closer look at the radicalisation and militancy of Indian anticolonialism at the time and the British authorities' response to this. The book, indeed, examines the workings of British intelligence and surveillance and the development of inter-imperial collaborations between European empires. Narrating the story of Acharya's escape from India, furthermore, enables a fresh view of the politics of exile and unveils both the brutality of British colonialism in India as well as of liberalism within Britain. It highlights the existence of anticolonial movements beyond the British empire, and the radical alliances that existed with sympathisers, anticolonialists, and other subject nations across Europe and Constantinople. Perhaps the most radical of exiled anticolonial movements was the Ghadar movement in North America. Tracing Acharya's flight to New York, his two years in North America, and return to Europe at the outbreak of the First World War, this biography asks:

3

how do we understand the global reach of Indian anticolonialism in the first decades of the twentieth century? What does this mean for our understanding of nationalism as an international project?

Acharya joined the Indian Independence Committee (IIC) in Berlin alongside Chatto, Har Dayal, Chempakaraman Pillai, L. P. Varma, and Taraknath Das, among others, and in 1915 ventured to Constantinople. Back in the Ottoman capital, Acharya took part in Indian-German missions across the Middle East to sabotage British war efforts, to recruit Indian soldiers into their fold, and to instigate a revolution in India from neighbouring Afghanistan. Despite German financial backing, none of these ambitious plans resulted in the armed revolution hoped for. Instead, Acharya and Chatto placed their faith in international socialism and world peace when they moved to Stockholm in May 1917 to attend the International Socialist Congress. However, after almost two years in the Swedish capital, negotiating Indian independence with European socialists and forging alliances with other anticolonial revolutionaries and subject peoples, they had made little progress and came up against the limits of international socialism.

The First World War raised several questions about anti-imperial struggles: if this was an imperialist war, why would Indian nationalists ally themselves with another European colonial power? They were not alone in this, so why is it important to understand how Indian anticolonialists forged new alliances with other colonial and subject nations? In what ways was Indian nationalism anti-British or anti-imperial? This biography deals with these questions. It explores the socialist bid to end the imperialist project as well as the complex relationship between socialism and anti-imperialism. Doing so, it argues that neither the German Kaiserreich nor the second international socialists were genuinely supportive of Indian independence, thus exposing the limits of European anti-British alliances and ideas of internationalism.

Revolution and communism

The Russian Revolution set in motion new forces that inspired hope for independence across the colonial world. Motivated by the Bolshevik promise for self-determination, Acharya and a group of Indian revolutionaries travelled to Russia in June 1919. After a fateful

INTRODUCTION

meeting with Lenin in July, the group left for Afghanistan, where Acharya soon broke away and set up the IRA with his comrade Abdur Rabb. While sympathetic to Bolshevism, the IRA remained independent from the new regime and refused to submit the struggle for independence to another foreign government. Having by then encountered several Russian anarchists, the IRA's independence and Acharya's changing political convictions brought him into disfavour with the Bolsheviks and the ICP, forcing him to flee another totalitarian regime in late 1922.

Acharya's time in Russia, Afghanistan, and Central Asia raises important questions about the turn from international socialism to Lenin's promise of self-determination. In other words, what was the relationship between Bolshevik communism and anticolonialism? How did the Russian civil war in Central Asia impact Indian anticolonial struggles in the area? How did Acharya remain independent from and challenge a new authoritarian regime? Most importantly, in the struggle for freedom, what was the relationship between Bolshevism, communism, and anarchism? Tackling these questions, the book contributes to a global history of communism from a South Asian perspective.

The first fifteen years of Acharya's life in exile were characterised by movement and action, resistance and reaction, always negotiating global revolutionary politics with the aim of liberating India from British rule. Wherever there was an exiled Indian revolutionary group, Acharya was there. In many ways, the struggle for Indian independence found its maturity outside India, among intellectuals, sailors, and workers in exile, in conversation with other colonised and subject peoples and inspired by global thoughts on revolution and self-determination. Revolutionaries like Acharya lived itinerant lives, often travelling under false names and nationalities, smuggling banned literature and arms, connecting and disrupting notions of periphery and centre, and, in doing so, contributed to shaping global anticolonial radical communities.[3]

Anticolonialism, anarchism, and anti-militarism in Weimar Berlin

While never a leader in the Indian revolutionary movement in exile, in Weimar era Berlin, Acharya became fiercely independent and

5

charted new intellectual territories. Where his first fifteen years in exile were marked by frequent mobility, nationalist agitation, and militancy in pursuit of Indian freedom, his twelve years in Berlin were characterised by a persistent intellectual engagement with the true meaning of freedom. What Acharya had learned from his experiences as an exiled Indian anticolonial revolutionary was that freedom, in any meaningful sense of the word, could only come from subject peoples themselves and without native rulers governing the lives of the masses. Indeed, whereas most anticolonial revolutionaries agitated along parliamentarian lines, appealing to governments for concessions or placing their faith in Bolshevism, Acharya articulated an entirely different understanding of freedom from all forms of oppression.

Shortly after his return to Berlin in 1922, inspired by anarchists he had met in Russia, Acharya attended the founding meeting of the anarcho-syndicalist International Working Men's Association (IWMA) and soon started sending anarchist literature to India's left-wing leaders and organisations. While not abandoning his friendships and connections with other Indians in Berlin, he leaned more towards anarchism, but synthesised his thoughts on anarchism with anticolonialism. Acharya relied on an ever-growing network of anarchists, within Berlin and across the world, including the German IWMA secretary Augustin Souchy, the British editor of *Freedom* Thomas H. Keell, the veteran Russian American anarchist Alexander Berkman, and the French anarchist and editor of *L'En Dehors* E. Armand (Ernest-Lucien Juin). Among the anarchists, Acharya occupied a unique position as the only Indian and the most prominent figure from the British colonial world. In conversation with such anarchists, Acharya weaved together the energies of anti-authoritarianism and anti-imperialism that mutated into a series of 'countercultural revolutionary practices' through the 'politics of friendship'.[4] At the same time, this is not to overlook the contentious dialogues and 'difficult solidarities', as Priyamvada Gopal notes, that transformed these affective and political communities.[5] Indeed, as the book reveals, Acharya was also subject to prejudice within the anarchist movement, although minor in comparison to the outright racism of German society in general.

In his pursuit of freedom, Acharya connected anticolonial anarchism with cooperativism and pacifism. From the mid-1920s, he took

INTRODUCTION

a great interest in cooperative and utopian experiments across the world and envisioned similar ideas for India. This was also partly inspired by Gandhi's notion of village communes and for Acharya led to a life-long engagement with pacifism, anti-militarism, and Gandhism. Abandoning the militancy of early twentieth century Indian nationalism, Acharya turned to pacifism and joined the International Anti-Militarist Bureau (IAMB) but remained ambivalent about Gandhi's *Satyagraha* campaign, then underway in India. Articulating these ideas in early 1930s Berlin, however, was dangerous. The rise of fascism and Nazism sent Acharya and Nachman on the run again. At the suggestion of Subhas Chandra Bose, and with the help of some exiled Chinese revolutionaries in Berlin, Acharya and Nachman escaped to Switzerland and France, living clandestinely for a year. Acharya returned to India in April 1935, and Nachman followed a year later. Acharya's life in Weimar era Berlin reveals a great deal about the spaces of anticolonialism that expanded beyond the British Empire, embracing new articulations of resistance, while being under constant threats from authoritarianism in various guises.

Though feeling isolated in Bombay after almost twenty-seven years in exile, Acharya remained in touch with comrades across the world but also dedicated himself to building an anarchist movement in India. For the first and only time, he invoked the idea of *nirajya*—the nearest Sanskrit equivalent to 'anarchy'—as distinct from *swarajya* but never developed this further. He published his memoirs, tales of fellow Indian nationalists, and wrote about anarchism for Indian periodicals. But anarchism was not in fashion in India then, and the outbreak of the Second World War put a stop to his activities. His first years back in India reveal a lot about the difficulties of starting an anarchist movement, even merely as an intellectual movement, in India. Unfortunately, as I argue, there were also missed opportunities to articulate anarchism from within Indian traditions, drawing on Indian ideas, beyond those imported through Acharya's experiences in Berlin and connections across the world. Viewed as such, the biography broadens the intellectual history of the 'age of entanglement' to reveal anarchism's rich but troubled relationship with anticolonialism in the interwar years.[6]

ANARCHY OR CHAOS

Freedom, violence, and anarchy

After the Second World War, Acharya threw himself into reconnecting with the international anarchist movement, sought out old and new friends, and represented India in the Commission for International Anarchist Relations (CRIA). Looking eastwards, he connected with Japanese, Chinese, and Korean anarchists, and even further afield to Australia, with the hope of establishing an anarchist magazine for Asia. It never materialised and neither did his attempt to set up an anarchist paper in Bombay with his friend D. N. Wanchoo. Having contracted tuberculosis in early 1948, the death of his wife, Nachman, in February 1951 dealt a devastating blow to Acharya, and his final years were spent in solitude, deep poverty, and illness. That did not stop Acharya from agitating for anarchism in India. In fact, in periodicals such as *Kaiser-i-Hind* and, more explicitly, *Harijan*, Acharya finally articulated and embraced Gandhism within the anarchist tradition. His tragic death in March 1954 put an end to anarchism in India. Nevertheless, as I conclude, while Acharya never published or edited his own anarchist periodical, his more than two hundred articles in Indian and international anarchist periodicals from 1923 to 1954 are testimony to a prolific writer and intellectual anarchist.

This biography of Acharya tells the story of Acharya's trajectory through Asia, Europe, North America, Russia, and Central Asia, connecting waves of revolutionary movements from the early twentieth century to the early Cold War period after Indian independence. Global and transnational in its scope, it follows the perspective of a unique figure who fought from exile, moving across vast distances, in search of the ultimate understanding and practice of freedom. In doing so, the book aims to open new temporal and geographical spaces, to explore the revolutionary nature of the Indian struggle for freedom, the First World War, the Russian Revolution, the rise of fascism and Nazism, and the question of Indian independence, among other events, through a unique but overlooked figure. An overriding theme throughout is the notion of 'imaginary futures', as Manu Goswami articulates it, in search of possibilities and solutions to chaotic times.[7] Or, as Acharya put it to his friend V. V. S. Aiyar: '[w]e

INTRODUCTION

are revolutionaries, and we don't know what we will be tomorrow, let alone what it will all be worth that which we can do, after all'.[8]

The main argument of this biography is that, by tracing Acharya's path from Indian nationalist to exiled anticolonialist, his alliances with other colonial and subject peoples and engagement with international socialists, his turn to communism and swift rejection of Bolshevism in favour of anarchism, we arrive at a more nuanced understanding of the multifarious nature of the Indian struggle for freedom. In fact, it is by examining the long history of his trajectory through to anarchism that allows us to account for anticolonialism's troubled relationship with this political and ideological movement. While Acharya fought to introduce anarchism into India's freedom struggle and succeeded in writing extensively about anarchism and 'anarchistically', as he said, in Indian papers, he never managed to build a broader movement. Not for want of trying, though: he made several attempts to start anarchist periodicals in India, which alas never materialised. The anarchist inroads into Indian anticolonial and postcolonial thought, however, were mainly intellectual as well as embracing the legacies of Gandhism without the mythology of Gandhi. At the same time, as the book ultimately argues, it is imperative to engage with Acharya's thoughts and activities within the international anarchist movement, operating from Berlin and Bombay, to fully appreciate the revolutionary impetus of anarchism as a global phenomenon—as a global idea of resistance and freedom from oppression—and as part of radical conversations with anticolonialism at the time.

Bringing Acharya back to life: stories of nationalism, anticolonialism, and anarchism

Despite his peripatetic life as the quintessential Indian anticolonial revolutionary, his central role in the formation of the ICP, and his unique place within the international anarchist movement of the first half of the twentieth century, Acharya's life has been relegated to relative obscurity and, in some cases, subject to mythology. This erasure has consequences for historical narratives today: where and to whom do these ideas really belong? I situate Acharya's life within accounts of Indian anticolonialism and of twentieth century anar-

9

ANARCHY OR CHAOS

chism. In doing so, I wrest his story away from a nation-state idea of freedom and emphasise the internationalism of anticolonialism that, for Acharya, led to anarchism as the only logical conclusion. Indeed, as Priyamvada Gopal insists, '[i]f colonialism might be broadly understood—in all its variety—as a project of expansionist racialised capitalism ... then anticolonialism emerges as the different kinds of resistance to this project'.[9] Guided by Gopal's insights, the book offers a fresh perspective onto the global circulation of ideas and movements that Acharya articulated and experienced and, by extension, the intellectual history of anticolonialism.

This is not the first biography of Acharya. However, C. S. Subramanyam's otherwise excellent biography of Acharya from 1995, while exploring Acharya's life in relation to India's anticolonial struggle and his years in exile, is remarkably scant on his life in Berlin and overlooks almost thirty years of extensive activity in the international anarchist movement. In fact, Subramanyam even goes so far as to suggest that

> [h]e seems to have come back [to India] having lost faith in political organisation and political parties. That probably accounts for the lack of any significant political activity of his that could be traced or any activity that had any relevance to the events and movements of this period 1935–1954.[10]

As this biography makes evident, Acharya was, indeed, extremely active during those years and his ideas gained significant relevance in the post-Independence period in India. Similarly, Bishamber Dayal Yadav's edited and introduced version of Acharya's memoirs, published as *Reminiscences of an Indian Revolutionary* (1991), sheds little light on the richness of Acharya's life beyond the few years covered in the memoirs.[11] In my research for this biography, I have benefitted from a privileged position and access to digitised resources and hitherto untapped archives across the world to build on the stories uncovered by Subramanyam and Yadav.

More recently, Maia Ramnath has opened new avenues of thinking about Acharya within an antiauthoritarian history of India's freedom struggle, paving the way for further research into this overlooked figure; this biography builds on Ramnath's efforts.[12] Andrew Davies's innovative work on geographies of anticolonialism in South India,

10

INTRODUCTION

which devotes an entire chapter to Acharya, is immensely useful for tracing the broader connections and spaces that Acharya carved out in praxis and theoretically.[13] This biography owes a great deal to such inquiries. Alongside Ramnath's and Davies' work, Lina Bernstein's biography of Magda Nachman adds significant layers to Acharya's personal life in Berlin and Bombay.[14] In many ways, this biography serves as a companion to Bernstein's work as well as to my own edited collection, a sourcebook of Acharya's essays.[15] At the same time, it extends these recent studies to explore longer trajectories, changing forms of revolutionary strategies, and shifting and developing ideologies to uncover Acharya's rich intellectual contributions to South Asian anticolonial thought.

Acharya's life overlapped with several prominent figures in the Indian freedom struggle that have been the subject of biographies lately: Dadabhai Naoroji, Shyamaji Krishnavarma, Vinayak Damodar Savarkar, V. S. Srinivasa Sastri, Jawaharlal Nehru, and M. N. Roy, to name a few.[16] It is instructive to read this biography of Acharya alongside these recent interventions to get a broader vision of the global scales of Indian anticolonial thought. In fact, if these studies have highlighted the intellectual inroads of liberalism, terrorism and violence, and communism, this book demonstrates that anarchism should be considered in conversation with these ideologies to give a fuller picture of India's road to freedom and the post-colonial nation.[17] I am, however, also interested in the act of recovering Acharya's life, which has been relegated to obscurity and, in some ways, silenced from certain narratives. In doing so, I hope to initiate conversations and make way for different narratives about the entangled worlds of anticolonialism and anarchism.

If Acharya remains an overlooked figure in the historiography of the Indian independence struggle and anticolonialism, he has not fared better within histories of anarchism. As the biography makes clear, Acharya was not on the fringes of the international anarchist movement but was a well-known figure across the world at the time. However, his name rarely appears in histories of anarchism in the twentieth century, though my own work and recent interventions by Ramnath and Mike Finn have made great strides in the right direction. In fact, as Finn argues, '[a]narchist praxis, if not anarchist ideas or

11

ANARCHY OR CHAOS

movements, played a role in India, even if that role was—at times—to be defined against the dominant approach to the independence struggle'.[18] Even in histories of Gandhian anarchism and the *Bhoodan* movement, Acharya is conspicuously absent.[19] This biography re-institutes Acharya into these traditions to engage in closer conversation between these histories and, in doing so, intervenes in current debates around the global networks of anarchism that have generated much new scholarship lately.[20] A major extension of this scholarship, however, this biography charts a more recent history into the twentieth century, often considered after the heyday of anarchism.[21] More importantly, while there has been a growing interest in uncovering and exploring anarchism across the colonial world, these have focused more on documenting their existence and less on integrating anticolonial thinkers into anarchist intellectual history. Following in Laura Galián's footsteps, this biography demands a rethinking of anarchist thought in the twentieth century to integrate ideas about freedom from anticolonial perspectives.[22]

Writing a life

In a 1935 essay on the German anarchist historian Max Nettlau's biography of Mikhail Bakunin, and more generally on Nettlau as a biographer, Acharya remarked: 'Bakunin himself could probably not explain why he was acting like he did at the time, because he was *acting*; however, Nettlau is an observer and can, therefore, be objective, as biographers should be'.[23] This biography heeds Acharya's call and aims to objectively reflect on Acharya's acting, activities, thoughts, conversations, life decisions, and reactions to global movements around him. While Acharya often wrote in conversation with others, interacting with anarchist writing in general, his thoughts were also primarily articulated from his own experiences. It is with that in mind that the form of biography is well-suited to tease out a life and experience, from which to better understand Acharya's intellectual development and contribution to anarchism's vibrant and challenging pursuit of freedom.

The global biographical approach, as Neilesh Bose suggests, 'assists the uncovering of broad-based macro-level changes ... within the

INTRODUCTION

purview of an individual's life'.[24] The globality of Acharya's biography, however, is not only a geographical idea, but also the global circulation of his thoughts and connections. Indeed, where Acharya's early nationalist career was marked by movement across the world, his activities within the anarchist movement emanated out of Berlin and Bombay, two micro-global cities themselves, but his writings and networks spanned the globe. Taking Bose's ideas seriously also means that tracing Acharya's itinerant and global life opens new avenues of thinking about transnational histories of revolutionary lives, of anti-colonialism and anarchism, of commitment to internationalism, and of how these strands of political thought and praxis were interwoven across the world. Anarchist internationalism, as Constance Bantman eloquently notes, 'captures two defining characteristics of the movement and its functioning: first, the central importance of multi-scalar flows of people, propaganda material, money, and ideas, as well as the predominantly—but not exclusively—informal nature of these exchanges'.[25] For Ruth Kinna, anarchist internationalism was not about transcending state division but rather about 'extending the principle of non-domination globally'.[26] Such notions of globality, internationalism, and transnationalism inform my approach to recounting Acharya's life. As the biography makes clear, however, such conceptions of internationalism did not always extend to the colonial world.

In search of archives

The biography relies on intelligence reports, newspaper reports, memoirs, correspondence, and primary texts. In a letter to the CRIA from September 1949, Acharya proposed:

> [a]rchives are necessary, but they should be distributed as they are likely to be confiscated by authorities or damaged in fire or wars. One archive for Asia and America in addition to several in Europe. The Labadie, Ann Arbor University, Michigan, USA is collecting all libertarian literature and must have a big collection by now.[27]

As this biography makes evident, Acharya knew the importance of establishing archives for anarchists through his involvement with the CRIA after the Second World War. However, despite such efforts to

ANARCHY OR CHAOS

preserve a legacy of Acharya's anarchism in India, there is no repository or collection of his papers anywhere. What is more, his peripatetic movements across India, Europe, Russia, and North America have made it difficult for historians to trace his life and activities. Guided by Nathan Jun's bold claim that 'without archives, anarchism in any manifestation is more than just ahistorical—it is functionally devoid of meaningful content', this biography relies on archival material from archives across the world to assemble a global, itinerant, and revolutionary life.[28]

If these archives are already uneven and ephemeral for anarchist scholars, the colonial archives present difficulties, too.[29] In fact, as the Indian parliament (Lok Sabha) debated in 1984, it appeared that intelligence files on Acharya, Har Dayal, and Aiyar, among others, had been destroyed in the UK.[30] However, the India Office Records (IOR) in the British Library, London, contains Acharya's passport applications from the 1920s and 1930s, which reveal a great deal about Acharya's activities up until his flight from Europe in 1935. Reading these alongside files on Acharya from the Politisches Archiv des Auswärtigen Amts (German Foreign Office Political Archives, PAAA) in Berlin shed light on his life during that period. The IOR, moreover, also hosts the Weekly Reports of the Director of Criminal Intelligence (WRDCI), which tracked the activities of Indian nationalists outside India in the early twentieth century. These provide important information about Acharya's life and movements at the time. Combined with the fact that there are few writings by Acharya's own hand, however, this also means that the first parts of the biography rely primarily on second-hand intelligence information. In other words, the first chapters of the book are focused on actions and movements, whereas the later chapters rely on primary texts and personal correspondence, giving voice to Acharya himself.

The absence of a repository for Acharya's papers also means that, in many cases, I rely on his letters to others while I rarely have letters addressed to Acharya. Therefore, we hear mostly his voice, his thoughts, without necessarily having the complete correspondence. Yet, these accounts still give invaluable insight into the global conversations he engaged in. Thus, missing information also provides an opportunity to give space to Acharya's own words through his writings and letters. What is more, these 'affective archives', as Razak

INTRODUCTION

Khan articulates it, reveal emotional and human aspects of Acharya's life that offer a fuller picture of the entanglement of the personal and the political.[31] At the same time, his correspondence and articles often provide clues to other people he was in contact with, to organisations he was involved in, to articles published in lost periodicals, or to events that I have not been able to explore further.

With such erasures in mind, researching and accessing material has required a 'contrapuntal reading', to borrow from Edward Said, to read between more dominant and prominent narratives to uncover Acharya's voice and life.[32] To give a few examples: in a letter from Augustin Souchy to Alexander Berkman from February 1931, we discover more about Acharya's translations for the German anarchist paper *Der Syndikalist*, and in a letter from Albert de Jong to M. A. Faruqui from September 1927 we learn about Acharya's initial involvement with the International Antimilitarist Commission (IAC).[33] It is at these interstices that Acharya's life extends beyond the self as a subject of conversation.

A related issue is the question of translation. Reflecting the transnational nature of the anarchist movement, as well as Acharya's own journeys, he wrote only in English but published in various languages in journals from across the world, including Kannada, Japanese, English, German, French, Spanish, Swedish, Portuguese, Italian, and Dutch, and some of his articles were published simultaneously in *L'En Dehors*, *Road to Freedom*, *Die Internationale*, and *La Protesta*, for example. Wherever possible, I have undertaken my own translations but, in some cases, I have relied on translators' assistance. In such instances, this is noted in the relevant footnote. In addition to published articles, I have uncovered several unpublished articles in archives and draw on these in the biography. In some cases, it is difficult to determine if an article was actually written by Acharya and in other cases articles were published anonymously. However, in his correspondence, he would often mention that he had published an article in a specific periodical, which has enabled me to identify him as the author.

Chapter outline

The book takes a chronological approach, allowing us to see broader developments unfold over times and spaces. While there may be recurrent themes in his writings throughout his life—for example, his continuing engagement with Gandhi, pacifism, and non-violence—these also developed through time. It is divided into five parts, each constituting an important phase of Acharya's life, with shorter chapters that examine distinct periods in Acharya's life but also in world history.

In Part I, 'Nationalism, Exile, and War, 1906–19', I explore Acharya's life in India, his entry into nationalist politics, escape into exile, and anticolonial revolutionary activities across Europe and North America until the end of the First World War. Chapter One situates Acharya in Indian nationalist politics of the early twentieth century, exploring his involvement with the nationalist paper *India* in Madras and Pondicherry, and his escape from India and life in London. The chapter traces his involvement with militant nationalists such as Vinayak Damodar Savarkar, V. V. S. Aiyar, Lala Har Dayal, and Virendranath Chattopadhyaya. Acharya's activities in London reveal a great deal about nationalism in the British empire and about how Britain, paradoxically, afforded more liberties to anticolonial nationalists than India.

Chapter Two takes us beyond the centre–periphery dichotomy of anticolonialism. After Acharya embarked on a misguided venture to Morocco in an act of anticolonial solidarity with the Rifs, he spent time in Lisbon before arriving in Paris in October 1909, and the chapter investigates the politics of Indian anticolonialism in Europe beyond the reach of the British authorities. It brings to light tales of arms smuggling, printing seditious literature, and the formation of anticolonial alliances with Egyptian nationalists in exile in Paris. The chapter examines Acharya's sojourn in Berlin and Munich, attempting to start new nationalist groups, while living precariously and with great uncertainty. Set against the Italo-Turkish war of 1911, the chapter concludes with Acharya's activities in Constantinople, where he sought to foment anti-British alliances with the Young Turks and foster connections between India's Muslims and the Islamic world. The chapter unveils the ways in which anticolonial politics in exile was often simultaneously militant and precarious, characterised by mobility and uncertainty, while consciously building anticolonial and inter-revolutionary alliances in the greater struggle against imperialism.

INTRODUCTION

Chapter Three starts with Acharya's hasty escape from Europe. As Acharya appeared in New York City and spent the next two years in North America, he became involved in the Ghadar Party and the Hindusthan Association of America (HAA). The chapter provides context to those organisations and to Acharya's engagement with radical anticolonialism that lead him to brief encounters with prominent anarchists Alexander Berkman and Hippolyte Havel. Ultimately, as the chapter highlights, those global anticolonial networks that Acharya was part of in Europe extended to North America and, in this case, were interweaved with the radical politics of anarchism.

When imperialisms clashed in the First World War, the scales of anti-imperialism also changed. In Chapter Four, I examine what the war meant for Indian anticolonialists such as Acharya, explored through his involvement with the IIC in Berlin and across the Middle East. The chapter provides a detailed account of the Indian-German conspiracy through Acharya's experiences across the Middle East, a daring mission to the Suez Canal, and internal disagreements within the IIC. As the chapter suggests, while posing a concerted threat to British rule in India, the creed of 'the enemy of my enemy is my friend' eventually failed for the Indians. The chapter unveils an anti-imperial history of the First World War that opens new ways of understanding the global scale of the war.

This failed attempt on behalf of Indian revolutionaries led to an engagement with international socialism. Chapter Five charts Acharya's and Chatto's two years among international socialists in the Second International. With the tides of the war turning, Acharya and Chatto sought out new allies in the freedom struggle and relocated to Stockholm in May 1917 to bring the question of Indian independence into the discussions of peace. They set up the Indiska Nationalkommittén (Indian National Committee, INK), found a small office, published propaganda in Scandinavian newspapers, and set to work among and within other colonial and subject peoples in the Swedish capital. The chapter explores how Stockholm became a hub of anticolonialism in the last years of the First World War, and how they engaged with social democrats and the limits of international socialism. At the end of the war, it was clear to Acharya and Chatto that they could not rely on help from Europe's socialist leaders in the struggle for Indian freedom.

ANARCHY OR CHAOS

Part II, 'Revolution and Communism, 1919–22', is devoted entirely to Acharya's time in Russia and Central Asia. Chapter Six focuses on his fateful journey to Moscow to meet Lenin in July 1919 and subsequent mission to Kabul with Mahendra Pratap and Abdur Rabb. Abandoning the bourgeois nationalism of Pratap, Acharya and Rabb set up the Indian Revolutionary Association (IRA) to agitate among the *Muhajirs* in the Afghan-Indian borderland. As a representative of the IRA, Acharya attended the Second Congress of the Communist International in July and August 1920 and here met Abani Mukherji, M. N. Roy and his wife, Evelyn Trent, and Mohamed Shafique, all representing different strands of Indian revolutionary groups. Acharya's presence at this event has been overlooked, but the chapter seeks to reinstate him into the early history of communism's relation to anti-imperialism.

Chapter Seven offers detailed insight into the collaboration between these Indian revolutionaries in Russia, the formation of the ICP, its relation to the Comintern, and early activities. While Acharya remained a member of the IRA, he was also instrumental in the formative months of the ICP, leading missions to Andijan, Skobelev, and Bukhara, and recruiting new members into the party. Roy's grip on the party and Acharya's continued membership of the IRA became a contentious issue, and only two months after the formation of the ICP, the Indians discussed Acharya's allegiance to the Bolsheviks. Expelled from the ICP in late December 1920, the division between the Indian revolutionaries grew wider as Chatto and a group of Indians from Berlin arrived in the spring of 1921 to propose an alternative to Roy's group. The chapter brings to light a fascinating and problematic history of the birth of Indian communism in exile.

In Chapter Eight, the book follows Acharya's association with anti-Bolshevik dissenters and anarchists in Russia. Acharya worked as a journalist, writing critical articles about the Bolshevik regime for Indian papers, and started working for the American Relief Administration (ARA) alongside his comrade M. A. Faruqui as well as the Russian anarchist Abba Gordin. Indeed, it was in Russia that Acharya first turned to anarchism, having worked with Nicolai Ragdaev in Tashkent and attended Peter Kropotkin's funeral in Moscow in February 1921, and developed a deep engagement with

18

INTRODUCTION

anti-statist politics that set him on a new path towards freedom. Acharya found love in Moscow, marrying the Russian artist Magda Nachman in 1922, but also found that his critical stance towards the Bolshevik regime was no longer tolerated, prompting the newly married couple to flee. Ultimately, the chapter illuminates how the Bolshevik promises of self-determination for colonial peoples turned into brutal repression for dissenters like Acharya.

Part III, 'Anticolonialism, Anarchism, and Anti-Militarism, 1922–34', covers Acharya's years in Weimar Berlin. Chapter Nine explores Acharya's ventures into anarchism, which tried to bring the political philosophy into India's independence struggle from afar, and to place India's freedom on the agenda of global anarchism. In the mid-1920s, Acharya was involved in a deportation case against Indians in Berlin, which was eventually abandoned, and in challenging the racism of German cultural politics in the Hagenbeck affair. In addition to translating for and frequently contributing to anarchist papers, his articulation of anarchism in Indian papers such as *Forward* and the *People* was unique and, eventually, evolved into a heated debate with Jawaharlal Nehru over the brutality of Bolshevik prisons. Acharya's different approach to the question of freedom, the chapter illustrates, brought together anticolonialism and anarchism in ways that open new ways of understanding the radical landscape of 1920s Berlin as a hub for the entangled world of anti-imperialism and anarchism.

Chapter Ten follows on from Acharya's spat with Nehru and examines his involvement with the League Against Imperialism (LAI) and the anti-militarist organisations the IAMB and the IAC. Despite being an early member of the LAI, set up by his old friend Chatto, Acharya had serious misgivings about the Moscow-backed organisation. Instead, his involvement in the anarchist movement brought him into the orbit of pacifism and anti-militarism and, by extension, the radical politics of Gandhi. The chapter elucidates some of the major tensions within the broader, left-wing anti-imperialist movement: how did anarchists view anti-imperial struggles? How did anarchists work with communist-backed organisations? How did anarchists connect anti-militarism and anti-imperialism? Acharya dealt with all these questions, as the chapter illustrates, by embracing Gandhism without Gandhi.

ANARCHY OR CHAOS

In Chapter Eleven, the biography examines Acharya's travels among Berlin's ultra-leftists and extensive engagement with questions of gender and sexual relations in the French anarchist periodical *L'En Dehors*. While Acharya had joined the ranks of the anarchists, he also associated with anti-Bolshevik dissenters and council communists, mainly through his connection with Karl Korsch's Kritischer Marxismus reading group, and he remained friends with revolutionaries he had met in Russia. In 1928, he published his key article 'Les Trusts et la Démocratie' in *L'En Dehors*, laying out the case for autonomous communes in India. As the chapter tackles these issues, it also offers a sustained reading of Acharya's thoughts on sex and gender relations. In *L'En Dehors*, he wrote extensively about women's freedom from the bonds of marriage and submission to men, and he defended homosexuality and the labour of sex workers. His thoughts open a window onto the entangled world of anarchism and free love, thoughts that extended to conversations across Europe and Asia.

In Part IV, 'Escape and Return, 1934–45', the book covers Acharya's flight from Nazi-era Berlin and return to India after almost twenty-seven years in exile. Chapter Twelve explores Acharya's experiences of the rise of Nazism, the repercussions for Indians in Berlin, and the decision to flee again. Acharya had applied for a passport to leave Berlin since the mid-1920s, but due to his long career as an anticolonial revolutionary, the British refused to grant him amnesty for his activities. However, in early 1934, he finally succeeded, and he and Nachman escaped to Zürich to stay with Nachman's sister, eventually living secretly in Zürich and Paris. The chapter unveils the difficulties of returning to India for exiled revolutionaries and the dangers of living underground.

Following on from this, Chapter Thirteen charts Acharya's first years back in India. Where his time in Berlin and exile were marked by close friendships and associations, his return to Bombay was characterised by isolation. While he still corresponded with anarchists across the world and engaged with the Spanish Civil War from an Indian perspective, he also found time to reflect on his long career as an Indian anticolonial revolutionary and wrote his memoirs as well as several articles on figures such as Chatto, Madame Cama, and Savarkar. In many ways, as the chapter makes clear, these accounted

INTRODUCTION

for his turn to and engagement with anarchism. In Bombay, Acharya found new ways to bring anarchism into intellectual, left-wing debates in India through his association with Ranchoddas Bhavan Lotvala and the Indian Institute of Sociology (IIS). The outbreak of the Second World War, however, put a stop to Acharya's efforts to spread anarchism in India.

The final part of the book, Part V, 'Freedom, Violence, and Anarchy, 1945–54', follows Acharya's re-emergence in the international anarchist movement and Asian connections, his views on Indian independence, Hindu nationalism, and the assassination of Gandhi, and the articulation of anarchy in India. Chapter Fourteen examines Acharya's attempts to reconnect with old friends in the anarchist movement, while also building a movement at home and looking eastwards towards Asia for new connections, as well as his involvement with CRIA. Now in his late fifties and suffering from health issues, Acharya worked tirelessly to build up an anarchist movement in India and to connect it to a global movement. This involved setting up a library in Bombay, asking friends to send anarchist literature for the reading room, and publishing a new libertarian journal with Lotvala. At the same time, Acharya debated the future of anarchist relations within CRIA and with Asian anarchists, as the chapter concludes, thus reorienting global conversations away from Europe and the Americas.

In Chapter Fifteen, the biography turns to the question of Indian independence and Partition, the assassination of Gandhi, and the rise of Hindu nationalism. As an avowed anarchist, independence and self-government for India did not equate with any meaningful sense of freedom. While Indian leaders negotiated their place in Cold War politics, Acharya's ideas gained more currency. His central article 'Les Trusts et la Démocratie' was reprinted in pamphlet form as *Principles of Non-Violent Economics* (1947), and he contributed an essay on 'What is Anarchism?' to Iqbal Singh and Raja Rao's stock-taking collection *Whither India?* (1948). At the same time, he had to face two old interlocutors: Gandhi and Savarkar. The assassination of Gandhi by Nathuram Godse, a follower of Savarkar's *Hindutva* ideology, shook India. Acharya despised the mythological status of Gandhi, even immediately following the assassination, but admired Gandhian tac-

ANARCHY OR CHAOS

tics; at the same time, he had admired Savarkar's revolutionary fervour but rejected the ethnic fascism of *Hindutva*. Post-colonial India, as the chapter elucidates, saw Acharya reconnect with old comrades from the early twentieth century nationalist movement, testifying to the longevity of revolutionary camaraderie and the role of these revolutionaries in the freedom struggle.

The final chapter sheds light on the last years of Acharya's life in Bombay. After Gandhi's assassination, Gandhians abandoned the principles of pacifism, according to Acharya. Instead, he found an outlet for his pacifism in French anarchist-pacifist periodicals, continued to connect with anarchists worldwide, and drew on this network for contributions when he and Wanchoo wanted to start a new anarchist publication in India. Poor health, poverty, and the tragic death of Nachman in February 1951 put an end to the project and, as the chapter makes clear, an end to India's own anarchist periodical. Instead, Acharya challenged Lotvala's individualist libertarianism and embraced the 'near-anarchists' around the *Harijan* group. As the chapter ultimately concludes, the key figures around the *Harijan* group, K. G. Mashruwala, Vinoba Bhave, and Maganbhai P. Desai, were approaching anarchism, partly through Acharya's ideas, and Acharya found an Indian expression of anarchism through the periodical. The tragic death of Acharya in March 1954, the book concludes, also meant the death of anarchism in India.

I end the biography with an Epilogue that reflects on how Acharya was remembered, initially, and subsequently forgotten as India's most important anarchist theoretician and proponent. Obituaries and tributes soon poured in from anarchists across the world, but only a few years after his death, Acharya's contribution to anti-imperialist and anarchist debates about the true meaning of freedom had been overlooked. This biography, then, is a recovery of a unique history with broader implications and histories—a journey through anticolonialism, communism, pacifism, and anarchism in the pursuit of freedom over imperialism. Indeed, if, as Adom Getachew notes, 'the universalization of the nation-state marked an important triumph over European imperialism, it has also come to represent a political form incapable of realizing the ideals of a democratic, egalitarian, and anti-imperial future', it is instructive to look to anticolonial freedom fighters such as Acharya,

INTRODUCTION

who rejected the universalisation of the nation-state.[34] That is, Acharya made a major contribution to our understanding of resistance to oppression, be it imperialist, authoritarian, totalitarian, fascist, or racist, as embodied by the nation-state.

PART I

NATIONALISM, EXILE, AND WAR, 1906–19

1

NATIONALISM IN THE BRITISH EMPIRE

A revolutionary from South India

Born on 15 April 1887 in the old neighbourhood of Triplicane, Madras (now Chennai), Mandayam Prativadi Bhayankaram Tirumal 'M. P. T.' Acharya belonged to a Tamil family of the Brahmin caste. His father, N. P. Narasimha Aiyar, worked as a supervisor in the Public Works Department in Madras, and his mother, Singammal, was a housewife.[1] He had two younger brothers and came from a family with a long tradition of nationalist agitation: he was the nephew of S. N. Tirumalacharya, founder of the nationalist journal *India*, later edited by the Tamil poet C. Subramania Bharati and C. Srinivasacharya, Acharya's cousin. Yogi Parthasarathy Iyengar was another of Acharya's uncles, and Alasinga Perumal, an ardent follower of the Hindu reformer Swami Vivekananda, was another cousin.[2]

Around 1897, Acharya entered Hindu High School in Triplicane. He passed the lower secondary examination in December 1901, taking the compulsory subjects of First Language (English), Arithmetic, Geography, and History of India, and optional subjects of Sanskrit and Geometry and Algebra, and graduated on 16 April 1902.[3] At the time, the renowned, later liberal politician V. S. Srinivasa Sastri was headmaster (1899 to 1905).[4] In his *Reminiscences of a Revolutionary* (1937) (hereafter *Reminiscences*), Acharya recalled: '[h]e was a stern

ANARCHY OR CHAOS

headmaster in our school and prevented every pupil from taking parts in politics. I was one of the few hard nuts for him to crack'.[5]

From an early age, Acharya became involved in nationalist activities. In 1906, he was proprietor and publisher of the paper *Bala Bharat*, then edited by Bharati. In August 1907, when his cousin Srinivasacharya was arrested for publishing sedition in *India*, Acharya briefly assumed editorship of the paper until November 1907, when he went to Poona (now Pune).[6] Acharya was a follower of Bal Gangadhar Tilak, a prominent member of the 'extremist' wing of the Indian National Congress (INC), and as he recalled in his *Reminiscences*: 'I went to Poona to study under Lokamanya Tilak. He used to recommend me books to read'.[7] After Poona, Acharya travelled to Bombay (now Mumbai), a city which did not impress him at the time.

Leaving Bombay a few weeks later, at the invitation of Tilak's friend G. S. Khaparde, Acharya attended the annual INC meeting in Surat in December 1907. At that meeting, 'moderates' from the INC prevented Tilak from speaking, as the meeting was held in his province and thus conducted the meeting in the spirit of neutrality. Tilak's ban caused great frustration among the 'extremists', and soon skirmishes broke out.[8] The 'moderate' Sastri was also present at the Surat meeting and later recalled:

> [a]s soon as the shoe was thrown, the scene became utterly tragic. The confusion was indescribable. When the shoe was thrown actually, the lathis on the one side began to play; and Tilak's followers mounted the platform and they rapidly got hold of the chairs and flung them freely. I was present among the persons. In those days I was a little more courageous than I am now, and as soon as the first chairs were flung, I rushed up on the platform. And what did I see? I saw a young fellow taking a chair and about to strike. I looked up at him. I met one of my own pupils, and old student of the Hindu High School. He had his chair ready to strike me. As soon as he saw me, he exclaimed, 'Is it you, Sir?'. The man became worse and worse afterwards among the Extremists.[9]

This 'young fellow' was Acharya, his former student, who had now joined the ranks of the 'extremists' armed with a lathi (a long, heavy stick).[10] In his *Reminiscences*, Acharya recalled meeting Sastri again in Bombay shortly after the Surat pandemonium:

28

NATIONALISM IN THE BRITISH EMPIRE

I told him on the stairs of the Sardar Griha [Tilak's home in Bombay—ed.], where he saw me limping and with the lathi from Surat that he was no longer my headmaster and the lathi in my hand must be proof of our belonging to opposed camps in politics. He simply smiled and went away.[11]

Acharya, too, went away—away from Bombay and soon away from India. By the time of the Surat congress in 1907, Indian nationalist resistance to British rule had grown more violent, and the circulation of literature played a significant role in the movement. In response, the British authorities implemented a series of laws to curb the publication of seditious literature, such as the Prevention of Seditious Meetings Act and the Newspapers (Incitement to Offences) Act. Deterred by these new acts, Srinivasacharya and Acharya moved their paper *India* to the French enclave of Pondicherry in September 1908 and continued to publish it outside the reach of the British authorities.[12] However, despite evading the British authorities, shortly after their move to Pondicherry, Acharya had to flee again.

Sedition, surveillance, and exile

By October 1908, Acharya's parents had arranged for his marriage. He returned to Madras for the wedding but came back to Pondicherry soon after, where Jnanendra Nath Chatterji joined him.[13] However, by then, the Government of India was pressuring the French Government to suppress seditious literature and extradite or deport Indian revolutionaries hiding in their territories. His cousin had already been imprisoned, and Acharya feared that he would be next, so he decided to flee again. 'Life in Pondicherry', he wrote in his *Reminiscences*, 'was not safe for refugees. There are many British spots with police stations where one could walk in unawares. Moreover, the Police or Police Chief tried to make the lives of refugees hell by telling people to tell us that we would be extradited'.[14] Acharya then cut off his hair to avoid being recognised, briefly said goodbye to his ailing father, and shipped off to Colombo in Ceylon (now Sri Lanka). Acharya initially planned on going to Java but was informed that no ships were leaving in that direction for a week, so instead he bought a third-class ticket for a Japanese vessel bound for Marseille and packed his trunk and 300 rupees.[15]

ANARCHY OR CHAOS

The vegetarian Acharya sustained himself only on bread and coffee and reached Marseille after twenty-two days. He immediately caught a train to Paris and sought out Julien Vinson, the Pondicherry-born French linguist and supporter of the Indian struggle for independence. Seeking work opportunities, Acharya explained to Vinson that he wanted to learn engraving and process work, and Vinson recommended Acharya to a process engraver but refused any financial help. Instead, Acharya tracked down Shyamaji Krishnavarma, the wealthy Indian nationalist whom he had heard of through the *India* group in Pondicherry.

Founder-editor of the nationalist paper *The Indian Sociologist*, president of the Indian Home Rule Society (IHRS), and proprietor of India House in Highgate in London, Krishnavarma was a central figure among exiled Indian nationalists in London and Paris. By 1907, the increasingly militant rhetoric in *The Indian Sociologist* had brought more attention to Krishnavarma's suspected radicalisation of Indian students in Britain, prompting an official investigation into the situation under the direction of William Lee-Warner, William Hutt Curzon-Wyllie, and Theodore Morison in May 1907.[16] Alerted to this investigation and fearing arrest for publishing sedition—thus risking the same fate as prominent nationalists Lala Lajpat Rai and Ajit Singh who had been imprisoned for sedition earlier that year—Krishnavarma fled London for Paris in June 1907 and settled in the affluent suburb of Passy. It was here that he received Acharya in December 1908.[17] However, wary of this unknown newcomer, Krishnavarma also denied Acharya financial help and instead sent him to another Indian nationalist in Paris. This person suggested that Acharya should contact V. V. S. Aiyar, whom Acharya knew as the London correspondent for *India*, then living at India House in London. Aiyar arranged for Acharya to come to India House only a week after his arrival in Paris.[18]

London and India House

Arriving without any money in this 'hot-bed of sedition', as Acharya recalled, Aiyar greeted Acharya at the station in London and offered him free lodging at India House. Located in the affluent North London

30

NATIONALISM IN THE BRITISH EMPIRE

area of Highgate, India House was a hostel for Indian students, but by 1908 it also served as a home for militant Indian nationalists. After Krishnavarma's departure, Vinayak Damodar Savarkar served as de facto manager of India House, with Aiyar as his right-hand man, and replaced the IHRS with the secret Free India Society, a London branch of the Abhinav Bharat (Young India) society he had established in Poona a few years earlier.[19]

Among the other residents and frequent visitors to India House were Chattopadhyaya, Har Dayal, T. S. S Rajan, Govind Amin, Asaf Ali, Haidar Raza, Joaquim de Siqueira Coutinho, H. K. Koregaonkar, Chandra Kanta Chakravarty, and Madan Lal Dhingra, the latter soon to become a notorious 'martyr' in the militant struggle against British rule. Paris-based Indians such as Sardarsinhji Ravaji Rana and Bhikhaiji Rustom Cama, known as Madame Cama, frequently travelled to London to attend Sunday meetings at India House. All these figures would play important roles in Acharya's life for the next few years. Rajan later described Acharya's arrival thus:

> [o]ne day, [in late 1908], another young man arrived unannounced at India House. He too came with all his belongings, a box, and a bed. He was thin and emaciated, but with a very intelligent face and sharp eyes. He looked twenty. He said his name was M. P. Tirumal Acharya and that he had come by third class in ship from India. Third class travel had affected him and hence his famished look. He said he was from Triplicane, Madras city. He had come with no assurance of any income and urgently in need of a job. He was prepared to do any work; all that he wanted was board and lodge at India House.[20]

The Indians at India House were known for their secrecy and militancy and were kept under close surveillance by the Special Branch of the Metropolitan Police, a unit of Scotland Yard established in 1907, separate from the British Department of Criminal Intelligence (DCI), which was responsible for surveillance in India. Shortly before Acharya's arrival, an Indian spy known as 'Kirtikar' had infiltrated the Free India Society but was exposed and prevailed upon to provide false reports of their Sunday meetings.[21] Although suspicious of newcomers, Aiyar and Savarkar welcomed Acharya. As Rajan later recalled,

> with the experience of Kirtikar (the Mahratta youth who proved to be a police spy planted in their midst), Aiyar and others were wonder-

31

ANARCHY OR CHAOS

ing if this newcomer too was not another police stooge, [but] it was decided to take Tirumal Acharya in. We needed a man to help in the cooking and to do our shopping and to supervise the maintenance of the House. So it was agreed that he should stay at India House on probation and that his expenses should be divided equally among the seven permanent residents of the place.[22]

Alongside working as a cook at India House, Acharya also enrolled as a student at the London County Council School of Photo-Engraving and Lithography. Unlike others such as Savarkar, Aiyar, and Chatto, for instance, Acharya had not come to London with the intention of returning to India with a degree in hand or to join the Indian Civil Service. Acharya became a valuable member of the Free India Society, and Aiyar and Savarkar soon used Acharya to provide false information to Scotland Yard and the DCI about the activities at India House.[23]

At India House, Acharya shared a room on the second floor with another newcomer, Joaquim de Siqueira Coutinho, a Goanese of mixed Portuguese and Marathi descent. As Coutinho did not speak any of the Indian languages, Acharya and Koregaonkar often translated for him and initiated him into the inner circles of the militant India House group. Coutinho and Acharya assisted Savarkar with the publication and translation of his revisionist history *The Indian War of Independence of 1857*. However, in the spring of 1909, Coutinho left London for Lisbon and burnt much of the seditious literature he had in his possession for fear of repression, leaving little trace of his involvement with India House.[24] Chapters from the book were frequently read aloud at the Sunday meetings at India House.

It was during this time that Acharya became greatly impressed by Savarkar: '[h]is lectures breathed the spirit of patriotism. Even those who did not like his patriotism sometimes dared to come to the lectures, as he was also a very good speaker, full of literary fluency and much learning of Sanskrit'.[25] Acharya even noted that 'his personal charm was such that a mere hand-shake could convert to his views such obstinate men as V. V. S. Aiyar and Har Dayal—not only convert but even bring out the best of them'.[26] However, while Savarkar may have been a charismatic speaker and the most prominent figure at India House at the time, his politics were not unproblematic. Despite arguing for Hindu-Muslim unity in the struggle against the

NATIONALISM IN THE BRITISH EMPIRE

British, the DCI reported that Savarkar would often let his anti-Muslim sentiments get away with him, especially in his quarrels with Raza, Asaf Ali's travel companion and close friend.[27]

Acharya's appreciation of Savarkar's rhetorical fervour is perhaps understandable, but his glossing over of Savarkar's anti-Muslim sentiments is problematic. Acharya would later revise his opinion of Savarkar's brand of Hindu nationalism, but even Asaf Ali acknowledged Savarkar's firebrand oratorial skills: 'Savarkar ... despite his careless English, had so genuine a ring of sincerity in his speech that he almost always made a memorable impact on the audience'.[28] Ali's appraisal of Savarkar is perhaps even more surprising in light of his friendship with Raza, but it suggests that, at the time, Hindu-Muslim divisions and disagreements were considered less important than the articulation of militant anticolonial nationalism. Indeed, as both Acharya and Ali allude to, and as Janaki Bakhle argues, 'Savarkar was less a skilled revolutionary warrior than a rhetorical revolutionary—i.e., a seditionist. His lasting impact on the Indian political scene had more to do with changing the terms and scale of the discourse of Indian history and, by extension, the British Raj as well'.[29] Despite inaccuracies in the work itself, Bakhle further argues, *The Indian War of Independence of 1857* was a direct challenge to the colonial logic of British rule in India.

While Acharya and some of the other India House residents helped with the translation of the book, the manuscript was so inflammatory that they struggled to find a printer in Britain. Instead, after initially contacting a German printer on the continent, the contract went to the Rotterdamsche Boek- en Kunstdrukkerij. The Dutch printer then sent the proofs to India House, and the book was hurriedly published in May 1909.[30] According to Koregaonkar, Acharya 'wrote out the corrected proofs of the Mutiny Book [and] Savarkar used to like him very much'.[31]

Around the time of Acharya's arrival in London, a rifle range had been installed in the back garden at India House and some of the members were involved in smuggling arms to India.[32] Alerted to the growing militancy, it was perhaps no surprise that Scotland Yard kept the Indians in Highgate under close surveillance. To evade or throw off detectives, Acharya would sometimes directly confront them.[33] The

ANARCHY OR CHAOS

pressure of constant surveillance combined with internal divisions amongst the Indian nationalists, however, meant that the lodgers and regular visitors to India House were decimated by the spring of 1909. By June, only Acharya, Aiyar, and Raza were staying at India House, and Raza would soon leave for Oxford. At the same time, *The Indian Sociologist* became more militant in its rhetoric. Indeed, Krishnavarma now defended political assassinations in India, which led to his disbarment from Inner Temple and subsequently in need of a new printer for the periodical. After first consulting Thomas H. Keell, the editor of the anarchist paper *Freedom*, and then Twentieth Century Press, the press of the Social Democratic Federation, the contract eventually went to Arthur Fletcher Horsley, who printed the May, June, and July 1909 issues of *The Indian Sociologist*.[34]

In late June 1909, the DCI reported that Acharya was being 'coached by Aiyar to become a martyr, and thus hand his name down to posterity'.[35] Perhaps exaggerating, the DCI also reported that Acharya had 'become careless of his life', that he 'spoke cheerfully but his voice had a ring of suicidal insanity', and that he was 'destitute and completely in the power of the India House party, especially of Aiyar, who is a close associate of Savarkar'.[36] Corroborating that assessment, according to Koregaonkar, Acharya was overheard saying that 'he is quite prepared to shoot any Englishman any day when he feels called upon to do so'.[37]

However, while Acharya was being coached to sacrifice himself, it was another regular India House visitor, Madan Lal Dhingra, who assumed the role of martyr. On 1 July 1909, the London-based National Indian Association hosted one of its 'At Home' events at the Imperial Institute in Kensington, London. As Curzon-Wyllie, the political aide-de-camp to George Hamilton, the Secretary of State for India, ascended the stairs to the Institute, Dhingra shot him five times. Dhingra tried to kill himself, but the Colt pistol failed. The DCI soon suspected that Dhingra had acted on orders of Savarkar to avenge his brother, Ganesh D. Savarkar, who had been sentenced to transportation for life for his involvement in arms smuggling in June 1909, but they could not prove this.[38] According to Acharya, Dhingra had come to India House the night before the assassination to see Savarkar who was not there. 'He was always of a brooding temperament when he

34

NATIONALISM IN THE BRITISH EMPIRE

was at India House', Acharya recalled, 'but not so that evening. But it is true that he spoke very little so that one could have no inkling of what was going on in his mind'.[39]

On 5 July 1909, a meeting was held at Caxton Hall to condemn the assassination of Curzon-Wyllie. While a resolution to condemn the act was widely supported by the Indians gathered there, at the end of the meeting, Savarkar rose and protested the motion. Skirmishes broke out, and when Edward Palmer, a retired Indian army officer, tried to eject Savarkar from Caxton Hall, Acharya intervened and struck Palmer with a stick.[40] *The Times* reported: 'there were loud and indignant cries of "Put him out!", a few chairs were brandished, and an East Indian gentleman, Mr. Palmer, received a blow from the cheek which caused blood to flow'.[41] In his *Reminiscences*, Acharya admitted that,

> [n]o sooner did the blow fall upon Savarkar, than I who was standing on a chair to see the commotion and happened to have a stick in the hand, instinctively struck him on the head. Naturally, I got into trouble with some of the proud loyalists around me, of whom a Sikh gentleman took me by my tie and began bravely to strangle me and the plain-clothes-policemen began to remove me out of the hall.[42]

Both Savarkar and Acharya were immediately expelled from the meeting but, to Acharya's surprise, not arrested. At the time, Acharya had moved away from India House and was lodging with Bipin Chandra Pal in Shepherd's Bush. Acharya was aware of potential repercussions and, not wanting to cause trouble for Pal, moved to rooms above an Indian restaurant at 17 Red Lion Passage.

After the assassination, India House came under even closer surveillance by Scotland Yard. Instead, for the next few months, the Indian restaurant became a central meeting venue for the Indian nationalists in London. On 21 July, Acharya, Aiyar, Chatto, G. C. Varma, and Niranjan Pal hosted a farewell meeting at the restaurant to convey their gratitude to Koregaonkar, who had witnessed Dhingra's assassination of Curzon-Wyllie, for his struggle for Indian independence. Koregaonkar left London a few days later and returned to India, where he was immediately arrested for his suspected involvement in the Curzon-Wyllie assassination. In return for leniency, he provided a detailed account on the activities of the Indian nationalists in London.[43]

ANARCHY OR CHAOS

The assassination of Curzon-Wyllie and subsequent arrest of Dhingra brought the Indian nationalists in London into contact with the British anarchist Guy A. Aldred. Writing from the safety of his Paris mansion, Krishnavarma had defended the politics of assassination in the July issue of *The Indian Sociologist*, prior to Dhingra's actions. Doing so, however, landed the British printer, Horsley, in trouble, and he was subsequently fined for printing sedition. Taking over from Horsley, Aldred assumed the printing of *The Indian Sociologist* in August, defending the principle of free speech, and he devoted the issue entirely to anti-imperialism and the case of Dhingra. As had happened to Horsley, Aldred's intervention soon yielded him a fine and a prison sentence of ten months, of which he served eight. It also led to a lifelong engagement with the Indian freedom struggle for Aldred (see Chapter 15).[44]

Acharya's brief sojourn in London brought him into contact with some of the most prominent militant Indian nationalists of the time. His early years and involvement in the Indian nationalist struggle, both in India and in Britain, are evidence of the increasingly radical nature of the movement. While for many Indian nationalists, paradoxically, Britain was freer for them than India, by the end of the first decade of the twentieth century, Britain's hospitality towards exiled, political refugees waned, and this 'hot-bed of sedition', as Acharya had put it, had become too dangerous. Acharya soon fled again.

2

EXILE IN EUROPE

Anticolonial solidarity and guerrilla warfare

London had become too dangerous for the Indian nationalists. Hence, at the suggestion of Savarkar and Aiyar, Acharya and Sukh Sagar Dutt, another India House regular, departed for Morocco to learn armed guerrilla warfare and to support the Rifs in their struggle against Spanish colonisers in the Second Melillan campaign in August 1909.[1] When Acharya applied to the India Office for a passport, he was asked why he wanted to go to Morocco. 'I said that I did not want to help the invaders but those who were defending themselves against them', he explained.[2] Indeed, the Rifs had successfully held off the Spanish colonisers for months, which greatly impressed Acharya and the Indian nationalists in London.

Acharya obtained a British passport valid for 'Europe and North Africa' on 16 August and set off for Southampton, armed with a Mauser rifle and a Browning revolver. Acharya and Dutt spent a night in Southampton before departing on the German steamer *Lützow* on 17 August.[3] Their weapons were immediately confiscated by customs when they arrived in Gibraltar a few days later. Undeterred, on 22 August, Acharya set off for Tangier on the *Gibel Dersa* and landed there on 26 August. He did not know that he was being followed closely by the DCI and a deputed French detective. Meanwhile, Dutt

37

ANARCHY OR CHAOS

abandoned their venture and returned via Marseille to London, leaving Acharya on his own in Tangier. He soon had no money left and started to doubt the mission to reach the Rifs. However, he made friends with a local Arab, Salim Atyyeh, who—unbeknownst to Acharya—happened to be an agent for the French detective working for the DCI. Atyyeh put Acharya up with a Spanish family instead of having him stay in an expensive hotel, and Acharya spent the next couple of days with his new friends.

Stranded at Tangier, on 27 August, Acharya applied to the British consul to send him back to Britain but was informed that he would be sent back to India instead. He wrote to Aiyar in London and asked for money to leave Tangier, warning Aiyar that his letters had been opened and that he had abandoned the plan to go to Melilla. His letters were intercepted by the French detective and handed over to the British authorities. Aiyar cautioned Acharya against coming back to London and sent him money to proceed to Lisbon, where he could stay with Coutinho. Meanwhile, on 22 September, the Government of India issued a warrant for Acharya's arrest for his involvement with *India* in Pondicherry. In addition to charges of sedition, the Government of India accused him of being involved in bomb-making and therefore demanded that he be arrested and extradited for prosecution in India.[4]

Leaving Tangier on 25 September on the Dutch steamer *Koning Willem III*, Acharya arrived in Lisbon the next day and soon gave a lengthy statement to the local British authorities about his intentions for staying in Portugal. Tired of 'a year of continuous wandering without a penny, tossed as it were by every wind and wave', as he noted in his *Reminiscences*, he explained to the British authorities that he intended to stay in Lisbon for a while to learn Portuguese and then eventually go to Brazil to 'settle, if possible, as a soldier'. Perhaps young and naïve, he was honest about his plans: '[m]y intention in going to Tangier was to fight in the Rif war to accustom myself to war'.[5] Alarmed by Acharya's militancy, the Portuguese authorities summoned him for an explanation and subsequently informed him that they would keep him under surveillance. By early October 1909, Aiyar had moved to Paris and from here wrote to Acharya through Coutinho, asking Acharya to join him in the French metropolis, where he would work with Govind Amin.[6]

EXILE IN EUROPE

The Paris Indian Society

On 4 October 1909, Acharya made his way to Paris, where many other India House alumni had also congregated since the assassination of Curzon-Wyllie. In Paris, Acharya lodged at 46 rue Blanche with S. R. Rana, a thirty-nine-year-old wealthy pearl merchant and financier of the Indian revolutionaries in Paris, and soon found secretarial work as a 'despatch clerk and postboy' with Rana's pearl company.[7] Alongside Rana and Krishnavarma, the forty-eight-year-old Madame Cama was a central figure among the Indian nationalists in Paris. She had extensive connections with Irish, Egyptian, Polish, and Russian exiled revolutionaries in the French capital, and travelled among French socialists Jean Jaurès and Jean Longuet and joined the Section Française de l'Internationale Ouvrière. Cama also espoused the struggle for Indian independence among international feminists and suffragettes, combining anticolonialism, socialism, and feminism into a unique articulation in *Bande Mataram*, a new periodical she had founded with Har Dayal in September 1909. Through her multifarious connections, Acharya and some of the other younger Indians were introduced to these networks, learning about socialism and anarchism for the first time, and the importance of interconnected struggles against oppressive regimes, be they imperialist, capitalist, or Tsarist.[8]

Back in India, on 21 December 1909, Anant Laxman Kanhere assassinated A. M. T. Jackson, the District Magistrate of Nasik, allegedly in revenge for Jackson's involvement in the arrest and transportation for life of Savarkar's brother, Ganesh, in June 1909. The DCI was quick to point out the similarities between the assassination of Curzon-Wyllie and that of Jackson and subsequently tried to connect Savarkar to both murders. However, rather than securing a warrant for Savarkar's arrest for his alleged involvement in these murders, the DCI charged him under the Fugitive Offenders Act for seditious speeches made in 1906, which meant that Savarkar could stand trial in India rather than in Britain.[9] Alarmed by this, Savarkar fled London for Paris in early January 1910. However, against the advice of other Indian nationalists in Paris, Savarkar returned to London in March 1910. He was immediately arrested upon his arrival at Victoria Station and incarcerated in Brixton Prison, while he awaited extradition for trial in India.[10]

39

ANARCHY OR CHAOS

In early January 1910, Acharya was involved in smuggling weapons and seditious literature into India. The plan had been discussed amongst the Indian nationalists in London for a few months. Chanjeri Rao, who had recently arrived in London, joined the nationalists and was soon, according to his own testimony, pressured into assassinating Lord Morley, the Secretary of State for India. Rao refused to do this but was instead prevailed upon to bring a letter to Acharya as well as twenty-five revolvers 'in a box with a false bottom'. Arriving in Paris on 4 January 1910, Rao stayed at Acharya's and Amin's place, who now lived together at 75 Rue du Faubourg du Temple, and in the following days, the three of them looked around for a new apartment where they could learn how to manufacture bombs. Acharya and Amin also introduced Rao to all the prominent Indian nationalists in Paris, and Krishnavarma urged Rao to bring the twenty-five revolvers and some books with him to India. Rao deemed it 'a dangerous task' but promised to bring the books and one revolver. Acharya had special access to private rooms at Rana's house and was responsible for packing up the books and the revolver, a task he had often overseen, Rao later confessed. Rao left Paris with the revolver, cartridges, and some books on 10 January. He was immediately arrested upon his arrival in Bombay on 28 January 1910 and provided the British authorities with an extensive account of his activities among the inner circles of the Indian revolutionaries in London and Paris.[11] While the attempt to smuggle seditious literature and arms into India failed in this case, the episode is evidence of the militancy of the Indian nationalists in Paris and London at the time and, indeed, of Acharya's central role in these ventures.

In the meantime, the British authorities had decided that Savarkar should stand trial in India. On 1 July 1910, he was placed in a cell on the British P & O steamer SS *Morea*, a commercial vessel destined for India. However, as the *Morea* docked outside Marseille on 8 July, Savarkar escaped through a porthole and swam to French territory. Running from the now alerted British authorities on the vessel, Savarkar approached a French policeman and claimed asylum in France. Perhaps misunderstanding Savarkar's appeal, the policeman handed Savarkar back to the British authorities on the *Morea*. Departing with Savarkar on board the next day, the vessel landed at

40

EXILE IN EUROPE

Bombay, and Savarkar soon stood trial for sedition. However, the Indian nationalists in Paris claimed that Savarkar's return to the British was a breach of international legal rights of asylum. The 'Savarkar affair', as it was called at the time, soon became a major international scandal that was eventually brought to the Permanent Court of Arbitration at The Hague in late October 1910.

Largely funded by Cama, the Indian nationalists hired Longuet as a legal advisor and garnered support from many corners of the world. Aldred, for instance, set up the Savarkar Release Committee, while British Independent Labour Party leader Keir Hardie brought the case of Savarkar in front of the socialists gathered in Copenhagen for the International Socialist Congress in August 1910. However, the court at The Hague decided in favour of the British Government on 24 February 1911 and thereby upheld the verdict to return Savarkar to the British authorities who sentenced him to double life in prison, a total of fifty years, in the Cellular Jail in the Andaman Islands.[12] If Savarkar had already assumed the role of rhetorical leader of the Indians in Europe, the trial and sentencing made him a martyr in the struggle for Indian independence.

Anticolonial alliances in Paris and Brussels

Acharya's activities among the inner circles of the Paris Indian Society also brought him into contact with some Egyptian nationalists in the French metropolis. To discuss their future cause of common action, Egyptian nationalists planned to hold a conference in Paris in September 1910 and invited several Indian and European supporters. In the days before the conference, Acharya, Chatto, and Aiyar frequently met the Egyptian nationalist leader Muhammad Farid Bey and, reportedly, began to 'wear the fez in imitation of the Egyptians'.[13] However, the British authorities prevailed upon the French authorities to prohibit the conference because 'it did not desire that Paris should become the centre of an anti-British crusade'.[14] Instead, the Egyptians decided to move the conference to Brussels, now to be held in the Brasserie Flamande from 22 to 23 September 1910.[15] The night before departing for Brussels, about a hundred and fifty Egyptians and Indians and twenty-five Europeans held a soiree at the Grand Palais

ANARCHY OR CHAOS

des Champs-Élysées. Just after midnight, Acharya, Aiyar, and Amin left together with the Egyptian nationalist Mansour Rifat, and then departed on the 8:20 train for Brussels the next morning.[16]

Drawing in Egyptians from all over Europe, the next two days also saw speeches from prominent European socialists such as Longuet and Hardie, Irish revolutionaries such as Charlotte Despard and Nannie Florence Dryhurst, as well as Cama and Har Dayal, and the event was capped off with singing from Perin Naoroji.[17] According to intelligence reports, Acharya attended under the name 'Mr. Bhayankaram', which, they stated, meant 'awe-inspiring'.[18] Acharya later recalled that at the congress, he and Aiyar had been in the company of Asaf Ali, Chatto, and Rifat, as well as Djelal Nuri Bey, a 'quiet, fair young man, with small moustache and low feminine voice at the "table" in Hotel de la Esperance, who used play Turkish tunes upon the piano after dinner in the evening, till rather late, and probably Misses Naoroji also sang before him and others present'.[19]

After the conference, Acharya went to Rotterdam to learn printing and engraving at the Rotterdamsche Boek- en Kunstdrukkerij, where he oversaw the second printing of Savarkar's *The Indian War of Independence of 1857*, this edition being financed by Cama.[20] The DCI reported that, 'the whole of the negotiations with this firm were conducted by Tirumal Acharya. The copies of Savarkar's book were sent to the Free Railway Station, Paris, where Acharya took delivery. He wrote from care of S. R. Rana, 46 rue Blanche, Paris, when sending the money for the bill'.[21] Meanwhile, returning to Paris, a life of wandering was not yet over for Acharya.

A sojourn in Germany

In July 1910, Acharya, Aiyar, and Amin had discussed moving to Brazil to start a nationalist group among the Indians there. They soon abandoned these plans, while Acharya was reported to be wanting to return to India in August and now associated closely with Aiyar in Paris.[22] In the meantime, Aiyar and Krishnavarma went to Copenhagen for the International Socialist Congress in late August 1910 to protest the arrest and deportation of Savarkar. Attending as unofficial guests invited by Longuet and Jaurès, they were not permit-

42

EXILE IN EUROPE

ted to address the audience, but Hardie spoke on their behalf, ensuring that the congress resolved to condemn the violation of the right of asylum in the Savarkar affair.[23] On his return from Copenhagen, Aiyar stopped in Berlin and met Jodh Singh Mahajan, a former India House resident, to discuss the formation of an Indian nationalist group in the German capital. According to the DCI, Mahajan had attempted to learn how to manufacture arms in Berlin, but failing to do so had left him disillusioned. Instead, he wanted to go to Brazil and start an Indian nationalist group there.[24] After Berlin, Aiyar returned briefly to Paris before he went back to Pondicherry in October 1910.[25]

Acharya's plans to return to India soon changed. In November 1910, he briefly lived with Chatto at 14 rue Montaigne and ceased working for Rana. At the suggestion of Aiyar and Cama, Acharya now moved to Berlin to replace Mahajan and to set up a revolutionary society among the Indians there. In Berlin, he found work as a tea-maker and salesman at the Allgemeine Teeimport-Gesellschaft, where his employer noted that 'he was always very industrious, willing, and reliable' and 'discharged his duties faithfully'.[26] Acharya was unable to set up a nationalist group in Berlin, and in April 1911, he moved to Munich. In the Bavarian city, he met the staunch anti-imperialist Walter Strickland, known as 'the Anarchist Baron' for his aristocratic heritage, and Strickland's protégé Padmanabha Pillai, whom Acharya knew from Pondicherry as a nationalist sympathiser.[27] A close associate of Guy Aldred and Krishnavarma, as well as a contributor to *The Indian Sociologist*, Strickland had renounced his aristocratic heritage and travelled the world before he ended up in Munich shortly prior to Acharya's arrival. Padmanabha Pillai studied Forestry and was on the fringes of the revolutionary movement, but according to Acharya, Pillai was 'all right as regards views … [and] he is a much better fellow than our London students'.[28]

Acharya soon found work with the Munich branch of the Allgemeine Teeimport-Gesellschaft. In April 1911, according to the DCI, he complained to a friend that he had not heard from Chatto for weeks, despite writing several letters to him, and he feared that Chatto had abandoned the revolutionary cause. In fact, back in Paris, Chatto was preoccupied with marital affairs, and he had fallen out with Cama. Indeed, there was tension within the Paris Indian Society,

43

ANARCHY OR CHAOS

partly caused by distrust because of suspected misuse of Cama's funds for the Savarkar case, and widespread dejection had set in following the decision against Savarkar at The Hague.[29] In August 1911, an old friend from Pondicherry, Jnanendra Nath Chatterji, arrived in Munich. Acharya and Aiyar considered calling him to Pondicherry: '[h]e will not be of much use to discuss, but for action he will be valuable', Acharya wrote to Aiyar.[30]

In late August 1911, the Allgemeine Teeimport-Gesellschaft went bankrupt, and Acharya lost his job. In need of help, he went to the British consulate in Munich, who suggested that Acharya should send a lawyer's notice to the liquidators of the tea company. Acharya could not afford a lawyer and instead wrote to Cama. In early September, she replied dismissively:

> [l]ast year this month I was begging you to go to Pondicherry, Indo-China, or anywhere in the East, and I had some arrangements made for your passage, but you were very cross with me and would not listen to go East; if I mentioned it you turned away. Now this year when you want to go, I am sorry I am perfectly helpless. Nobody pays you a *sou* [penny] for the cause; even the expenses of the paper *Bande Mataram* depend on my self-denial. All *deshbandhus* here are forsaking the cause and talking of famine in India and their own pleasure in Paris. Since the great master *Desh* Savarkar is lost the demoralised people have collapsed, and London friends are also having their quarrels.[31]

Cama did, however, strike a note of sympathy: '[m]y heart aches for you, my brother and son, but I cannot see my way how I can help you. The only thing for you now is to take up some other situation in Germany and wait for some time till you save your passage'.[32]

When Italy invaded Ottoman-occupied Libya on 29 September 1911, Acharya wanted to join the Tripolitanians—much as he had wanted to support the Rifs against Spain—in their struggle against the foreign invaders. He suggested this to Strickland, who gave Acharya a 'recommendation to Professor [Ármin] Vámbéry in Budapest requesting him to help me through his Turkish friends to get me over to Tripoli'.[33] Vámbéry had travelled extensively throughout the Ottoman Empire, spent a year in Constantinople, and made extensive connections with Turkish Pashas, and was therefore considered a perfect intermediary.

44

EXILE IN EUROPE

However, Acharya soon abandoned this venture. In late September 1911, he wrote to Aiyar that he wanted to return to India, and that he had asked his father for money. He also mentioned Cama's letter, noting that he had no grievances against Cama, and he thought that the disagreements in Paris were rather absurd. As for his situation in Munich, he reiterated that he liked Padmanabha Pillai, although he called him 'aristocratic' and 'diplomatic'. Acharya praised one of Har Dayal's friends, C. Khodadad, a Muslim from Delhi. 'In many respects he is even better than Pillai', Acharya noted to Aiyar and continued:

> [h]e will be quite with us, though at present, as a student of chemistry in Europe, he keeps his ideas (which are our own) in the background. I might say he is at least as good as Asaf Ali (I don't mean what Asaf Ali is at present for I hear nothing of him). Of course, Khodadad is not as rich as either Ali or Pillai, and even when they moved very closely with each other I don't believe Pillai knows as much of Khodadad as I do .... On the whole, I can say both of them are very good fellows and will be useful some time hence.

Acharya had his letters sent to Khodadad at Marsstrasse 7 in Munich, but nothing else is known of their friendship.[34]

In early October 1911, Acharya again wrote to Aiyar that he had heard from Cama that Aiyar might be in prison and, if that was the case, he would not return to India. At the same time, he was also increasingly frustrated with his life in Europe: 'I am extremely tired of European and Europeanised countries, be these America or Africa, I will get out of there quick at all risks. I prefer our country even inside its prison cells and penal settlements or on its gallows erected by the brutes'.[35]

Meanwhile, the prominent Indian nationalists Ajit Singh and Sufi Amba Prasad had fled India in 1909. They spent considerable time in Persia before Singh proceeded alone to Constantinople and arrived in Paris via Switzerland in August or September 1911. However, Singh soon returned to Lausanne under the assumed name Mirza Hassan Khan.[36] In mid-October 1911, Singh and Chatto discussed sending Acharya to Constantinople, as they considered it important to have an emissary there to stir up anti-British sentiments and unity amongst Britain's oppressed, and they suggested that Acharya should 'try to earn his living by giving lessons in English'.[37]

ANARCHY OR CHAOS

They first sent Acharya to Vienna to see Singh's friend Agha Rahim Zadah, while Singh procured further letters of introduction from acquaintances he had made during his time in Constantinople, including Saiyid Muhammad Tawfik, principal of the Persian School, Prince Bahman Mirza, the Persian vice-consul, and Sayyed Hasan Taqizādeh, a leader of the Ferqeh-e Demokrat party.[38] While Singh was planning this, Chatto was initially suspicious of Singh's motives and asked Acharya for his opinion. Acharya seems to have trusted Singh and responded to Chatto: '[i]t was indeed very kind—if not purely patriotic—of him'.[39]

Anti-British work in Constantinople

With letters of introduction from Strickland and the others in hand, Acharya arrived in Constantinople on 1 November 1911.[40] Writing to Aiyar a week later, he asked for Aiyar's opinion of his move to the city and made it clear that 'I have not been sent here to live hand to mouth or to live comfortably but for various reasons all in the interests of our common ideal'.[41] While the Italian-Ottoman War had been raging since late September 1911, Acharya reassured Aiyar that '[e]verything is still orderly, and the city seems to go on as usual'.[42] He also commented that '[a]ll classes and creeds are united in the hatred of the Italian Government and things, and seem to urge the Government to continue the war to the bitter end. This must be an example of real public opinion!'.[43] Acharya also noticed that Indian Muslims had collected money for their Ottoman 'co-religionists', and he asked Aiyar: '[a]re the Hindus doing anything to help Turkey, say, by way of finance? The idea should be set in motion by our revolutionaries that the Hindus should join the Muhammadans'.[44] Acharya went even further and suggested: 'we ought to have taken the lead before the Muhammadans, so to give the Italo-Turkish War an anti-European turn as far as possible, and to bring such Muslims as are patriotic enough to the Hindu revolutionary party'.[45] He warned, however, that this should not be an 'opportunity for the formation and strength of mere Pan-Islamism'.[46] While writing from a Hindu perspective, Acharya's militancy was unquestionable, and while he believed in 'freedom, unity, and revolution', as he wrote, he was

EXILE IN EUROPE

wary of the dangerous aspects of revolutionary struggles based on religious or ethno-nationalist unity.[47]

Slowly settling into life in Constantinople, a week later, Acharya wrote to Aiyar again that, despite the 'ugly things such as haggling in business, roads no good even for mules, all lanes, house in wood and ruins, stink and dirt', he liked 'the people better, as orientals can be expected to be more familiar'.[48] He soon tried to contact Djelal Nuri Bey and Muhammad Farid Bey but did not succeed. However, with the letters of introduction from Singh, Vámbéry, and Strickland in hand, on 10 November 1911, Acharya met Tevfik Fikret (Mehmed Tevfik), the poet and editor of the local paper *Tanin* and a strong supporter of the Committee of Union and Progress (CUP), as well as Mehmed Said Pasha, the newly instated president of the CUP. He presented them his reasons for stirring up united anti-European feelings, but they were hesitant and informed Acharya that, 'this being a time of war, when they have much business to attend to, and much trade is paralysed, and since I don't know Turkish, they would think it over and let me know'.[49] Acharya's hopes for united anti-European struggles were dashed as they also blamed India for 'most of the troubles in the Middle East and to Asia generally'.[50] The Ottomans wanted a major Asiatic power such as India to support them against Italy, but instead had to rely on Germany and Britain, according to Acharya, which explained their reluctance to support him. He did find Singh's friend Tewfik Beg very friendly, however. Acharya informed Aiyar that Beg could potentially be helpful with mobilising Indian Muslim support for the Ottoman struggle. These plans, of course, relied on money, but as Acharya lived 'by hook or crook', they would be difficult to carry out. Indeed, Acharya was well-aware of the uncertain nature of a revolutionary life: '[w]e are revolutionaries, and we don't know what we will be tomorrow, let alone what it will all be worth that which we can do, after all'.[51]

Acharya decided to remain in Constantinople until he felt it 'useless or impossible'.[52] He received long letters from his father, asking him to return to India, but Acharya felt that the revolutionary struggle was 'greater and stronger than family and personal feelings'.[53] In late November 1911, Acharya became desperate and asked Chatto for money: 'I have been thinking of suicide, though not with my own hand exactly'.[54] In early January 1912, Acharya fell ill and was con-

47

ANARCHY OR CHAOS

fined to his house for two weeks. He had no money left, but Fikret promised to find work for him at *Tanin*.[55] He also sought employment with the general supply company Altendorf, Wright & Darf and provided a letter of recommendation from Rana: '[h]e is the son of a very respectable family, well educated, intelligent, and possessing a knowledge of several languages, especially English, which he speaks and writes flawlessly', wrote Rana, and continued: '[h]e is an honest and well-mannered young man who deserves every possible encouragement. You can give him the position for which he has made an application without any misgivings'.[56] Beg also praised Acharya: 'I can say nothing that is not favourable in regard to him. He is a capable, honest man, who by reason of his commendable qualities would satisfy you in every sense of the word'.[57]

Meanwhile, by mid-March 1912, Acharya still languished in the Ottoman metropolis, now giving English lessons at the Shaikh-ul-Islamat but also, reportedly, considered leaving for Tripoli.[58] He remained in Constantinople and, as the DCI reported, behaved himself 'quiet and free from suspicion'.[59] Acharya's unsuspicious behaviour meant that the DCI relaxed their surveillance of him, for they soon reported that

> M. P. Tirumal Acharya, the young Madrassi revolutionary, appears to have given the slip to those who were watching him, and has left for some unknown destination. There is reason to suppose that he went first to Paris, and efforts are being made to pick up some trace of his movements there. He is known to be anxious to return to India. He was accompanied from Constantinople by a person whose name is given as Hassan Syed Hal, described as an Indian trader who has not been identified further. The latter was apparently well off and supplied the money for the journey.[60]

It is not known who this benefactor Hassan Syed Hal was, but they did not travel to Paris. In the French metropolis, internal disputes had undermined the revolutionary zeal of the Indian nationalists, especially after Govind Amin had stolen a large number of pearls from Rana and subsequently committed suicide in September 1912.[61] Instead, Ajit Singh suggested to Acharya that he should join Chandra Kanta Chakravarty, his former India House associate, who had arrived in New York City in February 1910.[62]

48

EXILE IN EUROPE

Acharya's peripatetic travels across Europe within a short span of time, associating with the most prominent Indian nationalists in exile, are exemplary of the itinerant lives of anticolonial revolutionaries at the time. Marked by uncertainty, frustration, and poverty, the constant movement was both in response to intelligence surveillance, geopolitical rivalries, and imperial ambitions of European powers but also the ultimate expression of anticolonial praxis—that is, forging anticolonial alliances with other nationalists in exile, producing nationalist literature and propaganda, and an allegiance to militancy and armed struggle. Meanwhile, Acharya's correspondence with Aiyar in India connected those networks across the globe, showing how Indian nationalism was not a territorial idea but transnational and cosmopolitan, yet also fraught with tension and precarity.

3

THE GHADAR PERIOD

Escape to the United States

On 24 June 1912, Acharya departed the Greek port of Patras on the steamship *Argentina*, travelling under Persian nationality, and arrived at Ellis Island on 12 July. In New York, he met Chakravarty and proceeded to George Freeman's offices at the *Gaelic American*, who apprised him of the case against Amin, and found lodging at 515 East 144th Street.[1] Soon after, he made his way to Prattsburgh, a small town in the north-western part of the state of New York, and from here wrote to Rana and lamented Amin's theft. Acharya had also heard from Chatto earlier, he wrote to Rana, that Amin was getting into trouble, and he worried that the theft would cause even further suspicion and division among the Indians in Paris. He wrote, however, 'I don't see any reason why the action of one misguided man after such a length of satisfactory conduct should bring the whole class into disrepute and mistrust, and therefore I hope that things will go on as usual, perhaps to fill the loss recently suffered'.[2] Acharya also conveyed news from Har Dayal who was 'living well' and Chakravarty who was 'now a Ph.D. in medicine and ... being very obliging whenever necessary'.[3] However, Acharya had abandoned his revolutionary life for the time being. He explained to Rana that he had 'been doing all sorts of hard labour, outdoor and indoor' and was now working on a farm in Prattsburgh.[4]

51

ANARCHY OR CHAOS

Meanwhile, the DCI was still clueless as to Acharya's whereabouts. By November 1912, the DCI reported that they had lost track of Acharya but suspected that he had gone to North America. To find him, the Indian-born Canadian intelligence officer William C. Hopkinson scoured Seattle for traces of Acharya but reported back: 'I could not learn anything of Acharya, as the name is apparently unheard of in and around Seattle; but, I have made arrangements of such a nature that should anything be heard of him I will be immediately apprised thereof'.[5] A few weeks later, Hopkinson wanted to continue his search for Acharya throughout the entire Pacific North West:

> [b]efore proceeding on this trip, I have considered the matter carefully; and I think it would be to the interests of the Government, in connection with Hindu affairs, to make this journey, inasmuch as—in addition to the inquiry re Tirumal Acharya—I am almost sure I shall be able to gather a deal of interesting information. It is more than a year ago since I was in that locality, since which period there has been a considerable influx of Hindu students to Berkeley.[6]

Hopkinson was right about the increased activity of Indians around Berkeley, but he would not find Acharya there at the time.

The Ghadar Party and Indian anticolonialism in North America

After leaving Paris in October 1910, Har Dayal had wandered the world and spent time in Algiers, Martinique, and Hawaii. He briefly studied Buddhism at Harvard University before he ended up in Berkeley at the end of April 1911 and joined Stanford University as Lecturer in Indian philosophy in January 1912. He soon resigned his post but continued to lecture among the radical circles in the Bay Area, including at the Radical Club, the Fraternity of the Red Flag, and the Bakunin Institute. It was here Har Dayal turned to anarchism and soon served as secretary of the Oakland branch of the Industrial Workers of the World (IWW), its members known as Wobblies.[7]

Bringing his philosophy of 'Hardayalism' into practice, Har Dayal and Pandurang Khankhoje, both of whom had joined the IWW in 1912, started organising among the Indian labourers on the West Coast, many of them Sikhs working in the lumber mills, and in late May 1913, the first meeting of the Hindusthan Association of the

52

THE GHADAR PERIOD

Pacific Coast (HAPC) took place in Astoria, Oregon.[8] Soon attracting a large membership, Har Dayal, Khankhoje, Thakur Das, and Ram Chandra, among others, swiftly set to work among the growing presence of Indian labourers and students in the United States. Like the Indian nationalists in London and Paris, the HAPC set up a propaganda paper, *Ghadar* ('Mutiny'), and henceforth the organisation became known as the Ghadar Party and its members known as Ghadarites.[9] The HAPC also purchased a house on 436 Hill Street in San Francisco, the Yugantar Ashram, which served as a meeting venue for Indians on the West Coast.

Modelled after the Free India Society in London—as well as the Society of Political Missionaries, a political organisation Har Dayal had proposed to Krishnavarma already in 1907—the HAPC adhered to rules of secrecy and inner circles but with branches across North America that were organised 'relatively informal, sans official hierarchy but with active leaders selected by consultation among core participants'.[10] Alongside the propaganda work in the Ghadar Party, Khankhoje directed the organisation's militant wing, drawing inspiration from Chinese and Mexican revolutionaries in exile, and advocated insurrectionary guerrilla methods against the British in India.[11]

Such anticolonial solidarities around issues of labour, race, and imperialism translated into closer conversations between the Ghadarites and the Wobblies. While the Ghadarites still organised around the idea of the nation and not class like the Wobblies, the two organisations shared tactics such as non-parliamentarian agitation, strikes, and boycotts, which signals important overlaps between anticolonialism and revolutionary syndicalism. These affinities, as well as Har Dayal's connections with prominent anarchists Alexander Berkman and Emma Goldman, established a historical lineage and a future direction that influenced Acharya.[12]

By the spring of 1913, Acharya had returned to New York City and lived at 515 East 144th Street with Freeman as well as 'Bamaghar, an East Indian, and German who goes by the name of Gore', all described as 'bad characters'.[13] He applied for US citizenship in New York on 15 March 1913. The affair caused some uproar as the county clerk struggled to pronounce Acharya's full name. Asked to repeat his name twice 'as thirty-six clerks crowded around' him, he was eventu-

ANARCHY OR CHAOS

ally 'persuaded to apply for citizenship under the name Tirusnab Acharya'.[14] In the end, however, his application was rejected as naturalisation required residence in the US for at least two years. By then, his reputation as a militant revolutionary had caught up with him. William Williams, the US Commissioner of Immigration, wanted to deport Acharya, but the British consul at New York, on Hopkinson's advice, had no specific charges against him. In case of deportation, the British consul said, Acharya would be sent back to Patras in Greece, as that was his last point of residence before arriving in the US.[15]

A year later, there were signs of more activity in New York City. As the DCI reported:

> [t]he Indian colony in New York, which has been very quiet for the past two years, is beginning to show signs of renewed activity. The New York branch of the Hindusthan Association of the United States, America, has some 12 members, prominent among whom are C. K. Chakravarty and M. P. T. Acharya .... George Freeman of the *Gaelic American* continues to associate with the Indian agitators.[16]

Set up in January 1914 as a successor to the Hindusthan Association of the USA, the new Hindusthan Association of America (HAA) was principally an organisation for Indian students in America, with some more radical members such as Acharya and Chakravarty.[17] Now living with Chakravarty at 494 East 141st Street, Acharya was brought on as councillor of the HAA's eastern section.[18] During a later raid of Acharya's and Chakravarty's home at 364 East 120th Street, copies of *Bande Mataram* and other publications, fake passports, photos, and letters from Chinese revolutionaries were recovered.[19] The two of them also visited Haines Falls in the Catskills Mountains, where Acharya befriended a woman referred to as 'Mother Logan'.[20]

Meanwhile, in the San Francisco area, Har Dayal was arrested on 25 March 1914 'on charges of being a member of excluded classes, an anarchist or advocating the overthrow of the United States government by force'.[21] However, with the help of the Paris-based Irish nationalist Maud Gonne, Madame Cama managed to put up the $1,000 bail for Har Dayal's release, who then fled the US for Switzerland.[22] In Zürich, he stayed with Chempakaraman Pillai, joined Pillai's organisation the International Pro-India Committee, and soon started writing for Mansour Rifat's publication *La Patrie Egyptienne*.[23] In June 1914,

54

THE GHADAR PERIOD

the DCI reported, Acharya had agreed to proofread the Tamil edition of the *Ghadar* and even contributed articles in Tamil to the publication.[24] Acharya's involvement with the Ghadar Party is somewhat unclear, but the DCI reported that in the autumn he had travelled to San Francisco to join the Yugantar Ashram.[25]

Indian revolutionaries and anarchists in exile

In New York, Acharya first met Berkman and his friend Hippolyte Havel, two of the most prominent anarchists of the period.[26] While Berkman associated with Har Dayal and the Ghadarites on the West Coast, little is known of Berkman's contact with Indians in New York. In the early 1910s, Berkman was involved in the Modern School movement, inspired by the Spanish educator and freethinker Francisco Ferrer, who had been executed by the Spanish government in July 1909, and the Ferrer School in New York.[27] Berkman went on a speaking tour in the late summer of 1914, and Berkman may have met Acharya on one of such occasions. Indeed, as Acharya admitted to the Swedish anarchist Bert Ekengren many years later, 'although I had read Kropotkin in 1909 in London and had known Alexander Berkman and his group in New York', he was not seriously interested in anarchism at the time.[28] Similarly, little is known of Acharya's connections with Havel at this point. Given that Havel and Berkman often worked together at the time, it is possible that Acharya met them on the same occasion. However, Acharya's later claim to have met the two prominent anarchists in New York at the time should perhaps be considered an attempt to establish a longer pedigree of anarchist activity on his behalf.

Indeed, while Acharya's two-year sojourn in North America was relatively quiet compared to his militant life in Europe, during his time there, he also consolidated some friendships and introduced him to new ideological avenues. Building on similar militant groups in Europe, the Ghadar Party was considered a major threat to the British empire, particularly through its inter-revolutionary connections and merging of anticolonial and anarchist politics. While Acharya, in some ways, was marginal to these developments, the pre-war Ghadar period was significant for his understanding of revolutionary strug-

ANARCHY OR CHAOS

gles. Meanwhile, the outbreak of the First World War in July 1914 changed Acharya's life dramatically. In November 1914, he departed New York, leaving behind traces of his life in India, Europe, and North America: his high school diploma from the Hindu High School in Triplicane, some letters of recommendation from Rana, Beg, and other former employees, his British passport from 1909, and several postcards addressed to him 'in most affectionate terms' by a German girl in Munich who signed herself as 'Faschoda Marie'.[29]

Acharya's two years in the US spanned some of the most important years of Indian anticolonial activity on the continent. While he initially abandoned the movement, upon his return to New York, he reconnected with the anticolonial networks and alliances there as well as the radical Ghadarites on the West Coast. His activities are evidence of the global scale of the Indian revolutionary movement as well as overlaps and antagonisms with the international anarchist movement that greatly influenced Acharya.

4

WAR AGAINST THE BRITISH EMPIRE

The Indian Independence Committee in Berlin

In November 1914, Acharya arrived in Berlin on a fake Persian passport provided by George Freeman. Two months earlier, in September 1914, the Auswärtiges Amt (German Foreign Office, AA) had approached Chatto with the prospect of obtaining Indian assistance in overthrowing the British in India.[1] For Chatto, the potential of German assistance to the Indian nationalists was nothing new. In an editorial in *Talvar* from March 1910, Chatto had intimated that a war with Germany could lead to British expulsion from India.[2]

Adopting the dictum that the enemy of our enemy is our friend, under the auspices of the newly-founded Nachrichtenstelle für den Orient (Intelligence Bureau for the East, NfO)—an office attached to the AA—Chatto set up the Indian Independence Committee (IIC) in Berlin in the autumn of 1914.[3] Among the early members were Dr Mansur Ahmed, Chempakaraman Pillai, and Moreshwar Prabhakar.[4] The Berlin group worked in close collaboration with Indian nationalists in Switzerland, led by Har Dayal, Birendra Nath Das Gupta, and Mahendra Pratap, and Chatto and Har Dayal travelled frequently between Berlin and Geneva to coordinate their activities in the autumn of 1914.[5] When the Ottoman Empire joined the war on the side of the Germans, Har Dayal went to Constantinople for

57

ANARCHY OR CHAOS

talks with Enver Pasha, the Ottoman minister of war, to sound him out about support for a German-Ottoman invasion of India but returned empty-handed to Geneva in October 1914. He and Pratap eventually went to Berlin in late January 1915 to join the IIC.[6] Throughout the autumn and winter of 1914, when Chatto and some of the other Indians in Berlin took out some apartments at Leibnizstrasse 42 in the Charlottenburg district of Berlin, around the corner from the IIC offices at Wielandstrasse 38, they reached out to Indians elsewhere in Europe and in North America to recruit them into the IIC. There was no formal membership, and the IIC comprised a revolving cast of members affiliated with the committee in Berlin. Egyptians, Persians, and pan-Islamists formed similar organisations under the auspices of the AA.[7]

News of the IIC's revolutionary ambitions reached Acharya in New York as well. On 31 October, provided with travel money from Dr Erich Kraske, the German Vice-Consul in New York, Acharya departed New York on the French steamer *Chicago* and arrived in Geneva a couple of weeks later, where Har Dayal received him.[8] He only stayed here for a few days, departing Zürich on 14 November, destined for Berlin via Munich. Though briefly held up at the border because of his Persian passport, he arrived in Berlin on 18 November and made his way to Leibnizstrasse, where Chatto and the other Indians took him in. Muhammed Barkatullah, Taraknath Das, L. P. Varma, Heramba Lal Gupta, Bhupendranath Datta, and Abdul Hafis also soon made their way from North America to Europe and joined the IIC's plot to overthrow British rule in India. In Berlin, Acharya's fake passport soon landed him in trouble when the local police visited him and asked for proper papers. As he was 'protected' by the German government, Acharya wrote to the NfO, he was not worried.[9] Two weeks later, both he and Gupta received proper German passports.[10]

Indian prisoners of war in Germany

When the war broke out, Indian residents in Germany were interned or had daily reporting requirement. The IIC was aware of this, so to recruit people into the organisation, the IIC sometimes intervened.

58

WAR AGAINST THE BRITISH EMPIRE

For example, Tarachand Roy from Leipzig had been interned in the early months of the war but, with the help of the IIC, released from prison and later allowed to be admitted to the University of Berlin in return for propaganda assistance for the IIC. By contrast, the IIC did not trust Dalip Singh Gill, a Ghadarite who was interned in the Rastatt camp, and Gill remained imprisoned throughout the war. At the outbreak of the war, the British Empire recruited around one and a half million Indians into the British army, and around 900,000 served in theatres of war in Europe, the Near East, and North Africa. After heavy battles in the early months of the war, thousands of Indians were captured and put into German prisoner-of-war camps such as Ruhleben and Zossen—the latter known as the Halbmondlager (Half Moon Camp) for its many Muslim prisoners. An early strategy by the IIC was to persuade Indian POWs to defect and join the Indian-German conspiracy against Britain. In early January 1915, Acharya, Dr Mansur, and Das visited the Halbmondlager and provided a lengthy report on the conditions of the Indian prisoners. Concerned particularly with Indian officers and Muslims, they made suggestions to the AA for how the prisoners should be treated and hoped that some of them would join the IIC if released.[11] In addition to such propaganda activities, a few days after their visit to the Halbmondlager, Rudolf Nadolny, the leader of the German General Staff responsible for arms and sabotage, asked Acharya and some of the other Indians to learn how to manufacture hand grenades and explosives.[12]

The Indian mission to Constantinople

The IIC soon plotted world revolution from Berlin. At their instruction, the AA sent money to the Ghadarites in North America to ship arms from the West Coast via Java and Shanghai to India. They made direct contacts with nationalists within India who were soon to be supported by Harish Chandra, Pratap's erstwhile assistant, and they planned missions to German East Africa.[13] However, after the Ottoman Empire entered the war in November 1914, the theatres of war in the Middle East became more important venues for the IIC. Prominent figures such as Pratap, Har Dayal, and Barkatullah all stressed the significance of revolution in India via the Middle East and

ANARCHY OR CHAOS

Afghanistan, entering through the North-West Frontier, supported by the Germans and working with Enver Pasha and the Ottoman government to realise their ambitions.[14]

The IIC set up a regional headquarters in Constantinople and rented an apartment from Abdullah Cevdet Bey, the famous poet and founding member of the CUP. Drawing extensive financial support from the AA, the Indians embarked on missions to Kabul, Baghdad, and the Suez Canal to persuade Indian soldiers arriving through these areas to defect and join the Indian Volunteer Corps, to be formed as a militant rebel group of Indians willing to march on India and fight against the British. In late February 1915, Acharya, Varma, and Das Gupta embarked on a mission to the Suez Canal via Constantinople. They had been provided with German East African passports— Acharya travelling under the name 'Haidar Ali', Varma as 'Hussain Ali', and Das Gupta as 'Muhammad Akbar'—given 3,000 Marks for the journey, and left Berlin in the evening of 25 February.[15] Before they left, Acharya swapped names with Das Gupta and now travelled under the name 'Muhammad Akbar'.[16] Another mission led by Pratap, which included Hormaz Kersasp, Kedar Nath, Basant Singh, Rishi Kesh Latta, and Chet Singh, set off for Kabul via Baghdad at the same time. A. C. Sharma, Kandubhai Nayik, and Acharya's friend Khankhoje joined that mission later.[17] Arriving in Switzerland in early March, Acharya returned to Berlin to care for other matters, while the rest of the mission pressed on to Constantinople.[18]

Having abandoned his first journey to Constantinople, Acharya soon embarked for the Turkish metropolis again, this time with Muhammad Rajab Ali in tow.[19] Travelling through Bulgaria, where his money (1,590 Marks) was confiscated, Acharya made it to Constantinople in late March 1915.[20] The mood was tense in the Turkish capital. Har Dayal telegrammed Acharya, Barkatullah, and Kersasp to avoid contact with any Egyptians and Turks not trusted by the Ottoman government and encouraged them to leave Constantinople as soon as possible.[21] Travelling under the name 'Jamal bin Sulaiman', Har Dayal arrived in Constantinople in early April and intended to join the mission to Syria and Baghdad.[22] Instead, he remained in Constantinople and took charge of the Indian mission there. Meanwhile, the Suez Canal mission had gone ahead without Acharya and when they arrived in Jerusalem

WAR AGAINST THE BRITISH EMPIRE

on 22 April, asked the IIC when Acharya would join them.[23] However, according to Har Dayal, Acharya was 'doing good work' in Constantinople, and he intended to keep Acharya there for the time being. Har Dayal noted that most of the work in the Suez Canal would have to be undertaken by the Egyptians anyway, so Acharya was not needed there for the time being.[24]

When Barkatullah had arrived in Constantinople in mid-March, he was instructed to wait for Pratap's Kabul mission to arrive from Berlin, so the Suez Canal mission subsequently became responsible for organising the Syria mission as well.[25] This change meant that Acharya and Varma were to be sent to Damascus via Jerusalem instead.[26] However, at Har Dayal's order, Varma stayed behind in Constantinople. Varma soon sent a letter to Chatto in Berlin, complaining about Har Dayal's selfish and dictatorial behaviour, which he had already noticed in Berlin. Varma questioned Har Dayal's 'spirit of democracy and ideals of Anarchism, which he used to preach in America', and accused him of conspiring against Chatto and Das.[27] Varma also explained that Har Dayal had poisoned Acharya's mind so that Acharya kept the money they had been entrusted for the Damascus mission to himself. What is more, Varma stated, the day before Acharya left for Damascus on 15 May, Acharya had asked Varma to hand over his passport which he would then give to Har Dayal. When he asked Har Dayal about it, Har Dayal said he did not have Varma's passport, so Varma was now stuck in Constantinople without money and a passport.

Acharya only remained in Damascus for about three weeks before he was called back to Constantinople, where he was asked to await Chatto's arrival.[28] Chatto arrived in mid-June and reported to the Berlin committee on the harmonious nature of the Indians in Constantinople but was soon called back to Switzerland by Das Gupta.[29] Meanwhile, Barkatullah and Pratap's mission to Kabul, officially led by the German officers Oskar von Niedermayer and Werner Otto von Hentig, had arrived in Baghdad via Aleppo in late May, proceeded a week later, and landed in Kabul in early October 1915. After long negotiations, the mission failed to receive any formal agreements from the Emir, who had struck a peace deal with the British, which meant that he could not support the Indians. However,

61

ANARCHY OR CHAOS

before the mission left in early 1916, they set up the Provisional Government of India with Pratap as president, Barkatullah as prime minister, and Ubaidullah Sindhi, an ardent pan-Islamist Indian nationalist, as home minister.[30]

The Suez Canal mission

In mid-June 1915, a report reached Constantinople that Acharya was needed in Jerusalem.[31] Less than two weeks later, with Acharya now in Jerusalem, the Suez Canal Mission telegraphed to Constantinople that Acharya should travel to Egypt with Ismail Hüsni, an Egyptian nationalist, right away.[32] As a protectorate of the British Empire, the Suez Canal was important for bringing in troops and supplies to the European theatres of war. At the time, the British had 70,000 troops in the region, mostly from the British Indian Army.

Acharya, Das, and Varma made it to Arish in Egypt in mid-July 1915 and set out to deploy local Bedouins as armed couriers. On 23 July, Acharya, Das, and Varma joined an Ottoman patrol, comprising twenty foot-soldiers, forty camels, and some Bedouins, and headed for the canal. The patrol reached Qantara five days later. They were wary of British soldiers in the area and realised that they would easily be overpowered if spotted. Consequently, they revised their original plans and resolved instead '(1) to do some destructive works; (2) to creep near the Sikh guards who [were] stationed on the side of the canal; (3) to make raids upon some of the Bedouin villages in which the English had placed their spies'.[33] Acharya, Das, and Varma decided to blow up the British-controlled railway with dynamite. However, the Bedouins convinced them—since the Indians would risk being caught by the British when swimming across the canal to reach the railway—that they should undertake the mission. Armed with revolvers and rifles, the band of Bedouins set off around midnight. 'We heard from a great distance a solitary but terrible explosion at 1.15 A.M. (night) which showed that the Bedouins did the work satisfactorily', Acharya later reported. He, Das, and Varma wanted to approach some of the Sikh guards that night as well but abandoned that plan as the explosion had alarmed everyone in the area. Instead, they embarked towards Arish, careful to avoid British airplanes in search

WAR AGAINST THE BRITISH EMPIRE

for them, and reached their destination three days later. In Arish, they persuaded local Bedouins and Ottoman soldiers to distribute propaganda for them, but soon after returned to Jerusalem.[34]

In Jerusalem, Das complained about the work of the mission. He would have been more useful in the Far East, he wrote in a confidential letter to the IIC.[35] Acharya and the Suez Canal mission notified the IIC two weeks later that they had no knowledge of Das' letter of complaint.[36] What is more, a month later, they notified the IIC that they did not believe Das' reasons for abandoning the mission—he also claimed health reasons—and they were worried that he would set a precedence for leaving the mission. However, Das was eventually allowed to retreat to Hebron for convalescence.[37] Meanwhile, after a brief mission to Beersheba in southern Palestine, Acharya informed the IIC that he wanted to return to Constantinople and proceed to Java.[38] However, on 3 September 1915, the IIC wrote to Acharya that he should 'continue his work at Suez Canal'.[39]

The Suez Canal mission was preparing to leave Jerusalem in mid-September. Their plan now also involved assassination of top British officials which, according to Das, had already been approved in Berlin.[40] However, in early October, Das returned to Constantinople and abandoned the plan. Varma and Das Gupta returned to Aleppo, while Acharya continued his work for the Suez Canal mission in Arish.[41] As the rift between Acharya and Das was greater than initially thought, Das was soon recalled to Berlin for work.[42] Instead, Abdul Hafis and Dr Mansur were sent to Constantinople, where Acharya joined them in mid-November 1915.

Restless and uncertain of his future, Acharya wanted to have a personal conversation with Har Dayal or Chatto as soon as possible. However, by then Har Dayal had returned to Berlin and left the IIC, signing letters instead as head of the Ghadar Party, and refused to work with the German authorities. After initially signalling reconciliation with the IIC, Har Dayal changed his mind. Instead, he wanted to go to Switzerland in January 1916, but the German authorities denied him permission to leave, so he was stuck in Berlin.[43] On his part, Chatto had left for Zürich in November 1915, ensnared by the British spy Donald Gullick, who tried to lure Chatto across the border into France where he could be arrested. Gullick's mission to

ANARCHY OR CHAOS

entrap Chatto was discovered by the Swiss police, and they were both briefly imprisoned for violation of Swiss neutrality. However, Chatto was considered innocent and released in mid-December but ordered to leave the country.[44] Thus, Acharya had to wait for Har Dayal and Chatto in Constantinople, uncertain of his future.

There was tension amongst the Indians in Constantinople. According to Das, this was due to Har Dayal's earlier refusal to work with Abdul Jabbar Kheiri and his separate Muslim Indian organisation that was working closely with the Ottoman government.[45] Someone like Dr Mansur, a friend of Jabbar Kheiri since India, would have been more diplomatic, Das felt, and Datta, who was a far more experienced revolutionary than Acharya, would have been better suited for their mission. Jabbar Kheiri had poisoned the ears of the Ottoman government, too, Das noted, and even stolen documents from Har Dayal. To move forward, Das wanted to establish more harmonious relations between the Hindu and Muslim Indians and to have formal relations with the Ottoman government.[46] Das' suggestions were taken on board, and the Young Hindusthan Association (YHA) was formally recognised by the Ottoman government in Constantinople in March 1916. To avoid accusations of the organisation being dominated by Hindus, the IIC settled on Hafis as president and Dr Mansur as vice president.[47]

The Baghdad mission

In early 1916, Acharya, Das Gupta, Varma, Rajab Ali, Sher Mohamed, and Maqbul Husain prepared to go to Baghdad, led by Dr Mansur in collaboration with Enver Pasha and the German commander Wilhelm von der Goltz. They would liaise with the Indian-Persian committee in Baghdad, led by Sufi Amba Prasad, and prepare to establish an Indian National Corps there that would join Ottoman forces and eventually march towards India.[48] Approved by the Ottoman government, the Baghdad mission was financed by the AA and intended to 'spread news of the war, and the political situation generally, in and out of India'.[49] However, the mission was delayed for weeks, owing to the Ottoman *councillor d'etat* Ali Bach Hamba's failure to pass on their requests for *wasiqas* (travel documents) to Enver Pasha. Finally,

WAR AGAINST THE BRITISH EMPIRE

with the help of the Haydarpaşa train station commander, they departed Constantinople at 5pm on 11 February 1916. Dr Mansur and Acharya travelled first class, while the others were seated in second class. Shortly before reaching Derince, a German officer in Ottoman uniform confronted Dr Mansur and Acharya, demanded their tickets and *wasiqas* and asked: '[w]ho are you to travel in first class? Get out at once'.[50] They refused to hand over their documents to the German officer, and at Derince, a train conductor boarded, checked their tickets and documents, and confirmed that everything was in order. The German officer refused to accept this, directed Dr Mansur and Acharya to leave the first class compartment, and eventually ordered his men to throw them off the train. With the German soldiers hesitating, an Ottoman officer intervened and pushed Dr Mansur out, prompting the German soldiers to join in and violently force the two Indians off the train with their luggage. 'Thus disgraced and insulted we were forced to discontinue our journey in Izmit', Dr Mansur reported to Hafis.[51] Spending the night in a hotel in nearby Izmit, where Sher Mohamed and Husain joined them, they received a new set of tickets and *wasiqas* the next day to travel on to Baghdad on 14 February. Full trains passed by the entire day, but they finally found empty seats in a first-class carriage at 8pm in the evening. As had happened a few days before, an Ottoman officer and a German officer refused the Indians admittance and forcibly pushed them off the train. Insulted and defeated, Dr Mansur and Husain returned to Constantinople the next morning, leaving Acharya and Sher Mohamed behind in Izmit.[52] They returned to Constantinople two weeks later. The episode was a stark reminder of the precarious position of the Indians, caught between German-Ottoman politics as British colonial subjects.

The mission eventually made it to Baghdad via Deir ez-Zor on 7 April 1916, nineteen days after leaving Aleppo, only to find that Halil Pasha, the governor of Baghdad, was away, and von der Goltz was ill. Even worse, the German consulate at Baghdad had no information about finances for the mission, and they had lost contact with Pratap's Kabul mission. Dr Mansur hastily telegraphed the IIC, who asked the AA to send 1,000 Ottoman Pounds to the mission immediately.[53] However, the mission was met with indifference by Halil

65

ANARCHY OR CHAOS

Pasha as well as the German authorities. This was not on account of the Ottomans, Acharya complained in a long letter to Chatto, but owing to the ineptitude of Dr Mansur. He was simply not suitable for the mission, making friends with the wrong people and 'enemies of clever and even sincere men', Acharya said, and even Rajab Ali and Husain were useless.[54] His complaints to Dr Mansur had fallen on deaf ears, and he worried that writing to Abdul Wahid—the new general secretary of the YHA in Constantinople—would be pointless, so he wrote directly to Chatto. Acharya felt that his presence there was futile, as he was only spending money like the others without doing any real revolutionary work. Dr Mansur had come under the influence of Inayat Ali, a Muslim Indian they had picked up in Deir ez-Zor on the way who was suspected to be a spy. In fact, when Acharya reminded Ali that they had met in Constantinople in 1911 or 1912, Ali denied this, which made Acharya more suspicious. Even worse, Dr Mansur and Husain had engaged local sex workers, causing a major scandal with the German authorities, and Dr Mansur had become hostile to Acharya, Varma, and Sher Mohamed along the way, due to Wahid's intrigues and Muslim resentment towards them, Acharya speculated.[55] Acharya was willing to remain in Baghdad, but only if Dr Mansur and the others changed their attitudes. If not, he wrote, 'I am determined to sever my connections violently whether I am going to be transferred to another centre or will be left to my fate here, or I should expect worse treatment'.[56] In mid-June, the German consul at Baghdad, W. G. Hesse, wrote to the AA about Dr Mansur's incompetence, too, and subsequently stopped funding the mission there. Hesse informed them that Acharya had returned via Aleppo to Constantinople, where he wanted to discuss the situation with Chatto.[57]

Meanwhile, Chatto and Datta arrived in Constantinople in late June. In their assessment of the tense situation in Constantinople, they wrote to Hafis that no work had been done in seven months, except for deputing the Baghdad mission, and no acceptable plan had been submitted to the authorities. Both the German and the Ottoman authorities, Chatto and Datta noted, felt that the Indians were wasting their money. In fact, internal disagreements and incompetence caused the Ottomans to stop funding Indian work in Constantinople. To

66

WAR AGAINST THE BRITISH EMPIRE

remedy the situation, a dramatic restructuring of Indian work was needed, which required Hafis to resign as president of the YHA. Doing so, Hafis also agreed, would allow Chatto and Datta to mend relations with both the German and the Ottoman authorities.[58]

The IIC laid out a new plan for Indian work in Turkey to the German embassy in Constantinople. Led by Pillai, it stated that Acharya and Varma should remain in Constantinople until further notice, while Dr Mansur would return to Berlin with Chatto. Rajab Ali was also dismissed from the new organisation. Maqbul Husain would carry out propaganda work in the Muslim POW camp in Islahiye, while Das Gupta and Nayik would work in the Hindu POW camp Ra's al-Ayn. Sher Muhamed would be asked to work as an interpreter in one of the camps. Two newcomers, Abdur Rabb and Mirza Abbas, would join the INP's work in the POW camps. Hailing from Peshawar, Rabb had worked as an interpreter for the British embassy in Baghdad for eighteen years, but when the war broke out, he defected and started writing anti-British articles for the periodical *Jahan-i-Islam*.[59] A month later, Acharya was still in Constantinople, but had still not been put to work and was uncertain of his future role in the INP. The IIC asked him to remain there until he was needed in Berlin.[60]

By December 1916, the IIC decided to terminate their operations in Constantinople altogether, for which Acharya and Das Gupta became responsible. They had to pay three months' rent to Abdullah Cevdet Bey, return documents to Berlin, pack revolvers and ammunition, and return furniture to the German embassy.[61] Das Gupta soon returned to Berlin, preparing to move to Switzerland to direct activities there, leaving Acharya with the responsibility to close the operation alone. Unwilling to do this single-handedly, Acharya asked for comrades from Berlin to come and assist him, which was agreed upon by the IIC, but this could not be done until mid-January 1917. The IIC asked the German embassy to pay Acharya 25 Liras per month and provide any assistance necessary. Acharya was now the representative of the IIC in Constantinople and was told to refrain from associating with any other Indians.[62] The situation was tense, and Acharya was the only reliable Indian in Constantinople. All communication between the IIC and the German embassy was to go through him.[63]

67

ANARCHY OR CHAOS

Acharya's last months in Constantinople proved difficult. He had to pay final salaries and give notice to the other Indians there, including Inayat Ali, Rajab Ali, and Husain, who all complained to the Tashkilat that Acharya had failed to do so. For the IIC, the question was whether it was the responsibility of the Germans or the Ottomans to pay the Indians. Acharya met Ali Bach Hamba and Dr Fuad Bey in the Tashkilat on 7 February to resolve the matter. He explained that the men had all been paid one month's expenses, and that he was duty bound by the IIC to stay away from the other Indians, but he would leave the final decision to the IIC.[64] The IIC refused to pay them more and asked Acharya to withhold any further payments until Chatto's arrival. However, the IIC worried that if they did not agree to pay these expenses, the Ottoman government would not allow Acharya, Varma, and Nayik to leave the country as planned at the end of the month. Therefore, they asked the AA to provide Acharya protection until the mission could be terminated.[65] The German embassy was not as forthcoming as the IIC had hoped, leaving Acharya without money to settle matters and terminate the mission, and it provided no protection from the Ottoman officials and the other disgruntled Indians.[66]

Chatto arrived in Constantinople on 11 March to resolve the situation. When he met Ali Bey in the Tashkilat the next day, Chatto felt that the Ottoman authorities were hostile to the Indian nationalists and refused to accept any responsibility for their joint activities. As for settling expenses and determining future prospects in Turkey or Germany, Chatto promised to help the dismissed Indians as much as possible.[67] Chatto settled the matters with Ali Bey in the Tashkilat on 17 March and reluctantly agreed to make minor payments to Rajab Ali and Husain. Chatto, Acharya, and Nayik finally left Constantinople on 10 April 1917.[68]

Acharya's activities across Europe and the Middle East during the First World War illuminate both the international scale of the war as well as an anticolonial history that upends conventional narratives. Despite the pursuit of global revolutionary missions directed from Berlin, the Indian-German conspiracies to overthrow British rule in India were not successful. As evidenced by Acharya's activities, efficient British intelligence on the one hand, and internal divisions

WAR AGAINST THE BRITISH EMPIRE

amongst the Indians on the other, thwarted many of these missions. Furthermore, the Indians found themselves to be pawns in a European imperialist game and soon had to look elsewhere for support.

5

INTERNATIONAL SOCIALISM AND WORLD PEACE

The International Socialist Peace Congress in Stockholm

After the February 1917 Russian revolution, the establishment of the Petrograd Soviet in March 1917, and the US entry into the war in April, various factions of the divided Second International—the Bureau of the Socialist International and the so-called Zimmerwaldians in the International Socialist Commission—arrived in Stockholm to negotiate a socialist peace in April 1917.[1] In agreement with other socialists from within the divided Second International, a Dutch-Scandinavian Committee (DSC) comprising, among others, the Belgian social democrat Camille Huysmans, the Dutch social democrats Henri van Kol, Willem Albarda, and Pieter Jelles Troelstra, and the Swedish social democrat Hjalmar Branting, was formed in early May 1917 to lead the negotiations.

Meanwhile, heeding the call from the Petrograd Soviet for self-determination for subject nations, the plans for a socialist peace congress also meant that nationalists from across the subject and colonial world arrived in the Swedish capital. Nationalist revolutionaries and representatives from Finland, Hungary, Ukraine, Poland, and Georgia, as well as anticolonial nationalists from India, Egypt, Persia, and Ireland soon made their way to Stockholm.[2] On 12 May 1917, equipped with German *Personalausweise* (ID cards), Chatto and Acharya

71

ANARCHY OR CHAOS

departed Berlin for the port city of Sassnitz. Here they boarded the SS *Drottning Victoria*, bound for the Swedish port town of Trelleborg, and proceeded to Stockholm, where they checked into Hotel Imperial, 'a very nice, clean, respectable, quiet and gentlemanly place where we pay about 7 SEK each (including bath) for our rooms'.[3]

International socialism, subject nations, and anticolonialism

In a letter to the IIC, Chatto outlined their activities and plans for work in Stockholm: first, to connect with the socialists in the city, they went to the publisher Bonnier to get some of Hyndman's material translated into Swedish and circulated among the delegates. A Swedish edition of all their pamphlets, Chatto stated, was necessary to 'enlighten people here and thus make our stay easier and more profitable'.[4] This could not be too politically charged, of course, as Sweden was neutral, and Bonnier refused to put its name to such material. Second, Chatto reported that they had already met both the Finnish and the Polish organisations in Stockholm. Emblematic of the nature of political agitation in the city, these organisations, Chatto remarked, 'always mean a couple of men who carry on the business energetically. So our outlook is not so bad'.[5] Whereas the Poles had decided not to press for further concessions and independence from Germany, the Finns were not satisfied with the Russian offer of autonomy and wanted complete independence. That was Chatto's and Acharya's standpoint too, a view they shared with Irakli Tsereteli and Georges Matchabelli, two members of the German-based Committee of Independent Georgia, whom they knew from Berlin. In fact, Tsereteli had suggested that, if the socialists were unwilling to consider the Indians' demands, the oppressed peoples gathered in Stockholm should hold a separate conference and send delegates to the socialists. With support from the Georgians, Chatto and Acharya were scheduled to meet van Kol and Huysmans the next day, 18 May 1917, and prepare the ground for their activities in Stockholm.[6]

The most pressing problem for Chatto and Acharya, though, was the fact that they still operated out of a hotel, and they needed an office for their activities and propaganda. They suggested renting an apartment with three or four rooms, which could be shared with the

INTERNATIONAL SOCIALISM AND WORLD PEACE

Persians and the Egyptians.[7] In all, they needed a furnished apartment at about 200SEK per month, a Swedish secretary who could speak English, French, and German, a typewriter, and one Indian and perhaps one Persian to reside at the place. Chatto also suggested that the AA should send an Irish representative, as 'it would be good to have two groups here—one anti-Russian and the other anti-British'.[8] To pay for this, he requested that the AA should send them 1,000SEK and prepare a Russian translation of their pamphlet *Indien unter der britischen Faust* for propaganda work amongst the Russians.[9]

The next day's planned meeting with Huysmans and van Kol was postponed until further notice, and Acharya and Chatto experienced another setback when, on 19 May, they visited the offices of the newspaper *Dagens Nyheter* to inquire if the newspaper would publish their articles. While they were well-received and the daily promised to publish their articles on India, Chatto also asked that his name not be mentioned for fear that their agenda in Stockholm would be revealed. However, the next day, *Dagens Nyheter* published an account of the Indians' visit and mentioned Chatto's name, though not Acharya's. Describing Chatto as a 'lively, seemingly intelligent young man', the orientalist rhetoric of the Swedish daily was also clear from the interview: '[i]n the last few days, Stockholm's colony of well-known strangers has gotten a new and exotic segment in a couple of representatives from the Indian nationalist party'.[10] The Indians were not in Stockholm to agitate for peace or socialism but for India's independence, Chatto stated in the interview. He also reiterated that, while they came from Berlin, they were not pro-German. Indeed, they had no illusion that German rulers would be better than British rulers: '[w]e Indians do not wish to swap masters', he said. 'We do not want any masters at all'.[11]

The new Indiska Nationalkommittén (Indian National Committee, INK) swiftly set to work among the socialists and arranged to meet Huysmans on 24 May. Chatto put two important questions to Huysmans: first, whether the ISC would take up the question of subject nations, and second, if India could not be represented at a potential peace conference, whether a resolution on Indian independence would be passed. Huysmans acknowledged that, even though some Indians had attended the congresses in Stuttgart (Cama and Rana) and

73

ANARCHY OR CHAOS

Copenhagen (Aiyar and Krishnavarma), that was only at the invitation of private citizens such as Hyndman. In fact, because the Indians did not have a socialist party, they could not be represented at the congress in Stockholm. What is more, Huysmans hinted that because the Indians had been based in Germany during the war, they might be suspected of working with the German government. Chatto countered that,

> [w]e were old workers and before the war denounced as 'anarchists' and now as 'German agents'. We said that we were against all Governments and had ultimately as little confidence in the Prussian as in the English or Russian Govt., but that as practical men it was a duty to profit from circumstances and work from the country where we could live most safely.[12]

In the end, however, Chatto felt that Huysmans was sympathetic towards their struggle for independence but insisted that their case should be raised by the British socialists.

In a revealing report to the IIC on 26 May, Chatto laid out the plans for future work in the Swedish capital along anticolonial lines. He suggested that, much like the Finns, Poles, and Georgians, who had constituted themselves into a group of subject nations of the Russian empire, 'the position becomes clear, logical, and forcible, if the Indians, Egyptians, and Irish form a similar anti-British group'.[13] In June 1917, the INK reprinted two pamphlets, *British Rule in India Condemned by the British Themselves* (1915) and *Selbstregierung für Indien: Gefordert vom Indischen Nationalkongress und der All-India Moslem League* (1916), and published a new one, *Speeches and Resolutions on India at the International Socialist Congresses* (1917). Acharya sent this to Huysmans as well as to Ture Nerman of the newly formed Swedish Social Democratic Left Party, which also included Carl Lindhagen, the mayor of Stockholm. To appeal to the socialists, the pamphlet summarised how the Indian question had been debated at the international socialist congresses in Paris, Amsterdam, Stuttgart, and Copenhagen. They stated in the Introduction: 'we earnestly trust that the International Congress now meeting at Stockholm, will once again devote its attention to the Indian question and use the whole force of International Socialism at the coming peace negotiations to insist upon the emancipation of the Indian people'.[14]

74

INTERNATIONAL SOCIALISM AND WORLD PEACE

Chatto and Acharya soon moved to Roséns Pensionat, a guesthouse run by Cecilia Håkanson on Grev Turegatan 22, a short five-minute walk from Artillerigatan 28B, where they set up an office on 7 July 1917 alongside the Friends of Irish Freedom.[15] While these groups had come to Stockholm specifically to carry out nationalist propaganda, Coleridge Kennard, the under-secretary to the British Legation in Stockholm, wrote, 'it is clear that the chief object ... is to attempt to get into contact with anti-English Russian Extremists with a view to starting an Indian and Persian independence movement in Russia'.[16]

'The day of the barbarians'

On 12 July, the DSC met the Indian, Egyptian, and Persian delegations, a day described by Huysmans as 'the day of the barbarians'.[17] Ahead of the meeting, the INK gave interviews to *Svenska Dagbladet* and *Aftonbladet* and publicly stated their agenda in Stockholm. Anyone interested in the Indian cause, they noted in *Svenska Dagbladet*, could obtain information from their newly opened offices at Artillerigatan. They did not expect much from the socialist peace conference, as they had been received 'dismissively' by Branting, 'who did not strike them as being a friend of the independence struggles in the British Empire'.[18] However, in an interview published the next day in *Aftonbladet*, Chatto conceded that when they had met Branting the day before, he was much friendlier than previously. 'Branting was the most feared man', Acharya later recalled, 'as he could make and unmake Cabinets owing to his party holding the key position in the Parliament'.[19]

Despite Chatto's efforts to articulate the importance of the Indian question in relation to the peace conference, the meeting with the DSC did not result in any substantial concessions. Branting made it clear that this was a socialist peace congress and only socialist parties were admitted but that, although they were interested in the viewpoints of the other nationalist parties, these representatives from the colonial world should put their demands in writing to the secretary. Troelstra asked Chatto and Acharya questions about economics, literacy, and agriculture in India, but Huysmans was more direct: how was the question of Indian independence relevant to the socialist peace congress? How could they practically resolve anything?

ANARCHY OR CHAOS

Huysmans reiterated that their demands should be put to the British delegation. Chatto and Acharya responded that, firstly, the British suspected them of being German agents and, second, that Indian interests at the peace congress should be represented by the Indians themselves. The INK's protests were met with little sympathy. 'The Indian question is important', acknowledged Troelstra, 'but it is irrelevant' to the peace discussions.[20]

Acharya reported to the IIC a few days after the meeting, however, and was more optimistic about the outcomes of the meeting and the compromises they had to make:

1) that we be allowed to be present at the [International Socialist] Congress when the English delegation should take up the Indian question, and if possible we be allowed to speak on our case;
2) that attempts be made to get a delegate from America to represent the Indian National Congress;
3) that the Congress should demand that a representative of India and not an Indian nominee of the Secretary of State for India be allowed to take part in the peace congress of the various governments.[21]

If they were allowed to be represented at the proposed peace congress for 15 August, Acharya suggested that Datta and Prabhakar should also attend, but for now they would focus on bringing the Indian question before the Zimmerwald conference.

Zimmerwald, antimilitarism, and anticolonialism

Throughout the summer of 1917, peace negotiations between the divided Second International socialists broke down. In August, the American, French, and British governments prohibited socialists from their countries to travel to Sweden to attend the peace talks.[22] This meant that the INK could not present their case to sympathetic British socialists, as the DSC had suggested, and they had to find other allies. At the same time, events in Russia meant that the Petrograd Soviet delegation had other plans for a socialist world revolution that changed the course of the peace talks in Stockholm.

From 5 September, Acharya and Chatto attended the weeklong third Zimmerwald conference. The event was dominated by the

INTERNATIONAL SOCIALISM AND WORLD PEACE

Russians, including Angelica Balabanoff, secretary of the Zimmerwald group, and the Russian-Ukrainian communist Konstantin Troyanovsky, but other groups such as the Swedish Social Democratic Left Party also attended. Unlike the social democrats, the Zimmerwaldians tied the war to the question of colonialism and principally supported anti-colonial nationalists in their struggle against imperialism. However, aside from discussing the relationship with the other socialists in the city and issuing a manifesto calling for a mass strike to end the war, which was not published until after the October revolution in Russia, nothing substantial was agreed upon at the Zimmerwald conference.[23] In addition to Lindhagen, Acharya and Chatto made contact with Balabanoff and Troyanovsky, thereby strengthening their commitment to Russian support for Indian independence.

In early November, the INK proposed that it would work with Troyanovsky to distribute propaganda in Russia. The INK considered him 'unfit for any practical organising work', but because of his personal relations with prominent Russian leaders, and 'on account of him being a literary man', they decided to pay him to work on behalf of India in Petrograd.[24] The INK argued to the AA that there were strong anti-British feelings in Russia, which the Russian leaders might use against the British in peace negotiations. If the Russian leaders took up the cause of India, they could establish anti-British organisations throughout Russia, smuggle letters and publications into India, and it would help the Germans negotiate with Russia. To this end, the INK proposed three points of action from their side:

1) Troyanovsky undertakes to keep up communication with Stockholm by sending trustworthy agents from time to time and try persuading all important men who happen to pass through Stockholm to us.
2) From our bureau in Stockholm, we shall send out every week or ten days articles, etc., to the Russian press as well as to the Ukrainian.
3) We shall distribute pamphlets on India in the Russian language amongst the Russians in Sweden and as far as possible in Norway and Denmark.[25]

As Troyanovsky was about to leave for Petrograd, the INK supplied him with pamphlets on India and suggested that he should

ANARCHY OR CHAOS

receive 7,000SEK for his work for now and more later, depending on his progress.

Breaking with the Dutch-Scandinavian Committee

The INK broke completely with the DSC in November 1917. On 15 October, the DSC had issued a peace manifesto that proposed certain resolutions about annexations, territorial divisions, war indemnities, the right to self-determination, and international economic measures and labour union rights. On the question of colonies, the DSC suggested that 'as a minimum, administrative autonomy is proposed for all groups of peoples, who have reached a certain cultural level'.[26] The manifesto was strongly criticised by the INK, who argued that the manifesto only considered European issues and ignored the national struggles for self-determination in the colonial world. The INK wrote a scathing letter to the DSC on 16 November, complaining that 'the "peace" manifesto lately issued by you has exposed once for all the insincerity of West-European Socialists and justifies us in looking upon the Dutch-Scandinavian Committee as agents of the subtle and cruel imperialism of the so-called Western democracies'.[27] The INK wanted to expose the hypocrisy of the DSC and charged that,

a) for West-European Socialists, as for all European Imperialists, the word mankind means only Europe;
b) that the West-European Socialists, just as the Imperialists, seek the establishment of a European truce, not a world peace, and that they regard all the splendid Asiatic and African lands stretching from Tangier to Peking as the legitimate booty of their European wars;
c) that only those countries are deemed by European Socialists, just as by the Imperialists, to be worthy of liberation, which have by the force of historical circumstances come under the banner of Christ—the problems of non-Christian countries being euphemistically termed 'questions of an economic character', and
d) that only those countries receive the generous consideration of the Committee which are not under the rule of England or France.[28]

The letter went on to challenge the DSC's peace manifesto in more detail, suggesting that the DSC had deliberately omitted India from

78

INTERNATIONAL SOCIALISM AND WORLD PEACE

the peace questions, and made comparisons between other subject nations and India. They argued for the centrality of India to several other international wars and grievances, suggested that the DSC was in the hands of British imperialists, and reminded them that British colonialism in India had been discussed at previous International Socialist Congresses. The INK asserted that 'no lasting world-peace is possible unless and until India and other countries in a similar position are granted their full political and economic rights, and an end is put to Colonial Imperialism'.[29]

Russian work and Brest-Litovsk

Quoting a press release from the INK, *Stockholms Dagblad* reported on 24 January 1918 that Leon Trotsky brought up the question of Indian independence at the peace negotiations at Brest-Litovsk on 15 January 1918. Trotsky declared that Russia would immediately acknowledge India's independence, if the British left, but not the existing ruling party, the INC, in India, as they acknowledged the legitimacy of the British empire.[30] Trotsky's interest in India's independence, the INK reported to the AA, was a direct result of Troyanovsky's work during his trip to Petrograd. In fact, Troyanovsky had approached Trotsky on behalf of the INK and, through instructions given to Vatslav Vorosky, the Bolshevik emissary in Stockholm, Trotsky expected at least one of the Indians to proceed to Petrograd as soon as possible. Chatto had already asked Vorosky if it would be possible to obtain permission to go to Petrograd, but Vorosky asked Chatto to wait for further instructions. Upon receiving Trotsky's letter, Chatto sent letters through Vorosky to Trotsky, asking him to arrange for permission from the Ministry of Foreign Affairs in Petrograd for the Indians to travel there. Troyanovsky told Chatto and Acharya that he would even house them. The Indians were keen to obtain permission directly from Trotsky and the Bolsheviks, as Balabanoff had criticised them vigorously for being in German pay.

Neither Chatto nor Acharya went to Petrograd at the time, but still set to work amongst the Russians and suggested six points of action:

1) Energetic literary propaganda in the press.
2) Founding a journal devoted to India.

79

ANARCHY OR CHAOS

3) Founding a permanent Russian-Indian Committee in Petrograd and Moscow.
4) Sending of literature (in Indian languages) to Afghanistan and India.
5) Work among Indian Muslims, particularly in Bukhara, where Indian merchants had a large presence.
6) From Petrograd as a centre, communicate with Japan and China.[31]

All of this, the INK suggested, could be done through the Russians, but it was 'simply a question of money and daring'.[32] From their end, the INK started sending Indian propaganda to Petrograd, but they also suggested that the AA should distribute Indian propaganda among Russian prisoners-of-war in Germany.

As Germany annexed the Baltic states from Russia, the negotiations at Brest-Litovsk demonstrated to the INK that they could no longer rely on German support for their cause: '[w]e have every reason to think that the Indian and allied questions have been completely given up by the German Government as they have their own axe to grind in colonial politics'.[33] Because of Germany's new-gained territories and imperial ambitions, the AA withheld payment for Troyanovsky's work.[34] For the INK, the refusal to pay Troyanovsky signalled that the Indians were just tools in the hands of the Germans and not considered sincere nationalists. However, the INK suggested that, until an Indian delegation could be sent to Russia, which was not possible as long as Chatto and Acharya were the only representatives in Stockholm, they should pay Troyanovsky a small amount and keep sending him propaganda material.

One of the constraints of the INK was that it was effectively run by only two people. Propaganda work in Switzerland was pointless at the moment, Chatto complained to the IIC, and Har Dayal should be brought to Sweden as soon as possible. Stuck in Vienna because of passport problems, Har Dayal wrote to Datta that he had been working with the Ukrainian nationalists there and suggested that they 'join the rear guard of the socialist parties' and start a socialist paper.[35] With the assistance of one of two 'socialists' from India, they could get a hearing as 'comrades' among the Ukrainians, as he could write 'in the regular socialistic style with quotations from Marx, etc.'.[36] However, Chatto wrote to the IIC that Har Dayal's idea of 'starting

80

INTERNATIONAL SOCIALISM AND WORLD PEACE

a socialist paper in Kiev or Bukarest is one of the most ridiculous that can ever be made. We should on no account follow the ostrich policy of believing we are hoodwinking European political parties by pretending to be anything else than nationalists'.[37]

Indian propaganda and Swedish socialism

In December 1917, the INK had reported to the AA that their propaganda activities were improving. Dismissing Har Dayal's plan for starting a socialist paper, they had wanted to start their own bimonthly bulletin in Sweden along the lines of *Das Neue Litauen* or *Ukraina*, but the AA did not provide funds and it would require more people in Stockholm. Instead, they sent 'socialist brochures' to several Swedish newspapers and passed their articles on to the IIC.[38] In February 1918, some Swedish sympathisers published *En Bok om England och dess Undertryckta Folk*, which included two essays by Chatto and Acharya entitled 'Det engelska väldet i Indien' and 'Birma'.[39] By the summer of 1918, dissemination of Indian propaganda became increasingly difficult, and the INK came under attack by the Swedish Social Democrats, who charged that the INK's propaganda in *Aftonbladet* presented a wrong picture of the benefits of British rule in India. In fact, wrote a Swedish journalist in *Social-Demokraten*, the British had introduced modern civilisation and culture to India, and if the British left, the country would erupt into civil war.[40] The INK swiftly retorted in *Aftonbladet*, criticising the so-called 'neutral' Swedish Social Democrats for being against Germany and pro-British. They had nothing against British anti-imperialists and liberal ideals, but their articles in various Swedish newspapers were intended to enlighten readers about the brutality of British rule in India.[41] Surprisingly, the otherwise sympathetic Social Democratic Left Party adopted a similar view to that of the Social Democrats and dismissed criticisms of British rule in India, blaming problems of poverty, hunger, illiteracy, and despotism on Indian princes and other native rulers. However, as a social democratic principle, they also supported complete independence for India, which Britain was gradually introducing, they noted.[42]

ANARCHY OR CHAOS

The Wilsonian moment

When US President Woodrow Wilson issued his Fourteen Points statement of principles for peace to the US Congress in January 1918, the principle of self-determination of nations reverberated across the colonial world.[43] For the INK, however, Wilson's call for self-determination rang hollow.[44] Responding to Irish nationalists' faith in Wilson's Fourteen Points, in an article in *Aftonbladet*, the Indians exposed how 'the American dollar world's sympathy for the Irish is over now that it clashes with American affairs in Europe. About the same would be true for the Indian question'.[45] By late October 1918, however, as the prospect of peace negotiations became more pressing, the INK took a different stance to Wilson's Fourteen Points and sent a telegram to him. They condemned British rule in India, as well as German atrocities committed during the war, and reiterated that world peace hinged on Indian independence. What is more, they demanded that Indian representatives be present at the upcoming peace congress and that Wilson use his influence to include India as a free nation of the proposed League of Nations.[46]

The German Revolution and the end of the war

A week after the formal end of the war in Europe in November 1918, Helmuth von Glasenapp of the AA travelled to Stockholm to consult with the INK about their future plans. The IIC in Berlin, they suggested, should be dissolved, the furniture sold, and books donated to the AA. If the AA agreed to support future Indian activities, Chatto and Acharya would either stay in Stockholm or relocate to Amsterdam and establish another propaganda paper there. Von Glasenapp also obtained statements from Chatto, Acharya, and Har Dayal about their own plans. Chatto wanted to remain in Stockholm and become a Swedish citizen, Har Dayal wished to get financial support to go to a retreat, while Acharya left for Berlin on 30 November and stated that he intended to become a German citizen.[47] Har Dayal soon denounced Chatto, Acharya, and the IIC, and retreated from Indian revolutionary work.

The IIC was officially dissolved on 6 December, and Acharya provided an account of the INK's activities in Stockholm to the AA.[48]

82

INTERNATIONAL SOCIALISM AND WORLD PEACE

Acharya reminded the AA that the INK was under a one-year contract and should be financed further to continue propaganda in the country, but the dissolution of the IIC in Berlin meant that the future was uncertain for many of the Indian revolutionaries who had collaborated with the Germans. Some of the Indians in the IIC had already stated their plans in a collective letter to the AA.[49] It took a few weeks before Acharya informed the AA that he wanted to return to his old craft and learn typography and photoengraving, that he wanted three years' expenses for his study and maintenance, and that he wanted to become a German citizen.[50]

However, Acharya was not ready to abandon his work for Indian independence. On 22 December, Acharya wrote to Romberg that it was imperative that India was represented at the next international socialist peace congress, scheduled for Bern in early February, as well as the Paris Peace Conference.[51] At the same time, the German Revolution was in full swing, led by the Spartacists Rosa Luxemburg and Karl Liebknecht. Spurred on by the Spartacists, the strikes and demonstrations in early January were met with fierce repression by the army and the Freikorps, a paramilitary, anti-communist group, and were swiftly crushed.[52] Acharya witnessed this but sought out the Spartacus leaders for help.[53] As Acharya later recalled: 'I left Chattopadhyaya and went to Germany to see what could be done with the Spartacus leaders; Liebknecht and Rosa Luxemburg and also with the President of the Bavarian Republic, Kurt Eisner'.[54] At the direction of Friedrich Ebert, the Social Democratic Party leader and president of the German Republic, Liebknecht and Luxemburg were assassinated by the *Freikorps* on 15 January, shortly after Acharya met them.

The International Socialist Congress at Bern

After a brief stay in Berlin, Acharya made his way to Munich. The AA recommended that Acharya should present the Indian cause to Kurt Eisner, leader of the People's State of Bavaria, and then proceed to Bern to address the International Socialist Congress to be held there from 3 to 10 February 1919. The AA would arrange for travel documents from Munich to Bern and back to Munich.[55] Out of the ashes

ANARCHY OR CHAOS

of the failed Stockholm conference, European socialists sought to reconcile their wartime disagreements and reconvene the social democratic alliances at the International Socialist Congress at Bern. Held at the Volkshaus, the headquarters of the Swiss socialists, the British delegate Ethel Snowden sat 'at the back of the room', she recalled, and '[a]mongst the listeners of every nationality I observed Indians with turbans and Turks wearing the fez'.[56] Indeed, there were listeners of many nationalities, including Acharya, Das Gupta, and Pratap. Snowden was not just observing these Indians. Summing up his experiences at the congress, Acharya recalled that, 'Jean Longuet, leader of the French Socialists, who was known to us in France and Charles Rappoport before the war were sympathetic towards India, but the Socialists discussed only European questions. Mrs. Snowden was also sympathetic towards India'.[57] While the British delegation resolved to support Indian self-determination, Ramsay MacDonald was hostile to the Indians, and Acharya, Das Gupta, and Pratap achieved little at Bern, except getting noticed in the Italian Socialist Party paper *Avanti!*.[58]

When Acharya returned to Berlin on 3 April, he informed the AA that, since world events had changed drastically since November 1918, he had now decided to abandon his plans of studying printing and photoengraving. As he could no longer rely on financial assistance from the Germans, he had to seek other means of employment that would allow him to continue political agitation at this opportune moment in history: 'The next few months are very important and hopeful and therefore I, among others, must agitate anywhere to get the means for our propaganda, which will necessitate me going here and there'.[59]

Acharya's two years in Stockholm, Munich, and Bern revealed the limits of international socialism. Despite extensive propaganda activities, newspaper interviews, articles, and publications, as well as meetings with European socialists, Acharya and Chatto were dismissed either as irrelevant or as German agents. They lacked socialist credentials but built on their anticolonial networks and formed new alliances with Russian revolutionaries, especially after the 1917 Russian Revolution. The end of the war spelled new directions for Acharya, who tried his luck with the Spartacus leaders and socialists at Bern, but to no avail.

PART II

REVOLUTION AND COMMUNISM, 1919–22

6

REVOLUTION IN RUSSIA

From Berlin to Moscow

Uncertain of his future after the war and the socialist conference at Bern, Acharya found himself in Munich again. Pratap had also made his way to the Bavarian city after a brief sojourn in Russia, but the two of them soon returned to Berlin.[1] On the evening of 10 May, the Indians in Berlin held a meeting at the Klindworth-Scharwenka Conservatory in Charlottenburg to commemorate the 1857 revolt. Indian songs were played on a gramophone, Acharya and Nayik sang a few songs, and Pillai gave a speech on the 1857 revolt.[2] At the meeting, according to the DCI, it was resolved that Acharya, Mahendra Pratap, Abdur Rabb, and the Turkish officer Alif Khan should travel to Moscow to support Barkatullah's work there.[3] Barkatullah had remained in Afghanistan after the war ended and gained the Emir's trust. As an emissary of the Emir, Barkatullah went to Moscow in March 1919 where he met Lenin on 7 May and subsequently went on propaganda tours for the new Soviet International Propaganda (Sovinterprop) and the Provisional Government of India.[4] With the outbreak of the Afghan-British War in early May 1919, the Indians' hopes for Bolshevik and Afghan assistance gained even more ground. 'What Germans could not do, I thought, will now be done by Soviet Russia and the new Afghanistan', Pratap remarked.[5]

ANARCHY OR CHAOS

Travelling to Russia in 1919 was difficult and dangerous. The usual route through Sweden or Finland was risky as the British navy controlled the Baltic Sea. Instead, the group decided to travel through the war-torn Baltic states and left Berlin sometime in June. While Pratap, Acharya, and Rabb were planning their venture in Berlin, Gill, who had been released from the Ruhleben internment camp at the end of the war, inquired suspiciously about their travel plans.[6] During his imprisonment, according to Khan, Gill had become acquainted with Karl Liebknecht as well as some Russian officers who encouraged him to travel to Russia as a representative of the Hindu Sabha, a new Indian revolutionary group led by Dr Mansur that would replace the old IIC. Gill had told some of the other Indians in Berlin that his plan was supported by the Bolsheviks. This was not true, Khan stated, but Gill kept observing Pratap's group. They eventually invited Gill to join their mission, which he refused, so they secretly boarded a train in Berlin to avoid attracting attention. However, travelling by plane, Gill caught up with them at Kovno (now Kaunas) in Lithuania. Upon reaching Kovno, Gill's travel companion, Markofski, the Russian deputy ambassador to Berlin, was arrested. Markofski believed that Gill had betrayed him. Pratap's group thought so too. What is more, they were suspicious of how Gill could have crossed the German border. In his defence, Gill produced a letter from the German army commander General Ludendorff, which stated his purpose of travel to Russia on behalf of the NfO. Satisfied with this explanation, Pratap's group allowed Gill to join them.

On 14 June, the group reached Bauska in German-occupied Latvia and sent a note to Helmuth von Glasenapp through his brother, Wilkin, who was stationed there, and asked for help to cross the border.[7] The group was allowed to proceed, but then held back at Jakobstadt (now Jēkabpils) at the eastern front, where the Latvian border commander had been given notice to prevent a British spy from crossing. However, as Gill carried his British passport and a letter of permission from the German authorities in Latvian, he was permitted to continue into Russian-held territory. Conversely, the DCI reported that Acharya had been shot while attempting to cross the border:

> [w]hen Mahendra Pratap and his friends, among whom were 'Mandayam' Acharya, Dalip Singh Gill and Abdur Rabb, failed to cross the Lettish lines to the Bolsheviks early in June, they were sent

REVOLUTION IN RUSSIA

to [Rüdiger] von der Goltz headquarters at Mitau because they had German passports. But Acharya returned to the Letts, showed an English passport and said he believed that he could get through without danger. The Lettish commander, who supplied this information, put him charge of an escort to take him to the Esthonian Staff. The escort shot him on the way.[8]

As it happened, Acharya's group was sent back to the German authorities at Mitau (now Jelgava) in Latvia, where Khan abandoned the venture and returned to Berlin.[9] Soon after, as reported in several British newspapers, the German authorities helped a group of Indian emissaries that had been halted at the Latvian border to cross into Russian territory by airplane. Indeed, Rabb wrote to Khan that they had found a way to cross the border, which was only an hour away.[10]

Upon their arrival in Moscow in early July, Pratap, Acharya, and Rabb stayed at the Gutchkov Mansion, the 'palatial building of the former sugar-king', where Barkatullah had set up office, and were 'right royally feasted' at a time when food was scarce in Russia.[11] Gill had arrived on 6 July a few days earlier with some Russian peasants and was immediately imprisoned by the Soviet authorities on suspicion of being a British spy. When Barkatullah discovered this, he visited Gill and concluded that he was harmless. Barkatullah, who carried some authority with the Russians, convinced the People's Commissariat for Foreign Affairs (NKID) that Gill should be released. In the meantime, Pratap's mission had arrived and related their story about Gill to Barkatullah, but they all took pity on Gill and, after his release, asked him to return to Berlin. Before returning, on 26 July, Gill met Lenin, who, Gill said, promised support for the Hindu Sabha in Berlin. Gill returned to Berlin in early August 1919 and boasted about meeting Lenin and receiving promises of financial support from the Bolsheviks. In his report on their journey to Russia, Khan concluded that Gill was not an Indian patriot but a British spy.[12]

Pratap, Acharya, and Rabb also met Lenin in July. About a year later, Acharya recalled: '[w]hen I arrived in Moscow and went with some friends on business to see him, he was not found to be so terrible as he appeared to many people, even "socialists" of Western Europe. He was very smiling and pleasant even to his opponents'.[13] In his memoirs, Shaukat Usmani related how the meeting had been told to him:

ANARCHY OR CHAOS

[l]ong accustomed to see big officials of various countries, they filed up in a single line while the servant was behind them. Lenin came out of his room and they bowed. It displeased him. Moreover, their treatment of the servant incensed him. Instead of shaking hands with these distinguished guests, he went behind them and embraced the servant and seizing him by the hand brought him in front and explained to the servant that he was as much a man as the Raja [Pratap] and the Moulvi [Barkatullah]. He enthusiastically explained to him that Soviet Russia did not recognize any social barriers. After that he shook hands with the four who apologised for their misbehaviour.[14]

Datta corroborated this story, as told to him by Acharya.[15] Pratap recalled that '[i]t was after this interview that the Foreign Office decided that I must accompany His Excellency Mr Suritz, the first Russian Ambassador to the Court of Afghanistan'.[16] With Igor Reisner, the secretary to Suritz, now on board, the mission left Moscow in September 1919, destined for Kabul.[17]

Travelling through Herat, Kandahar, and Tashkent in October and November, the mission arrived in Kabul on 26 December 1919.[18] Impressed by what he had seen, Acharya sent a letter to his family:

[a]s an Indian patriot and as a man who has lived among the working people of Europe and America for some time, I have full sympathy with the present revolution .... Russia is now a common country of the common people with intelligent and work-loving people at their service .... It is, of course, only a beginning, what they are making there, but it is a promising and successful experiment .... If this government ceased to exist, then woe unto mankind.[19]

By contrast, Pratap had different opinions about Lenin and the Bolsheviks and believed that an intellectual vanguard was necessary to work on behalf of the proletariat.[20] Soon after their arrival in Kabul, Acharya and Rabb fell out with Pratap over the direction and leadership of their mission.[21] Instead of following Pratap's nationalist-bourgeois leadership, Rabb and Acharya formed the Indian Revolutionary Association (IRA) in late December 1919.[22]

The Indian Revolutionary Association

Mohammed Ashur, a fallen IRA member, gave insight into the workings of the organisation in 1922. According to Ashur, the aims and objects of the IRA were:

REVOLUTION IN RUSSIA

1. To work against the English in all possible ways and to use all possible means and resources which may lead to ultimate emancipation of India.
2. To keep well informed the Russian public in special, and Europe in general, with regard to the actual conditions prevailing in India under the English regime. For this purpose, a representative Committee of this Association shall be established in Tashkent.
3. To establish friendly and secret communication with all the revolutionary societies of the oppressed nations of the world, and to co-operate with nations who are actually struggling for the freedom of their countries.[23]

The IRA comprised twenty-six ordinary members, with Rabb serving as president and Fazl Kadir as secretary. It had both a Propaganda Section, devoted to producing and distributing literature, and an executive Active Section, aiming to 'carry on a guerrilla warfare with the English on the Indian border and to incite and help border tribes to fight the English Government'.[24] The Propaganda Section consisted of Mohammed Ashur, Nazir Siddiq, and Mohammed Amin Faruqui, who later served as secretary of the IRA. The executive Active Section consisted of Acharya, Ghulam Habib Wafar, and Daud Khan. Significantly, Acharya was the only non-Muslim Indian in the organisation.

Initially based in Kabul, the IRA was at the mercy of Amanullah Khan, who had succeeded his father as Emir of Afghanistan in late February 1919. The IRA was aware of the Emir's troubled relations with the British and intended to stay away from domestic and foreign politics, but still declared its intention to recruit sympathetic subjects and to establish revolutionary branches throughout Afghanistan. The IRA worked in full cooperation with the Afghan Foreign Ministry and promised to report regularly to the Ministry about its activities. Perhaps more importantly, regarding its relations with Russia and other nations, the IRA remained open to establishing connections with 'all those Governments which sympathise in the aims and objects ... and it can take all kinds of help from such Governments for the achievement of these aims and objects'.[25] This did not mean, however, that the IRA would 'bind itself to enforce the political policy of these Governments in India. If the help were conditional it cannot accept this help, nor any help can be accepted as debt. It can only be accepted as a free grant'.[26]

ANARCHY OR CHAOS

While the IRA clearly wanted to remain politically independent from Russia and other sympathetic nations, they were also aware of the necessity of international alliances. The IRA declared that, 'as the Association is convinced that India can only be freed through pure and real socialism which embraces true internationalism, the Association shall therefore try to educate the Indian public opinion in all possible ways to accept socialism as the only true salvation of India and of the world'.[27] Recognising the diverse composition of Indian society, comprising primarily peasants and workers, hundreds of races and ethnicities, various languages and religions, the millions of untouchables, and the tyranny of the caste system, the IRA also stated that it was their duty to 'try and establish equality and preach fraternity of the human race'.[28] Indeed, the IRA conceded that earlier Indian revolutionary movements had been led primarily by educated upper and middle classes, but the masses of India were now becoming active in their resistance against not only the British but also native ruling princes. The way forward for India was a 'Federated Soviet Republic' as far as it was compatible with local conditions. In practice, this would mean a return to the 'old Socialistic institutions (Communal Councils of Five) and the electorates of Art and Labour Unions', which had been destroyed by British rule, and 'union elective bodies and self-governing communal councils'.[29]

At the second meeting of the IRA on 17 February 1920, they drafted a message for Lenin:

> [t]he Indian revolutionaries express their deep gratitude and their admiration of the great struggle carried on by Soviet Russia for the liberation of all oppressed classes and peoples, and especially for the liberation of India. Great thanks to Soviet Russia for her having heard the cries of agony from the 315,000,000 people suffering under the yoke of imperialism. The mass meeting accepts with joy the hand of friendship and help extended to oppressed India.[30]

Although the organisation was not affiliated with the Comintern, Lenin was initially happy with the work of the IRA and in May sent them a congratulatory note:

> I am glad to greet the young union of Muslim and Hindu revolutionaries and sincerely wish that this Association will extend its activities among all the workmen of the East. When Indians, Korean, Japanese,

REVOLUTION IN RUSSIA

Persian, Chinese, and Turkish peasantry and working people will stretch to one another their hands and will fight together their common cause of freedom—only then is assured the decisive victory over the exploiters. Long live free Asia![31]

Only three months after the IRA had been established, the British Government and the Emir agreed to an armistice. The British offered financial assistance to the Emir on condition that he change his attitude towards the Bolsheviks and repress the Muslim revolutionaries in the country. Consequently, Acharya and the IRA were expelled from Afghanistan in late May 1920.[32]

Meanwhile, at the invitation of the recent Mexico-returned Comintern agent Mikhail Borodin, M. N. Roy (Manabendra Nath Bhattacharya) and his wife Evelyn Trent had arrived in Moscow via Berlin as delegates from the Mexican Communist Party to attend the Second Congress of the Comintern to be held in Petrograd and Moscow in July and August 1920.[33] In Berlin, Roy had met Abani Mukherji, who was also on his way to Moscow at the invitation of the Dutch communist Sebald Justinus Rutgers. While in Berlin, Roy contacted Datta and some of the other Indians to discuss plans for an Indian communist party. However, Datta was aware of Roy's dubious activities during the First World War and asked Roy to account for the money he had received from the AA. Roy brushed him off. He did not need the support of the Berlin Indians anymore and had found new allies among the communists. Indeed, Roy also met the prominent German communist August Thalheimer and the Dutch communist Henk 'Maring' Sneevliet, who was also on his way to Moscow as a delegate of the Dutch Indies. While rumours of Roy's intrigues and questionable wartime activities followed him from Mexico to Berlin and Moscow, in the company of these prominent communists, Roy transformed himself into a modern, transnational revolutionary who had abandoned militant nationalism.[34]

Meanwhile, the IRA relocated to Tashkent, where they continued their work for armed revolution in India among the *Muhajirs*. Tashkent was also home to the Turkestan Bureau of the Comintern, which was actively supporting revolutionary activities in India and China. Mohammed Shafique and Muhammed Ali of Barkatullah's Provisional Government of India, now working with the Sovinterprop, had also

93

ANARCHY OR CHAOS

arrived in Tashkent on 31 March 1920. With the help of the Bolsheviks, the IRA approached Indian traders, smugglers, and seasonal workers in the region. They also set up two propaganda periodicals, *Zamindar* and *Azad Hindustan Akhbar*, and started training Indian Muslims who had recently come to the area in guerrilla warfare. These activities strengthened the IRA's connections with the Comintern in the lead up to the Second Congress.[35]

The Second Congress of the Communist International

In early June 1920, in preparation for the Second Congress, Lenin solicited advice for his 'Draft Theses on National and Colonial Questions', which reached Roy through Balabanoff. After the failed revolution in Germany, Lenin was convinced that world revolution depended on the question of self-determination in Asia. In his 'Draft Theses', Lenin argued that to overthrow European colonialism in the 'backward countries' of Asia, proletarian parties and the Comintern should enter into temporary alliances with bourgeois democratic forces in the colonial world and that communists should support peasant movements to draw them into Bolshevik visions of organisation.[36] In response to Lenin's thesis, Roy drafted a supplementary note in which he argued that 'bourgeois democratic' forces actually comprised a variety of progressive movements in India, but he suggested that these were reactionary forces and unreliable allies in the struggle for Indian independence, thus the Comintern should not support these movements indiscriminately. What is more, he assigned a much greater role to India and Asia—refuting the term 'backward countries'—in the struggle for world revolution.[37]

Acharya was deputed to the Second Congress on behalf of the IRA with a consultative vote, but he did not know whether the Soviet Government or the Comintern had invited him.[38] He was clearly taken with Lenin and the Russian revolution. In fact, reading Lenin's *The State and Revolution* (1917), Acharya wrote, had such an effect on him

> that it took me two or three days before I could accustom myself to the new way of thinking—I was literally transported to another world .... The final result of my reading Lenin's one work was that from a national or political revolutionary, I became a convinced

94

REVOLUTION IN RUSSIA

communist and found that I was a revolutionary for 15 years without ideas.[39]

Acharya was convinced that 'India will put into practice Lenin's teachings within a year or at the most two, for India has always been ripe of modern communism and internationalism and will certainly never be for Capitalism' and speculated that '[p]erhaps the Indian revolution will be the precursor even of European revolution as the Russian Revolution was and is of Germany. When it comes, it will certainly be the peasants' and workmen's revolution in India in the sense of Lenin—and nothing else'.[40]

Departing Tashkent on 12 July, on the train he met Shafique, who attended as a representative of the Indian Section of Sovinterprop, and on their way they heard about Roy's presence in Moscow. Staying at the Delovoy Dvor hotel in Moscow, as they were having dinner one evening, Acharya recalled, 'I saw a bearded Indian face next to a well-dressed European lady. Someone told me he was Roy, and the lady was his wife, and they were living under the name Allen and had come as delegates of the Communist Party of Mexico, the lady as one for the women's section'. They struck up a conversation, Roy having heard about Acharya and Shafique from Lev Karakhan, the Deputy Commissar of the NKID, and one day Roy and Trent took Acharya to Karakhan's offices at the Gutchkov Mansion where they met Borodin.[41]

While Mukherji attended as a communist representative of British India with a consultative vote, it was Roy who attracted the most attention and caught the ear of Lenin.[42] At the Congress, with the approval of Acharya and Mukherji, Roy was put forward as a member of the Commission on the National and Colonial Question, chaired by Sneevliet.[43] Acharya had also originally been proposed for this commission, alongside Roy, but was ultimately left out.[44] Photos from the opening session show the five Indian delegates sitting together, and footage shows Mukherji and Acharya standing up and clapping after a speech by Lenin.[45]

On the day of the opening session in Moscow on 24 July, Roy's rejoinder to Lenin was put forward to the Commission on the National and Colonial Question. But Lenin's 'Draft Theses' also elicited a reply from Acharya. On the same day, Acharya wrote to Lenin on behalf of the IRA on the subject of 'The Struggle against Pan-

95

ANARCHY OR CHAOS

Islamism'. Drawing on more than a decade of anticolonial work among Indian, Egyptian, and Ottoman Muslim nationalists, Acharya argued that 'pan-Islamism, like all similar -isms—pan-Germanism, pan-Slavism and so on, is now a Utopia which exists only in the brains of a few perhaps idealist but misguided, un-practical but harmless people, however persistent their efforts may be'.[46] The different strands and nations within Islam would not be able to unite against colonial oppressors, as had been seen during the First World War, and they would only turn against and exploit each other. Acharya argued instead for communism and internationalism:

> [i]t is Soviet propaganda and Soviet successes in Islamic countries which can, if at all, make for the possibility of Islamic unity. But in that case, Islam as a religion and politics will become harmless, because a new generation will spring up, which will be openly irreligious and thoroughly international.[47]

Internationalism and unity against capitalism and hierarchies was important for this new generation:

> [i]t is not enough to encourage the younger generation of these struggling nationalists to fight not only against the foreign imperialists but also against their own politicians who are chiefly Mullahs, nobility, or businessmen …. Let us encourage the toleration and co-operation between the masses of both [Muslims and non-Muslims] for Soviet ideas and ideals. That will counteract the effects of pan-Islamic propaganda more than any fight of a different nature.[48]

Acharya was clearly worried about Bolshevik support for pan-Islamic propaganda but encouraged an inclusive vision of anticolonial struggles. A few months later, Acharya wrote to Chatto to apprise him of his letter to Lenin and noted that 'this attitude [pan-Islamism] … must be strongly protested against'.[49] In response to Acharya's letter, Chatto wanted to travel to Moscow to discuss the matter directly with Lenin but could not leave Stockholm at the time.

During the congress, Acharya, Roy, and Sneevliet joined forces to address the question of 'contract coolies' and the indentured labour system in place in many colonies. Calling out European socialists for celebrating the coming communist system, they reminded the Comintern that 'a condition of actual slavery prevails amongst hundreds of thousands of workingmen and women who have been suffer-

REVOLUTION IN RUSSIA

ing under what is known as the "contract coolie" and "indentured labour" systems of exploitation'.[50] Labourers from across the colonial world were contracted into exploitative master-slave relations, brutally enforced by colonial government regulations, and unable to defend themselves. They also warned that

> the whole governmental machinery is always on the side of the employers, and generally, it is the government itself which maintains this system as a profitable monopoly, and which is therefore the party most interested in preventing any improvement of conditions or organization of the coolies in self-defence.[51]

They specifically addressed the communist delegates from various imperialist countries and charged that, 'so long as such conditions prevail in any part of the world, the universal emancipation of the working class cannot be realised'.[52] In doing so, they held the delegates accountable for truly addressing the question of universal emancipation and self-determination.

In the manifesto of the congress, Lenin assured that '[t]here is a promising convergence of the Muslim and non-Muslim peoples, who are everywhere welded together by the common chains of British and foreign domination .... Their struggles are waged not only against the foreign oppressors but simultaneously against their own landlords, feudalists, clerics, and usurers'.[53] The manifesto also called out the socialists in the Second International who did not support anticolonial struggles:

> [t]he Socialist who directly or indirectly supports the privileged position of one nation at the cost of others, who has made his peace with colonial slavery, who makes a distinction between peoples of different races and skin colours, who helps the bourgeoisie of the metropolis to preserve its domination over the colonies instead of helping the cause of armed rebellion of the colonies, the British Socialist who fails to support by all possible means the rebellion in Ireland, Egypt, and India against the London plutocracy—such a Socialist deserves, if not the bullet, then certainly the mark of infamy, and no mandate or confidence from the proletariat.[54]

It is easy to trace the influences of anticolonial revolutionaries like Acharya, Roy, and Sneevliet in the manifesto.

ANARCHY OR CHAOS

The Provisional All-India Central Revolutionary Committee

In early August 1920, under the auspices of the Sovinterprop, the Indian revolutionaries in Russia joined forces to form the Provisional All-India Central Revolutionary Committee (PAICRC), led by Roy, Mukherji, and Shafique, while Acharya and Rabb also joined but simultaneously remained members of the IRA.[55] Mukherji explained that Roy had been appointed by the Comintern to centralise the work of the Indian revolutionaries and that the main purpose of the PAICRC 'is to call the Congress of Indian revolutionary parties, organizations and individuals from within India, which will formulate the program of the Indian Revolution, and which will form the first real, All-India Central Revolutionary Committee to act as the supreme body for directing the Indian Revolution'.[56] The organisation also recognised that 'the real freedom of the Indian people will not be achieved by the establishment of an independent government alone'.[57] The PAICRC worked for the economic and social emancipation of the masses, 'aiming at the unification of all the communities which compose the Indian people, irrespective of their religious beliefs, and the establishment of such conditions, after the overthrow of foreign rule, as to prevent the exploitation of [one] community by another'.[58] Working for these political, economic, and social principles, the PAICRC would also seek to arm the masses to prevent a counter-revolution by establishing a 'revolutionary Dictatorship' and work in 'economic cooperation with all revolutionary proletarian republics, such as Russia'.[59] The PAICRC was a temporary organisation, uniting the Indian revolutionary groups in Soviet Russia, but all funding from the Comintern was funnelled through this organisation and Roy.

The Baku Congress of the Peoples of the East

The Congress of the Peoples of the East was held in Baku from 1 to 8 September 1920. Conceived by Comintern Chairman Grigori Zinoviev to intimidate European imperial interests in the oil-rich, newly-independent Azerbaijan, British intelligence wrote off the Congress as an 'utter farce', and Roy was against the event altogether as 'it could serve only the purpose of agitation' and achieve little in

REVOLUTION IN RUSSIA

terms of bringing about a revolution.[60] However, it signalled a stronger commitment to the liberation struggles across the colonial world.[61] In preparation for the Baku congress, Rabb sent a note to the Comintern on behalf of the IRA: 'The Indian Revolutionary Association of Tashkent requests on behalf of the 315 million of the oppressed in India, that the delegates of this Congress and Soviet Russia who are gathered here together in order to liberate their fellow beings, the help for which India craves and begs'.[62] Offering the IRA's help in questions on India, Rabb also warned against religious divisions between oppressed peoples in India and stated that the future of the world depended on the freedom of India.

Of the almost 1,900 delegates to the Baku Congress, there were fourteen attendees from India, half of them from the IRA, including Acharya, Ashur, and Siddiq, and the rest from other groups, including Mukherji as the Indian communist delegate.[63] In the proceedings from the Baku congress, Acharya is listed as an official representative from India and, curiously, as from the communist faction.[64] This seems to suggest that the Bolsheviks considered Acharya a communist, although he had no official relations with the Comintern yet. At the congress, Acharya was elected to the Council for Action and Propaganda in the East (CAPE) as a communist representative from India.[65] Acharya's friend Nikolai Ragdaev, a Russian anarchist sympathetic to the revolution, later joined Acharya in the CAPE (see Chapter 8).[66] In the months after the congress, however, the CAPE lay dormant and in terms of actual propaganda or action, little materialised from the Baku congress.[67] The Indian delegates also achieved little from the Baku congress as all Indian communists were in exile and there was no communist movement within India yet.[68] To remedy this, the Indian Communist Party (ICP) was formed shortly thereafter to bring the struggle for Indian independence under the direction of the Comintern.

While sympathetic to the Bolsheviks, Acharya's first year in Russia, traversing Central Asia and setting up a new revolutionary organisation, the IRA, saw him navigating international revolutionary alliances and forming new connections that replaced the old nationalist ones. By now an experienced revolutionary in his own right, as he attended the Second Congress of the Comintern and the Baku Congress,

99

ANARCHY OR CHAOS

Acharya remained independent from Moscow and was not entirely convinced of the Bolshevik experiment yet. This independent attitude soon brought him on collision course with some of the other Indians in Russia. Through Acharya's activities in Russia, we arrive at a more nuanced understanding of communism and anti-imperialism.

7

THE INDIAN COMMUNIST PARTY

The Indian Communist Party

At the suggestion of the Executive Committee of the Communist International (ECCI), the various Indian groups in Russia were encouraged to unite under the Bolshevik banner and form a communist party to be affiliated with the Comintern. However, Acharya was sceptical of this proposed venture. In fact, in an article in *Izvestia* from 19 September 1920, Acharya offered an overview of the multifarious nature of the Indian revolutionary movement— ranging from workers, peasants, and even the nationalist bourgeoisie—and argued that if revolution would break out in Europe, India would follow, and all classes, not just communists, would take part in such a revolution. The British had to be ousted from India before any form of communism could emerge.[1]

Acharya and Mukherji returned to Moscow after the Baku congress and there met Shafique and Roy, who in the meantime had been elected to the Small Bureau of the Comintern. On 20 September, Acharya, Shafique, Mukherji, Trent, and Roy left Moscow, arriving in Tashkent on 1 October, and the first meeting of the ICP took place in Tashkent on 17 October.[2] According to Roy, it was Acharya and Rabb who had proposed the formation of the ICP.[3] This contradicts the historical records. In fact, only two weeks prior to the formation of the ICP, Roy had written to Suritz:

ANARCHY OR CHAOS

> I have been authorised by the Soviet Govt. to take charge of all the Indian propaganda, political and military works in co-operation with you .... I have also been appointed by the Communist International [as] its representative in the Middle East in conjunction with Shkolnikoff (President of the Turk Comm. and commandant of the Turkestan Forces) and Com. Safaroff. We are authorised to organise here a Bureau of the Communist International for the works in the East.[4]

Roy emphasised that, 'besides the organisation of a Central Revolutionary Committee, the time is ripe for the formation of a Communist Party in India. A country with a growing proletarian movement must have the political direction of a Communist Party'.[5] Even further, Roy explained that the various Indian revolutionary groups in exile should 'adopt a common programme and elect a Central Revolutionary Committee to which every organisation must be subordinated'.[6] In other words, Roy was pushing for the establishment of the ICP and to bring other Indian revolutionary bodies in Central Asia under this party.

In addition to Roy and Acharya, the first members were Trent, Mukherji and his wife Rosa Fitingov, Muhammad Ali, and Shafique, the latter being elected secretary of the ICP. As Rabb still disagreed with Roy on the question of converting to communism, he was not admitted until a few weeks later. At the first meeting, it was agreed that, as soon as a political programme had been drafted, this would be communicated to the Comintern in Moscow. The meeting adjourned with the singing of 'The Internationale'.[7] It took another two months for the group to draw up a programme and inform the Comintern, while waiting for more members to join, and the ICP was not formally registered until early January 1921.[8]

To train and educate the Indian *Muhajirs* who had come to Tashkent, members of the ICP started giving lectures on capitalism, imperialism, and Marxism, thus preparing the ground for revolution in India. They could only join the Military School after this training. The idea was that, upon return to India, the *Muhajirs* would spread communist propaganda, enlist the masses, and then receive arms from Russia for a revolution.[9] One of the lecturers, Shaukat Usmani, who joined the ICP in late November 1920, later recalled: '[t]he Indian in charge of work here [Tashkent] was M. P. T. Acharya', who was working with Shkolnikoff, 'a brilliant Russian comrade' well-versed in Marxism.[10]

102

THE INDIAN COMMUNIST PARTY

'The India House at Tashkent', Usmani wrote further, 'became virtually the property of Maulana Abdur Rabb, M. P. T. Acharya, Amin Siddiq (Rabb's secretary) and one M. A. Faruqui'.[11]

Throughout the autumn of 1920, Acharya and Roy corresponded frequently and worked together in harmony towards stirring up Indian revolution from the Russian borderlands. After the first meeting of the ICP in Tashkent, aside from a brief trip to Skobelev (now Ferghana) in late November or early December, during which he suffered from a high fever, Acharya was mostly based in Andijan and worked with the Kashgars. On 28 October, Acharya wrote to Roy about the difficulties of recruiting Indians into their fold, and he requested rifles, a typewriter, and some fresh underwear.[12] Roy responded a few days later, aware of the difficulties of finding true revolutionaries rather than religious fanatics, and asked Acharya to remain in Andijan. Roy asked Acharya to organise a mission to Kashgar to set up another centre with the object of producing propaganda literature and scouting for routes to India through the mountainous border regions.[13] Acharya explained to Roy a few days later that it was difficult to obtain information about routes to India as many of the locals were illiterate and only knew the territory in practice. Indeed, many of the local Indians were willing to help in some way, but they would need more education to be of use for revolutionary purposes. Another problem in the Kashgar region was the interference of some of the *Aqsaqals* (elders, village leaders) who threatened their recruitment in the region.[14]

Writing from Tashkent on 11 November, Roy sent Acharya a mandate appointing him

> the representative of the Tashkent Bureau of the International in Andijan. The second paper authorises you to draw money from the funds of the Soviet International for secret Indian work. The third paper is the announcement that the Soviet International Propaganda is liquidated and the Bureau of the International established here, and that you are sent to Andijan to reorganise the branch there.[15]

Acharya was to equip some of the arriving Indians with arms and clothing. The responsibility of sending a mission to India now in Acharya's hands, he informed Roy that he had received information from a local Kashgar about routes to India. Acharya was working

103

ANARCHY OR CHAOS

under difficult circumstances in Andijan. 'Owing to heavy though early snow, there is neither telegraph, electricity, or telephone working here', he explained to Roy.[16] In another letter, Acharya informed Roy that he was joining the Indian mission to Skobelev but that he could not acquire horses, rifles, and clothes for the expedition.[17]

Departing for Skobelev on 19 November to organise the mission to be sent to India, Acharya informed Roy that the Indian centre in Osh had been terminated, so Acharya suggested that the men from there should scour the area for possible routes to India. Some of the younger men, he explained, were more suited for military training, which should be done in Tashkent, but many of the men in Andijan were unfit for proper revolutionary work. Asking Roy for maps of the region, Acharya also complained that they had not received the promised funding from Roy.[18] Arriving in Skobelev a few days later, Acharya soon realised that their mission was doomed. After discussing the situation with members of the Soviet Revolutionary Military Council, Acharya explained to Roy that it would be impossible to travel via the Badakhshan mountains 'whether escorted or otherwise on land or by airplanes'.[19] There were heavy snowstorms in the area, the mountains would be too high for airplanes to cross, and local soldiers might be hostile to their mission. Consequently, Acharya and Shkolnikoff would return to Andijan, leaving the rest of the mission in Skobelev. Acharya complained again that they had not received any clothes and asked Roy to sort it with the Oblast Revolutionary Committee. More urgently, he again alerted Roy to the fact that they had still not received the promised funding from him.

Shortly after Acharya's return to Andijan in early December, Usmani arrived to assist him. Usmani later recalled:

> M. P. T. Acharya was a good-natured revolutionary. He came to the railway station to receive me. The first question that he asked me was whether I was a member of the Communist Party. On my replying in the negative, prompt came the remark, 'Then you're a diplomat'. At that time, I took this for a compliment, but what Acharya meant to say was that I was shrewd enough to avoid the controversies between his and Roy's group.[20]

Usmani's later account of his time with Acharya in Andijan strikes a different tone from his letters at the time. Nine days after his arrival

THE INDIAN COMMUNIST PARTY

in Andijan, Usmani complained to Roy that he was 'doing nothing but idling away the time. C. Acharya could not show me the procedure of work nor could he give sufficient instructions to me to begin the work'.[21] He did not entirely blame Acharya, however, but noted that many of the Hindus in Andijan were just as bad as the Muslims—'idlers, drunkards, debauchees'—all looking to take advantage of the mission and obtain a free return to India.[22]

Usmani's account of the growing disagreement between Acharya and Roy, however, proved more accurate. Arriving in Andijan on 3 December, after suffering a high fever and gruelling weather on the way back from Skobelev, Acharya received the promised money from Usmani and informed Roy of the treacherous conditions in the area. More importantly, having received a letter from Chatto, who was still in Stockholm with Nalini Das Gupta, Acharya said that Chatto would be a valuable addition to their efforts in Moscow or Afghanistan. Chatto had to settle some financial debt in Stockholm, but Acharya suggested to Roy that Karakhan should intervene and take care of that, thus allowing Chatto to join them in Russia. Chatto made a brief trip to Russia in November 1920 to discuss plans with Mukherji for uniting the Berlin group with the PAICRC. They agreed to bring eight or nine Indian revolutionaries from Berlin to Russia to strengthen their work within the PAICRC as well as to establish a sub-committee in Berlin.[23] Acharya's friend Abdul Hafis was also about to join them. 'Hafis is not good for political work but is a good chemist and metallurgist', Acharya explained to Roy. 'He is a "good" bourgeois or aristocratic revolutionary—that is all', Acharya said.[24]

Meanwhile, perhaps worried about the arrival of Chatto and Hafis, both of whom were friends of Acharya, Roy tightened his grip on the ICP. This became evident at an IRA meeting on 5 December where Acharya and Rabb explained:

> [t]here was no need at all to make most of the Indians sign on as hospital guards or become Communists .... We are not against Communism, (and) we do not make a distinction between a Communist revolutionary or just a revolutionary. All we object to is forcible conversion (to Communism). We have respect for convictions and object to the use of force. Comrade Roy cut off supplies to the Indian Revolutionary Association and immigrants from 3rd instant.[25]

105

ANARCHY OR CHAOS

Indeed, while Acharya clearly still found someone like Hafis a good and useful revolutionary, Roy wanted to bring the Indian struggle for independence under the ICP and, by extension, the Comintern, and to exclude non-communist elements from the movement.

At another meeting on 15 December 1920, Acharya was appointed chairman of the Executive Committee of the ICP, while Shafique was appointed secretary, and Roy became a member of the Executive Committee. At the same time, Shafique resigned from the PAICRC, being too busy with the military school, and Acharya assumed the role of secretary.[26] To move the ICP forward, Acharya was to take steps towards officially registering the ICP with the Comintern while Roy and Mukherji were in charge of drafting a party programme.[27] It was also resolved that the ICP 'would be always an independent body. Only those members who are specially deputed to join any special Indian Organisation, shall be under the command and discipline of the latter'.[28] Furthermore, it was agreed that '[t]he Communist Party as a body will be subject to no other organisation and its members are not free to join other political organisations unless with the permission of the Party or unless specially deputed to do so'.[29]

These last points, of course, had direct consequences for Acharya and Rabb, who were still members of the IRA. In fact, as Usmani explained, whereas Roy's group wanted all Indian revolutionary activities to go through the ICP and take directions from Moscow, Acharya and Rabb's group 'insisted all revolutionary work should be conducted through a revolutionary party in which all the Indians, whatever their political convictions, should be included. This left room for anarcho-communists as well as the extreme type of nationalists'.[30]

The meeting was quickly followed by the first regular Sunday meeting of the ICP on 18 December held jointly with the PAICRC. By then, Roy had seized control of the PAICRC and was upset that the NKID still supported the IRA. It was resolved that '[t]he Comintern should be requested to inform the Indian Revolutionary Association, and all Indian revolutionaries in Tashkent, that henceforth its relations with the Indian revolutionary movement will be through the medium of the PAICRC having its headquarters in Tashkent'.[31] At the ICP meeting, Roy and Mukherji promised to draft a programme within the next ten days, while and Acharya and Trent were tasked with

106

THE INDIAN COMMUNIST PARTY

drawing up a constitution of the ICP.[32] However, Roy also questioned whether 'a member of the ICP can maintain any official relations with any other non-Communist organisation without the official consent of the ICP, and as such, whether Comrade Acharya can continue to be the member of the Indian Revolutionary Association, while he can produce no official permission from the ICP to this effect'.[33] The question was discussed intently at the meeting, with Acharya initially trying to mediate, but he eventually argued that 'he had been a member of the IRA prior to the formation of the ICP, and he declared his desire of continuing his former relations with that body in order that he might be able to reconcile it with the ICP and the PAICRC'.[34] Acharya's proposition was met with furious opposition from the others, and 'he was told over and over again that he was not authorised to do it until he receives official permission of his co-operation with that not only non- but anti-Communist organisation'.[35] In his defence, Trent suggested that Acharya should continue to work with the IRA but not remain a member of the IRA. In doing so, she noted, Acharya could be the connecting tissue between the two organisations. It was agreed that 'Acharya should be asked to resign from the IRA, but at the same time carry on working with that body till further notice'.[36]

The issue of Acharya's membership was raised again at the next regular ICP meeting on 26 December. He and Trent had drawn up a constitution but asked for more time, and he had even taken steps towards registering the ICP formally with the Comintern. More pressingly, there had been inquiries about Acharya making statements against communism. At the meeting, Acharya admitted that he had done so, but said that 'he was joking'.[37] In Soviet Russia, such accusations were serious, so a special meeting of the ICP was called on 28 December. Acharya delivered a longthy defence of himself, knowing well, he said, 'that his statement would be absolute rejected and no attention would be paid by the prejudiced party to his complaints'.[38] He explained how he and Rabb had gone to Kabul to form the IRA but had to retreat to Tashkent to set up the organisation there. Roy's denouncement of the IRA, Acharya said, was unjustified, to which Trent immediately replied that 'no special personalities or organisations were censured, but on account of their parasitic behaviour, the Indians as a whole, were charged'.[39]

107

ANARCHY OR CHAOS

Acharya explained that, when he went to Moscow to set up formal relations with the Comintern at the Second Congress, Roy was already there, preparing to go to Kabul as the head of the Indian section, but Acharya felt that 'Roy would absolutely fail to do any national work in the cause of revolution'.[40] Though Acharya and Roy travelled together to Tashkent, Acharya's prophesies soon came true, according to him, and Roy succeeded in conspiring against Rabb and gathering supporters around himself. When Acharya was sent to Andijan, the rift between Roy and Rabb grew wider, and, although Acharya tried to mediate, 'in his absence things went from bad to worse through the tactless and tyrannical policy of Com. Roy'.[41] Acharya stated that anti-communist propaganda had been attributed wrongly to Rabb and that it actually stemmed from other intriguers. Upon his return to Tashkent after Moscow, Acharya again tried to mediate between Roy and Rabb, even joining the ICP to better relations, but also failed to get along with Roy. Ending his defence, Acharya charged that the ICP as a whole 'is nothing but a religious sect'.[42]

In response, Roy dismissed Acharya as disgruntled and called his accusations baseless and without any evidence. 'Almost every charge was stupid enough', Roy retorted, 'and he thinks it below his dignity and not necessary to make any reply to it'.[43] He stated that he had discussed the potential of the Afghan revolution before Rabb and the other Indian revolutionaries, 'thinking them to be revolutionaries at least'.[44] When he arrived in Tashkent, Roy stated, he had tried his utmost to collaborate with Rabb, but failed to find common ground.[45] Acharya was formally expelled from the ICP at the meeting held on 28 December 'on account of actively supporting people engaged in frankly anti-communist propaganda and on account of bringing groundless accusations against all the party members for which you refuse to present any proof.'[46] At a meeting on 31 December 1920, Acharya elaborated on his resistance to forcible conversion to communism: 'Indians must be told that they will be taught Communism here, but not forcibly recruited into the Party'.[47] He repeated his charge that Roy 'must be dismissed from his job ... because he has lost his prestige among the Indians'.[48] In the end, Acharya and Rabb lost out to Roy and his supporters.

THE INDIAN COMMUNIST PARTY

Divisions between the Indian revolutionaries in Russia

On 20 January 1921, Roy, Rabb, and Acharya left for Moscow, staying at the Hotel Lux, to discuss the rift between the various Indian groups in Russia further, now that Chatto's group from Berlin was expected to arrive.[49] However, only a few days later, Acharya was also expelled from the executive committee of the PAICRC for 'making groundless accusations against the Committee members and the condition of Indian work as a whole'.[50] The PAICRC also charged that he had 'done this in an underhanded and sneaking manner, tale-telling, back-biting, and otherwise lowering the dignity of the Indian revolutionaries, only coming out to the Committee with your allegations after having been to several Soviet officials'.[51]

To purge Acharya completely from revolutionary work, on 30 January, Shafique wrote to Acharya to demand that he return the original letter that had granted him status as the chairman of the ICP and notified him that the ECCI had been informed of these actions.[52] On the same day, Acharya wrote a letter to the ECCI and explained that an Indian communist party was unnecessary: '[w]hen Comrade Roy proposed the setting up of an Indian Communist Party, I declared clearly and openly that it would be better not to have a party so named at all than to have one composed of different sorts of people calling themselves Communists'.[53] The next day, he wrote to directly to Lenin, enclosing a six-page document on the work in Central Asia, 'just to show the rotten condition of Indian work entrusted to Com. Roy and pointing out how the work can be done'. He asked for a personal meeting with Lenin and noted that he could bring 'personal and written evidence to show that Com. Roy has mismanaged the Indian work to such an extent that it can no longer be saved by him'.[54] Acharya was not granted a meeting with Lenin, but the quarrel between the two Indian groups soon became a sore topic for the Comintern. On 11 March, an ECCI group comprising Karl Steinhardt, Konstantin Zetkin, and Yakov Peters convened in Moscow to resolve the disagreement. They accused Acharya and Rabb's group of pan-Islamist propaganda, and therefore anti-Bolshevism, and consequently supported Roy's side against Acharya and Rabb.[55] A few weeks later, Acharya responded to the ECCI's decision and explained how Roy

ANARCHY OR CHAOS

and Borodin intrigued against Chatto's group in Berlin by withholding money from them with the hope that the group would not come to Moscow. Acharya explained:

> when Comrade Roy was compelled to go to Moscow for the settlement of the conflict against him, I surmised that possibly he might put an end to the hopes for the India conference, for he knew that the comrades in Europe were neither agreed with the plenipotentiary powers conferred upon him from the People's Commissariat for Foreign Affairs nor with his choice or method.[56]

According to Acharya, Roy was clearly worried that he could not bring Chatto and the Berlin group under his wing. To support his claim, Acharya quoted from a letter he had received from Chatto: '[w]e have tried to bring together all forces again (Communist and National) …. I do not agree with Comrade Roy or his methods, no one does. Again, we must work now. Do not leave Moscow. Most important to have you there'.[57] Upon receipt of Chatto's letter, Acharya urged the ECCI to arrange for Chatto and the Berlin group to travel to Moscow right away.

Shortly thereafter, the remaining Indian revolutionaries in Tashkent held a meeting where Mukherji accused Rabb and Acharya of being spies and agitators, implicating Faruqui in their intrigues as well, and even suggested that they were working for the British government. Their indictment against Acharya was spurious:

> Acharya came out of India as an English spy to spy over the Indian students in London. After a year's work there, he was discharged by the British Government on account of his drinking habits, after which he became an Indian revolutionary. This fact about Acharya we have heard only from the verbal report of Comrade Mukherji who says that he heard it himself from Acharya and from some other English Comrades in the Comintern, Moscow.[58]

Despite having no evidence for the accusations, the group concluded that '[w]e have no reason to disbelieve Comrade Mukherji'.[59]

The Berlin Indians in Moscow

The Berlin group of Indians arrived in Moscow a few weeks later, staying at the Hotel Lux, and on 25 May, the Indians from the various

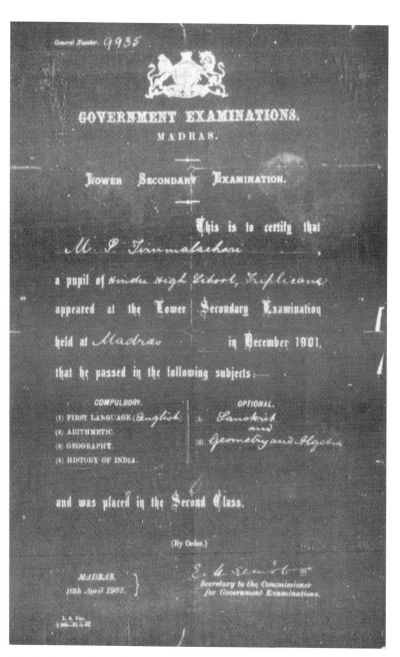

Fig. 1: Lower Secondary Examination Diploma, Hindu High School, Triplicane, 16 April 1902.

Fig. 2: M. P. T. Acharya, United States, c. 1914.

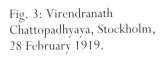

Fig. 3: Virendranath Chattopadhyaya, Stockholm, 28 February 1919.

Fig. 4: A group of delegates arrive in Petrograd for the Second Congress of the Communist International, Petrograd and Moscow, 19 July–8 August 1920. An official greets the French communists Marcel Cachin and Louis-Oscar Frossard, flanked by Karl Radek on the left and Grigori Zinoviev on the right. Behind Radek, looking at the camera, is M. P. T. Acharya.

Fig. 5: Delegates leaving the Smolny, Petrograd, for the formal opening session of the Second Congress of the Communist International, 19 July 1920. Acharya can be seen at the bottom left-hand corner.

Fig. 6: Opening session of the Second Congress of the Communist International, Tauride Palace, Petrograd, 19 July 1920. Indian delegates sitting second section from the bottom of the photograph, third row of desks. From the aisle and left to right: Abani Mukherji, M. P. T. Acharya, Evelyn Trent, M. N. Roy, Mohamed Shafique.

Fig. 7: After the opening session at the Tauride Palace, the delegates marched to the Square of the Victims of the Revolution, Petrograd, 19 July 1920. Acharya can be seen in the lower left-hand corner.

Fig. 8: Procession to the Square of the Victims of the Revolution, Petrograd, 19 July 1920.

Fig. 9: M. P. T. Acharya, wedding photograph, 1922.

Fig. 10: Magda Nachman, wedding photograph, 1922.

Fig. 11: IWMA founding meeting, Berlin, 25 December 1922–2 January 1923. Back row, left to right: Hermann Ritter; Theo Schuster; Armando Borghi; Edvin Lindstam; Johan Gerhard van Zelm; Theo Dissel. Middle row, left to right: Orlando Ángel; Augustin Souchy; Alexander Schapiro; Rudolf Rocker; Alibrando Giovannetti; Bernard Lansink Jr. Front row, left to right: Frans Severin; Virgilia d'Andrea Borghi; Diego Abad de Santillan.

THE INDIAN COMMUNIST PARTY

factions met to discuss their differences. The Berlin group comprised Chatto, Agnes Smedley, Khankhoje, Datta, Hafis, and Ghulam Ambia Khan Luhani. Acharya and Faruqui aligned themselves with Chatto's group.[60] The two Indian factions accused each other of spying and counter-revolutionary work and did not reach any agreements. In the wake of the meeting, Roy asserted his power over the ICP and Indian revolutionary work. Roy informed the Comintern that Chatto's group were old guard nationalists and not communists, hence they should not receive support from the Bolsheviks.[61]

While Acharya had split from the ICP and aligned himself with anti-Bolsheviks and anarchists, he attended the Third Congress of the Comintern in Moscow as 'a confirmed Communist'.[62] Footage from the event confirms Acharya's presence there, and he later wrote to the British anarchist Tom Keell that he had met Rose Witkop, Guy Aldred's partner, when he stayed at the Hotel Lux during the Third Congress.[63] By the summer of 1921, most of the Berlin group had left Moscow, but Chatto, Luhani, and Datta remained to attend the Third Congress. After the congress, Chatto, Luhani, and Datta presented a 'Thesis on India and World Revolution' to a new commission of the Comintern, in which they laid out the anticolonial struggle in India, the role of British imperialism, and the task of the Comintern to support the Indian freedom movement. The 'Thesis' outlined the heterogenous nature of Indian society, including bourgeois nationalists as well as peasants and workers, and the need to overthrow British rule before any form of communism could be introduced. In a follow-up 'Memorandum' by Chatto, Luhani and Khankhoje, they criticised Roy's ICP and emphasised that this organisation, having been founded outside India, should not determine the direction of the freedom struggle, and that any talk of communism in India was premature, but that with the help of the Comintern, a new group under Chatto's leadership could pave the way for communism in India. India was not ready for communism yet, they argued. The group's 'Thesis' and 'Memorandum' were largely ignored by the ECCI and perceived as nationalist and even bourgeois, without a real grasp of Marxism and the revolutionary potential of the international working class.[64]

Before they returned to Berlin in September 1921, Chatto and Smedley met Emma Goldman and Alexander Berkman in Moscow.

111

ANARCHY OR CHAOS

Smedley did not know them personally but greatly admired these two anarchists and insisted on visiting them in their house arrest.[65] In her memoirs, Goldman recalled:

> I had heard a good deal about Agnes in the States in connexion with her Hindu activities, but I had never met her personally. She was a striking girl, an earnest and true rebel, who seemed to have no other interest in life except the cause of the oppressed people in India. Chatto was intellectual and witty, but he impressed me as a somewhat crafty individual. He called himself an anarchist, though it was evident that it was Hindu nationalism to which he had devoted himself entirely.[66]

Their meeting in Moscow laid the grounds for a close friendship that continued in Berlin.

While Acharya stayed out of the discussions between Chatto's group and the ECCI, after the Third Congress, he again wrote to the ECCI to explain his side of the conflict and noted that documents he had given to Mikhail Kobetsky of the ECCI and to the NKID to support his case had disappeared from the Comintern archives. He reiterated that Roy had worked against Rabb from the beginning of his arrival in Tashkent, that Roy had refused to work with the IRA and a mixed committee of revolutionaries of various shades, that he had expelled everyone who was not willing to work under his orders, and that he had even spread a rumour that Acharya and Rabb had been arrested to discredit them. With the arrival of Chatto's group from Berlin, Roy became even more obstinate and, Acharya stated, 'he has been doing everything persistently, systematically, and with impunity to break up everything and disperse everybody concerned with the Indian work of the Comintern', all with the help of the prominent communists Borodin, Karakhan, and Santeri Nuorteva.[67]

A few days later, now staying at the Hotel Dresden in Moscow, Acharya laid out the conditions for the Comintern for achieving anything in India:

1. The Indian Communist Party must throw out all 'infantile' and so-called extreme communists, esp. Roy, Mukherji, and the members of the self-styled Provisional Government of India who are now in it, namely Shafique, Zacharia, Muhammad Ali, and a couple of others.

THE INDIAN COMMUNIST PARTY

2. A mixed Commission of Indian Communists and pro-Communist Indian 'nationalists' as well as one or two Russian comrades representing the Comintern—or only one Russian comrade and another representing the French, German, or any other strongly revolutionary party interested in the immediate destruction of the British Empire—such a commission must be nominated to make plans for organising, acting, and controlling all activities with regard to India.

3. Until a successful political revolution is made in India, all the activities of the Communist and non-Communist revolutionary organisations must be strictly subordinated to the decisions of this commission.[68]

Acharya warned again that, '[a]s Indian comrades are not experienced in labour organisation and communist propaganda and activity ... I am firmly convinced that any encouragement to "left communism" in countries like India is an encouragement to counter-revolution in those countries now'.[69] He emphasised lastly that

> [i]f the above suggestions are not accepted by the Executive [ECCI] or the Small Bureau of the Comintern, I for one refuse to have any part in the Indian activity of the Comintern, although I have no intention or desire to go out of Russia but will be glad to serve any other Communist party in any capacity.[70]

In other words, while Acharya broke definitively with the ICP and had a different vision of the Indian anticolonial struggle, he still had faith in communism. The close collaboration between the various Indian revolutionary groups in Russia, which eventually led to intense disagreements and the fragmentation of the ICP, reveal a great deal about the troubled history of the birth of Indian communism in exile. Acharya's role in this history, moreover, illuminates the ways in which totalitarianism and internal power struggles hampered the true meaning of freedom for colonial subjects.

113

8

ANTI-COMMUNIST ACTIVITIES

Anti-Bolshevik dissent

After his expulsion from the ICP, Acharya associated with Bolshevik dissenters and critics, among them Balabanoff and Alexandra Kollontai. After the failed peace congress in Stockholm, Balabanoff travelled to Russia in 1919 and became a central figure in the Bolshevik revolution. As a member of the ECCI, she led the Women's Section of the Comintern alongside Kollontai but also took an interest in colonial questions. By the time of the Second Congress of the Comintern, however, she had fallen out with Lenin and the Bolsheviks, and she was soon expelled from the ECCI. Acharya's association with Balabanoff was probably brief, but he later remarked:

> [t]hose who knew Balabanoff (as the writer knew), know how reli giously scrupulous, and unselfish she is, even to the point of martyr- dom. She looks at the proletariat like an ascetic with pity, but that did not prevent her from co-operating with and justifying the actions of a newer state for a couple of years—because of the danger to the Russian proletariat from *other* states.[1]

However, despite Acharya's admiration for Balabanoff, he also criti- cised her and said that 'she was responsible for the betraying of the proletariat to a new set of oppressors and exploiters instead of liberating them'.[2] As an anarchist, he accused her of being naïve, 'for she hopes another state will be required to emancipate the proletarians'.[3]

115

ANARCHY OR CHAOS

It was also through Balabanoff that Acharya first met Kollontai in Moscow. As he later recalled:

> I had the privilege of being taken by Mme Balabanoff into Mme Kollontai's room in the Hotel National and being introduced to her when the latter was head of the women's section of the Communist International ... Mme Kollontai told me that there was no more emancipation movement among the women in Russia proper but only in Muslim Russia. The Russian women think, she said, that with the success of the Bolshevik Revolution, emancipation is over and want to drink, dress, and dance. She was a charming woman and very graceful and was simply dressed at the time I met her.[4]

While Acharya disagreed with the politics of these two prominent women, there is also a sense of admiration and respect for their courage to dissent from the Bolshevik party. He later wrote about Balabanoff to Boris Yelensky: 'I knew her since Sweden in 1917. Pity she will die Marxian. A kind of Marxian ascetic'.[5] About Kollontai, he later said: 'at a party congress meeting when Mme Kollontai complained against want of party and proletarian democracy, Trotsky got up and threatened her with concentration camp. She was the first workers' opposition movement'.[6] In some ways, Acharya's association with Balabanoff and Kollontai is not only indicative of his encounters with anti-Bolshevik dissenters in Moscow, but also explains why he still took part in revolutionary work and propaganda for India. Meanwhile, Acharya eked out a living as a journalist, a profession that was initially tolerated by the new Bolshevik regime, and published articles about the Indian revolutionary movement in publications such as *Pravda* and *Vestnik NKID*. Like all other foreign journalists in Russia, the Cheka kept him under surveillance to ensure his anti-Bolshevik criticism did not damage the new regime.[7]

The NEP and the American Relief Administration

Three years after the October Revolution, war communism and the ongoing civil war in Russia had brought the country to the brink of economic breakdown. The Kronstadt Rebellion in early March 1921 made it clear to Lenin that a new economic policy was needed. In March 1921, Lenin introduced the New Economic Policy (NEP), which ceded some agriculture, small trade, and light industry back

ANTI-COMMUNIST ACTIVITIES

into private hands, and he invited foreign aid organisations to help with the famine. After the introduction of the NEP, Acharya later wrote—on the authority of Mikhail Reisner, who had seen Lenin at the time—'Lenin had a shock as the consequences of NEP and his mind was so paralysed that he looked blank and vacant-minded'.[8] Indeed, Lenin fell ill in late 1922, leaving the country in limbo and in the hands of Stalin, Zinoviev, and Trotsky.

The introduction of the NEP could not alleviate the widespread famine, and soon Lenin needed relief aid from abroad. Under the direction of Herbert Hoover, the American Relief Administration (ARA) had been set up in February 1919 to provide relief for the war-torn European countries. In August 1921, at the invitation of Maxim Gorky and the Bolsheviks, the ARA moved some of its operations to Russia. Lenin was obviously worried about accepting aid from the US but hoped that Russia's peasants would see that the Bolsheviks provided bread and food for them again. By the summer of 1922, the ARA provided food and help to more than ten million people a day. The large-scale relief operation required assistance from local interlocutors and interpreters and often relied on former Russian emigres and anti-Bolshevik dissenters, including anarchists such as Theodore Kushnarev and Abba Gordin.[9]

From April to September 1922, Acharya and five other former members of the IRA—Rabb, Faruqui, Kadir, Nazir, and Abdul Aziz—worked as interpreters in the Russian unit of the ARA.[10] Due to personnel reductions, Acharya was dismissed along with the Indians in September 1922, but his superior, John J. Mangan, provided a letter of recommendation for Acharya: '[a]ll the time, Mr. Acharya was found to be accurate, reliable, and conscientious and his services were performed satisfactorily'.[11] By then, the IRA was in disrepute with the Comintern, but through his work in the ARA, Acharya became friends with Gordin and did useful work in Russia without becoming part of the new Bolshevik regime.

Among the anarchists in Russia

After leaving the ICP, Acharya drew nearer to the anarchists in Russia, including Berkman, who had been deported from the United

ANARCHY OR CHAOS

States and arrived in Russia in December 1919. For Berkman, the significance of the Indian revolutionaries in Russia is evident from a conversation he had with Karakhan already in late February 1920:

> [t]he subject changed to India, Karakhan remarking that a delegate had just arrived from that country. The movement there was revolutionary, though of nationalistic character, he thought, and could be exploited to keep England in check. Learning that while in California I was in touch with Hindu revolutionists and Anarchists of the Hindustan Ghadar organization, he suggested the advisability of getting in communication with them. I promised to look after the matter.[12]

After another meeting with Karakhan on 9 March 1920, Berkman noted in his diary: '[d]iscussed especially the Hindu question; also Ireland. Suggested to him the advisability of encouraging real Hindu revolutionists rather than Nationalists'.[13] Indeed, Berkman was aware of the Bolshevik revolution's attraction to revolutionaries from the colonial world.[14]

In Tashkent, Acharya had encountered the two veteran Russian anarchists Nikolai Ragdaev and Izya Shkolnikoff. A follower of Kropotkin, Ragdaev had initially taken a prominent role among anarchists in the Russian Revolution. On his part, after a few years in the US, Shkolnikoff had returned to Russia in 1917 and been active in revolutionary work across the country. Supportive of the revolutionary fervour of the Bolsheviks, Ragdaev and Shkolnikoff had taken roles in the government and been sent to Tashkent for Soviet propaganda and 'cultural work' in the Commissariat for Education and worked with the IRA.[15] In fact, Acharya also recalled that he had met the two of them in Tashkent—'we were together in Tashkent and Andijan'—and then again in Moscow, where Shkolnikoff told Acharya that 'he would be arrested as he fell into the trap of a provocateur who proposed they should go to Berlin for the IWMA conference'.[16] Symptomatic of the fate for many anarchist supporters of the Bolshevik government, Shkolnikoff was imprisoned sometime in 1921, suffered greatly during his incarceration, and eventually suffered from a mental breakdown, while Ragdaev died in exile in Tashkent in 1932.[17]

The veteran anarchist Peter Kropotkin had returned to Russia in May 1917 but fell ill in January 1921 and died on 8 February that

118

ANTI-COMMUNIST ACTIVITIES

year. Lenin offered Kropotkin's family a state funeral, which they declined, and an anarchist-led funeral committee was established instead. Acharya and Usmani were also in Moscow at the time of Kropotkin's death and attended the funeral. As Usmani recalled, the Indians in Moscow were granted permits to attend the 'funeral of Prince Kropotkin, the famous anarcho-Communist leader ... in Moscow's Trade Union House'.[18] Shortly after Kropotkin's funeral, the Petrograd strike and subsequent Kronstadt Rebellion cemented the Bolshevik grip on the Russian Revolution and crushed the dissent of workers and sailors. While the Kronstadt Rebellion was not led by anarchists—a mix of Bolsheviks, Socialist Revolutionaries, and anarchists took part—it embodied the anarchist spirit and rejection of party-line dictatorship advocated by the Bolsheviks.[19] For Acharya too, 'the Kronstadt Rebellion of March 1921 was the end of the Revolution'.[20]

Marriage and escape from Russia

At some point in 1921, Acharya met the Russian artist Magda Nachman, and by early July 1922 they had married.[21] Born on 20 July 1889 in Pavlovsk to Maximillian Julianovich Nachman, a wealthy lawyer of Jewish descent, and Klara Alexandrovna of German Lutheran descent, Nachman enrolled at the E. N. Zvantseva art school in 1907. A talented artist, Nachman's paintings and sketches were soon included in various exhibitions, and in 1913 she spent the summer at the cottage of the well-known poet Maximilian Voloshin in Koktebel in the Crimea, where she befriended the poet Marina Tsvetaeva and the actress Elizabeth Efron, among others. She moved to Moscow in 1916, still spending her summers at Voloshin's cottage, but when the 1917 February Revolution broke out, the Russian metropolis became too expensive and work scarce, so she moved to Ust-Dolyssy with Efron. Working random jobs to support her artistic career and relocating frequently, Nachman returned to Moscow in November 1920, still pursuing her artistic career, and here met Acharya in 1921.[22]

By late November 1922, the situation had become impossible for Acharya in Moscow. Stranded there since early January 1921, work-

119

ANARCHY OR CHAOS

ing variously as a journalist and for the ARA, while still receiving financial assistance from the NKID, his presence in Russia was no longer tolerated by the Bolsheviks. Now that the Russian civil war had ended, so too did the NKID's assistance to the non-Bolshevik Indians. According to the British emissary in Moscow, Acharya and the Indians had requested permission to leave Russia, but were prohibited from doing so: '[n]ot being communists ... they are useless from the point of view of the International and that they cannot be allowed to leave since it is certain that, once away from Moscow, they would form centres of propaganda directed against the Soviet power'.[23] However, when Karakhan raised the matter of the stranded Indians in Moscow with Zinoviev, Karakhan was informed that, despite the fact that he had come to an agreement with the Russian State Political Directorate (GPU; the successor to the Cheka), the Bolsheviks wanted to expel Acharya and the Indians from Russia. Nevertheless, Karakhan made a case for them and allowed Acharya and two other Indians to leave for Germany.[24]

But leaving Russia in 1922 was no easy task. In a letter to Igor Reisner from 18 December 1922, written a few weeks after the couple's arrival in Berlin, Acharya explained that Karl Moor, the Swiss socialist and double agent, had ordered Acharya's detention because, according to Dalip Singh Gill, who had returned to Moscow, Acharya had been responsible for Gill's arrest in April 1921.[25] This was because of Gill's intrigues and Moor's personal grievances against anti-Bolshevik revolutionaries.[26] Acharya's intervention was proof, according to Moor, of Acharya being a spy and a counter-revolution-ary. 'As a result', Acharya wrote, 'real revolutionaries go to prison and counter-revolutionary agents get released'.[27] In fact, Moor had instructed the GPU to prevent Acharya from leaving Russia and sent a telegram to the border police to that effect as well. Despite Moor's intrigues, Acharya and Nachman managed to leave Moscow for Berlin in late November 1922. 'I must have been lucky, and I was able to leave Russia', wrote Acharya.[28]

Acharya's three years in Russia were important for his development as an international anticolonial revolutionary. Expelled from the ICP for anti-communist activities, Acharya eked out a living in Moscow, working for the ARA and witnessing the end of the revolution up

120

ANTI-COMMUNIST ACTIVITIES

close, and eventually drew nearer to anarchism through personal encounters with prominent anarchists. Having fled colonial oppression in India almost fifteen years earlier, Acharya and his new wife now had to flee again—this time from totalitarian, Bolshevik oppression.

PART III

ANTICOLONIALISM, ANARCHISM,
AND ANTI-MILITARISM, 1922–34

9

ANTICOLONIALISM AND ANARCHISM
IN WEIMAR BERLIN

Indians in Charlottenburg

In mid-November 1922, Acharya and Nachman arrived in Berlin on Russian passports. As Acharya was known to the Auswärtiges Amt, they easily obtained permission to stay in Germany.[1] A few weeks after their arrival, Acharya wrote a long letter to Igor Reisner and clarified his hasty departure from Russia. He explained that the GPU had been ordered to detain him and given notice to the border police to prevent him from passing in case he tried to flee, but miraculously they still managed to escape. He accused the Bolsheviks of repressing true revolutionaries; the strong revolutionaries were arrested, and the weak ones were turned into counter-revolutionary spies. The real revolutionaries, in his opinion, were the anarchists and syndicalists. However, in his view, even Rudolf Rocker and Alexander Berkman, whose books on the Russian Revolution he admired, did not entirely understand the political and economic bankruptcy of Soviet Russia. Perhaps not entirely convinced by Rocker's and Berkman's analyses of the events in Russia, Acharya also exposed the hypocrisy of Russian revolutionaries who only wanted to hold on to state power, much like any other capitalist statesmen they initially fought against. Acharya resisted the Bolshevik seizure of the means of the state and defiantly declared:

125

ANARCHY OR CHAOS

'let them call me an anarchist'. As a final break with Bolshevism, he challenged that, unless the Bolsheviks stopped persecuting revolutionaries, and unless Roy was rendered harmless, he would continue to expose the true nature of the conditions in Russia. To this end, he and Chatto would start a newspaper agency in Berlin that would analyse the Russian Revolution from an Indian perspective.[2]

Acharya and Nachman arrived shortly before the economic collapse in Germany and settled at Leibnizstrasse 42 in Charlottenburg, the same address where Acharya had lived with some of the other members of the IIC in 1914. Like many other new migrants, they often moved from place to place in search of cheaper accommodation. In July 1923, they moved briefly to Bochumer Strasse 5, just north of Leibnizstrasse, and then on to Kantstrasse 90 in Charlottenburg in September 1923. In a letter to his friend P. Parthasarathy in Bangalore (now Bengaluru) from September 1923, Acharya revealed about their Kantstrasse 90 apartment:

> I occupy one room, the next room is occupied by two girls and in a third room has now removed one Indian from Mathura [Uttar Pradesh], I have very little to do with my landlady except for paying her bills when she asks for it, the girls in one room are busy working somewhere and the Indian is also working to learn in some automobile factory.[3]

By October 1925, they had moved across the street to Kantstrasse 77. Informally known as 'Charlottengrad', the area was mostly known for its substantial Russian population—around 250,000 Russians had flocked to the city—but it also attracted a considerable number of the approximately two hundred Indians in Berlin at the time as well as Persians, Egyptians, and Chinese.[4] Though surrounded by many of his friends, Acharya initially withdrew from the Indian community, as he explained to Parthasarathy:

> I go to very few Indians and very few come to me—as all are busy enjoying themselves with those who can afford to pay for enjoyment and have a mind to do so. Still sometimes, some fellows pay a visit now and then, like Bhupendranath Datta (Vivekanand's brother) with whom I have very little business to transact or pleasure to enjoy.

He also noted, probably referring to Faruqui, 'I have got an excellent friend in a Peshawar young Mahomedan, he and I worked

126

ANTICOLONIALISM AND ANARCHISM IN WEIMAR BERLIN

together in Kabul, Tashkent, and Moscow, and who came here a few days after my arrival. He is married to a Lettish girl. He is in a very poor condition'.[5]

Roy and Mukherji, now enemies, had also relocated to Berlin in 1922. As Acharya related to Reisner: 'Roy lives in a first-class pension on the corner of Kurfürstendamm and Uhlandstrasse. Just like a Kurfürst in the Middle Ages. I saw Mukherji driving around in an automobile, must be about that international support of the workers'.[6] While these two caused great concern for the British intelligence services, the most prominent figure among the Indians was Chatto. As Acharya stated in his letter to Reisner, he wanted to start a news agency with Chatto to expose the truth about Roy and the Bolsheviks. Before Chatto had departed for Moscow in 1921, he had founded the Indian News Service and Information Bureau (INSIB) with the aim of sending political, economic, and cultural news to India.[7] To do this, the INSIB published the *Indo-German Commercial Review*, which soon changed name to *Industrial Review for India* and then *Industrial and Trade Review for Asia*. These were ostensibly focused on trade and commerce between India and Germany, but also featured more political articles, which soon attracted the attention of the British authorities. Smedley and, from 1923, A. C. N. Nambiar, who was married to Chatto's sister, Suhasini, assisted Chatto in these endeavours.[8] Acharya helped Nambiar and Chatto with secretarial work and translated French and German texts into English for the *Industrial and Trade Review for India*.[9]

In addition to this commercial organisation, in early 1923, the Hindusthan Association of Central Europe (HACE) expanded from being merely an Indian student organisation to include more prominent figures such as Chatto, Pillai, Datta, as well as Acharya. Initially setting up a club house at Georg-Wilhelm-Strasse 7–11 in Halensee, partly funded by Chatto, throughout the next decade, the HACE would serve as a social organisation with monthly meetings, many of which Acharya attended.[10] Alongside helping Chatto and Nambiar, Acharya supplemented his income by working as a personal secretary to B. Rosenthal, the director of the record company Zonophon A.G. in Ritterstrasse 111, handling the English correspondence and general office work. Rosenthal noted in a letter of reference for

127

ANARCHY OR CHAOS

Acharya that he was 'a very pleasant employee', dutiful and industrious, and a reliable person.[11] Acharya worked for Rosenthal for two years, until Rosenthal moved to England in 1925.

However, Acharya was still struggling financially. While he may have withdrawn from many of the other Indians in Berlin, he remained friends with Mansour Rifat. 'Dr. Rifat was also with me for some time in Stockholm', Acharya wrote to Parthasarathy. 'He is here in much straitened circumstances but certainly not so bad as I am'.[12] To supplement his secretarial work, Acharya typed and translated letters and manuscripts for Rifat and helped him with the publication of *Die Ahmadia-Sekte* (1923).[13] Thus, slowly finding his footing in Berlin, in the summer of 1923, the German authorities extended Acharya's permission to stay in the country.[14]

Indians among the anarchists

In the early 1920s, Berlin was not just home to Indians and Russians, but was also a hub for German and international anarchists. In his memoirs *Revolución y Regresión (1918–1951)* (1952), Rocker later recalled of Berlin in the 1920s:

> Berlin was at that time a centre for political refugees as Paris, Geneva, Zürich or London were in other times. In those years there were also a large number of Indians. They had their own circle in the eastern part, which served mainly as a point of reference and mostly had the task of financially helping its most destitute members. Most of the members of the club were Indian students, who were sent to Germany during and after the war and continued their studies at the University of Berlin. Almost all were declared nationalists, but among them there were also some who expressed a keen interest in libertarian ideas, like our young comrade Acharya, well known in our environment. Acharya lived for a few years in Berlin and then returned to India, where he continued to participate very actively in the libertarian movement.[15]

As Rocker noted, Acharya was well-known among the anarchists in Berlin. However, it was Chatto who interested Rocker the most:

> The soul of the circle was the well-known Hindu nationalist Chattopadhyaya, or Chatto, as it was customary to call him. He lived

128

ANTICOLONIALISM AND ANARCHISM IN WEIMAR BERLIN

in Berlin then with the American writer Agnes Smedley, who later became famous as a journalist and author of some books on China. I had met them through Emma Goldman, who was seeing them in Moscow, and Milly and I often met with them …. Chatto was a very charming man, an excellent and brilliant conversationalist, who gave flavour to every meeting and always offered good incentives. He also possessed a broad political vision and clearly recognized that a social transformation in the West would never happen unless the problem of colonial politics was not overcome and if the slave peoples of Asia did not enjoy the same rights as the Western nations.[16]

Indeed, in the early 1920s, Chatto and Smedley associated with many well-known anarchists, including Goldman, Berkman, Rocker, and Armando Borghi, and attended a reading group with these figures.[17]

In late December 1922, the International Working Men's Association (IWMA) was founded at a series of meetings held at various locations in Berlin to evade police surveillance. However, the Berlin police interrupted several meetings and arrested some of the attendees who had travelled to Germany illegally. Set up by anarchists and revolutionary syndicalists as a rival to the social democratic International Federation of Trade Unions (Amsterdam International) and the Comintern, the IWMA brought together anarchists from across Europe, North America, and South America, and had Souchy, Rocker, and the Russian syndicalist Alexander Schapiro as secretaries.[18] While the IWMA was committed to internationalism and anticapitalism, and had affiliated groups in Europe, North America, and South America, as well as contacts with Japanese and Chinese anarchists, it did not necessarily extend this commitment to internationalism to the colonial world.[19]

Nevertheless, Acharya and a group of Indians in Berlin attended some of the formative meetings of the IWMA. It is not certain who the other Indians were, but it is likely that Chatto was among them. At the meetings, it was decided to set up an affiliated group formed of Indian revolutionaries in Europe, although not formally attached to the IWMA, with the aim to send anarchist literature to India.[20] To that end, Acharya began translating for and contributing to the *IWMA Press Service*.[21] Due to Acharya's work, an article on the salt tax and civil disobedience movement in India, on the use of terrorism in the struggle against the British, and on May Day celebrations in India

ANARCHY OR CHAOS

appeared already in the July 1923 issue of the *IWMA Press Service*.[22] In response to the formation of this Indian group in Berlin, the Government of India banned the import of IWMA literature in March 1923, but the June issue of the *IWMA Press Service* made its way into the United Provinces. The Indians' first 'success', the IWMA noted sarcastically, was to get IWMA literature proscribed from India.[23] However, while British intelligence took notice of Acharya and the IWMA, they confused the anarchists with the communists at the time, mistaking these Indians for belonging to Roy's communist group.[24]

Despite the ban on anarchist literature in India, Acharya soon set to work and wrote a scathing critique of the political ideas that Roy had presented in his 1922 'A Programme for the Indian National Congress'. Acharya wrote:

> [i]n this programme, it is also proclaimed contrary to all accepted principles of his Russian Bolshevik party that the first and foremost objective of the national struggle (our movement for national liberation is freely used in this programme) is to secure the control of the national Government by the elected representatives of the people. The principle of election is also declared to be the democratic principle of universal suffrage. All these principles are boldly, rather audaciously, and falsely proclaimed—probably to accept his programme or at least to draw others into a discussion on them.[25]

Acharya also denounced Pratap who, he claimed, called himself 'the servant of mankind and the latest incarnation and prophet of God'.[26]

According to a British intelligence report, in early 1923 Acharya contributed to Sylvia Pankhurst's *Workers' Dreadnought* and Grigori Maximoff's Berlin-based publication *Rabochii Put*, an anarchist paper affiliated with the IWMA.[27] At the same time, to influence the various left-wing and labour organisations that had recently formed in India, Acharya started sending anarchist material to them, somehow circumventing the government ban. In June 1923, he wrote to the Indian trade unionist Malaypuram Singaravelu Chettiar in Madras and requested to join the newly-founded Labour Kisan Party of Hindustan, explaining that he was an anti-capitalist, anti-Bolshevik writer, giving an account of his expulsion from the ICP and denouncement of Roy as a British agent, and he offered to set up a

130

ANTICOLONIALISM AND ANARCHISM IN WEIMAR BERLIN

European branch of the Labour Kisan Party of Hindustan and to affiliate it with the IWMA.[28] In July 1923, he sent a copy of *Workers' Dreadnought* to M. P. S. Velayudham and explained that

> [t]he new International Working Men's Association is anti-political and federal. It is an improvement far ahead of the Third International with which I am at loggerheads after cooperating with hope for a whole year. I know all the personalities there well including Lenin, whom I had met twice. I am fighting them all in every writing and talk everywhere.[29]

However, as the Labour Kisan Party of Hindustan was decidedly communist and soon aligned with Roy, none of Acharya's plans materialised. Similarly, a few years later, he sent some of his articles to N. M. Joshi, leader of the All-India Trade Union Congress (AITUC), who, though much interested in Acharya's writings, declined to affiliate the AITUC with the IWMA.[30] Also in July 1923, he wrote to the veteran Indian nationalist Chittaranjan Das, declaring his political beliefs to be 'anarchism, pure and simple'.[31]

Acharya's attempts to associate these communist and left-wing organisations with the IWMA might also explain why the British intelligence lumped him in with the other Indian communists in Berlin. As one report stated:

> though he now ostensibly a member of the Fourth International, Acharya is of course purely personally interested in Eastern unrest. This is recognized by the Third International authorities in Berlin, who treat him accordingly and do not consider him an enemy as they do other definite members of the Fourth International.[32]

Whether the Comintern in Berlin treated Acharya any differently from other anarchists is uncertain, but Acharya's association with these Indian left-wing and labour leaders should be interpreted more as an attempt to affiliate these organisations with the IWMA and thus bring anarchism into India's labour and freedom struggles.

Deportation of Indians in Berlin

Acharya's association with other Indians in Berlin soon landed him in trouble with the authorities. By the mid-1920s, Berlin looked significantly different than it had only a few years before. Antisemitism and

ANARCHY OR CHAOS

racism became more overt, and some of the Indians in the city feared physical assaults due to what had happened to some Egyptians.[33] This prompted Chatto and Pillai to send a petition to the AA in July 1924: '[s]ince the war, foreign refugees, and particularly Indian political refugees, have enjoyed full rights in Germany, but the Indian revolutionaries fear that now in the future they may also be arrested and insulted on suspicion, as has happened in the case of the Egyptians'.[34] In fact, owing to political agreements between the British and German authorities, the German police frequently searched some of the Indians' homes and confiscated papers.[35] During a search of Acharya's Kantstrasse home in 1925, the police found his private office littered with manuscripts for Egyptian revolutionaries, but none of them were considered offensive to the German authorities.[36]

Acharya's association with the other Indians in Berlin manifested itself clearly when, at the request of the British authorities, the German authorities looked into deporting Acharya, Chatto, Pillai, Mukherji, and Roy to India on grounds of their political activities in Berlin.[37] The British assessed that Acharya was a more dangerous man than Pillai and eventually issued a warrant for his arrest should he enter India. In January 1925, however, the German authorities validated Acharya's residency permit, which allowed him to remain in Berlin.[38] The Indians in Berlin were soon caught up in a high diplomacy game between Britain and Germany. Although initially sympathetic to the British request, the German authorities eventually decided that they could not betray the Indians who had helped them during the war, and the British conceded that it would be better to allow the Indians to remain in Germany where they could keep track of them rather than to expel them to other countries.[39]

For Acharya, the affair highlighted the ways in which the British authorities were less concerned with the potential threat of anarchism to British rule in India but perceived communism to be a major ideological challenge to their colonial regime. Nevertheless, while the deportation request was abandoned and Acharya had been granted permission to stay in Germany, in January 1926 he applied for a British passport. Asked by the British consul in Berlin to provide more information about his activities, Acharya stated that he had left his nationalist activities behind him and declared: 'I am also a convinced anti-

ANTICOLONIALISM AND ANARCHISM IN WEIMAR BERLIN

Bolshevik. I am further free from the politics of any kind of party or government'.[40] In February 1926, the British consul granted Acharya an emergency certificate valid for a single journey to India on the most direct route but refused to offer a guarantee that no action would be taken against Acharya upon his arrival in India. Without this guarantee of amnesty, Acharya abandoned the idea of returning to India.

Anarchist experiments in cooperative living

While Acharya now travelled amongst many well-known anarchists in Berlin, he also took great interest in utopian and workers' cooperative communities across the world. To this end, he established contact with Warren Brokaw, editor of *The Equitist*, as well as E. Z. Ernst, the founder of the cooperative Freedom colony in Kansas, who sent him Labor Exchange founder Giuseppe B. de Bernardi's publications.[41] In the mid-1920s, Acharya contacted the British anarchist Ernest Bairstow, secretary of the British Llano Circle (BLC).[42] While the BLC had not established a cooperative colony at that time, the group laid down the principles for a future community in its pamphlet *The Comradeship of Economic Equality* (1926). The BLC was not the only experiment in cooperative living in Britain. The Whiteway Colony had been established in the Cotswolds in 1898, and Thomas H. Keell, editor of *Freedom*, moved there in 1928, becoming secretary of the colony, with his partner Lilian Wolfe.[43] When Acharya first approached Keell in August 1925, he wrote that he had obtained Keell's contact details from Bairstow.[44] At the same time, the BLC's *The Comradeship of Economic Equality* made its way to Acharya, who wrote to Bairstow on the BLC's experiment in cooperative living:

> I agree with you—have always thought and thus imbibed respect for Llano Colony—an ounce of practice is worth ten tons of theory and rules. But the only defect I see in the methods of the Colony is that it still has to educate itself in scientific rather than humanitarian outlook or sentiment.[45]

As one of its strongest supporters, Acharya wished their experiment continued success and compared it to the Whiteway Colony, 'which is interesting as individualist and anarchist, but not scientific'.[46] In contrast to the Whiteway Colony, he argued later, 'I consider Llano

133

ANARCHY OR CHAOS

the only socialist point today in the world'.[47] He was firmly convinced 'that the Llano system can be applied at this age not only on an isolated but world-scale with benefit to all mankind'.[48] In fact, 'Llano is an experiment which be improved if all villages try it, but if Llano fails— as some predict—the fault will be because of the experiment being too small to be independent'.[49] To spread the ideas of the Llano colonies, Acharya later wrote to 'friends in India to convert every village into Llano (750,000 villages!) if they want to succeed in improving conditions peacefully'.[50] Acharya's correspondence with Bairstow and interest in the Llano cooperative experiment continued throughout the 1930s and inspired his ideas of communal living in India.

Anarchism, communism, and class struggle in India

In August 1925, Acharya contacted Keell and asked for copies of *Freedom* 'for propaganda in India, as I am an Indian. I think it will do a great benefit if you can make that sacrifice'.[51] As he only had precarious work, Acharya could not pay Keell for the periodical, but he promised to send money when he had any. However, he felt that India needed English-language publications, and Acharya offered to provide Keell with addresses of interested subscribers and serve as a conduit for anarchism to India. He explained that he knew Berkman, Goldman, and Havel, and asked Keell if he knew anyone in Berlin who could lend him Berkman's *The Bolshevik Myth* (1925) and Goldman's *My Disillusionment in Russia* (1923). As both Acharya and Berkman were living in Berlin, Keell was puzzled by Acharya's request and inquired with Berkman. In response, Berkman 'made inquiries about M. Acharya and was told that he is OK', and he listed several publications for Keell to send to Acharya.[52] Keell sent Acharya the requested copies, for which Acharya thanked him and, in return, offered to do translation work for *Freedom*.[53] When Acharya wrote to Keell the next month, he noted that

> [m]ost literature went to India of course where they get very little news of them. Of course, I sent only to select people whose views I more or less know and think worthwhile sending and know what to send or not. Some went to Turkey and I would like to make some reach the Negro world in South Africa.[54]

134

ANTICOLONIALISM AND ANARCHISM IN WEIMAR BERLIN

Through his initial conversations with Keell and Berkman, Acharya was keen to introduce anarchism into India's left-wing struggles and to spread the political message of anarchism to India and South Africa. In the pages of the *IWMA Press Service* and other IWMA-affiliated papers such as *Der Syndikalist* (Germany), *De Syndicalist* (Netherlands), *Road to Freedom* (USA), *L'Adunata dei Refrattari* (USA), *La Protesta* (Argentina), and *La Voix du Travail* (France), Acharya threw himself into debates about working-class struggles in India from an anarchist perspective. As was customary with the transnational circulation of anarchist literature at the time, Acharya's texts were often reprinted across these periodicals in different languages and thus reached a global anarchist readership.[55]

Meanwhile, communism was making a greater impact in India. The ICP formed in Tashkent was not recognised as a communist party in India, as it had been formed outside the country, and Roy's status was challenged by other left-wing leaders. In late 1925, Satya Bhakta set up an Indian Communist Party at a conference in Cawnpore (Kanpur). While the party soon attracted many other left-wing leaders, including S. A. Dange and J. P. Begerhotta, it was decided to change the name to the Communist Party of India (CPI) and affiliate it with the Comintern. Bhakta was against this move and later dissociated himself from the new party. However, Roy was not happy with Bhakta's new party, called Bhakta a bogus communist, and denounced him as an apologist for British imperialism.[56]

Acharya followed the events from Berlin, having contacted Bhakta and Begerhotta, and soon articles denouncing Roy's dictatorial and counter-revolutionary manners appeared in *Der Syndikalist*, the *IWMA Press Service*, *Freedom*, and in Guy Aldred's periodical the *Commune*.[57] As Acharya remarked to Keell: '[t]he articles are more interesting as the working methods of "Communists" treachery and the gang which does so than as history of Roy alone'.[58] In the *Mahratta*, Acharya challenged readers to understand the real meaning of communism:

[i]t is evident to any child, not quite wholly depraved and deprived of intelligence, that Communism and socialism are not party and government affairs or methods but social and communal 'government' of all affairs (i.e., social self-government) but without any *uppermost government*. To say that any party or government represents

135

ANARCHY OR CHAOS

Communism is an absurdity, being evidently contradictory to this social, communist (common) idea.[59]

In fact, criticising the Bolshevik experiment in communism, Acharya claimed that '*Communism can only come through and beyond Anarchism* not before and behind it'.[60] Relying on Acharya's opinions, Bhakta defended himself against Roy's charges and called Roy a 'British spy'.[61] Bhakta's retort and Acharya's article from *Der Syndikalist* did not go unnoticed by Roy and his associates, who called Acharya's article 'the production of a deranged mind' and asked: '[w]hy should [Roy] bother to take notice of a raving lunatic, as Acharya is?'.[62] They concluded that 'Satya Bhakta does not improve his position the least by calling Roy a British agent on the authority of Acharya'.[63]

Acharya refrained from commenting further on the internal debates among the communists in India but instead articulated an 'Anarchist Manifesto' for India. Originally published in the *People* (Lahore), Acharya's text was reprinted in *Road to Freedom*: 'I am convinced that no unity can come out of constitution mongering either for the present government or for any future government. Constitutional schemes can only regroup the quarrels, but not avoid them'.[64] Acharya set out four points to attain 'unity, peace, and harmony':

1. Give up looking for political or economic central government, of any kind whatever.
2. Give up looking for any kind of constitution, legislature, even village legislature.
3. Give up all religious, political, party groupings.
4. Mind your immediate living affairs from birth to death—such as food, clothing, housing, work, instruction, recreation. Assure these for yourself in common with others.[65]

Acharya elaborated on how to assure these necessities and comforts for all. In doing so, he envisioned a different path to freedom and independence than other left-wing or communist parties.

The Hagenbeck affair

In the meantime, Acharya was fired from the *Industrial and Trade Review for Asia*, as Nambiar was not satisfied with his translations, and Acharya and Nachman soon moved to Ringbahnstrasse 4 in the

ANTICOLONIALISM AND ANARCHISM IN WEIMAR BERLIN

Halensee area of Charlottenburg.[66] He picked up work as an English teacher and, briefly, as a translator for the Deutsche Film Union. The manager A. C. Berman recalled: '[w]e found his work most satisfactory and take pleasure in recommending him to anyone needing a first class, high grade, serious minded translator'.[67]

By then, Acharya had joined the HACE and socialised at the regular meetings, some of which attracted more than five hundred guests from various nationalities and backgrounds and hosted songs and dance performances.[68] Berlin, and the Charlottenburg area in particular, was clearly a multicultural metropolis in the mid-1920s, but the Indians were also acutely aware of the racial hierarchies of European colonialism and popular discourse. This became abundantly clear in the summer of 1926, when the German animal collector John Hagenbeck, the brother of Carl Hagenbeck, who was infamous for putting humans on display in zoos, put around a hundred 'native Indians' on display at the Berlin Zoo to show everyday life, performing the roles of fakirs, street magicians, and snake charmers.[69] The 'Indians in the Zoo'-affair, as it was known in the German newspapers, did not go unchallenged by the Indian community in Berlin.[70] Before the exhibition opened, Acharya had warned in the *Bombay Chronicle*:

> [n]o doubt, Carl Hagenbeck wants to make money out of the business of 'Indian poverty', of culture. No doubt, the British Government thinks it good to give these 'fellow' citizens of the Empire passports and 'protection' for the benefit of C. Hagenbeck and its own propaganda purposes. No doubt, also, that the Europeans believe that those Indians come to show what their country and people, their highest 'really' are 'like'.[71]

Acharya had seen similar shows in Munich and at Coney Island in New York City before the war, which may explain why he confused the two brothers in his article. Acharya was acutely aware of the racist representation of Indians, but he also laid blame on capitalism and imperialism: 'so long as the Indians are kept poor whether by Indians or their British masters you cannot ask these poor specimens of Indian culture not to hope to earn a little more money than in India'.[72] For Acharya, British imperialism and poverty in India should also be considered in the protest against Hagenbeck's dehumanising venture.

137

ANARCHY OR CHAOS

Acharya was not the only Indian to protest the Hagenbeck exhibition. The HACE protested to the AA but was met with little sympathy. German newspapers, however, showed more understanding of the Indians' protest, while Chatto, Nambiar, and Smedley soon vented their opinions in Indian papers such as *Bombay Chronicle*, *The Hindu*, *Forward*, and the *People*.[73] Incensed by the protests of the Indians in Berlin, Hagenbeck took Smedley to court for libel. Smedley had criticised the meagre earnings of the Indians, but Hagenbeck claimed that they earned more in six months working for him than they would earn in five to ten years in India.[74] Acharya defended Smedley and retorted: 'there is no question of damages because Miss Smedley has not at all *injured* the business of Mr. Hagenbeck after the troupe has left. The damage done, if any, is to the reputation of the *British Government*'.[75] The dispute between the Berlin Indians and Hagenbeck was eventually settled out of court when Smedley withdrew the 'exaggerated aspects', according to Hagenbeck, of her articles and apologised to him. For Acharya, the settlement was a sham and should 'serve as a warning to law makers to show how every action, statement, and thought is likely to prevent the public even from breathing, for the laws are intertwined and anything may be liable to prosecution by twisting anyone of the laws'.[76] In other words, for Acharya, the laws of the state were stacked against colonial subjects, and the whole affair only demonstrated the bigotry of both the British and the German governments. By 1927, it was clear that Berlin was central to the articulation of Indian anticolonialism in exile. Nationalist newspapers such as *Forward*, *Bombay Chronicle*, and the *People* frequently carried special news sections from Berlin. Alongside Nambiar, Acharya became Berlin correspondent for *Forward* and *Bombay Chronicle*, though he soon fell out of favour with *Forward*, which, he wrote to the Dutch anarchist Albert de Jong, was dominated by the communists.[77]

Anarchism as socialism

Developing an anarchist critique of politics in India, in one of his first articles for the *People*, Acharya took the British socialist Wilfred Wellock to task for not challenging the notion of usury and taxation

138

ANTICOLONIALISM AND ANARCHISM IN WEIMAR BERLIN

completely. For Acharya, the difference between usury and taxation was irrelevant as long as the state was allowed to collect taxes. '*Socialism and state idea cannot be harmonised*', Acharya argued.[78] 'If people want Socialism', he continued,

> they must act for a society without the state—which can only be managed in small independent communes acting together for common benefit by production and 'uniformisation' of consumption without of course separate ownerships, barter, exchange, profits and money. Otherwise usury will exist in some form and name or other.[79]

This was a classic anarchist argument: that socialists often do not go far enough in their understanding and articulation of freedom. As long as the state existed and, by extension, was allowed to collect taxes, people would be bound in oppressive power structures that fall short of true freedom. This was also true, he argued against Diwan Chaman Lal, then-president of the AITUC, and N. M. Joshi in another article for the *People*, for the ways in which wages and salaries provided no relief, even if wages increased, for the workers. 'Working for wages is slavery', Acharya wrote,

> for the slave's body is not taken care of by the master who does not own him (and calls his slave a free labourer) but at the same time makes the living of the slaves impossible by both keeping the wages as low and nominal as possible and the prices of his goods and services as high as he can.[80]

Having learned these lessons from witnessing European colonialism and exploitation of workers, Acharya called for Indian workers to challenge these structures of inequality and bondage and for revolutionaries to abandon constitutional struggles.

A protest against Nehru

In the *People*, Acharya soon fell out with Jawaharlal Nehru, who had arrived in Europe in March 1926 with his wife, Kamala, who was ill and sought retreat at a Swiss sanatorium. During his time in Europe, Nehru visited Chatto in Berlin, which initiated a long friendship between the two prominent figures. Jawaharlal Nehru's father, Motilal Nehru, the soon-to-be president of the INC, arrived in

ANARCHY OR CHAOS

Europe in the autumn of 1927, and in November that year, the Soviet Ambassador in Berlin invited the two of them to visit the Soviet Union to commemorate the tenth anniversary of the revolution. While the Nehrus were initially hesitant in their support of Russia, Jawaharlal Nehru also saw a country that could solve the problems of the world.[81] As he wrote to his sister Vijaya Lakshmi: '[w]e are in a topsy-turvy land .... But the spirit of equality is rampant and pride in the Revolution'.[82] He was impressed with the 'extraordinary absence of different classes' and remarked that there was no difference between the president and the workers.[83] During their three-day visit to Moscow, the Nehrus visited the Butyrka Prison—Soviet Russia's notorious prison for political dissenters—and Jawaharlal was impressed with what he saw. While he acknowledged that, '[p]robably, only the rosy side was shown to us', Nehru also wrote to his sister that 'what we saw created a very favourable impression. The jail was not treated as a place for punishment but as a place of detention'.[84] The barber shop, the basketball court, and the absence of warders were evidence of the lenient conditions in Russian prisons.

Acharya read the *Bombay Chronicle* report of Nehru's trip to Moscow and scorned him for not criticising the conditions in Russian prisons. 'Even without the arrest and deportation of famous Bolshevik comrades', Acharya said, 'it would be preposterous on the part of any freedom-loving man to speak about the good conditions of any prisons in any "advanced" country'.[85] He accused Nehru of pointing out how bad prisons in India were by, conversely, praising them elsewhere. Taking an anarchist approach, '[i]nstead of that', Acharya charged, 'they must make common cause with all sufferers in the world and demand that all prisons, punishment and police—and the constitutions and laws which make these tortures inevitable—be uprooted and destroyed'.[86] By contrast to the Nehrus' Soviet-sponsored visit to Moscow, the IWMA had delivered a protest to the Comintern headquarters in Berlin and issued a statement on the persecution of political prisoners in Russia, Acharya also remarked. Indeed, taking an anarchist stance, he concluded that 'servility to one Government leads to servility to other Governments also'.[87]

About a month later, Nehru responded to Acharya's criticism. Nehru stated that the letters to his sister were not intended for publi-

ANTICOLONIALISM AND ANARCHISM IN WEIMAR BERLIN

cation and that he did not want to absolve the entire Russian prison system, but he also reiterated that 'I merely described what I actually saw in a particular prison which was stated to be the largest in Moscow. I must say that I was very favourably impressed by this visit'.[88] Calling Acharya's critique of him a 'monstrous perversion', Nehru continued his defence and referred to an American friend of his who had toured Russia's prisons and reported that 'the general conditions prevailing there was a very favourable one'.[89] Indeed, while Nehru admitted that anti-Bolshevik political prisoners may be 'badly treated', this had no bearing on what he experienced in Moscow.[90]

Nehru's poor defence, in Acharya's eyes, just confirmed Nehru's problematic account of the Russian prisons. In response, Acharya bombarded the *People* with rejoinders to Nehru, but the periodical only printed a few of them. In these articles, Acharya again took Nehru to task for so blindly giving a favourable impression of the prison he saw—even if it was just one prison—and trusting the Bolshevik guided tour of the prison. Even further, Acharya repeated his criticism of the prison system altogether and chastised Nehru for supporting Bolshevism: '[f]or me, even the best prison in paradise do not convince me of the "good treatment of criminals"'.[91] Indeed, for Acharya there was no difference between British imperialism and Soviet Bolshevism—both were statist forms of oppression. Acharya pressed on:

> I see clearly that by your defence of prisons, Russian or other, you only work for those who want to establish prisons for all. I have no respect for such reformism as your socialism and the Marxist Bolshevism. Therefore, I feel compelled to denounce it till such humbugs are exposed and blown up. You and your friends behind want to reform and 'socialise' people in prisons, and I want to see them reformed in freedom.[92]

Nehru refrained from responding further to Acharya's criticisms and neither did Acharya attack Nehru again on this account.

His criticism of the Nehrus, however, soon cost him dearly. In late May 1928, Acharya was reportedly 'on the verge of starvation' and 'dangerously ill'. To help him out, Smedley wrote to Motilal Nehru and asked for assistance. However, when Smedley learned of Acharya's harsh criticism of the Nehrus, she withdrew her support for him.[93]

141

ANARCHY OR CHAOS

Acharya's anarchist anticolonialism and anti-Bolshevism, moreover, soon brought him into disrepute with his old friend Chatto. Indeed, Nehru was not the only sympathiser of Russian society. By late 1926, Chatto had abandoned anarchism and veered towards communism. By contrast, Acharya's turn to anarchism, associating and corresponding with anarchists in Berlin and beyond, was unique and soon mutated into global conversations around the true meaning of freedom and internationalism. Viewed this way, Acharya's ventures into anarchism opens a window into understanding Berlin as a hub for different anti-authoritarian radical landscapes.

10

ANTI-IMPERIALISM AND ANTI-MILITARISM

The League Against Imperialism

Acharya's spat with Nehru spilled over into disagreements with Chatto and Smedley and the establishment of the League Against Imperialism (LAI) in 1927. The LAI had its roots in the Rathauskeller meeting in Berlin on 10 February 1926. Conceived by the German communist Wilhelm Münzenberg as an anticolonial organisation to bring together various German socialists and anticolonial activists in Berlin, including Chatto and Nambiar, the Rathauskeller meeting led to the formation of the League Against Colonial Oppression (LACO).[1] The LACO was backed financially by the Comintern and aimed to operate as a centre for anticolonial activity in Europe and then liaise with activists across the colonial world. In addition to spreading propaganda, Münzenberg wanted to organise international conferences to highlight the atrocities of colonial policies, the importance of anticolonial struggles, and the position of the international proletariat.

In the early stages of the LACO, M. N. Roy acted as intermediary between Münzenberg and the Comintern to ensure that the new organisation followed the Comintern's policy on the colonial question. However, when the Comintern dispatched Roy to China, he left the LACO. Chatto also joined Münzenberg's efforts and was crucial to reaching Indian anticolonial leaders, most prominently Joshi, Nehru,

143

ANARCHY OR CHAOS

and Shapurji Saklatvala.[2] However, Chatto was initially wary of the Comintern's control over the LACO. On 30 April 1926, a group of anticolonialists in Berlin met with the aim of 'liberating it from Communist control'.[3] Chatto stated that 'the League was an instrument of Soviet diplomacy' and that 'the representatives of the Eastern peoples should have their own independent organisation to capture the League for their own purpose'.[4] By saying this openly, Chatto inadvertently revealed the LACO's connection to the Comintern, which caused concern in Moscow. In the future, Roy and the ECCI wrote to Münzenberg, 'the work for the organisation of the League should be conducted with great prudence' and it was considered 'necessary to act very carefully in establishing relations with the emigrant groups in Europe'.[5] While Acharya assisted Chatto and worked as a typist and secretary in the eastern section of the LACO, he was also sceptical of its methods and objects.[6] According to Acharya, British intelligence services reported, the LACO aimed to 'bolster up the Soviet Government against other capitalist Governments', and he was reportedly 'convinced that the organization is run from Moscow and that its main object is pro-Communist propaganda'.[7]

The Brussels congress held at the Palais Egmont in February 1927 brought together 174 delegates representing thirty-one states and 134 organisations, and aimed to build political solidarity across colonies and among oppressed peoples. Now operating under the name League Against Imperialism, the organisation soon became the biggest anti-imperialist organisation ever seen, fostering inter-imperial, anti-colonial alliances across the colonial world that laid the foundation for organised resistance to colonialism in all its guises for decades.[8] After the Brussels congress, the LAI set up headquarters in Berlin, with Münzenberg as head of the international secretariat alongside Chatto, who became a key figure in the organisation.[9]

However, despite Chatto's prominent role in the LAI, for Acharya and the other Indians in Berlin, the question remained: if and how they should affiliate with the LAI? A few weeks after the Brussels congress, the HACE met to discuss the issue at their new headquarters at the Alexander von Humboldt-Haus in Fasanenstrasse. It was decided that any member could join the LAI individually, but the HACE would not join formally as an organisation.[10] At the meeting,

ANTI-IMPERIALISM AND ANTI-MILITARISM

Acharya spoke out against the LAI on several fronts. First, he criticised the LAI for inviting the League of Nations but neglecting to invite anyone to represent the oppressed peoples of Russia such as those from Georgia, Ukraine, Azerbaijan, Turkistan, or Kyrgyzstan, or anyone to represent anti-Bolshevik prisoners in Russia. Acharya referred to his experiences with the Second International socialists at the peace congress in Stockholm and pointed out that, when similar anti-imperialist and socialist conferences had been held during the First World War, the Entente powers only invited delegates from subject nations oppressed by the Central powers. The Indian nationalists had opposed this policy already then, so why should they now accept such one-sided understandings of subject and oppressed nationalities and not invite oppressed peoples of Russia? Second, Acharya argued that

> it was not enough to cry in chorus how the nationalities were oppressed and exploited by foreign powers—however much that demonstration of wounded backs might excite pity among sections of European peoples—but there was no hope of the Congress taking up energetic action even in Europe against the oppressors.[11]

For example, the British Independent Labour Party, Acharya said, took no action in Britain after the Brussels congress. He agreed with the comments made by a black delegate at the congress and said that 'there was nothing to expect from the Communists to Nationalists in Europe—for they all want business with Asia and Africa for employment and the business policy of the Governments suits their purposes'.[12] Third, Acharya condemned the Brussels congress 'as a "dangerous move" to take the wind out of the sails of Asiatic and other movements of the oppressed by turning the attention to their emancipation from their own countries to the offices of the League [against Imperialism] in Europe'.[13] Acharya saw this as another elitist organisation and argued: '[i]t is not propaganda in Europe that has to be done by the intelligent leaders of oppressed orient and Africa but work in their own countries which require all their intelligence and devotion'.[14] Too many different agendas were at stake. 'The Congress as it consists of all kinds of interested party leaders cannot arrive at any united action but will be led into channels or crying hoarse in foreign lands about the woes of their people'.[15]

145

ANARCHY OR CHAOS

Anti-militarism and pacifism

By the mid-1920s, Acharya travelled in Berlin's pacifist circles, attending meetings in the War Resisters' International (WRI) and the pacifist youth organisation Weltjugendliga, and even gave talks at the Quakers in Berlin.[16] As a staunch pacifist, Acharya sent Weltjugendliga pamphlets to the *Bombay Chronicle* and articles to the organisation's own periodical *Weltjugendliga: Blätter der Weltjugendliga* as well as articles to the Internationale der Kriegsdienstgegner, the German section of the WRI.[17]

Soon after the founding congress in Brussels, Acharya left the LAI and instead joined the International Anti-Militarist Bureau against War and Reaction (IAMB) and the International Antimilitarist Commission (IAC). Composed of revolutionary antimilitarist organisations, the IAMB was led by Augustin Souchy, Albert de Jong, and Arthur Müller-Lehning.[18] While the IAMB was committed to global, anti-imperialist struggles against military oppression and economic exploitation across the colonial world, the organisation struggled to establish contacts with anticolonial revolutionaries. Throughout the 1920s, the IAMB conducted its politics in resolute defence of its principles by constantly supporting imprisoned conscientious objectors, revolutionaries of various left-wing persuasions, and persecuted antimilitarists. Given its predominantly Dutch origins and membership, the IAMB devoted great attention to Dutch colonialism in Indonesia.[19] To establish stronger ties with the IWMA, in 1926 the IAMB and the IWMA resolved to set up the IAC with de Jong and Müller-Lehning as secretaries. The purpose of the IAC was to cooperate more effectively between the IWMA and the IAMB and to 'initiate a wide propaganda of an educational nature, embracing the question of war, its causes and objects, and its effects upon mankind on general and labour in particular'.[20] To do this, from May 1927 the IAC started publishing a monthly *Press Service* in French, German, English, and Dutch.

In late May 1927, M. A. Faruqi, Acharya's old friend from the IRA and the ARA in Russia, attended a WRI conference in Amsterdam. Faruqui delivered a talk on anti-militarism in India and tied it inextricably to anticolonial resistance. His talk was published in the proceedings *Verslag van het Internationale Congres voor Dienstweigering* (1927)

146

ANTI-IMPERIALISM AND ANTI-MILITARISM

alongside essays by IAMB members de Jong and Hendrik Jan Mispelblom Beyer.[21] The publication of Faruqui's text gives rise to some confusion as it closely resembles an article written by Acharya. In fact, Acharya's article 'India's Man Power and the Next Imperialist War' from *Forward* (August 1927) is almost verbatim the same text as that of Faruqui's. Even further, an article attributed to 'M. A.' entitled 'Der Antimilitarismus in Indien', which is also almost identical to the other texts, appeared in the IWMA-organ *Die Internationale* in German in May 1928.[22] It is uncertain whether Acharya and Faruqui coordinated their essays or if there was confusion between the editors as to whether 'M. A.' was M. Acharya—who sometimes published under the initials M. A.—or M. A. Faruqui.

Prior to the conference, Faruqui had written to de Jong and asked for IAMB material in English. Soon after, de Jong invited Faruqui to join the IAMB and write for the *IAMB Press Service*, and asked Faruqui for addresses in India to which he could send anti-militarist propaganda.[23] Faruqui provided de Jong with the addresses of editors at the *People*, *Swarajya*, and Gandhi's publication *Young India*, and advised de Jong that '[t]he chief thing is that you should approach the masses and not the middle class, intellectuals and for that you ought to be in touch with local vernacular papers which are directly distributed in the factories and workshops'.[24] He also asked de Jong: '[d]o you send you publications to M. Acharya, Berlin-Halensee, Ringbahn Str. 4. This comrade is very active and will be very useful to you in every respect, for he has good connections all over India?'.[25]

On Faruqui's advice, de Jong contacted Acharya, who showed de Jong's letter to Souchy, and a few weeks later, Souchy vouched for Acharya to de Jong: 'Acharya has worked with us for years, he showed me the letter that he received from you, he is also willing to join the IAC, he is an anarchist'.[26] Faruqui also wrote to de Jong that he had asked Acharya to send relevant Indian addresses to de Jong and that Acharya wanted Faruqui to send de Jong's material to him. When Faruqui returned to Berlin in November 1927, he joined the German Communist Party (KPD) and still received the *IAMB Press Service*, and his article 'Anti-Militarisme en "Brits"-Indië' appeared in the *Internationaal Anti-Militaristisch Jaarboek* (1928).[27]

147

ANARCHY OR CHAOS

Anti-militarism and anti-imperialism

Through his involvement with the IAMB and the IAC, Acharya became a fierce critic of the LAI. In agreement with the IAMB and the IWMA, the IAC joined the LAI, and Müller-Lehning and de Jong represented the IAC at the Brussels congress in February 1927.[28] In their statement to the congress, they tied anti-imperialism inextricably to anti-militarism: '[c]olonial oppression and modern imperialist wars are only possible by the union of the white proletariat with their governments, oppressing them too, by the same imperialism, when they serve as sailors on men-of-war, as soldiers in the army, and as workers in war industries'.[29] The European and colonised working classes, they argued, should work together against imperialism and for a world revolution. They warned, however, that

> the struggling colonial people should take care that they do not create a new form of exploitation through a nationalist State in place of exploitation through their present 'motherlands', and that they do not set up the dictatorship of a political party in place of that which they have now.[30]

Such new states could only lead to militarisation, the permanent danger of war, and new economic conflicts. The position of the IAC was that, rather than fighting for a new nation-state, colonial peoples should seek, through revolutionary struggles such as boycott, strike, refusal to pay taxes, and non-cooperation, to make war and exploitation impossible.[31]

Having attended the Brussels conference, de Jong remained sceptical of the LAI's ties to Moscow and asked Acharya for his advice.[32] Acharya showed de Jong's letters to the IWMA and responded to de Jong: '[w]hile principally we must have nothing against the idea, I am afraid that the League will not tolerate us to agitate anti-militaristically and for free communism'.[33] Abandoning the 'united front' policy, disagreements between the Second International and the Comintern soon played into a political rift within the LAI as well. Picking up on this division, in a letter to Joshi of the AITUC, Acharya attacked Saklatvala and the LAI as a front for the Comintern again:

> [w]hile the IFTU and the Second International men behind it told this truth, there is no doubt that they were serving the imperialist ends of

ANTI-IMPERIALISM AND ANTI-MILITARISM

their own governments while Saklatvala wanted to serve <u>both Bolshevik and British interests at once</u> by inducing the trade unions in India to join the League and the Red International.[34]

He went further: '[i]t is a well-known fact that the League "Against" Imperialism is an organ bound to the Bolshevik state for its foreign propaganda purposes'.[35] Acharya also charged:

> [i]t is possible that the League will manage to establish good capitalist relations between the Bolsheviki and their rival imperialist capitalists by its agitation in the name of colonial and oppressed peoples (from which category the Russian colonial and oppressed people who form 99% of Russia, whom the Bolshevik exploit by selling their confiscated properties to foreigners as 'socialisation', are excluded!).[36]

In other words, for Acharya, there was no difference between capitalist imperialism and Bolshevik imperialism; it was all the same and remained the greatest threat to Indian independence and to the freedom of the peasants and workers of India.

Acharya soon fell out with Chatto and Smedley over the direction of anti-imperialism. In fact, as Berkman related to Goldman, Acharya had written to him that Chatto had been expelled from Belgium and France and that he was working indirectly as an agent of the Bolsheviks and that Smedley was stuck in Shanghai. Berkman conveyed Acharya's message to Goldman with some reservation: '[b]ut you know that in some respects those Hindoos are even worse than the Italians, very suspicious of each other'.[37] Berkman even suggested that

> with Chatto and Agnes, as with numerous others, it is purely economic pressure that is making them friendly to the Bolsheviks. I mean, both economic need and the need of doing something. Between the tendency to idealism and economic necessity, the latter is certainly far stronger the factor with the greatest majority of even libertarian people.[38]

Berkman's letter to Goldman betrays a sense of prejudice, of seeing the Indian struggle as problematic and troubled, without acknowledging the complexities of anticolonial struggles and the global left. In view of Acharya's harsh criticism of the LAI, it was perhaps not surprising that, when he applied to Chatto for work in October 1928, Chatto turned him down.[39]

149

ANARCHY OR CHAOS

Between 1928 and 1932, Acharya had extensive correspondence with de Jong and supplied him with contacts in India, including S. Srinivasa Iyengar, B. S. Pathik, K. S. Karanth (editor of *Vasantha*), and N. S. Hardikar (editor of *Volunteer*), to whom Acharya soon sent IWW pamphlets, and Acharya managed to feature articles by and about the IAMB and Dutch colonial oppression in Indonesia in *Forward* and the *People*.[40] In return, Karanth translated and published Acharya's article 'Murder as Basis of Modernism' into Kannada in *Vasantha* (see also Chapter 16).[41] When de Jong visited Berlin in August 1928, he met Acharya for the first time, and Acharya soon served as a conduit for anti-militarist propaganda to India. He passed on one of de Jong's pamphlets to Sarojini Naidu and later sent his own writings to Gandhi, receiving 'only a few personal lines' back, while de Jong in return showed Acharya's articles to Bart de Ligt.[42] Their frequent correspondence and extensive attention to India and the colonial question prompted an idea for Acharya to start a press service for Asia and Africa:

> [n]ow I find it is absolutely essential to start a special press service of articles for Asia and Africa in English, including for China and Japan. These articles may be translated also by the anarchist press of Europe and America. With this we can make very good propaganda for Anarcho-pacifism in all Asia and Africa.[43]

Acharya had tried to set this up for some time but needed money and assistance. None of this was forthcoming from de Jong and the IAMB, and the idea never materialised.

The LAI was now involved in various campaigns across the colonial world and had set up regional chapters, but it was also increasingly dominated by Moscow's political ambitions. By the July 1929 LAI congress in Frankfurt, the IAC had left the LAI but been replaced by the IAMB. Müller-Lehning, de Ligt, and Lambertus Johannes Bot Jr. represented the IAMB at the Frankfurt congress. As the communists had made 'the League subservient to the Third International', the IAMB reported afterwards, 'our delegates had a very difficult task'.[44] The Chinese civil war, fought between communists and nationalists, was high on the agenda at the Frankfurt congress, and Müller-Lehning reiterated some of his points from the Brussels congress, warning against the conjunction between statism and milita-

150

ANTI-IMPERIALISM AND ANTI-MILITARISM

rism and the seizure of the means of the state apparatus, all of which had come true in China.[45]

Acharya was critical of the IAMB's attendance at the Frankfurt congress and voiced his concern to de Jong and Müller-Lehning. However, as Müller-Lehning replied to Acharya:

> [t]he League issue is indeed a very difficult one and we are always concerned with the question of whether we can stay in the League or not. Anyway, it was not without significance that the IAMB was present in Frankfurt, and we had the opportunity to defend our views there. We would have stood even stronger, though, if the IWMA would have been represented there. As you know, many affiliated organizations, the most important ones, such as in India and Indonesia, are not Communist. It is not unthinkable to form an opposition to communist domination.[46]

More important for the IAMB, Müller-Lehning responded to Acharya,

> thanks to the League we for the first time came into real contact with the colonial peoples .... We are aiming to work within the League as long as it is possible, not because we could so much like to co-operate with the Communists, but since we believe that otherwise we would lose every contact to the colonial peoples.[47]

Müller-Lehning was certainly receptive to Acharya's views, he said, and wanted to discuss it further with him when he visited Berlin in October. Müller-Lehning's admission that the LAI allowed them to establish contacts with the colonial world is significant. Indeed, while the IAMB and the IAC were committed to anti-imperialism and internationalism, these organisations struggled to get a foothold in the colonial world, but Acharya proved to be a unique conduit for establishing such connections to India. The Frankfurt congress, however, also led to the Comintern's complete takeover of the LAI, thus submitting non-communist member organisations to Moscow's politics.[48]

Anti-militarism, anti-imperialism, and Gandhi

Through his involvement with IAMB and the IAC, Acharya engaged extensively with non-violence and pacifism more broadly, as well as with India's most famous pacifist: Gandhi. Prominent IAMB and IAC members such as de Ligt, de Jong, and Müller-Lehning frequently

151

ANARCHY OR CHAOS

commented on Gandhi's struggles in the *IAC Press Service*.[49] Acharya's own engagement with Gandhi's politics was lifelong, but he remained ambivalent about the Mahatma's ideas and practices. For example, in 1928, Acharya criticised:

> [w]hile [Gandhi] is violently opposed to violence in general, he is more opposed to the mass liberation from violence than to the violence of Governments. He does not believe that the violence established by Governments at their expense creates and necessitates the violence of the people at times. While he wishes to abolish the violence of individuals and groups, he believes that violence of governments is impersonal, necessary—nay perhaps in the end good …. If any group of people is entitled to establish or having established—to maintain their violence in the name of Society, nation, and order—what prevents other morally to overcome their violence with other violence in order to impose a new violence of their own?[50]

Acharya critiqued Gandhi for not denouncing the idea of the state *in toto*.[51] However, he also admitted:

> I do not mean to say that Gandhi is himself directly concerned in this or any other Governmental violence against people, but still—so long as he does not denounce all governments, i.e., parts of Society over the whole and at the same time countenances some government against others, he is indirectly with that violence.[52]

Acharya conceded that, while many people in India resisted the British government's call to arms, as long as governments existed, the threat of militarisation and war would always loom large. The only remedy was to abolish all governments.

In 1930, Gandhi took on the British government in a way that set an example for the world in anticolonial practice. Since the mid-nineteenth century, the salt tax in India had given the British government a monopoly on manufacturing and collecting salt, despite salt being readily available for people living by the coast. In January 1930, in response to growing calls for self-determination and following the failure of the Simon Commission, an all-British committee sent to India to devise new constitutional reforms, the INC resolved to fight for *Purna Swaraj* (complete independence) rather than dominion status.[53] On 12 March 1930, with the INC's blessing, Gandhi set off from the Sabarmati Ashram in Gujarat bound for Navsari (now Dandi)

152

ANTI-IMPERIALISM AND ANTI-MILITARISM

by the Arabian Sea to collect salt from the sea in defiance of the British salt tax. Arriving at Navsari on 5 April and attracting thousands of followers along the way, Gandhi's salt march demonstrated the defiance of the masses to the British authorities and the world.

Acharya admired Gandhi's tactics in this new phase of achieving *Purna Swaraj*.[54] For Acharya, the salt march was a major victory: '[w]ithout being a follower of Gandhi, I am an admirer of Gandhism as practiced today in India'.[55] In the *IAC Press Service*, Acharya further praised Gandhi: 'Gandhi denounced rightly the salt-tax as theft .... But Gandhi is prepared to become a thief in the eyes of the "law"'.[56] In fact, Acharya said Gandhi's salt march demonstrated to the world the praxis of anarchism in action:

> Gandhi by sanctioning and initiating passive polite and unarmed violation of salt monopoly law intervened successfully between governmental and popular violence and led the violent energies of the people into channels of unconquerable solidarity against the government and its laws. He overtook and unnerved the government and its readiness to use and justify its own violence over all. As such he acted like an Anarchist tactician of the first magnitude.[57]

Indeed, the salt march was a master lesson in anarchism, because 'Gandhi made the movement go without and against leadership'.[58] Gandhi's marches were open schools of practical political action, which meant that even arresting Gandhi could not stop the pacifist movement in India. 'In one stroke he killed off both Marxism and its opposite authoritarianism', Acharya rejoiced, celebrating Gandhi's salt march as 'the birth of popular Anarchy in the world—not only in India.'[59]

Gandhi was arrested a month after his arrival at Navsari, but the civil disobedience movement continued to grow throughout India, leading also to the boycott of other British goods and taxes. In retaliation, the British arrested more than sixty thousand Indians, including Sarojini Naidu and Jawaharlal Nehru. On 6 May 1930, the HACE held a protest meeting at their headquarters in the Alexander von Humboldt-Haus.[60] A photo from the meeting shows Acharya sitting on the floor in the back next to Jaya Surya Naidu, perhaps waiting to speak after Saumyendranath Tagore.[61] Acharya had no illusions that Western governments would support their struggle:

153

ANARCHY OR CHAOS

[t]hese workers in America and Europe, at the behest of their so-called workers parties, wait for socialism and fail to take action against the militarism of their exploiters in the Far East, in Africa, and South America, because the struggle of the peasant masses there in the colonial and semi-colonial countries is supposedly not a socialist struggle.[62]

Gandhi's salt march should be a lesson in antimilitarist direct action for all. He went further:

[e]ven though Europe's socialists talk day in and day out about class struggle on an international basis, they do not fight on the side of the enslaved farmers of India and other Eastern countries, but instead condone wage reductions, as well as the production of armaments, because they are scared of otherwise losing their bread.

If the workers of England and Europe had a real sense of their own interests, they would refuse the production of armaments and move towards a general strike against the capitalist attacks on Asian, African, and South American farmers and workers.[63]

In other words, Acharya connected the fate of workers across the world to antimilitarist resistance and challenged European workers to solidarity:

[i]n order to struggle against capitalism, militarism, and imperialism abroad, one has to begin a struggle in one's own country against those who, in one way or another, band together with these powers. That is the lesson that the politically confused European workers must learn from the great struggle against European imperialism and militarism that is underway in Asia.[64]

In the same vein, Acharya also accused the European press for not reporting accurately on the struggles in India. Only the anarchist and anti-militarist presses reported truthfully on Gandhi.[65] Thus sceptical of other presses, upon a visit to Souchy in September 1932, he gave Souchy an article on Gandhi's hunger strike intended for the Swedish syndicalist paper *Arbetaren*. Souchy sent it to the editor Albert Jensen with an introductory note: 'Acharya is a solitary Indian anarchist, whom I have known for 12 years, he is an honest man, but a bit strange, "oriental"'.[66] As is evident, despite the anarchist press' honest reporting on India and Gandhi, sometimes Eurocentric and orientalist stereotypes still prevailed, even among Acharya's friends.

154

ANTI-IMPERIALISM AND ANTI-MILITARISM

Whereas Acharya's involvement with the LAI was brief and tumultuous, he remained involved with the IAMB and IAC throughout the 1930s and served as a conduit for these organisations to India and the colonial world. His ideas about anti-imperialism, anti-militarism, and non-violence illuminate the tensions within left-wing anti-imperialist movements as well as within the Indian radical community in Berlin. As Acharya embraced Gandhism, without Gandhi, he weaved together global strands of radical politics into a unique articulation of anarchist-pacifist anticolonialism.

11

ULTRA-LEFTISTS AND OUTSIDERS

Among the ultra-leftists in Berlin

While Acharya had joined the ranks of the anarchists, he still associated with other left-wing radicals and ultra-leftists such as Magnus Schwantje, the founder of Bund für Radikale Ethik, Gavril Myasnikov, the founder of the Workers Group in Russia, and council communists and members of the Kommunistische Arbeiter-Partei Deutschlands (KAPD) Karl Korsch, Ruth Fischer, Käthe Friedländer (later writing as Kate Ruminov), and her Russian-born husband Basil Ruminov.[1]

Korsch had been expelled from the German Communist Party (KPD) in May 1926 and set up the Kritischer Marxismus study circle, which included anti-Bolshevik dissenters of various revolutionary creeds.[2] Among this group were also Souchy and Acharya as well as Roy. According to Souchy, the group's informal weekly meetings in the Café Adler sometimes attracted up to fifty left-dissidents.[3] After a failed mission to China, Roy was back in Berlin by 1928 and expelled from the Comintern in 1929. Acharya wrote to de Jong that he had seen Roy in Berlin, but he had not spoken to him since 1921.[4] At one meeting, Acharya later recalled, Korsch argued that Marx only described capitalism and not socialism or communism, and therefore it was up to them to arrive at definitions of socialism. Furthermore, Korsch believed that they should correct mistakes in Marx's thought,

ANARCHY OR CHAOS

but Acharya retorted that, in doing so, there would be nothing left of Marx in Marxism.[5] Korsch later conceded about Acharya: '[t]here was never any doubt about his revolutionary straightforwardness, but he was quite apt to mix things up both theoretically and in matters of practice'.[6] Korsch described himself as an 'ultra-leftist' at the time and later conferred this description to Acharya:

> [h]e was a somewhat bewildered 'ultra-leftist' in the late twenties and the early thirties—as were so many of us in that chaotic period in Germany. I did not think so much of him then, but I can see today that his position as an Indian exile was an even more bewildering one than was ours.[7]

Acharya's involvement in the Kritischer Marxismus group allowed him to flex his intellectual thoughts on anarchism and communism in conversation with Berlin's ultra-leftists.

Both Friedländer and Ruminov had attended the Second Congress of the Comintern in July 1920, then worked in the Internationale Arbeiterhilfe in Moscow for two years, before they returned to Berlin and joined the KAPD. In the spring of 1925, however, both Friedländer and Ruminov were expelled from the KAPD for their 'reformist position, connection with the Third International, and betrayal of the organisation'.[8] Having met them in Moscow, Acharya associated with Friedländer and Ruminov in Berlin through the study group around Korsch. Henry Pachter said of Basil Ruminov:

> he proved as indomitable in the West as he had been in the East …. The trouble was that at our meetings he defined democracy as his freedom to hold the floor indefinitely; not even the authority of Korsch, whom he worshipped, could silence him. We all loved him, though.[9]

Acharya gave a similar characterisation of Ruminov: 'I know him since 1921 in Moscow. But he is a Marxian, never learns anything. But I like him: He is a sincere fanatic'.[10]

Acharya later stated that he knew Myasnikov well in Berlin and also described him as 'a sincere fanatic'.[11] Myasnikov was a genuine dissenter and a critic of Lenin's and Trotsky's dictatorial line of Bolshevik party politics, and consequently he had been expelled from Russia. Arriving in Berlin in June 1923, he associated with both the KAPD

ULTRA-LEFTISTS AND OUTSIDERS

and the KPD, but returned to Russia in the autumn of 1923, only to be arrested immediately and imprisoned for the next three years.[12] Given that Myasnikov only spent a few months in Berlin in 1923, Acharya's claim that he knew him well in the German capital might be an overstatement.

Acharya's travels among Berlin's ultra-leftists may also have brought him into the orbit of Trotsky in early 1932. By then living in Istanbul, Trotsky had published critical articles about Roy and his activities in relation to China.[13] Having read Trotsky's criticism of Roy, Acharya sent Trotsky some of his own articles, explained his connection with Roy in Russia, and denounced Roy as a 'provocateur and saboteur of imperial England'.[14] Acharya had been proven right by Roy's and Borodin's activities in China, he wrote, and stated that, 'I have circumstantial proofs enough and can argue that they are not revolutionaries but Azefs—like Azef provocateurs and saboteurs coming as revolutionaries', in reference to the Russian double agent Evno Azef, who was active in Paris in 1910, when both Acharya and Trotsky lived there.[15]

Anarchism and autonomous communes

While Acharya travelled in these ultra-leftist circles, his commitment to anarchism was evident, finding clear expression in his writing on the colonial question, as well as on a broad range of topics, mostly gender relations and sexuality, but also, to a lesser extent, caste and religion. In doing so, he entered into conversation with other anarchist exponents and debates across countries and continents. For instance, in return for Acharya's help with translating for Berkman's *Bulletin of the Relief Fund of the International Working Men's Association for Anarchists and Anarcho Syndicalists Imprisoned or Exiled in Russia*, Berkman agreed to write for the *People*. 'I am an internationalist', Berkman declared in his article, 'and I am entirely opposed to Great Britain's policy in her colonies. As a matter of fact, I stand for the entire emancipation of all colonies from foreign rule'.[16] But Berkman did not support the nationalist struggle in India. As he explained: '[e]ssentially it is the same whether the masses are exploited by native or foreign masters. It is most near-sighted to pretend that a native tyrant

159

ANARCHY OR CHAOS

is preferable to a foreign one'.[17] Instead, India and all colonised nations needed 'freedom from governmental oppression and economic exploitation .... It is not a change of rulers that India needs, but the abolition of every rule which keeps the people in chains'.[18] Berkman's indictment of nationalism's strong hold on India was emblematic of anarchists' stance on anticolonial nationalism.

Throughout the next few years, Acharya continued to write extensively on strikes, the conditions of workers in India, and the colonial question in general for anarchist periodicals such as *Der Syndikalist*, *IAA Pressedienst*, *La Voix du Travail*, *Acción Social Obrera*, *Road to Freedom*, and *Man!*.[19] Not only did Acharya bring the question of colonialism and India's struggle for independence into anarchist debates, but his articles and thoughts circulated globally and reached well beyond audiences in Germany and India. For example, his general report on the political situation in India for the *IAA Pressedienst* was circulated and reprinted in *La Revista Blanca* (Spain), *Acción Social Obrera* (Spain), *La Protesta* (Argentina), and *Le Libertaire* (France).[20] While writing from the perspective of an Indian anarchist, Acharya also engaged in debates beyond India and colonialism. For example, his articles on the Stalinist shift from 'united front' to 'class against class', as well as the execution of martyred Italian American anarchists Nicola Sacco and Bartolomeo Vanzetti in August 1927, reveal a broader interest in issues of totalitarianism and oppression of anarchists across the world.[21]

However, it was his article 'Les Trusts et la Démocratie' in the French anarchist periodical *L'En Dehors* (April–May 1928) that proved to be one of his most significant. Criticising the French syndicalist Francis Delaisi's ideas of state socialism, Acharya compared it to Bolshevism and argued that '[i]n every system of the national economy, the interests of the consumers should be the basis for the organisation of production—not the advantage of the manufacturers, the state, or even a limited number of workers in limited trade unions'[22] Reminding readers that 'peoples are not born to be objects of exploitation and domination in the interests of a few individuals and group', Acharya argued for the establishment of autonomous communes through the 'abolition of the privileges of property (state, private, and combined), and the dissolution of ownership of these organisations

160

ULTRA-LEFTISTS AND OUTSIDERS

peaceably, violent, or otherwise'.[23] It was only through such communes that 'social solidarity and social work … and universal "democracy"' would be possible on an international scale.[24] Acharya advocated for a decentralised society, local autonomy, and diffused democracy: '[i]n a society, a nation, an international humanity divided into communist-social groups without authority, such groups can easily be led to coordinate their economic efforts voluntarily, needless to say, in view of their common and equally profitable aims'.[25] Two years later, the article was reprinted in the anarchist periodicals *Die Internationale*, *L'Adunata dei Refrattari*, and *La Protesta*, signalling the transnational circulation of Acharya's ideas. Acharya would return to this text throughout his writings in the next decades, eventually leading to its republication in India in 1947 (see Chapter 14, Chapter 15, and Chapter 16).

On the question of Asia and world revolution, Acharya's extensive articles on the Chinese revolution open a window into the importance of revolutions in Asia to the international anarchist movement. Arguing that '[t]he trouble in China is only another form of Bolshevik disruption in a far off country', Acharya denounced the likes of Karakhan and Borodin as treacherous counter-revolutionaries who exploited the Chinese masses.[26] While promising a workers revolution, the Kuomintang, Acharya argued, would betray the workers and resort to oppression like any other government as soon as they had seized power.[27] Fortunately, Acharya noted in the Dutch paper *De Syndicalist*:

> there are intelligent comrades in China who see through these things and make the Chinese people aware of the facts. Anarcho-syndicalist propaganda has gotten a foothold in China. It is directed against the foreign capitalists, England, Japan, America, as well as against the red imperialism of the Bolsheviks. After all, the Chinese are not so stupid that they will let themselves be satisfied with the meaningless reforms that the Kuomintang has written in its banner.[28]

Indeed, under Chiang Kai-shek's leadership, Sun Yat-sen's political philosophy of Three Principles of the People—nationalism, democracy, and the people—had failed to mobilise and represent the masses, Acharya stated. Instead, engaging with a bulletin from the Berlin-based Chinese News Agency, '[t]o realise these objects at

ANARCHY OR CHAOS

once, the Chinese must abolish any and every central authority', Acharya argued in *Forward*, and agitate for a 'thorough decentralisation'.[29] Ultimately, he lamented, '[t]he trouble with Asiatic revolutionists, as with the Euro-American, is that they spoil the attempts at betterment by thinking governmentally instead of socially as if the Government represents society organically'.[30] Rather than fighting for the Three Principles under the current regime, Acharya argued that

> [i]t is only when the Chinese revolutionists think in terms of society and nation—as an organic, dynamic, integrating whole, instead of the dead symbolic way of Government makers—that the principles of socialism and communism, of transferring the political power to the peoples themselves and of economic advantages to them, can be properly appreciated and realised. They must think non-governmentally—anarchically—as the society and nation requires.[31]

Dismantling sex and gender relations

Thinking anarchically was also Acharya's approach to issues around gender and sex relations. From early on, Acharya devoted considerable attention to gender equality and women's issues in India. In fact, one of his earliest essays, 'Die proletarierin in Indien', appeared in the November 1926 issue of the German publication *Der Frauen-Bund*, a feminist monthly appended to the Freie Arbeiter Union Deutschlands's paper *Der Syndikalist*. Offering an analysis of 'the lot of Indian women' and the working class in India, he argued that, because Indian women bear the brunt of menial labour, work long hours, and take care of children, they were locked into debt to men and employers simultaneously.[32]

He developed these ideas more extensively in the French anarchist E. Armand's periodical *L'En Dehors* in the late 1920s and early 1930s. Armand had long participated in debates around free love and sexuality in his paper and set up the Association Internationale de Combat contre la Jalousie et l'Exclusivisme en Amour in May 1926. Corresponding frequently with Armand, both privately and through *L'En Dehors*, Acharya joined this organisation and debates from sexually freewheeling Weimar Berlin.[33] According to Acharya,

162

ULTRA-LEFTISTS AND OUTSIDERS

repressing debates around sex, sexuality, and gender relations only perpetuated false notions of perversity, abnormality and, ultimately, freedom.[34] Acharya's arguments centred on women's oppression, not only by patriarchy but also capitalism and the West's corruption of the mind. Capitalism forced women to adorn themselves, Acharya argued, to attract the attention of men to whom they would be in debt through marriage or another uneven partnership. Clothing and toiletries, in this way, created a rift between men and women while nudity, the natural state of being, would create equality between the sexes.[35]

In one of his most insightful essays, Acharya argued that marriage was no different than sex work: '[p]rostitution is the public use of a certain body while marriage is the private monopoly of a certain body'.[36] The contract between a woman marrying a man—often predicated on money and wealth—differed only from the contract between a sex worker and a client in terms of duration. In fact, Acharya argued, sex workers had more freedom than married women, as they could leave their clients when the sexual arrangement was over. Acharya's argument commented both on how women would often have to marry due to financial pressures (an exploitative capitalist contract) as well as on the hypocrisy of the public perception of sex workers at the time. That said, observing the nude cabarets in Paris, Acharya argued that

> [n]ude cabarets have nothing in common with voluntary associations of nudists. If the young women were showing off their bodies for their own pleasure, or even from vanity, there would be nothing mercenary in that, even if curious persons handed over an entrance fee to them or to the owner of the place where they expose themselves.[37]

Entering such capitalist associations as workers, however, they were no different from any other worker offering her or his body as labour. Even more, Acharya asked, 'why stigmatise prostitution as immoral or incompatible with ethics? It is in this sense that the young women showing their nakedness in the cabarets are as respectable as any wage-earning woman'.[38]

Even further, marriage had corrupted the meaning of sex. Sex should only occur within the confines of marriage, according to normative society, and this effectively distorted the natural meaning of

ANARCHY OR CHAOS

sex as an act of love and pleasure between two equal individuals.[39] In fact, marriage often led to jealousy—the man taking possession of the woman—and even misery and death, because of society's rules about sex.[40] At the same time, referencing the central themes of the Indian epic *Mahabharata* as well as a contemporary legal case against the sociologist R. D. Karve in Bombay, Acharya noted that Indians seemed more liberated and objective when it came to sexual matters than Europeans.[41] Even in so-called liberated Russia, Acharya noted with reference to notable revolutionaries like Kollontai and Vera Figner, women were not free.[42] Matriarchal societies, Acharya said, were historically more equal and non-hierarchical and would pave the way for more anarchic communities.[43] Indeed, it was only when women were equal to men, in all respects, that these problems of marriage, sex, love, and freedom would be resolved.

Acharya's thoughts on sexuality and gender relations extended to questions around homosexuality—an issue that had come up in the summer of 1934, when Hitler's rival, Ernst Röhm, the openly homosexual leader of the German Stormtroopers, was assassinated on Hitler's orders during the so-called Night of Long Knives. Acharya accused the left of condemning both Hitler's hypocrisy and Röhm's homosexuality: '[w]ithout there being any question of defending homosexuality', he said, 'let us be careful not to use homosexuality as a pretext to play politics and to use politics as a pretext to condemn homosexuality'.[44] He argued that, when existing society had disappeared and anarchy prevailed, 'another "romanticism" will be born—that of an equal association'.[45] Under these conditions, 'the feelings of shame, perversity, and obscenity that currently accompanies homo- as well as heterosexuality will vanish in the face of the poetry of sexual excitement—or blood or of life—poetry that is neither masculine nor feminine, but human and universal'.[46]

Acharya's articles on gender and sexuality received much attention also beyond the readership of *L'En Dehors*. His article 'De la Jalousie' was reprinted in the Japanese anarcho-feminist Takamure Itsue's periodical *Fujin Sensen*.[47] Responding to Acharya's article, Takamure criticised Acharya's thesis as 'just another male view on sexuality'.[48] The news of Takamure's criticism soon reached Acharya, who then wrote to Armand:

164

ULTRA-LEFTISTS AND OUTSIDERS

I received information from Japan the other day that my defence of the thesis of our Association to combat jealousy was published in the January issue of *Fujin Sensen*, edited by Anarchist Comrade Miss Takamure Itsue in Tokyo and it is being discussed eagerly in her circles. If, as I expect, I get a few copies of the issue, I shall send you one. Hope the discussion will be fruitful.[49]

Having then read Takamure's response, Acharya wrote to Armand: 'I am writing an answer to the Japanese Women's Front (journal) [*Fujin Sensen*], where they criticised the anti-jealousy propaganda of our association. I think they will publish it and reproduce other articles'.[50] Whether his response was republished in *Fujin Sensen* is uncertain, but the conversation between Acharya and Takamure is evidence of the global circulation of Acharya's views at the time.

Religion, caste, and class

While Acharya was preoccupied with issues of gender and sex, he devoted less attention to questions of religion and caste. For example, whereas Gandhi's position on the question of untouchability and the caste system in India was problematic, Acharya did not devote much attention to the question at all. Although Gandhi fought against the caste system and founded a new journal *Harijan* (Gandhi's term for Dalits) devoted to the question in 1933, he did not necessarily disavow the issue of untouchability. In essence, Gandhi envisioned that there would be no enmity between castes, thus retaining the *varna* of the caste system, while the prominent anti-caste activist Bhimrao Ramji Ambedkar fought to abolish the caste system altogether.[51] Acharya later argued that Ambedkar's fight for Dalits and minority rights was exploited by the British as an excuse to continue their rule in India and that Ambedkar's struggle was intellectual rather than one concerned with workers.[52]

When analysing India's multi-religious composition and explaining how the many religions in India co-existed peacefully, Acharya often overlooked the structural inequalities of the caste system, with a few exceptions: in a letter to the INC from April 1928, Acharya declared that all castes should be 'guaranteed to be on a footing of perfect equality' and 'on the same par as of civil right equality, religious belief

ANARCHY OR CHAOS

equality, and similarly the status of untouchables'.[53] At the same time, in an article in *Der Syndikalist*, he noted that some Christians in India perpetuated the caste system to maintain order and separation between religions. The caste system was an impossibility in and of itself, due to the intermixing of nations and races, Acharya argued.[54] When the Austrian anarchist Albert Bruhl criticised the Indian caste system and argued that there was nothing like it in Europe, Acharya took offence.[55] He reminded Bruhl that Gandhi's non-violence campaign cut across class and caste, that it united the masses of India against the British, without Gandhi assuming the role of national leader.[56] In stating that, Acharya may have failed to acknowledge inherent differences between class and caste. Perhaps too naïvely, Acharya felt that anarchism in and of itself would abolish such hierarchies and the caste system.[57]

The *Indian Press Service*

In late 1930, Indulal Yagnik, a Gandhian and member of the Bombay Congress Committee and the All-India Congress Committee, arrived in Berlin. Yagnik wanted to start a new periodical with German financial help to propagate the Indian freedom struggle and, to do so, sought out some veteran Indian radicals in Berlin.[58] Yagnik greatly admired Chatto's revolutionary credentials but did not get along with him on a personal level. He also befriended Pillai, who was now a close associate of German industrialists and certainly not a communist. However, Yagnik failed to get Pillai's support.

Instead, Yagnik contacted Acharya, 'an old but poor patriot of south India, ... [who] maintained himself by working as a translator'.[59] Yagnik later explained that, 'when I met him in 1930–31 in Berlin', Acharya had become disillusioned with 'what he saw of Bolshevik terrorism [and] returned to Berlin a confirmed anti-communist, and was attached to the Amsterdam School of Anarcho-Syndicalism'.[60] This account has given rise to some confusion about Acharya's whereabouts, even to suggest that Acharya lived in Amsterdam at the time.[61] This was not the case—Acharya did not have a passport and would not have been able to leave Germany—but Yagnik's claim perhaps suggests that Acharya was associated with the IAMB in Amsterdam or had connections with Dutch anarchists.

166

ULTRA-LEFTISTS AND OUTSIDERS

The first issue of Yagnik's *Indian Press Service* appeared in December 1930, and Acharya soon helped him prepare the manuscripts.[62] Despite being destitute and on the brink of starvation, '[h]e showed willingness to type them without remuneration', wrote Yagnik, but '[a]fter a few weeks Acharya's enthusiasm for this work was reduced'.[63] According to Yagnik, Nachman had intervened and objected to Acharya doing this work for free, which meant that, '[f]inally, Acharya bluntly refused to continue typing the work'.[64] Appearing only under Yagnik's name and carrying general news from and about India, including paragraphs from the *War Resister*, but with no trace of Acharya's influence, the *Indian Press Service* ran for seven issues until 14 February 1931. Without Acharya's typist skills, Yagnik found the work too laborious and eventually returned to India in July 1931.[65]

Acharya's poverty also led him to a fateful encounter with Ranchoddas Bhavan Lotvala, an associate of Yagnik, during his visit to Berlin in 1932. Lotvala was a wealthy socialist and financer of notable communist ventures such as Dange's paper *The Socialist*, and during his many trips to Britain in the 1920s, he befriended Saklatvala. However, while travelling to Europe again in the early 1930s with his son, Nitisen, and now taking an anti-Stalinist line, Lotvala progressively moved away from communism and fell out with Saklatvala. By contrast, he was impressed by Acharya's anarchism, which planted a seed in Lotvala.[66] He did not embrace the libertarian tradition at the time, but he helped Acharya financially by hiring him to tutor Nitisen.[67]

By the early 1930s, as Acharya travelled among ultra-leftists and outsiders and engaged in global discussions about China, sex and gender, and caste and religion, all the while trying to make a living, the political climate in Germany was rapidly changing. Indeed, Acharya's activities in early 1930s Berlin suggest that he carved out different avenues of anticolonial thought than his contemporaries and engaged in conversations beyond anti-imperialism and anarchism that spanned across Europe and Asia. In fact, he often approached these issues through his particular articulation of anarchist anticolonialism, which later influenced Lotvala, and contributed to the global development of anarchism.

PART IV

ESCAPE AND RETURN TO INDIA, 1934–45

12

ESCAPE FROM EUROPE

Anarchism in the time of Nazism

In the July 1932 elections, Hitler's Nationalsozialistische Deutsche Arbeiterpartei (Nazi Party) became the largest party in the German parliament. Before the results of the elections were known, however, Acharya wrongfully assessed the gravity of the situation and argued:

> [t]he situation in Germany is different from the description given of it by all political parties, and even by the anarchist papers, which still think in the capitalist and political way. Fear of fascism and hope for Bolshevism are still held among us, even by the opponents of fascism and Bolshevism. Anarchists and syndicalists are themselves obsessed by those two fears, preferring the second as 'the lesser evil'. But clear-sighted observation shows that neither is possible in the situation of 1932, which is different from that of Russia in 1917 and Italy in 1922.[1]

In a call to awakening, he charged anarchists for not being prepared for the situation and questioningly concluded that 'anarchy is very close to carrying the day in Germany. But what is the proletariat going to do?'[2]

While Acharya rarely addressed the rise of Nazism and Hitler in Germany in his public writings, perhaps out of fear of persecution by the German authorities, he was more direct and worried in his private

171

ANARCHY OR CHAOS

letters from that period. For instance, corresponding with Armand in the winter of 1932, Acharya cautiously wrote:

> I am afraid I must return to India at all risks, since I cannot manage to live here. I am however trying to wait here till I can no longer do so. It is also difficult to leave for want of passage. But I think it will be easier if only I hold out this winter.[3]

In another letter to Armand from Christmas 1932, speaking about the hopelessness of the events in Germany, Acharya even wrote that he thought that there would be a revolution in Germany and that 'I feel that the situation will be sharper everywhere, without anyone knowing what to do'.[4]

The situation in Germany did resemble a revolution—not the left-wing revolution that the anarchists were hoping for, but a totalitarian overthrow of the existing Weimar system, leaving the socialist and radical left shattered. In fact, although the 6 November 1932 elections were not as convincing as Hitler had hoped for, in late January 1933, he was appointed Chancellor by the German President Paul von Hindenburg and immediately called for the dissolution of the Reichstag and new elections to be held. Unleashing a campaign of violence against the left in the weeks that followed, the Reichstag Fire on 27 February effectively granted Hitler the excuse he needed to seize power and suppress any opposition.

On 28 February 1933, the Berlin police notified Souchy that the *IWMA Press Service* was banned in Germany, initially for three months, which prompted the editorship to move to the Netherlands under de Jong, and then on to Madrid in the summer of 1933.[5] Rocker and Souchy left Germany after the Reichstag fire too.[6] Before leaving, Souchy was responsible for packing up the IWMA archives and bringing them to safety, but on 15 March 1933 the Nazis confiscated and destroyed a great deal of the archives.[7]

For the Indians in Berlin, the brutality of Hitler's rise to power also became clear when Nambiar and Jaya Surya Naidu were arrested on 28 February. By 1933, Nambiar was living at Acharya's former address at Kaiserplatz 17. Nambiar later recounted the circumstances of his arrest:

> I was arrested in Berlin in my flat on the 28th of February the day following the evening on which the Reichstag caught fire under mys-

172

ESCAPE FROM EUROPE

terious and controversial circumstances, and which was to prove as signal for a general action by Nazi Storm Troopers. About seven in the evening, when I was reading the afternoon papers, six Storm Troopers entered my flat. With loaded revolvers raised to my face and threat of being shot immediately in the event of any resistance, they asked me to follow to a car that waited outside.[8]

Nambiar was brought to the police station where he was assaulted by two Stormtroopers, and his typewriter was confiscated, as were numerous manuscripts, newspaper cuttings, and periodicals deemed 'subversive'. Naidu was released after a few days, but Nambiar was imprisoned for weeks without charges brought against him. On 4 March, the British Embassy in Berlin was informed of the arrests, and after three weeks of negotiations between the British and the Germans, Nambiar was released without trial on 25 March. However, he was directed to leave Germany immediately, a decision that was later overturned, but Nambiar chose to leave Berlin anyway. After giving an account of his life in Germany to the authorities and denying any involvement in anarchist or communist organisations, Nambiar left for Prague and here met Subhas Chandra Bose, who was on his way to Berlin.[9]

The Reichstag Fire provided the pretext for the 5 March 1933 elections, in which the Nazis seized power with a small minority, and was followed a few weeks later by the Enabling Act, which granted Hitler the right to enact laws without the approval of the Reichstag, effectively giving him dictatorial power in Germany. In the months that followed, the Nazis banned other political parties such as the KPD and the KAPD as well as the LAI and the IWMA. Acharya's friends Saumyendranath Tagore and Faruqui were expelled in April 1933.[10]

Escape to Switzerland

With the rise of Nazism, life became too dangerous for Acharya and Nachman in Berlin. At the suggestion of Bose, whom Acharya had met through Lotvala shortly after Bose's arrival in Berlin in July 1933, Acharya was encouraged to leave Berlin, so he applied for a passport again in September.[11] Bose had told Acharya that 'at the most [you] may be arrested and imprisoned' in India, in which case someone

ANARCHY OR CHAOS

would take care of Nachman.[12] 'Who they will certainly be is not suggested by him', Acharya noted that Bose had told him.[13] 'He did not offer any such care himself. Of course, he would recommend her to "others"'.[14]

It was time for Acharya to move on, but he needed passports for himself and Nachman. Since the late 1920s, Acharya had appealed to Indian leaders in *Forward*:

> [t]he position of the exiles is this. Most or all of them are ready to go back—having found their life after the War impossible of maintenance. Some of them are ready under any conditions. But almost all of them are willing to return home only when freedom from persecution for past 'offences' is guaranteed if not complete immunity to talk what they want.[15]

Refused a guarantee of political amnesty, Acharya denounced his former militant and revolutionary activities and declared himself 'to be perfectly and logically a consistent pacifist by whatever name I may be called or condemned'.[16]

At the time, the couple was living at Landgrafenstrasse 3a in Berlin, but soon after moved to Ringbahnstrasse 4, and by 1929 had moved to the Atelierhaus, a hub for artists at Kaiserplatz 17. In late August of that year, Acharya applied for a British passport again, asking to be treated on the same conditions as L. P. Varma, his associate from the IIC, who had now been granted a passport to return to India. The British FO stated, however, that Acharya's revolutionary career was much longer than Varma's and initially refused to consider Acharya's case on the same lines. Acharya inquired whether there were any outstanding warrants out for him in India. As the 1909 and 1925 arrest warrants were still in effect, the British authorities asked Acharya repeatedly about his destination, and Acharya eventually stated that he wanted to return to India but that he had no concrete travel plans. As his case dragged on for a few years, Acharya insisted in various declarations given to the British authorities that he was an anarchist and a pacifist, fervently against the communists, probably aware that communism constituted a greater threat to the British in India than anarchism.

Having moved to Grossbeerenstrasse 56C sometime in 1930, Acharya reached out to the British WRI and LAI member Fenner

174

ESCAPE FROM EUROPE

Brockway in July 1931. Inquiring why Acharya's case was held up, Brockway wrote to Hugh Dalton, the Under-Secretary of the Foreign Office: '[f]rom his letters he appears to be a pacifist Anarchist, quite a harmless sort of person .... He is known to the Pacifist circles in Germany and to Mr. Carey of the Quakers' International Secretariat. He is certainly not a Communist although he has been to Russia'.[17] Dalton replied that Acharya had to apply for travel to a specific country to be issued a passport, but Brockway was not satisfied and raised the matter again with Samuel Hoare, the newly appointed Secretary of State for India, in late September 1931: 'I understand that he is a pacifist anarchist and wishes to go to India to preach integral co-operation. He was married in Russia in 1921 but his wife is a non-political entirely concerned with art'.[18] Acharya had to apply to the British consul in Berlin, Hoare replied, and again state where he wanted to go.[19] Brockway communicated this to Acharya, and Acharya soon after applied to the British consulate at Berlin for a passport for all European countries except Russia for him and Nachman.

At the suggestion of Vallabhbhai J. Patel, whom he had met in Berlin, Acharya wrote to Gandhi for help, complaining that INC leaders were not willing to assist him, and asked Gandhi to intervene on his behalf:

> [a]s I am completely at the end of my tether, I have every duty to myself to press upon them for immediate help, whether they utilise my services or not. I think you can at once demand and get help instead of telling me, as a dying man, to wait till India is saved. A dying man cannot afford to wait.[20]

However, when Gandhi did not reply, Acharya was more than a little mad:

> [i]f it is politeness to keep quiet, it is 'politeness' with brutality to one who is suffering without help. It is want of courage not to say yes or no and at the same time a cover to conceal it .... I am very sorry great public men—even sincere ones—take recourse to such callous, brutal silence to avoid an unpleasant answer. I know even you cannot or will not save the millions of sufferers with Charka, negotiations, constitution, and Swaraj. You had at least a chance to save or answer one.[21]

175

ANARCHY OR CHAOS

When Acharya and Nachman were eventually granted passports for all European countries except Russia in late October 1931, Acharya could not afford the fees, so he asked the AA for financial assistance. At the same time, he was concerned about the situation in India, where the British authorities had recently repressed and imprisoned hundreds of dissenters, including Sarojini Naidu, to whom Acharya had also written for help. Indeed, even Brockway warned Acharya against returning to India: '[y]ou are certain to be regarded with suspicion in India and to be dogged by the authorities'.[22]

Moving to Kronprinzendamm 19 in 1933, from here Acharya applied to the British consulate in Berlin for a passport for himself and Nachman valid for India, and he again wanted to know if there were any charges out against him in India. The couple could no longer afford to stay in Berlin, he informed the British consulate, and they intended to go to Switzerland to live with Nachman's sister as soon as possible. In accordance with the decision on his 1931 application, in early January 1934 the British consulate granted Acharya and Nachman passports valid for Europe, allowing them to travel to Switzerland, and in late February 1934 they were granted passports for a direct journey to India. Although the arrest warrants from 1909 and 1925 were still out on him, the British FO deemed that 'as an extremist Acharya can be regarded as a spent force' and promised that, while no act of oblivion would be granted, he would be left alone unless he embarked on 'treasonable and seditious courses'.[23]

Tarachand Roy helped Acharya and Nachman with the final arrangements with their landlord and, with British passports in hand, they escaped to Zürich in mid-February 1934, where they stayed with Nachman's sister Adele Felder.[24] The German authorities kept Acharya under close surveillance and wanted to prevent him from re-entering Germany in case he could not find work or stay in Switzerland.[25] While Acharya was grateful to his sister-in-law for letting him stay, he was also aware of the burden it created. As he wrote to Armand:

> [t]hese are poor people and they offered roof for some weeks. They have at present no money at all. Fortunately, the sister-in-law has a job. I had to take advantage of their offer as I had no income and was in danger of arrest perhaps. They had to borrow money to pay railway fare.[26]

176

ESCAPE FROM EUROPE

It was impossible for Acharya to find work in Switzerland, as the Swiss Government did not allow for foreigners to work there, and Acharya and Nachman were only permitted to reside in the country for two months until the end of March 1934.[27]

Desperate to earn money, he wrote to Souchy in Spain and asked for work as an English teacher or translator, but to no avail.[28] Commenting on the political turmoil in Spain, Acharya wrote to Armand:

> I consider Spain is on the throes of a grand convulsion and much preparation of mind has to be done among anarchists on economic subjects. Otherwise they will end in bloodshed uselessly as in Austria. I think also Spaniards are better fit for social revolution than industrial unrest. The workmen want money only.[29]

Though Acharya had been granted a passport to India, he could not afford to buy tickets for the journey.

Over the years, Acharya had accumulated a collection of anarchist literature, which he could not bring with him to India. He left behind his collection of *L'En Dehors* with Nachman in Zürich and donated all his anarchist books to the Sino-International Library in Geneva. 'They were glad to take it—3 cases—at their own expense', he wrote to Armand.[30] Someone from the Sino-International Library helped Acharya retrieve the rest of this belongings from Germany, which suggests that Acharya had contact with some Chinese activists in Berlin.

Among the 'outlaws' in Paris

Forced to leave Zürich, Acharya and Nachman went to Paris in mid-April 1934 and lodged at 30 Rue Parmentier in the Neuilly-sur-Seine suburb. Acharya had already contacted Armand in mid-February and asked him to place a notice in *L'En Dehors* offering his services to anyone interested in discussing politics in return for board and lodging.[31] In mid-April 1934, the following text appeared under the heading 'Hindou':

> [m]iddle aged Indian, writer in this paper, experienced in 3 continents but without chance of work anywhere must have for some weeks or months roof and board free. Can speak German, French, English and can translate into English (also from Swedish). Shall gladly hold con-

177

versation and discussions on many a subject, social, sexual or economic besides also on various countries and people. Pleasant companion to persons, who has own ideas, but are seriously interested in extending vision about events, peoples and psychology. Would like to help at anything in country or town. Will go to any country, preferably Western or South Europe.[32]

He asked Armand to not mention his name, 'as that would be a cause for any troubles they may want to make for my stay here'.[33] He wrote to Armand a week later that in May he would earn some money by giving English lessons to two German students.[34]

Relying also on financial help from Armand and comrades in the French anarchist scene, Acharya received 250 Francs from Armand and met him whenever he visited Paris from Orleans as well as other anarchists, including 'a comrade from Arpajon' and a figure referred to as 'Com. Lesage'. Serendipitously, he also met Ernest Bairstow for the first time in Paris. 'Recently my wife and I had the privilege of meeting in Paris an Indian comrade who has been associated with the Circle for many years', wrote Bairstow of their encounter.[35] 'For a long time, he lived in Berlin. He now writes that he may be going to India before long. Wherever he is he can be relied upon to keep the ideals of the colony viewpoint to the fore'.[36] Indeed, only a couple of years later, Acharya wrote a long article on the history and principles of the Llano colony in the United States, arguing that 'sooner or later, every country will have to live according to the principles of social organisation as introduced in the American colony mentioned, for there is no solution to the selling system', and advertised that more information about the Llano colony could be had from Bairstow.[37]

Returning to Paris after twenty-five years also gave Acharya the opportunity to reconnect with Madame Cama. By then in her mid-seventies, Cama still lived at Rue de Ponthieu, and Acharya recalled how he escorted her down the Champs-Élysées, where she was known to all the café owners.[38] Having sustained a skull fracture in a taxi accident, Cama was ill and frail, suffering from facial paralysis, and looking to return to India to spend her final days there.[39] According to Acharya, she was also worried that she would die any day in Paris and had even purchased a lot at the Père Lachaise Cemetery. Cama brought him there one day and showed him the

178

ESCAPE FROM EUROPE

grave and the tombstone, which had her famous dictum 'Resistance to Tyranny is Obedience to God' inscribed in both French and Gujarati. 'That was the principle of her life', Acharya wrote.[40] After a prolonged visa application process, Cama returned to Bombay in August 1935, where she died a year later.[41]

'Anarchy or Chaos'

Shortly after he had arrived in Zürich, Acharya wrote in an optimistic yet biting article on the rise of fascism and global depression in Marcus Graham's journal *Man!* that 1934 would see the closing down of all business and states, leaving the way open for anarchism, whether anarchists were ready or not.[42] 'Preventing the teaching of anarchism', he wrote, 'cannot prevent the coming of anarchy. They who "prevent" only create chaos, even when losing their own lives in doing so'.[43] Anarchy or chaos was a frequent dichotomous proposition in Acharya's writings at the time. In fact, in the autumn of 1934, in his article 'Anarchy or Chaos?', Acharya proposed that

> the governments don't want revolutions—but by making conditions for living impossible they are inevitably bringing revolutions about—against themselves. By conspiring to keep people blind about their own dangers and dangers to their lives, they are calling forth a revolution which will be social, which will put all wars and Bolshevist bloodshed into shade. They are creating experimentally economic conditions which make people psychopathic and more blood thirsty than ever. And yet they cry in horror against revolutions and condemn anarchy—as if anarchy if consciously arranged would be worse than the chaos into which they are precipitating mankind in order to prolong their systems if it were possible.

Anarchists, Acharya argued, were trying to prepare for social, pacifist revolutions, where 'man will have, will be compelled, to give up arms in favour of the plow'.[44]

Escape from Europe

While Acharya and Nachman had been granted passports to return to India, they did not take up the offer immediately. In fact, Acharya called on the British consul in Paris in mid-May 1934 to confirm

179

ANARCHY OR CHAOS

travel plans for the couple to return to Bombay on the SS *Victoria*, scheduled to depart from Genoa on 28 May and arrive on 8 June 1934. However, when they did not arrive in Bombay as scheduled, the British Government of India was suddenly concerned. As had happened before, Acharya could not raise the necessary money to travel even to Genoa and had to abandon his plans. In the autumn of 1934, Acharya returned to Zürich for a few months, but was back in Paris again by December and wrote to Armand:

> [m]y case is so bad that I think we will soon have to quit this god's own country of plenty and peace. Perhaps I will have to leave my wife in Zürich and go to India to take chances. There is no standing peace in Europe. This may happen in December or January. So I will see you once—for the last time I believe.[45]

He hoped to meet Armand on 2 December 1934.

Acharya's underground life in Paris almost landed him in prison. 'I have been nearly taken to the lock up for want of regular papers. But this time I somehow managed to be free. But I may be asked to pay fine and take papers', he wrote to Armand.[46] Acharya was aware that prospects in Europe were clearly becoming untenable:

> I am probably going away from here soon, since I and my wife cannot earn but by chance and that will compel us to beat retreat together or one by one (I first). Even there in Zürich we cannot stay more than a few weeks. Where to go next, if we at all are allowed to go? For we will have not enough money. However, distant programmes are useless for those who don't know what next day! But every day is itself an anxiety—thanks to police and money whose authority none can usurp. Things will be alright as I think.[47]

Acharya received 100 Francs from Armand in early February 1935 but was still worried about the police hunting him down. 'I think I will have to leave France as a *pis-aller* whatever may come', he wrote to Armand.[48] He had also contacted a figure known as 'Gigou' in the Swiss town of La Chaux-de-Fonds, just across the border from France, asking for money and shelter. If that failed, Acharya continued, 'I must go to India end of the month leaving my wife away. It is both dangerous and a matter of luck for to go there—I don't know which is likely so I must go into the vague'.[49] If, however, he could get at least 100 Swiss Francs a month for three to four months, he

ESCAPE FROM EUROPE

could stay with his sister-in-law in Zürich and write up his memoirs. Adding to his troubles, although he had booked a journey to Bombay, he needed at least 500 Francs for two tickets, even leaving their luggage behind, and petty money for the voyage itself, and this depended on receiving funds from an unknown benefactor in Zürich. A week later, Acharya received money from Armand and was offered board and lodging from Gigou, an offer he would only take up if the other plans did not work out. However, he was still waiting to hear from the unknown benefactor, who demanded that Acharya board that ship as promised, but he could only do so by going to Zürich first. He was negotiating 'because it is yet too early to go to Genoa and meanwhile it means expense to stay here and I cannot leave my wife in this condition'.[50] He also had to find money for the train ticket from Zürich to Genoa and, failing to do so, he would have to postpone his trip until next month.

In late February 1935, Acharya returned to Zürich to make the final arrangements for going back to India. He still needed to raise 500 Francs to be able to travel, otherwise his ticket would be lost again.[51] Staying in Zürich was a great financial burden on Nachman's sister and her family who were 'anxious we both leave as soon as possible, since we cost them twice as much as their usual expenses and they are earning less and less. Quite understandable', Acharya wrote to Armand.[52] If they could raise 50 Francs a month, Nachman could stay with her sister, he noted, and the Swiss authorities had even granted them permission to stay until the end of May. Soon after, Acharya received 250 Francs from Armand and confessed: 'I didn't think you would get more than 50 and therefore think now that our circle is more sacrificing than more "disciplined" and bigger organisations. Yes, we outlaws have more solidarity than statutorily enforced organisations and therefore are the best of all in the world'.[53]

Acharya also reached out to the IAMB for help. In February, he wrote to Han Kuijsten who, given the IAMB's financial trouble, instead approached Acharya's acquaintance Henriette Roland Holst, the president of the Dutch organisation Vrienden van India.[54] At the same time, Acharya also contacted Hendrik Jan Mispelblom Beyer, the treasurer of the IAMB and also a member of Vrienden van India. Having discussed Acharya's case at the annual meeting of Vrienden

ANARCHY OR CHAOS

van India without any success, Beyer instead wrote to the IAMB secretariat on 4 March 1935 on behalf of Acharya:

> M. Acharya, a British-Indian, who has lived in Europe for many years, is now in financial trouble. He had worked in Berlin but had to flee the Nazi terror. He is an anarchist and has written for many magazines and he is well known in the movement in India .... Acharya has obtained the travel costs for a Trieste-India ticket. He should have left by the end of February but could not find any money to pay the travel expenses to Trieste. It concerns an amount of 100 Swiss Francs. Even if he gets this money, he still has to leave his wife behind in Zürich with people who themselves are in very bad financial position.[55]

Because of the IAMB's financial trouble, Beyer was sceptical that they could raise any money for Acharya, but he wanted to make them aware of Acharya's dire situation.

As Beyer alluded to, Acharya was worried about of leaving Nachman behind and about his fate in India. 'If nothing comes I will have to go back to India to get into prison or gallows, for the government does not give safe crossover', Acharya had written to Armand back in February 1934.[56] Despite the fact that they had both obtained passports, the couple decided that Acharya should travel alone and settle in before asking Nachman to join him in Bombay.[57] Perhaps through Beyer, Roland-Holst, and the Vrienden van India circle, Acharya managed to obtain the required amount of money, and, on 26 March 1935, he left for Genoa to board a ship destined for Bombay. He had asked Armand to send him a copy of Restif de la Bretonne's *Les Plus Belles Pages* (1905) directly to the SS *Victoria* for him to read on the voyage back, sarcastically remarking: 'I hear that Mussolini does not forbid foreigners from carrying any book he likes'.[58] Having obtained a guarantee from the British authorities that he would be left alone by the authorities in India, he wrote to Armand: 'On April 8, I will reach Bombay. Then the lottery begins'.[59]

The story of Acharya's escape from Nazi-era Berlin and difficulty returning to India illuminate the complexities of itinerant, exiled lives. It was almost impossible to escape past lives and activities, and it was certainly impossible to stay in Berlin. This also shows a pattern of revolutionary lives, of having to flee oppression and totalitarianism in its various guises, sometimes living underground. The political

182

ESCAPE FROM EUROPE

networks of anticolonialism and anarchism, indeed, helped Acharya and Nachman flee to safety; the political, then, was personal. Acharya had already fled India in 1908, then Russia in 1922, and now he had to flee Germany to escape the brutality of the Nazis.

13

RETURN TO INDIA

Arriving in Bombay

Acharya's first few weeks back after more than twenty-six years abroad proved to be relatively quiet. The British authorities had guaranteed that, 'while no act of oblivion will be granted, he would be left in peace unless he embarks on treasonable and seditious courses'.[1] He arrived in Bombay on 8 April 1935 and gave an interview to the *Bombay Chronicle* two days later. 'Mr. M. P. T. Acharya, who left India nearly 26 years ago and had spent his life in various parts of the world, returned to India on Monday', the article read.[2] 'On the continent, Mr. Acharya distinguished himself as a linguist and is thoroughly conversant with several continental languages and has also mastered the North European languages'.[3] In his peripatetic travels across the world, the article continued, Acharya had 'had intimate glimpses of the customs and manners of almost all peoples in the world. Mr. Acharya thinks that the Spanish in their temperament, outlook and ideas, resemble the Indian somewhat closely'.[4] Acharya commented on the world he left behind and assessed that, 'at present, political and economic conditions in Europe were quite unsettled', but he was also convinced that, 'though preparations for war and manufactures of armaments were going on at a brisk pace, it was not likely … that war would break out in the near future'.[5]

185

ANARCHY OR CHAOS

Acharya explained in the interview that he was planning to stay in Bombay, but he soon proceeded to Madras to visit his mother. He stayed in Madras for two weeks and made another week-long stop somewhere on his way back before he arrived in Bombay in early May 1935 and settled at 192 Hornby Road.[6] Left alone by the British authorities as promised but still worried about what life would bring for him, Acharya wrote to Armand: 'I am yet not quite free, but I am not troubled. I am, however, well received. A consolation'.[7] However, reality soon set in for Acharya, and he missed Nachman terribly. 'Since two weeks I have no news from my *compagne*, which makes me anxious. If I get any news of her, I shall let you know again', he wrote to Armand in June.[8] Correspondence with Nachman may have been sporadic, but in September, he sent her a photo of himself with a descriptive note of the AEG electric fan on his bedside table. The photo echoes his complaint to Armand: '[i]t is too hot here'.[9] The heat and loneliness aside, he soon regretted returning to India. In June, he wrote to Armand that he wanted to return to Europe: 'I am now regretting why I came here, as I have no chance of earning'.[10] However, he remained in Bombay and started preparing for Nachman's arrival. In December, two of her paintings, 'Russian Peasant' and 'Oriental', appeared in the *Bombay Chronicle* with a short biography of her artistic career.[11] It is uncertain exactly when Nachman arrived, but according to Bernstein it was between April 1936 and January 1937.[12] Though now stuck in Bombay, Acharya remained in touch with the IAMB group and Armand as well as with other anarchists across Europe and the US.

Self-government or no-government

While Acharya longed to go back to Europe, the situation there soon escalated into war, when Mussolini's fascist regime invaded Abyssinia (now Ethiopia) in early October 1935. In response to the invasion, the Dutch pacifist paper *De Wapens Neder* put together a special Christmas issue on imperialism, fascism, and militarism. Acharya's essay on British imperialism in India appeared alongside articles by the Japanese anarchist E. K. Nobushima's analysis of the rise of Japanese imperialism, the Algerian anarchist Sail Mohamed's essay

186

RETURN TO INDIA

on French colonial violence in Algeria, and Mispelblom Beyer's essay on Dutch colonialism in South East Asia.[13] Acharya commented on the increasingly militarised political situation in both Europe and Asia and argued:

> the explosive conditions caused by economic and political indignation, far too strong to be overcome by poison gas, tanks, and bombs, naturally has as few common purposes with the various socialist currents in present-day Europe. If all socialists agree on the necessity of socialism in Europe, all Asians agree on the destruction of foreign tyranny and exploitation. Just as the agreement in the various socialist currents stops with the abstract goal, the agreement with the Asian dissatisfaction also goes no further than that goal, and there are contradictions in methods and in immediate social and political ends.[14]

Praising the non-violent movement in India, Acharya warned that neither in India nor in Europe had people dared to live outside the protection of the state. The long-held trust in the notion of *swarajya* (self-government), he argued, had to be replaced by *nirajya* (no-government): '[e]verything indicates that nirajya will come before any other form of Swarajya, not only here, but also in Europe. The only other alternative is chaos, where everyone's hand will be against all, the real basis of all contemporary and past civilizations'.[15] For Acharya, there was clearly chaos across Europe and India already, and the only response would be *nirajya*. For the first and only time in his writings, he invoked the nearest Sanskrit equivalent to 'anarchy', namely *nirajya*, as a politically different ideology from decades of nationalist struggle for *swarajya*.

Acharya's distinction between *swarajya* and *nirajya* is significant. Within anarchist scholarship, 'anarchy' is often conceived as 'self-government' of the individual, but in the context of India, 'self-government' meant independence from British rule and a new Indian government replacing colonial masters.[16] For Acharya, this clearly would not do. The true government of the 'self', the individual, had to take on a different meaning in India. The 'self' had to be decoupled from the nation-state and the idea of constitutional government and instead handed back to the people to attain the meaning of 'no-government'. Acharya's articulation of *nirajya* as 'anarchy' in India is intriguing and an important theoretical intervention into anarchist

187

ANARCHY OR CHAOS

debates. Unfortunately, Acharya never developed this notion of *nira-jya* any further, but instead concerned himself with more practical matters and current events.

The Spanish Civil War and anticolonialism

In July 1936, the Spanish Civil War broke out and the IWMA moved its headquarters to Madrid. The rapid development of events in Spain, however, caused divisions within the antimilitarist wing of the international anarchist movement, and the IAC was discontinued in late August 1937 due to disagreements with the IWMA over the justification of armed struggle.[17] Being in India did not prevent Acharya from following the events in Spain. He received the *CNT Boletín de Información* and argued in an article in *Man!* that even anarchists were not prepared for the reconstruction of Spain. Civil war would spread across Europe and Russia, but 'Spain is the battlefield of all dictatorships with democracy—politically—switched in. The field for Spanish anarchists will be free and open. But mental preparation is wanting even in Spain for planned reconstruction. It may therefore even lead to chaos'.[18] The situation was worse in India: '[t]his country is the most rotten ripe for chaos, for it is poorer than any other including Spain and Russia'.[19] The people of India sympathised with 'the radicals' in Spain, but the war was also 'necessary to make anarchist revolution ripe when the war shall have forced all to the equal, Democracy in the anarchist sense would sprout, never to be smothered'.[20] Peace would also lead to oppression and death in Spain, but there was hope after the war: '[l]ong live Spain for showing to the world that all is not lost yet. The mental depression has been broken by Spain throughout the world .... Spain has lifted mankind out of the slough of thought: something new is still possible in the world and is coming'.[21] This was revenge for the Kronstadt Rebellion, he concluded, thus making comparisons between Bolshevism and fascism and extending the prospect of anarchist revolution to India.

Reminiscences of a Revolutionary

While the events in Spain occupied most of the international anarchist movement, Acharya was also concerned with issues closer to home.

188

RETURN TO INDIA

When Nachman joined him, they moved to 56 Ridge Road in the Malabar Hill area of Bombay, and Nachman soon set to work amongst Bombay's thriving artist community.[22] During his time in Zürich, Acharya had wanted to write his memoirs, which he expected to be sold across the world, but instead they appeared in eight instalments in the *Mahratta* from July to October 1937.[23] Acharya hoped that they would be published in book form later and wrote to Armand that the first volume on his experiences in Britain had attracted interest from a publisher.[24] However, outside of the *Mahratta*, his *Reminiscences* were not published elsewhere at the time and only appeared in book form as *Reminiscences of an Indian Revolutionary* in 1991.[25]

In addition, Acharya also published a series of essays on some of the figures he had met during his wanderings in Europe—notably Savarkar in London and Walter Strickland in Munich—and his obituary of Madame Cama offered great insight into his associations, activities, and role in the Indian revolutionary movement in Europe twenty-five years earlier.[26] Acharya's friendship with Cama, and Cama's role in the Indian struggle for independence, was underlined by a celebration of the flag that Cama had unfurled at the 1907 Stuttgart Congress on 18 August 1938. To mark the occasion, a meeting was held at the Tilak Mandir in Bombay where Acharya was 'specially invited for delivering a lecture', since he had been a close associate of Cama in Paris. 'He narrated vividly several incidents which evinced the fearless spirit and love of independence of Madame Cama', a report of the event noted.[27]

Most illuminating, though, are Acharya's recollections of Chatto and their activities in Sweden during the First World War. Chatto had returned to Russia in 1931 to answer to the Comintern for his activities during the First World War and his association with the now-disgraced Roy. His passport was confiscated, and Chatto was forced to stay in Russia, where he ended up working for the Institute of Anthropology and Ethnography in Leningrad (formerly Petrograd; now Saint Petersburg).[28] In the summer of 1938, a rumour that Chatto and a hundred Indians in Russia had been rounded up by the authorities reached Indian newspapers. In response to these reports, the British embassy in Moscow made an inquiry to the NKID about Chatto's whereabouts in October 1938 but was told that 'no trace could be found of the missing man'.[29]

ANARCHY OR CHAOS

Acharya picked up on the report of Chatto's disappearance in the *Mahratta* and soon wrote several articles about his old friend for that publication. Despite their ideological differences, he exonerated Chatto from accusations of being a Trotskyist agent and celebrated his revolutionary career:

> Chatto is not known as an effective public speaker but his powers of silent organisation are tremendous. He was ever ready to help and guide Indian students abroad but men and women of all nationalities who sought his assistance. His knowledge of European politics is immense. He has come in intimate contact with diplomats and politicians of various countries. He also has first-hand information about the poorest strata in European society. Big and small men alike cherish his company and he impresses everybody as a friendly, bright and helpful gentleman.[30]

This article was printed simultaneously in the *Oriental Review*, the organ of Indian Institute of Sociology (IIS).[31] When the Government of India re-opened the case on Chatto's disappearance in May 1947, they concluded that '[i]t seems very possible that he was "purged" in Russia in 1937 or thereabouts'.[32] This was indeed the case. Chatto was executed during Stalin's purges on 2 September 1937.[33]

However, Acharya's reminiscences of these figures—Savarkar, Strickland, Cama, and Chatto—should not be interpreted as a turn to nationalism, but instead, in some ways, sought to account for his turn to anarchism.[34] Having worked with militant Indian nationalists, European socialists in the Second International, and the Bolsheviks in Russia, these essays seemed to confirm that the only way forward for true freedom and independence was through anarchism.

The Indian Institute of Sociology

While Acharya continued to publish in the *Mahratta*, he also started writing for the *Oriental Review*, edited by Gajanan Yashwant Chitnis.[35] Acharya's acquaintance from Berlin, Lotvala, was also involved with the IIS and funding the organisation's library, and was responsible for commissioning foreign articles for the publication. After Chitnis' disappearance in 1939, Lotvala assumed editorship of the *Oriental Review*. Acharya's ideas had a great impact on Lotvala, and Lotvala

190

RETURN TO INDIA

soon began to advocate for libertarianism and anarchism in India and published anarchist texts in the *Oriental Review*.[36] Through Acharya's connections, Lotvala approached Rudolf Rocker in June 1938 and asked for permission to publish excerpts or chapters from Rocker's *Nationalism and Culture* (1937) in the periodical.[37] Lotvala confessed to Rocker that he was neither a communist nor a fascist but a believer in social democracy and noted: 'today things have gone to such a pass that anarchic individualism does not seem to be a practicable proposition surrounded as we are by psychology that has taken root in our mind of fear, suppression and oppression of ruling nations and helplessness of a subject people'.[38] Lotvala described the social and political conditions in India and continued: '[i]n India we are doubly exploited by our foreign British rulers and Indian princes and bourgeoisie'.[39] Lotvala was keen to publish the entire book or excerpts from it in India and assured Rocker that, if granted permission to reprint these excerpts, these would only be read in India and not affect sales in other parts of the world. Indeed, he would even promote Rocker's work more widely in his magazine, 'because I wish that your ideas should be spread in India'.[40] From reading *Nationalism and Culture*, Lotvala was aware that Rocker was against nationalism, but he explained that under existing British rule in India, nationalism was the only way to mobilise Indians against the British.[41] He was also doubtful that anarchism would work in a large country like India, but, as he was still learning about anarchism, he remained open to discussing this. Rocker eventually granted Lotvala permission to print excerpts from *Nationalism and Culture* in the *Oriental Review*, but these never appeared.[42] However, at the hand of Acharya, the *Oriental Review* carried news of the American anarchist Marcus Graham's arrest in 1938.[43] Through Acharya's and Lotvala's efforts, international anarchism reached India in the late 1930s.

Cooperative living and global language

While Acharya became involved in the IIC and actively agitated for anarchism in India, at least intellectually through publications alongside Lotvala, he was also interested in co-operative living as an anarchist praxis. After his return to Bombay, Acharya maintained contact

ANARCHY OR CHAOS

with Bairstow, and in June 1939 he wrote for the BLC's paper *Community Life* about Dayalbagh, a cooperative village commune near Delhi. Acharya had sent a copy of *Community Life* to the village leader, Gurcharan Das Mehta, and explained that Dayalbagh had been founded in 1917 by the wealthy Sahabji Maharaj (Anand Swarup)

> to train young men in professions of land-work. They make laboratory balances, electric fans, kettles, cutlery, gramophones, bolts, leather goods, cloth, hosiery, jewellery, etc., and, I hear, conduct a dairy farm. It is considered very up-to-date and is mentioned highly by Paul Brunton, in a book on India, as idealism and practical sense combined.[44]

In his book *A Search in Secret India* (1934), Brunton (Raphael Hurst) wrote at length about his visit to Dayalbagh in 1930. Acharya referenced Brunton's account of Dayalbagh and concluded his report in *Community Life* by stating that he intended to visit the village. After his visit, he later informed Armand, he wrote two articles on Dayalbagh.[45]

While Armand took an interest in 'proletarian colonies', as he explained to Acharya, he does not appear to have been particularly attracted to the cooperative village in India. Perhaps reflecting a Eurocentric worldview, Armand instead debated with Acharya about the introduction of the Latin alphabet in India. Acharya had already explained to Armand in a letter from June 1935 that it was impossible to translate an Indian text into Latin script, 'as none will understand it, since it makes reading difficult owing to English pronunciation attached to the letters'.[46] Acharya returned to the question of introducing Latin script in India and wrote a lengthy article 'Latin Script for India' in the *Mahratta*, arguing that, even within European languages with Latin script, there were great differences in terms of pronunciation, which hampered mutual understanding across languages. Similar problems would arise in India if Latin script was to be introduced there.[47] After Acharya's article was reprinted in *L'En Dehors* (May–June 1938), the French anarchist Paul Jauzin responded to Acharya that, statistically, more people in the world used the Latin script and uniformisation across the world would ease communication.[48] However, Acharya did not agree. In a letter to Armand, he noted that

> I agree the Latin script is more widely used internationally than any other. That does not mean its use is convenient internationally, for

192

RETURN TO INDIA

even in Europe they use different letters and combinations of letters in different countries for the same sounds, and some of the letters are redundant in the same language. Latin script cannot be rationalised for the same sounds in all European languages. That it has come to be used widely does not give it any advantage. On that principle, we might as well argue that capitalism used widely is good or permanent.

Conversely, in India, he argued, 'Sanskrit and Dravidian languages are based on phonetic script and wherever they are used, i.e., in all languages, they are pronounced in the same way from Himalaya to Cape Comorin, whatever the language be'.[49] Acharya's arguments were not phrased in anti-European or Indian nationalist terms but resisted the linguistic hegemony of European languages as a colonial enterprise. In other words, within the international anarchist movement, Acharya had to combat Eurocentric notions of language as a tool of imperialism.

War, fascism, and the end of anarchism in India

After Franco's victory in Spain in April 1939 and the outbreak of the Second World War in Europe in September 1939, the IWMA moved its headquarters to Stockholm where John Andersson of the syndicalist Sveriges Arbetares Centralorganisation (SAC) became secretary. Acharya's assessment of the rise of fascism and the prospect of war rested on an anticolonial perspective drawn from his experiences in the First World War. During that war, Germany complained against Britain and France for deploying colonial troops in Europe, thus betraying European solidarity, but now Germany engaged in another imperialist adventure with the ambition to join the other European imperial powers. However, European colonialism was dead, even from an economic standpoint, Acharya wrote: '[t]he colonies of today are the future graves of the mother country. It is no longer a question of obtaining free raw materials or holding markets for manufactures but only one of saving partly investments sunk in them'.[50]

Acharya elaborated on his perspective and wrongly predicted in 1938 that war could not break out again. As he explained:

> there are arguments why a world war is impossible in spite of large scale war preparations on all hands. The history of last year and this

193

ANARCHY OR CHAOS

year shows that while bankrupt countries like Italy and Germany are prepared to swallow up any country, the big powers are just looking on helplessly and recognise every *fait accompli*. That must be proof enough. That a large scale war is becoming more and more difficult. It is not a war when an up-to-date armed Power swallows up distant or near helpless countries. War is possible when equally powerful nations enter into a conflict.[51]

While Acharya conceded that, 'it is also true that Italy has annexed Abyssinia and Germany Austria while Japan is trying to swallow up China', his argument rested on an economic analysis of these fascist countries, highlighting the global economic depression and his experiences from the First World War: '[b]efore the last war the nations, i.e., Governments, had collected fat which they expended in 4 years. Today all Governments and the nations are on trade and treasury deposit. To make war without substantial sums is out of question even for desperates like Hitler and Mussolini'.[52] Acharya clearly underestimated the danger of German, Italian, and Japanese militarism, their imperialist ambitions, and the rise of fascism in these countries.

However, shortly after the outbreak of the Second World War, Acharya revised his position. In a long, two-part article in the *Mahratta*, Acharya analysed the rise of fascism in Europe:

[t]he birth of Fascism presupposes the following conditions; in the first place, the state must be in a state of crisis, i.e. radical social changes must have taken place which are utter irreconcilable with the old political system. In the second place, the crisis of the state must be of such a nature as to be of most immediate benefit to the socialist movement, to which the masses must be irresistibly drawn feeling it to be the only movement capable of creating a new world; in the third place, the socialists, when confronted with their responsibilities, must turn out to be utterly inadequate to the arduous task before them and do nothing but increase the general confusion, completely failing to fulfil the hopes reposed in them. When these three conditions are fulfilled, Fascism appears on the scene as a *tertius gaudens*, the interloper who steals the plum. Unless its leader is a complete idiot, his prospects are excellent.[53]

Acharya's sharp analysis of the situation stemmed from his experiences in Europe, negotiating with the Second International socialists in Stockholm during the First World War, and the complicity of

194

RETURN TO INDIA

Allied governments in enabling fascists like Hitler, Mussolini, and Stalin. In Weimar-era Germany, he noted, the German government was in a state of crisis, which allowed Hitler to seize power, because the communists and socialists had not been able to respond adequately to the economic crisis.

The outbreak of the Second World War ended Acharya's livelihood as a journalist and, for the time being, the advocacy of anarchist ideas in India. While he published an article on the failure of the Cripps Mission in *Kaiser-i-Hind* in April 1942, the only other trace of Acharya during the Second World War was that he appeared on the list of subscribers to *War Commentary*, the war-time successor to *Freedom*.[54] In India, the war brought back age-old fears of sedition and anti-British agitation, so the Government of India quickly introduced censorship and banned literature on socialism, communism, and anarchism under the Indian Press (Emergency powers) Act of 1931.[55] Acharya had already had a copy of Wilfred Foulstone's *The Strange Case of Major Vernon* (1937) seized by the British authorities in May 1938.[56] With the outbreak of war, the Indian Press Act led to the termination of the *Oriental Review* in May 1940, but the IIS continued its activities.[57]

While cut off from his friends in Europe, Acharya's correspondence with anarchists across the world is evidence of an internationalism that was rooted less in travel and mobility but rather the exchange of ideas. It was a similar notion of internationalism he brought to his *Reminiscences* and recollections of friends from the earlier nationalist movement. These accounted for his turn to anarchism, which mutated into promises of an intellectual anarchist movement in India through his association with Lotvala and the IIS, as well as anticolonial perspectives on the Spanish Civil War, the emergence of fascism, and the outbreak of the Second World War. These perspectives stemmed from Acharya's experiences with socialists in the Second International as well as witnessing the rise of fascism in Europe.

PART V

FREEDOM, VIOLENCE, AND ANARCHY, 1945–54

14

TOWARDS FREEDOM

An artist and an anarchist on Walkeshwar Road

When the lines of communication between India and the rest of the world were shut down during the Second World War, Acharya was also cut off from the international anarchist movement, and he struggled to find work or outlets for his writings. While Nachman managed to stage a few exhibitions in Bombay and worked with her friend the Austrian dancer Hilde Holger on a ballet production during the war, it is uncertain what Acharya did those years.[1] In various letters to Armand, Aldred, and the Chicago-based Russian American anarchist Boris Yelensky, he explained that he had not worked since the war broke out in 1939. He was ill and on the brink of starvation. The famine had brought death to millions across India, he noted in a letter to Armand, and he was concerned that he would soon be among them.[2]

By 1945, Acharya and Nachman had moved to a small apartment at 63C Walkeshwar Road. They had become friends with the painter Li Gotami and her husband, the German-Bolivian painter Anagarika Govinda (Ernst Lothar Hoffmann), who even held their wedding reception at the Acharyas' in 1947. In their apartment, Govinda later recalled, Nachman and Acharya had plenty of cats that 'seemed to be equally at home here as the paintings, among and on which they

199

ANARCHY OR CHAOS

walked and sat nonchalantly, as if to say that after all *they* were the masters of the house'.[3] Visiting one day, stepping over the cats as he ascended the stairs to their apartment, Govinda wrote that he was greeted by Acharya,

> who with a lively sense of humour related the story of their wanderings in Europe; how they left Russia after the Revolution, the hard times through which they went there and in Berlin, their travels in Germany, France, and Switzerland, and their final decision to settle down in India, which was just about to win her freedom and independence.[4]

Reconnecting with the international anarchist movement

Soon after the war ended in Europe, Acharya wanted to reconnect with the international anarchist movement and slowly reached out to old friends. He contacted Armand in July 1945:

> I am very glad to see your circular and it gladdens my heart to know that you have miraculously escaped death under occupation and concentration camps. I am also anxious to know what became of A. Souchy, A. Schapiro, A. Borghi, R. Rocker, de Santillan, M. Graham and others who know me and, if possible, I would like to get into touch with them also.[5]

He updated Armand on his life during the last six years:

> I am still suffering from chronic intestinal troubles—it is now 25 years, but I think I will get rid of it any time now. I have been during all this war in Bombay. Fortunately, we had no trouble except some shortages and increase in prices. I think India had the best time during the war—militarily. Poor Europe! Its troubles are not yet over. We read very little about the conditions in Europe, but I think I can imagine what they are.[6]

Acharya was aware of the chaotic situation in Europe but also lamented: 'I feel like Robinson Crusoe—alone—in India. I would like to return to Europe to plunge into some useful work among our friends. Now, it is impossible to think of it, but I still expect it will be possible'.[7] In his next letter, he asked Armand to place a few lines in his new journal *L'Unique*, expressing his wish to get in touch with 'A. Souchy, M. Graham, de Santillan and the IAMB people if they are still alive'.[8] Acharya's request appeared in *L'Unique* of May 1946.[9]

200

TOWARDS FREEDOM

Similarly, in December 1945, Acharya wrote to Aldred and asked him to put him in touch with Souchy who, he hoped, could be reached through Albert Jensen: 'I want to get in touch with all resurrected comrades and thinkers in Europe'.[10]

Through his request in *L'Unique*, Acharya soon reconnected with Souchy, who had moved to Mexico City in 1942. In July 1946, Souchy wrote to Rocker, then living in Crompond, New York, that he had received news from Acharya: '[s]urely you remember him. He translated the *IWMA Press Service* for us in Berlin. He was first with Chattopadhyaya but distanced himself from him when [Chattopadhyaya] became a Communist'.[11] Acharya had also sent Souchy his articles on Chatto from 1938, which Souchy passed on to Rocker. Pleased to hear from Acharya again, Souchy remarked upon Acharya's unique position in the international anarchist movement: 'I think he is the only comrade we have in India'.[12] Rocker responded about a month later:

> [o]f course, I remember Acharya, and it was very interesting for me to hear from him through you. I think you are right: he is probably the only Indian comrade we have. There are a number of intellectuals who are close to our thought, but we do not know how that develops. Nationalism has flourished there, as it has everywhere in Asia, and this ghostly light must probably burn out before people become receptive to other ideas.[13]

Rocker also appreciated the news about Chatto. 'Your message about Chatto surprised us both greatly', Rocker replied. 'We always thought that he returned to India, and since he went completely missing, we believed that he might have died because he was no longer a young man either. It was certainly not wise of him to venture back into the Russian cauldron'.[14] Rocker's comments reflect his friendship with and admiration of Chatto. In another letter to Rocker, Souchy remarked about Acharya: '[h]e is very active, despite being 62 years old. In the *Bombay Chronicle*, he publishes work by Emma Goldman, by you, by me; in all, he does an extraordinary amount of work to spread anarchist ideas in India'.[15] In addition to these old friends, Diego Abad de Santillan, too, must have made contact with Acharya soon, for in December 1946, de Santillan wrote to Rocker about Acharya's publishing plans in India.[16]

201

ANARCHY OR CHAOS

Acharya also reached out to his ultra-leftist friends. In early 1947, he reconnected with Ruth Fischer and her secretary, Kate Ruminov (nee Käthe Friedländer). Having moved to New York in 1941, Fischer dissented from the Stalinist communist line and soon became involved in secret work exposing communists for the US government and was writing her book *Stalin and German Communism* (1948).[17] Ruminov, Acharya shortly after wrote to Yelensky, 'is a very capable woman'.[18] Acharya sent Fischer some of his articles and in return received Fischer's *Newsletter* and *International Correspondence* for reprint in Indian magazines and was placed on Fischer's regular mailing list. Ruminov also inquired about Nachman's artist career and asked Acharya for his opinion on Roy's new periodical *The Marxian Way*—a paper that 'smacks of the old German social-democratic publications of the last century', Acharya had said to Aldred—and invited Acharya to contribute analyses of Stalinist influences in India for Fischer's publication.[19] Basil Ruminov, then separated from Kate and living in New York, had also sent greetings to Acharya through Guy Aldred's paper *The Word*.[20] Shortly after, however, Acharya appears to have lost contact with Fischer and the Ruminovs. As he wrote to Nicolaas Steelink only seven months later:

> I do not know what became of Ruth Fischer in New York who was going to publish a book on Stalin and was conducting the *Russian State Party* bulletin. I do not get these anymore. I suppose she is also persecuted because she exposed a commie agent. I had another friend, a Russian and his German wife there, who stopped writing me suddenly. They were in touch with Fischer. The German wife was translator to Ernst Toller in California and had a translation office in Los Angeles. She is a very capable worker.[21]

From Acharya's letter to Steelink, it is also apparent that he was in contact with the Australian council communist James Dawson, editor of the *Southern Advocate for Workers' Council*, a paper that Acharya placed in the libraries of the Bombay Union of Journalists and the Royal Asiatic Society alongside Steelink's *Industrial Worker* bundles. In fact, Steelink had suggested to Acharya that he should start an IWW group in India, which Acharya found impossible at the moment. However, by importing anarchist and council communist periodicals from across the world and making them available to these libraries,

202

TOWARDS FREEDOM

Acharya tried to introduce anarchist philosophy into India's intelligentsia, aware of the importance of libraries for this project.

Acharya's warnings against Roy, however, did not prevent Fischer from maintaining correspondence with him. In fact, when Fischer visited India between October 1951 and March 1952, she met Roy, and she must have considered visiting Acharya as well, as Korsch asked her to send his greetings to Acharya.[22] Whether Fischer did so is uncertain, but their correspondence, as well as the letters from Ruminov and Korsch, is evidence of the continuance of the global 'ultra-leftist' networks that Acharya had established twenty years earlier in Berlin. At the same time, the break in communication with Fischer and the Ruminovs also suggests that some of these connections and solidarities were fragile.

Building an anarchist movement in India

Acharya was not the only one to resume contact with the international anarchist movement (see Chapter 13). Lotvala soon reached out to Rocker again, asking for copies of *Nationalism and Culture* and *Anarcho-Syndicalism* (1938).[23] Whereas Lotvala was sceptical of anarchism when he read about it in the late 1930s, having since read the important works of Proudhon and Kropotkin, he was now 'very much impressed' by anarchism and wanted to publish extracts from Rocker's work in his paper *The Indian Sociologist*, the new organ of the IIS.[24] As he said: 'India is a vast country, and it will be very useful if we do our bit to spread libertarian ideas'.[25] In late November 1946, Lotvala sent Rocker six copies of the pamphlet *Socialism and the State* (1946), excerpted from *Nationalism and Culture*, lamenting that the proofs were bad 'due to the pamphlet published in a small country town due to the difficulty of printing in Bombay'.[26]

Throughout 1947, Lotvala remained in contact with Rocker, asking for permission to print *Anarcho-Syndicalism* in India, preferably with a new epilogue by Rocker, and informing Rocker that he had founded the Libertarian Publishing House with the aim of spreading anarchist literature. He explained that 'India is backward. Almost in a feudal state due to Imperialist domination and we expect great help from you Americans for our Renaissance. Ours is the poorest country

ANARCHY OR CHAOS

in the civilized world'.[27] Rocker obliged Lotvala's request and wrote a new epilogue for the book, which was published by Modern Publishers in Indore in August 1947.[28]

The Indian Sociologist soon became an anarchist organ, featuring articles by classic anarchists such as C. A. Smith and W. J. Taylor as well as advertisements for *Freedom*, Guy Aldred's *The Word*, William B. Greene's *Mutual Banking* (1850), Mikhail Bakunin's *God and the State* (1882), and an article entitled 'What is Libertarian Socialism?', among other things, all of which could be purchased at the Libertarian Book Depot, Arya Bhavan, Sandhurst Road in Bombay.[29] However, Acharya did not contribute to the periodical and, aside from Lotvala's editorial comments, there were no other Indians among the contributors.

Acharya had joined the managing committee of the IIS in October 1945 but had little immediate input into the organisation and *The Indian Sociologist*.[30] Indeed, as he wrote to Armand: 'I am the only man in India who writes from a libertarian standpoint. But recently one or two bourgeois fellows are interested in propagating libertarianism'.[31] However, he still joined Lotvala's efforts to build up an anarchist library within the IIS and asked Armand for works by Malatesta, Bakunin, Nettlau, a copy of Sebastian Faure's *Encyclopedie Anarchiste* (1934), as well as Armand's new periodical *L'Unique*. He explained more about Lotvala's project and conversion to anarchism to Yelensky:

> [t]here are no syndicalists or anarchists here: The result of foreign rule. But since some years, one rich man is interesting himself in anarchism and has published Bakunin's *God and The State* recently and is bringing out Rocker's *Anarcho-Syndicalism*. He is keeping a stock of *Freedom* publications for distribution and selling. It took me 12 years to bring him to the present view.[32]

In return, Acharya received the Chicago-based Russian-language anarchist paper *Dielo Truda-Probuzhdenie*, edited by Grigori Maximoff, from Yelensky and explained:

> [w]e want to make a collection of anarchist and syndicalist literature even in non-English languages for the library he is conducting. We would like to have all the works of Nettlau, if possible, in German. If you can get a copy of James Guillaume's *Internationale*, he will buy it. I select the books for the library. Even the University of Bombay

204

TOWARDS FREEDOM

wants to buy all anarchist classical literature in English and even some in French and German. Russian is useless for them.[33]

Acharya explained to Yelensky that his wife was Russian and could translate the contents for him. While Acharya helped Lotvala establish a library with anarchist literature at the IIS, he had to find other venues for his own writings. Since sometime during the Second World War, Acharya was writing regularly for the daily *Kaiser-i-Hind*, often under the pseudonym Marco Polo. As he confessed to Yelensky:

> I do write in a weekly one article a week and sometimes in a monthly. I shall send you cuttings of such articles. They pay poorly, but I go on because I can tell something. I generally discuss the problems anarchistically, although they are capitalist papers. Even labour papers will not publish such articles. I want to stir up a discussion on anarchist economics, which I think will be useful. I have my own ideas on it.[34]

In his extensive correspondence with Yelensky throughout 1947 and 1948, Acharya recounted his involvement with many prominent anarchists and left-wing radicals in the US, Russia, and Berlin. He had known Berkman and Havel in New York and met Berkman again in Moscow, he said. In Russia, he had worked with Mashidsky and Nicolai Ragdaev as well as Sam Shulman—an 'anarchist in the US before he returned to Russia. I think he is executed!', Acharya wrote—and Izya Shkolnikov 'who was a union organiser of clothing workers in the USA. He was implicated in a bomb plot against Lenin. He was arrested in Moscow in 1922 and I heard he died in prison after he became mad'.[35] Acharya lamented the recent deaths of Alexander Schapiro and Luigi Bertoni and asked Yelensky for news about Max Eastman's wife Elena Krylenko as well as Jacques Doubinsky, Borghi, Volin (Vsevolod Mikhailovich Eikhenbaum), and Myasnikov.[36] Through Yelensky, Acharya also made contact with John Cherney, another exiled Russian anarchist in the US, to ask for information about Abba Gordin, with whom he had worked in the ARA.[37]

Acharya's correspondence with Yelensky and Armand bear witness to his extensive networks and interactions with the global radical left throughout his long revolutionary career. At the same time, while Acharya received anarchist literature from across the world and in many languages, through these contacts he soon contributed to inter-

205

ANARCHY OR CHAOS

national anarchist periodicals such as Armand's *L'Unique*, *Tierra y Libertad* (Mexico), *Der Freiheitliche Sozialist* (Germany), and *Inquietud* (Uruguay), and delivered public talks on anarchism in Bombay.[38] Many of his articles from *Kaiser-i-Hind* were reprinted in *Freedom* and *L'Adunata dei Refrattari*, which is further evidence of the global circulation of Acharya's anarchist thoughts in the post-war period.

At the same time, Lotvala's political ideology was undergoing some change due to Acharya's influences.[39] As Lotvala explained to Rocker: 'I am trying my comrades here to change the name of the Indian Institute of Sociology to Libertarian Institute and the name of our journal to *Libertarian Socialist* so that it may have a definite characteristic nomenclature'.[40] On the eve of Indian independence (see Chapter 15), the IIS decided to change its name to the Libertarian Socialist Institute (LSI) and the name of its organ to the *Libertarian Socialist*. Advocating libertarian socialism, Lotvala explained that 'in order that it may be distinguished from the totalitarian or dictatorial one, it had to be named Libertarian Socialist Institute'.[41] The LSI had a clear anarchist profile and declared that '[w]e offer no blueprints of future society, no handed-down programme, no ready-made philosophy. We do not ask you to follow us. We ask you to stop depending on others for leadership and to think and act for yourselves'.[42] While Acharya's ideas influenced Lotvala, and he was on the managing committee of the LSI, Acharya never published in *The Libertarian Socialist* but soon sought out different anarchist relations across the world. Indeed, the differences between Lotvala and Acharya, and Acharya's exclusion from both *The Indian Sociologist* and *The Libertarian Socialist*, were detrimental to the formation of an indigenous Indian anarchist movement.

International anarchist relations

Acharya was not the only figure who had been disconnected from the international anarchist movement by the war. The movement itself had been shattered. To re-establish international relations, in February 1946 European anarchists held a preliminary meeting in Paris and set up the Secrétariat Provisoire aux Relations Internationales (SPRI). In early 1948, the SPRI started planning for a world congress of anar-

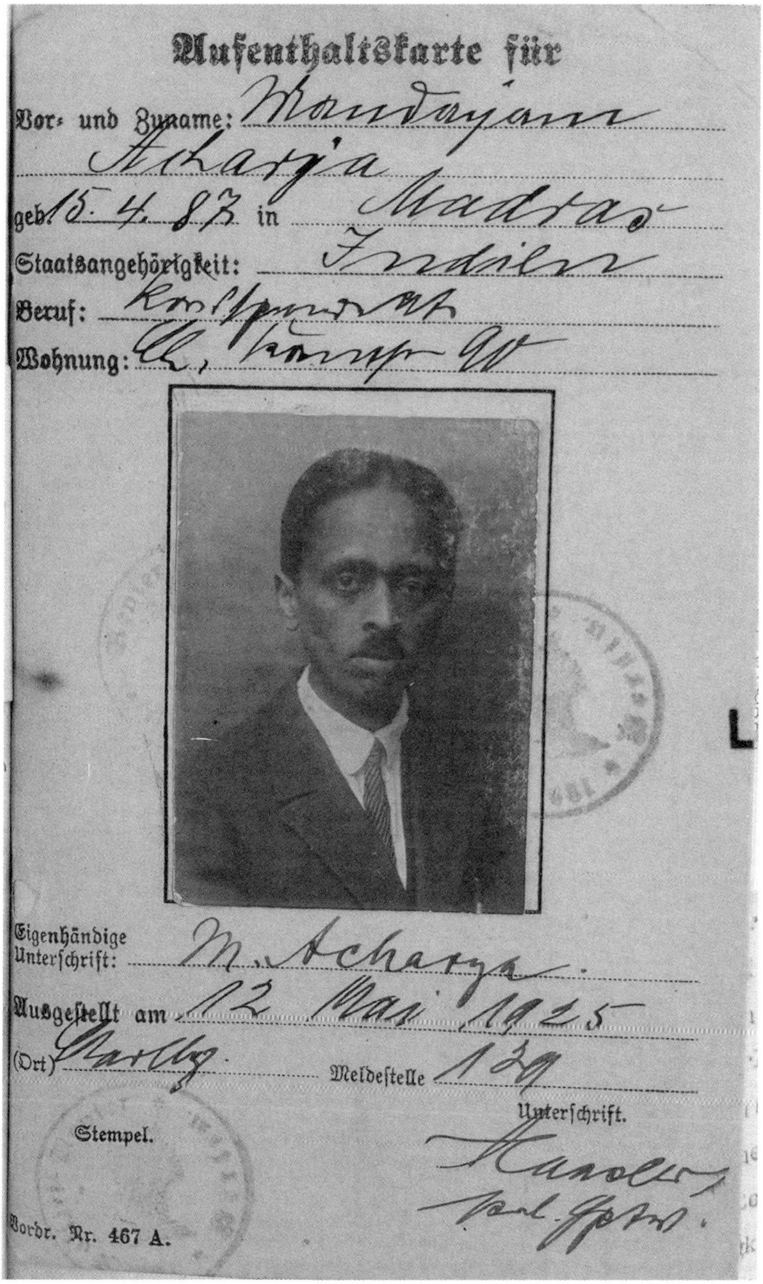

Fig. 12: Mandayam Acharya, residence permit, Berlin, 12 May 1925.

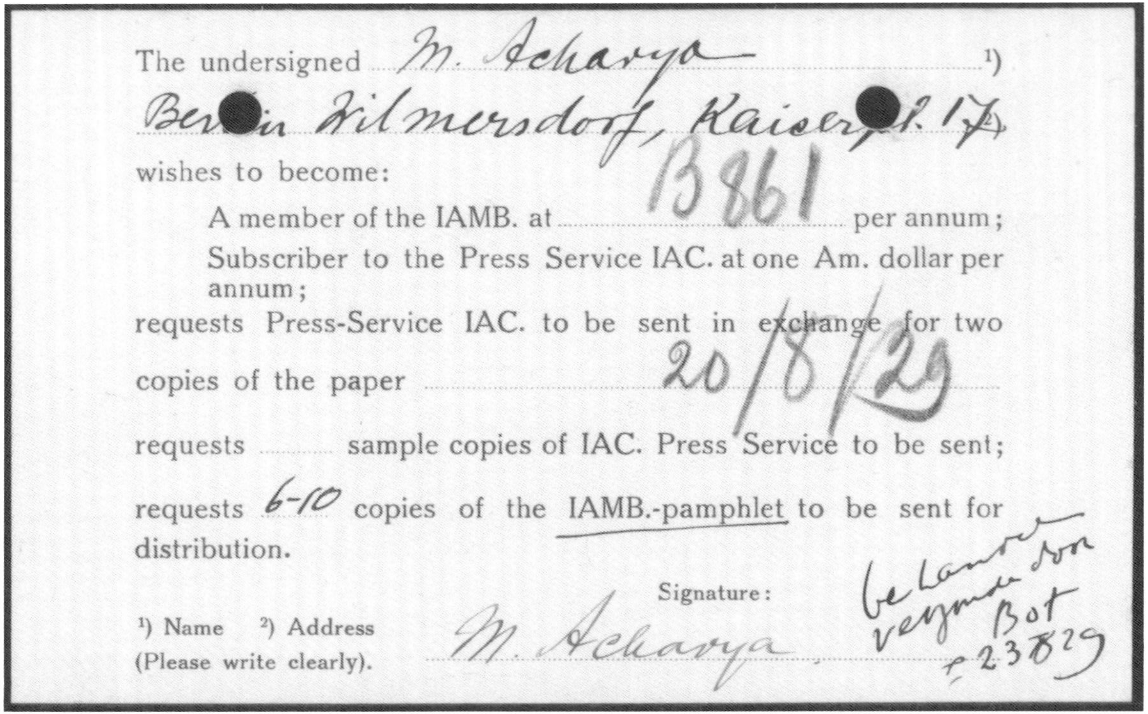

The undersigned *M. Acharya*   [1]

Berlin Wilmersdorf, Kaiser A. 17

wishes to become:

   A member of the IAMB. at .... *B 861* .... per annum;

   Subscriber to the Press Service IAC. at one Am. dollar per annum;

requests Press-Service IAC. to be sent in exchange for two

copies of the paper .... *20/8/29* ....

requests .... sample copies of IAC. Press Service to be sent;

requests *6-10* copies of the IAMB.-pamphlet to be sent for distribution.

                                          Signature :

[1] Name   [2] Address   *M. Acharya*
(Please write clearly).

Fig. 13: M. Acharya, IAMB membership card, 20 August 1929.

Fig. 14: Hindusthan Association of Central Europe, Berlin, protest meeting against Gandhi's arrest, 6 May 1930. Saumyendranath Tagore is speaking, Acharya is sitting on the floor in the back, and to the right is Jaya Surya Naidu.

Fig. 15: M. P. T. Acharya, Bombay, c. 1935.

Fig. 16: Close-up of M. P. T. Acharya, Bombay, c. 1935.

Fig. 17: M. P. T. Acharya, Bombay, 13 September 1935. Back of the photo reads: 'Myself on a hot night on my bed. Before me on the table an AEG electric fan'.

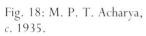

Fig. 18: M. P. T. Acharya, c. 1935.

Fig. 19: Magda Nachman outside their home at 56 Ridge Road, Bombay, c. 1937.

Fig. 20: Institute of Foreign Languages, Bombay, 13 April 1951. Nachman exhibition, the day after her death. Acharya with the back to the camera.

Fig. 21: M. P. T. Acharya, *c.* 1950s.

TOWARDS FREEDOM

chists to be held in Paris. In preparation for this world congress, Araceli Rodriguez, treasurer of the SPRI, contacted Acharya and asked for his opinions on this proposition. Acharya agreed 'with the necessity for an international Anarchist Congress and also its urgency'.[43] He felt that war or civil war would soon break out, economics and states would collapse, and that neither Bolshevism nor capitalism would re-emerge after the chaos. 'Hence the anarchists alone have the chance of putting society on a living basis', he argued.[44] 'Although anarchism is the oldest socialist movement, it will be the final movement to succeed'.[45] However, Acharya foresaw several problems with hosting a world congress: first, 'anarchists may have no money to come there. Then the passport and visa difficulties will arise. Only a few could manage to come illegally or under false passports'.[46] Second, he was concerned that 'the police, the communists, the socialists, and liberals and Fascists will try to prevent its being held or will even break it up'.[47] Lastly, he felt that 'as the Congress cannot last more than a week or fortnight, it cannot finish discussing and resolving all questions within that time'.[48] Ultimately, however, Acharya conceded that 'it is good to hold as big a congress as possible'.[49]

Before proceeding with the congress, Acharya suggested that it would be good 'to ask all individuals, groups, and organisations to send in writing to the SPRI to say what they want as anarchist society'.[50] He felt that anarchists should agree on what to do after the revolution, after states had been overthrown, and provide workable solutions. Otherwise, there would be 'chaos among anarchists on the morrow of the revolution'.[51] These propositions would then have to be circulated among anarchists in advance of the congress and the SPRI should serve as a 'clearing house of all such information'.[52] The chief issue to be discussed among anarchists, Acharya said, was the question of economics. The theories of Bakunin, Proudhon, and Kropotkin were no longer viable unless anarchists devoted more attention to organising economics, an issue he had tackled in his article 'Les Trusts et la Démocratie', which he appended to his letter to Rodriguez. Acharya concluded that

> I would like to come to an international anarchist congress, but I doubt very much if I can manage to do so, firstly, because I have weak health, secondly, I cannot pay the expenses, and, thirdly, because one

207

ANARCHY OR CHAOS

Congress cannot finish the subject, even if police troubles will not cut it short.[53]

Two months later, from 15 to 17 May 1948, the European Anarchist Congress was held in Paris at which the Commission for International Anarchist Relations (CRIA) replaced the SPRI.[54] In addition to preparing for a world congress, CRIA established three aims: '(a) to publish a regular bulletin of correspondence in various languages; (b) to induce into practical solidarity the disconnected federations, groups, and militants of the International; (c) to start the setting of international archives and of an exchange net of publications all over the world'.[55] Based in Paris, the new CRIA would be staffed by three figures, 'respectively appointed by the French FA, the Spanish movement in exile, and the Spartacus group of German-speaking anarchists of Paris'.[56] Although initially centred in Europe, CRIA was a concerted attempt to create a globally connected anarchist movement with no centre of power that allowed for connections between and across regional anarchist groups and individuals.

Asian anarchism

While efforts were underway to establish an international anarchist movement, Acharya reached out to anarchists across Asia and Australia.[57] In late November 1948, he contacted the Japanese anarchist Taiji Yamaga, secretary of the Japanese Anarchist Federation (JAF), having obtained his address from the Chinese anarchist Li Pei Kan (Ba Jin), requesting copies of the *Proleta Jurnalo*, the organ of the JAF, and asking Yamaga to publish his articles in their periodical. Unsatisfied with Lotvala's hold on the *Libertarian Socialist*—'I cannot get this old man to publish what I write', Acharya said—he suggested to Yamaga:

> I think we must have a magazine of discussion for Asia. It can only be in English for the present. If such a magazine is started, I can write much on anarchist problems, but from the economic angle .... I think we can make the magazine useful even for Western comrades.[58]

Yamaga agreed to translate and publish Acharya's articles and asked Acharya for news about Li Pei Kan's situation in Shanghai. In the meantime, one of Acharya's articles had appeared in Dawson's

208

TOWARDS FREEDOM

Southern Advocate for Workers' Council, which he appended to his next letter to Yamaga, and he had asked Dawson to contact Yamaga as well. Another contributor to the *Southern Advocate for Workers' Council* was the Australian author and pacifist Kenneth Joseph Kenafick, whom Acharya also urged Yamaga to contact.[59] Acharya confessed to Yamaga that 'I do not know what became of Com. Li Pei Kan in this turmoil in Shanghai and I hope he will go to a safe place and will write me from there'.[60]

In his initial letters to Yamaga, Acharya recollected his activities within the anarchist movement in the 1920s to 1930s, mentioning Souchy, Berkman, and Rocker, as well as Japanese anarchists Takamure Itsue, Yoshi Aso, and E. K. Nobushima, to assert his anarchist credentials.[61] Shortly after writing to Yamaga, Acharya contacted Roger Nash Baldwin, the founder and executive director of the American Civil Liberties Union, whom he had met in Berlin in the mid-1920s, and requested material for dissemination in India. Acharya informed Baldwin that he knew K. B. Menon, the first general secretary of the now defunct Indian Civil Liberties Union, originally set up by Nehru in 1936, and lamented that Baldwin had not visited India after his visit to Japan and Korea.[62] Baldwin also regretted that he could not visit India but wrote that 'my job in Japan and Korea was all I could handle'.[63] He sent Acharya the requested material and urged him to contact Kailash Nath Mehra, who was reorganising the Indian Civil Liberties Union. At the same time, Baldwin wrote to Mehra and suggested that he should contact Acharya.[64]

Acharya's correspondence with Li Pei Kan, Yamaga, Dawson, and Kenafick, as well as Baldwin in the US, suggest that he was also looking eastwards to build up new anarchist connections that would re-orient the radical dialogues both within India but also across Asia. His extensive correspondence with anarchists across Europe, North America, South America, Asia, and Australia is evidence of Acharya's unique position as a relatively solitary anarchist in India but at the same time a well-known figure connected globally.

World anarchism

Acharya brought his new connections across Asia into debates about international anarchism. In May 1949, CRIA solicited responses to

ANARCHY OR CHAOS

specific questions from anarchists across the world in preparation for the World Congress of Anarchists to be held in Paris in November 1949.[65] As Acharya had suggested to Yamaga, he was keen to strengthen anarchist connections across Asia and made this clear in his response. In his statement, Acharya, 'belonging to no group, at home or abroad', gave a brief account of the situation of anarchism in India and mentioned the LSI's efforts to publish anarchist literature and set up a library as well as some vague interest in anarchism.[66] He reiterated many of the points provided to the SPRI the previous year, but emphasised the need to focus on economics, internationalism, and non-violence to reach a broader audience beyond anarchists.

CRIA had asked for opinions about anarchist ideological principles. Acharya felt that ideology could not be debated until economic principles had been settled. In fact, anarchists would have to appeal to other movements to show how their systems were wrong and that, conversely, anarchist economics, i.e., the abolition of wages and prices, would be the only workable system. Following the collapse of the present wage-price system, '[t]here would rather be chaos. Anarchists are trying to prevent it'.[67] Putting anarchist economics into practice would mean abandoning the wage-system, thus abolishing employer/employee relations and the class system altogether, Acharya argued that anarchists were not 'trying to do what is impossible which is what all political parties are trying to do and only try to do what is possible'.[68] This was central to Acharya's thesis: '[t]he choice between mankind is either <u>anarchy or chaos</u>'.[69]

While he felt that federalism and cooperatives were effective non-hierarchical structures, these were often promoted on a national basis. Anarchism and CRIA itself had to be an 'international organisation with an international system of liaison', Acharya argued, and suggested that '[w]e should have three liaison centres [in] Europe, America, and Asia. For Asia, India or Japan may be chosen'.[70] These centres should serve only as clearing houses for distributing and exchanging information, and members should be nominated according to regional convenience. In India, however, 'where there is no group', Acharya noted, 'there can only be an individual who may be recognised'.[71] To build up a truly international movement, it was crucial to establish archives and publish literature. The Joseph A. Labadie Collection at the

TOWARDS FREEDOM

University of Michigan was already doing great work, Acharya said. However, he recommended that these archives 'should be distributed as they are likely to be confiscated by authorities or damaged in fire or wars'.[72] To ensure this, Acharya proposed '[o]ne archive for Asia and America in addition to several in Europe'.[73] On the question of spreading anarchist literature, it would be necessary to print classics by Bakunin, Malatesta, and Guillaume in addition to regional literature. However, the issue of language was difficult, Acharya admitted. Korean, Japanese, and Chinese anarchists often used Esperanto in their foreign correspondence, but this was not widely understood outside those countries.[74] English, French, Spanish, and German were more widely spoken languages, according to different colonial histories, but even these were unevenly distributed across the colonial world. By contrast, the Korean anarchists submitted to the CRIA that it was necessary to use Esperanto to spread propaganda.[75] What is more, said Acharya, illiteracy was widespread in many Asian countries, making it difficult to reach the masses, but an intellectual movement would still be valuable initially.

Acharya advocated a broader movement that included anarchist youth movements and women's movements as integral to the international anarchist movement itself. Similarly, he did not want to antagonise religious anarchists, e.g., Tolstoyans, and proposed an open, inclusive movement. In the wake of the Second World War, questions of violence, armed resistance, and non-violence remained central to anarchist debates. Having been involved in anti-militarist debates since the 1920s, Acharya advocated methods of 'strike, boycott, passive resistance, and civil disobedience on a large scale'.[76] However, he also conceded that, 'if violence is used against them, they must defend themselves even with violence in order to disarm violence'.[77] Anarchists, he argued, 'depend more on social solidarity to establish Anarchy'.[78] He warned, though, that 'armed defence may be organised in an emergency but should not be continued because organised armed defence, if maintained, will lead to a class of people who live only by maintaining themselves by arms'.[79] While Acharya foresaw many problems facing CRIA and the establishment of an international anarchist movement, he remained involved in this organisation (see Chapter 16). However, CRIA struggled with inter-

ANARCHY OR CHAOS

nal differences between anarchist groups across France and the UK, which illuminated the difficulties of anarchist organising after the Second World War. Similarly, while it was resolved to establish an Asian branch of CRIA at the World Congress of Anarchists in November 1949, this never materialised.[80]

Cut off from the international anarchist movement by the war, throughout 1945 and 1946 Acharya reached out to friends across the world while also attempting to build an anarchist movement in India. Connecting India's libertarian tradition to global anarchism, for the first time he looked to Japan, China, Korea, and Australia for solidarity and conceptions of Asian anarchism. These networks extended to the new CRIA, where Acharya debated the future of anarchism in the post-war era, bringing India into global conversations around freedom and independence. In doing so, Acharya reoriented the global trajectories of anarchism away from Europe and the Americas to Asia and Oceania.

15

VIOLENT INDEPENDENCE

Whither India?

The US entry into the Second World War in 1941 changed the course of the war for Britain and, soon after, the Atlantic Charter inscribed the commitment to independence for many of Britain's colonies. The deployment of millions of Indian soldiers to defend the British Empire put even more pressure on the British to grant independence after the war. Shortly after the war ended, Britain initiated talks with INC leaders Jawaharlal Nehru, Vallabhbhai Patel, and Rajendra Prasad, leading to the promise of independence in 1947.

For Acharya, talks of independence and self-government had nothing to do with the real meaning of freedom. As he argued: 'the fact is that a Centralist Government cannot be self-government; will not allow individuals and nations to govern themselves. Yet, the notion, the superstition, persists that a Government, a nation, and an individual are identical—with or without representation'.[1] In India, the village councils had lost their autonomy to a central government when, in fact, Acharya argued, '[u]nless every village is self-governing there can be no country-wide self-government'.[2] The war had proved that nation-states would inevitably fail to deliver freedom, that Bolshevism and capitalism had failed, and that empires would fall. Instead, by putting anarchism on an economic basis, this would pave the way for anarchism as the only way forward.[3]

ANARCHY OR CHAOS

Acharya was partly right in his assessment that nation-states would fail to deliver freedom. Even before independence in August 1947, there were labour strikes and social unrest across the subcontinent.[4] The trade unions in India were divided, Acharya noted, all vying for the attention of the workers, but the workers would often go on strike without approval of the trade unions. All this showed 'a certain sense of solidarity without class consciousness'.[5] Workers in India were more inclined towards anarchism, but labour leaders would crush any anarchist movement to prevent their freedom and lead them down a blind alley. Without an anarchist movement 'this country will go Fascist and go to the dogs .... This country is in a wilder state than any other and any bloodshed might take place here'.[6]

Indian independence also led to partition of the subcontinent and the creation of a new nation-state in South Asia: Pakistan, led by Muhammad Ali Jinnah. While Acharya defended the right to self-determination on principles of freedom, he was immensely critical of Jinnah and, as Acharya saw it, the attendant Muslim nationalism that lay behind this new republic. This was no different than Hindu nationalism as a driving force behind patriotism and the idea of self-determination. Before the Second World War, Acharya had been sceptical of Jinnah's politics, criticising Jinnah for not aspiring for complete independence—and any meaningful sense of freedom—and only agitating against the INC. If Jinnah wanted complete independence, Acharya argued, he should boycott the constitution and constitutional methods altogether.[7] As Acharya saw it, the failure of Jinnah to do so—and of Nehru and the INC as well—led to sectarian violence in the wake of Partition:

> [t]he real solution will come only when all warring states or weak states are not supported or strengthened but fought down by their own subjects; instead of helping to make war against one another a general, social strike against states in every country. If, for example, the Pakistanis fight against their own state and the Indians to likewise, there can be solidarity between the former united people. Otherwise, there will be no peace in India and Pakistan, not to speak of peace between India and Pakistan. If such a union among peoples is attempted, both the states will unite against their respective peoples, instead of fighting one another. That is the nature of all states, whether capitalist, communist, Hindu, Muslim, theocratic, or cultural.[8]

VIOLENT INDEPENDENCE

Nationalist leaders such as Jinnah and Nehru, Acharya felt, had betrayed their own people and now pitted them against each other in defence of the state.

At the same time, with the British gone, Acharya argued, India was now under the hegemony of the US through the United Nations but still faced a threat from Russia's imperial ambitions: '[b]efore this war, "world" meant Europe even for socialists. For the communists, it means only World under Stalin's hegemony. Stalin's regime is also colonial, for the Asiatic colonies of Russia are adjoining the "mother country"'.[9] However, 'even now', Acharya also noted, '"world" means to Anglo-Americans and other Europeans only Europe and North America. Of course, other continents like Asia, Africa, and South and Central America belong to the world only as adjuncts to Anglo-American finance capital'.[10] The solution, for Acharya, was non-violent economics.

Principles of non-violent economics

When Acharya resumed contact with Armand in July 1945, he urged Armand to reprint his key article 'Les Trusts et la Démocratie' in *L'Unique*. 'It will interest people now', he hoped.[11] Nine months later, he wanted to develop his ideas further and asked Armand for a copy of the article for himself.[12] Acharya was right that the article would interest people now. Throughout 1947, Acharya corresponded with the Gandhian scholar and political philosopher Kalidas Nag and sent him a copy of the article, which by then had appeared in *Kaiser-i-Hind*.[13] Nag found Acharya's arguments intriguing and wanted to republish a part of the article with his new International University of Non-Violence. In late 1947, the second part of Acharya's article appeared as the pamphlet *Principles of Non-Violent Economics*. In the Introduction, Nag explained that,

> [w]hile developing my thoughts on the International University of Non-Violence, I got many criticisms from Educationists and Philosophers. But I was surprised to receive the first constructive ideas on the economics of non-violence from Mr. M. P. T. Acharya, prolific writer on economic subjects, of Bombay. Exchanging ideas with him, I felt that he has something very positive and useful to communicate to our generation.[14]

ANARCHY OR CHAOS

Describing Acharya as a 'Renegade Bolshevik' and 'thoroughly sceptic about the State and its capacity to adjust to the critics of human history', Nag conceded that,

> [o]ne may not agree with him, but he goes on dinning into our ears that the State of whatever form with its paraphernalia of Exchange, Money, Wages, Price level, etc., has been found wanting and that Society might replace the State as the main supreme governing agency of human relations which should be mainly regulated on the basis of production for common and direct consumption.[15]

Nag avoided the term 'anarchism' but hoped that Acharya's ideas would 'rouse the attention of many a progressive thinker'.[16] Acharya later fell out with Nag, who by 1950 disavowed the pamphlet. As Acharya wrote to the Uruguay-based Romanian anarchist Eugen Relgis (Eisig D. Sigler): '[t]he man who wrote the introduction enthusiastically does not now want to know the pamphlet! For they consider it is too idealistic, even if correct. It is not "practical immediately"'.[17] Such later disagreements aside, *Principles of Non-Violent Economics* was important as Acharya's only stand-alone published pamphlet.

What is anarchism?

With the publication of the pamphlet, Acharya reached a wider audience in India. In April 1948, the two prominent authors and frequent collaborators Iqbal Singh and Raja Rao published the anthology *Whither India? (Socio-Politico Analyses)*. Compiled at the cusp of independence, the editors noted that, '[i]n so far as Indian politics has evolved an ideological basis, it can be claimed that this has resulted in the emergence of two major trends. These are Gandhism and Marxism'.[18] Of these two trends, they claimed that Gandhism was the dominant ideology, which had its 'roots in the tradition of moral humanism of the Indian thought', but also found inspiration from 'European Utopian Reformism ranging from Rousseau through Proudhon and Kropotkin to Ruskin and Tolstoy'.[19] Their invocation of Gandhism in the tradition of utopian and anarchist thinkers such as Proudhon and Kropotkin perhaps explains why they invited Acharya to contribute a chapter on anarchism.

216

VIOLENT INDEPENDENCE

Of all the contributors to the anthology—including Nehru, Jinnah, Sastri, and Jayaprakash Narayan, among others—Acharya was the only one to write an original article. 'We must also thank Mr. M. P. T. Acharya for having been kind enough to write for us his article "What is Anarchism?"', they noted.[20] The invitation to contribute alongside these more prominent Indian leaders signals the relative dearth of anarchism in India and, at the same time, Acharya's status as a unique and authoritative figure on the subject.

In the essay, Acharya outlined the basic tenets of anarchism and its distinction from other political and philosophical ideas, especially republicanism and Bolshevism, as well as the different strands of anarchism. Writing in the context of post-colonial India, Acharya explained that government and society are inherently incompatible and that governments are, by nature, violent. By contrast, he argued, '[t]he anarchists want everyone to be rulers in their own right. They do not believe that there can be separation of interests between the representatives and represented'.[21] To speak of self-government in India was a contradictory illusion. 'Hence proxy-government is not self-government by the people', Acharya said. 'In order to have self-government by the people, each has to represent himself directly. That can be done through no state, however radical'.[22] Speaking directly to the political climate in India, Acharya argued that nation-states were born out of violence and defended their existence through violence—army, police, and jails:

> a non-violent state does not, cannot exist. All states in essence are violence, concentrated violence over society—whatever their forms and shades, just as much as autocratic absolutist kings are. To speak of non-violent society and state in the same breath is mutually contradictory. Non-violent society can therefore come into being only with the abolition or 'withering away' of states of every kind .... The anarchists are therefore the only ones who want to abolish violence over and within society.[23]

In contrast to constitutional forms of government, he emphasised, '[t]he anarchists, when they insist on non-governed society, mean government of the people, by the people, for the people, directly by the people themselves without any intermediary'.[24] Thus also giving a blueprint for how to organise post-colonial India after independence,

ANARCHY OR CHAOS

Acharya's essay provided insightful and provocative arguments. However, as he tried to give a comprehensive account of what anarchism is, Acharya failed to provide a clear and concise manifesto. Instead, the essay is somewhat repetitive and unstructured, covering ideological tenets within anarchism, methods and tactics, historical struggles, and the current state of anarchism in India. Nevertheless, the inclusion of Acharya alongside more prominent figures, in some ways, suggests that anarchism was taken more seriously in India after independence. If Gandhism was steeped in the anarchist tradition, as the editors noted, Acharya's ideas were no longer marginal but central to the future of India's political debates (see Chapter 16).

The death of non-violence

While Acharya was a committed proponent of pacifism, seeing it as integral to anarchism, and had often praised Gandhi's efforts in the 1930s, by the mid-1940s he was critical of Gandhi's saintly fame and his adherence to parliamentarian politics. 'He borrowed a few pages from Thoreau and Tolstoy, mixing their views with popular Indian conceptions of peace and "ahimsa"', Acharya had noted in March 1946.[25] However, as Gandhi still called for 'a national state, with an army, and non-violence for the people', Acharya argued, Gandhi differed from the Tolstoyans and had 'nothing to offer'.[26] By contrast, he stated, 'the anarchists and Tolstoyans of the West have fundamental ideas about pacifism that Gandhi does not want to know of'.[27] The Tolstoyans, indeed, 'do not believe that peace is possible as long as the large landed property, the sense of property in general, and the caste system remains or is left untouched'.[28] Acharya was critical of the 'Gandhist cult of non-violence' that had emerged around Gandhi and accused Gandhi of 'quackery' which meant, he feared, that everyone would lose faith in non-violence.[29]

But Acharya was not the only Indian who was upset with Gandhi. Shortly after his release from house detention in Ratnagiri in 1937, Acharya's old associate Savarkar had emerged as the leader of the right-wing Hindu nationalist party the Hindu Mahasabha, which vehemently opposed Gandhi's civil disobedience movement and had a great following in the immediate post-war years. On 30 January

VIOLENT INDEPENDENCE

1948, Nathuram Godse, a devoted Savarkar-follower and member of the Hindu Mahasabha and the extreme right-wing group Rashtriya Swayamsevak Sangh, assassinated Gandhi in New Delhi.[30]

During his imprisonment in the Cellular Jail in the Andamans, Savarkar frequently petitioned the British for mercy, even turning away from his anti-British militancy of his youth. Instead, his new enemies were India's Muslims. While Savarkar at times had vented his anti-Muslim sentiments at the weekly meetings at India House during Acharya's tenure there (see Chapter 1), these evolved into the articulation of *Hindutva* in his *Essentials of Hindutva* (1923). Distinguished from the pluralistic notion of Hinduism, *Hindutva* was ethno-religious, territorial, and violently militant, steeped in ideas of blood and soil, and conceived Muslims as India's internal enemies. What is more, as Shruti Kapila argues, *Hindutva* was 'pitted against the dominant form of nationalism [and] emerged strictly in the context of Gandhi and his political ideas and practices'.[31] Since the early 1930s, Godse had come under the spell of Savarkar, who was once again pulling the strings behind the scenes rather than acting himself, and consequently Godse internalised the anti-Muslim violence espoused by the Hindu Mahasabha and the Rashtriya Swayamsevak Sangh.[32] The assassination sent shockwaves throughout India, prompting Savarkar to condemn Godse and the act.[33] Godse and his co-conspirators were immediately apprehended after the assassination and stood trial in late May 1948. Despite his denunciation of Godse, Savarkar was soon implicated and faced trial alongside Godse. However, through a carefully crafted confession and legal circumventions, Godse assumed sole responsibility for the assassination, denying a larger conspiracy and thus ultimately absolving Savarkar of any responsibility.[34]

While Gandhi's assassination shook India, one dissident anarchist was less upset. In the pages of *The Word*, Guy Aldred covered the trial extensively and defended Savarkar and the Hindu Mahasabha:

> [t]he outstanding fighter for Indian Freedom has been V. D. Savarkar, whose struggles and sufferings and thought overshadows even the work and character of Tilak, who was no mean fighter and an outstanding hero of the Independence movement. The [Hindu] Mahasabha was and is the outstanding nationalist organisation of India.[35]

ANARCHY OR CHAOS

Throughout the next few years, Aldred, in turn, received praise from Hindu Mahasabhists such as Om P. Kahol, the general secretary.[36] Lotvala, it seems, also supported the Hindu Mahasabha against the INC. As he wrote to Aldred: '[i]t is regrettable that the Hindu Mahasabha has a good number of rich persons as its members, but [they] are very stingy, and it is therefore that this organisation cannot fight the totalitarian and reactionary Congress Organisation'.[37]

Acharya, on the other hand, was more critical. He reminded Aldred that it was Gandhi who put the independence movement on a mass basis. Recounting his association with Savarkar in London, Acharya conceded that he had respect for Savarkar for 'having suffered 15 years in the Andamans' but also noted that, because of his imprisonment, 'his mind has not grown'.[38] However, Savarkar's greatest mistake, Acharya stated, was that he became leader of the Hindu Mahasabha instead of agitating outside party politics. While taking the opportunity to criticise Jinnah's agitation for a separate Muslim state, Savarkar's articulation of *Hindutva* did not 'justify Savarkar in putting religion before politics'.[39] The Hindu Mahasabha, Acharya argued, had no social political programme and sided with 'Brahmin landlords'. In leading this organisation of 'blacker reactionaries', Savarkar had wasted his political fervour and 'ended politically nowhere' and was now 'old and too decrepit to do anything'.[40] Aldred would later criticise Acharya for not siding with him in his support of Savarkar (see Epilogue). However, in his unwavering support of Savarkar in the name of anti-imperialism, Aldred failed to acknowledge the authoritarian tendencies in Savarkar and the Hindu Mahasabha and allowed *The Word* to become an outlet for religious hatred and bigotry.[41]

Reminiscences of Indian revolutionaries abroad

While Acharya refrained from commenting further on Savarkar, he reconnected with old friends from the Indian revolutionary movement of the early twentieth century. In fact, in his letters to Souchy, Acharya noted that he had been in touch with his old friend Khankhoje, who had migrated to Mexico in 1924 and become a renowned agricultural scientist: 'I wrote to my friend Khankhoje to find how you

VIOLENT INDEPENDENCE

are doing. But it appears that Khankhoje left for India for good soon after.'[42] Khankhoje went to India in 1951 and returned to Mexico in 1953, before settling in Poona in 1954 and spending the rest of his life in independent India.[43] In the letter to Souchy, Acharya also lamented the death of Heramba Lal Gupta on 28 April 1950 in Mexico City. Gupta had gone to Mexico even before Khankhoje and spent the rest of his life there.[44] From Acharya's letters, it appears that Souchy knew these two veteran Indian revolutionaries in Mexico, although nothing further is known of their connection.

It was perhaps through Khankhoje that Acharya also came into contact with Lanka Sundaram, who set up the Indian Revolutionaries Abroad Commemoration Committee (IRACC) in August 1950 with the aim of collecting and publishing information about the Indian exiled revolutionary struggle.[45] Sundaram invited the public to send 'information anecdotes, documents, pictures, etc., dealing with the activities of Indian revolutionaries abroad'.[46] The IRACC included contributions from Acharya, Khankhoje, Pratap, Taraknath Das, and S. R. Rana, while Savarkar was conspicuously absent. To persuade Rana, Sundaram remarked that 'Sri M. P. T. Acharya, Sri Pandurang Khankhoje and others of the Old Guard are recording these reminiscences'.[47] The commemorative project was 'expected to take over three years to complete', and a notice in the *Indian Daily Mail* confirms that Acharya contributed some documents to the IRACC.[48]

In the tumultuous years after independence, as violence erupted across the subcontinent, Acharya's life and political ideas gained more currency within India. The chaos of independence, Acharya felt, was to be replaced by anarchy and non-violent economics, and not a new nation-state. At the same time, connecting four decades of revolutionary activities abroad, Acharya's letters to Souchy—and vicariously Khankhoje—signal the entangled lives of Indian anticolonialists and anarchists in exile. However, it was clear that Acharya was committed more to anarchism than Indian nationalism. Indeed, his denouncement of both Gandhian party politics as well as Savarkar's Hindu Mahasabha is evidence of a different vision of freedom, rooted in non-violence and internationalism rather than the violent and nationalist convulsions that had characterised India's newly gained independence.

16

ANARCHY

The hypocrisy of Indian pacifism

After Gandhi's death, his ideas soon disappeared from mainstream Indian politics and attention was diverted towards positioning India in Cold War politics.[1] However, Acharya did not abandon pacifism and non-violence but articulated a different vision of anarchist non-violence in the post-colonial and global context. In the early Cold War period, Acharya felt that another war was on the horizon, which would cause chaos and class and caste conflict, eventually leading to the dictatorship of one group. Against this, Acharya warned, '[i]f we do not want dictatorship, we should get on without States, which means without money and exchange. The question is whether we will get even dictatorship. We may get only banditism'.[2]

In December 1949, pacifists from across the world met in the small Indian town of Santiniketan for the World Pacifist Meeting.[3] Originally planned by Gandhi in collaboration with the WRI, the conference was purportedly held in the spirit of Gandhian non-violence and internationalism. For Acharya, who did not attend, however, it was doubtful that the conference would follow Gandhi's ideals. As he said: '[t]he followers of Gandhi are more respectable than Gandhi himself. Now Gandhiji is no more. They have constituted themselves as authorities (Dictators) of Gandhi-ism and pacifism. Their pacifism will be of the status quo type, for the Indian Gandhians have now a state in their hand to wield'.[4] In contrast to Tolstoy's ideals of refusing to obey governments, these Gandhians were hypocrites for holding on to state power and perpetuating violence through government institutions. While the British were now gone, Acharya charged, '[m]asters are masters, whether native or foreign, and there can be no peace with master and servant relations, whether that relation is voluntarily accepted or not. Voluntary servitude is still servitude'.[5]

After the conference, Acharya reflected on the event, noting that the president of the meeting, Rajendra Prasad, also the president of the WRI, defended himself for abandoning Gandhian principles, as Gandhi was no longer alive, and stating that the establishment of an army was necessary. For Acharya, indeed, these Gandhians had 'completely abandoned the pacifist camp and are organising vast forces to oppress and dominate the people into subordination and misery for the benefit of an increasingly strong state'.[6] The new government of India under Prasad, Acharya criticised, 'under the pretence of "rights to independence", takes away civil liberties, and is worse than the previous British imperialist constitution'.[7] To the Sweden-based German anarchist Helmut Rüdiger, Acharya was even more blunt: '[t]hese Gandhians have become humbugs: They are tasting political power, which they are allowed to do owing to foreign governments. They have to fight as subordinates of Anglo-Americans whether they like it or not'.[8]

Anarchism in exile

Acharya's letters to Rüdiger signalled an internationalism in his articulation of pacifism that led to extensive correspondence with the French anarchist pacifist movement. He had resumed his longstanding correspondence with Armand and received *L'Unique* regularly. In *L'Unique*, *La Vie au Soleil*, and *Le Libertaire*, Acharya wrote about Japanese customs around nudity and the body, and in *Etudes Anarchistes* he wrote about the trade unions in India.[9] His article on the World Pacifist Meeting for the French pacifist paper *Les Nouvelles Pacifistes* brought him into contact with the editor Louis Louvet, a staunch

ANARCHY

anarchist pacifist, which carried on through the periodical *Contre-Courant* a few years later.

Another contributor to *Les Nouvelles Pacifistes* was Eugen Relgis, the South American representative of CRIA. Through the contacts of the Galician anarchist José Tato Lorenzo, editor of the Uruguayan anarchist paper *Inquietud*, to which Acharya had contributed, Relgis wrote to Acharya in early 1950 and sent him his book *Los Principios Humanitaristas* (1922).[10] Acharya responded in late March, giving an account of his international revolutionary life across several continents and countries and wrote that '[a]lthough I agree with you in your humanitarian and pacifist views I find after my experience with pacifists and working with them that something is wanting'.[11] He criticised prominent pacifists such as Bertrand Russell, Aldous Huxley, and J. B. Priestley for thinking in dualist terms, either fascism or Bolshevism, and not economic terms. Acharya included a copy of *Principles of Non-Violent Economics*, which he had also sent to Lorenzo, and reiterated his thoughts on anarchist economics. His unorthodox ideas, Acharya also noted, often fell on deaf ears in India, and at the time he found more sympathetic readers in the international anarchist movement.

In mid-September 1949, *Freedom* editor Lilian Wolfe wrote to the Swedish anarchist Bert Ekengren, an editor on the SAC daily *Arbetaren*, that Acharya wanted to 'correspond with him in English or German'.[12] When Acharya first wrote to Ekengren in late October 1949, as when he wrote to Relgis, he gave a lengthy account of his international revolutionary life, noting that he had lived in Sweden during the First World War, where he had visited Stockholm, Jönköping, and Gothenburg and met several notable Swedish socialists (see Chapter 5).[13] Acharya recounted his association with Albert Jensen, John Andersson, and Rüdiger during his time in Berlin, and noted that he had sent a copy of *Whither India?* to Andersson and, in return, received the *IWMA Press Service* (in Swedish) but, alas, no written reply from Andersson. Andersson was ill, Ekengren informed him, thus he could not reply. Through Rüdiger, Ekengren arranged for *Die Freie Gesellschaft* to be sent to India, and Acharya also received the Swedish anarchist papers *Arbetaren*, *Brand*, *Fritt Forum*, and *Storm*, as he could read Swedish but not write it, he said. Shortly after, he asked

ANARCHY OR CHAOS

Ekengren for a Swedish-English small dictionary with next shipment of anarchist papers.[14]

Acharya lamented that, whereas Japan and China had longer histories of anarchist movements, '[i]n India, there is no libertarian movement', though the LSI's efforts to build up a library and print anarchist literature were making progress.[15] Indeed, he noted, '[a]s the economic conditions are getting worse and the labour parties and trade unions are making a muddle, some people will be influenced by reading libertarian books and journals'.[16] However, this was an intellectual movement: '[a]s 95% of the people are illiterate and they have no chance of reading even in their own mother tongue, only intellectuals can approach them. As I do not speak or write in any Indian language well, I can only try to work on intellectuals'.[17] While Acharya was trying to convince intellectuals and trade union leaders to take up libertarian ideas, he had to write for capitalist papers such as *Kaiser-i-Hind* 'but from a libertarian point of view'.[18] His articles, he said, were 'an attack against both capitalists and Marxians at the same time, showing that both of them are trying unworkable, bankrupt, and therefore doomed economics. When the capitalist editors sleep, they publish such articles by me'.[19] While in India, he noted, 'one has to sail under the non-violence flag to be heard at all', and complained that the socialist papers refused to publish his articles and the libertarian papers were only read by those already convinced.[20]

A new libertarian review for India

In the late 1940s, Acharya was in touch with the short-lived North East London Anarchist Group, and in the early 1950s, he was involved in the Asian Prisoners Aid Group with the British anarchist Albert Meltzer.[21] A staunch anti-imperialist, Meltzer was a regular contributor to *Freedom*, where he would publish many of Acharya's articles and, in many of his own pieces, he often referred to Acharya's struggles in India. They had only met twice, during Meltzer's trip to India, but had regular correspondence.[22] In February 1950, Meltzer and Vernon Richards, editor of *Freedom* alongside Wolfe, were planning to start a new bulletin, aiming to provide general news for a broader and global audience, but from an anarchist point of view. In addition

226

ANARCHY

to Acharya, they wanted to enlist Herbert Read, George Woodcock, Alex Comfort, Reginald Reynolds, and George Padmore for contributions.[23] This new publication never materialised, but the fact that Meltzer and Richards had Acharya in mind signals Acharya's position as a well-known figure within the global radical left as well as his close friendship with Meltzer.

Acharya instead wanted to start an anarchist publication with D. N. Wanchoo, the son of one of his friends from Lucknow. Acharya had given Ekengren's and Rüdiger's addresses to Wanchoo who wanted to 'start a magazine to propagandise anarchism in all Asia', he explained to Ekengren.[24] In the summer of 1950, Acharya and Wanchoo placed a note in *Freedom* and asked for anarchist periodicals to be sent to them. In their announcement, they noted that an idea for an anarchist periodical 'in the English language circulating in Asia generally' had been pondered for some time by Acharya, but Wanchoo now asked 'comrades to let him have articles and translations for reproduction but also original material'.[25] The publication, they hoped, would 'have a broad basis of appeal among Anarchist writers and those of Anarchist tendencies'.[26]

Acharya and Wanchoo also contacted the American socialist Irving S. Canter, a prominent member of the Workers' Socialist Party and a frequent contributor to *The Western Socialist* under the pseudonym 'Karl Frederick', which was the first name of Canter's son. However, Acharya and Wanchoo assumed that 'Karl Frederick' was Karl Korsch when they invited Canter to contribute to their paper.[27] Canter had met Korsch once in 1949 and now wrote to Korsch to inform him of the mix-up and Acharya and Wanchoo's request. Korsch replied to Canter that he remembered Acharya from the Kritischer Marxismus study circle in Berlin in the late 1920s but 'there was no other link between us' (see Chapter 11).[28] He conceded, however, that, '[i]t is quite possible that he does more useful work in India today than he was in a position to do in Berlin around 1930. Since you intend to write him about his mistake, I'd like you to add my regards to whatever you will write to him'.[29] The mix-up between 'Karl Frederick' and Karl Korsch surprised Korsch because, when Acharya had approached George Gloss, the national secretary of the Workers' Socialist Party, a few years earlier, Acharya remembered Korsch's

ANARCHY OR CHAOS

name correctly. The name confusion aside, Korsch explained to Canter that, as they wanted articles written by 'Karl Frederick', they would surely be satisfied with articles by Canter.[30]

Acharya and Wanchoo also contacted Souchy to ask for his contribution:

> [y]ou probably know that a friend of mine wants to start a monthly which will publish anarchist and critical Marxian articles. We want to call it *Crucible: A Journal of Polemics*. I hope it will come out but if a war starts, we will get no paper and printer. He has no money but wants to make it pay through advertisements. He says many advertisers have promised to pay for 6 months. It is intended for Asia chiefly.[31]

To help Wanchoo, Acharya asked Souchy to send him a message and to relay to the IWMA, to continental anarchists, and to Swedish anarchists and syndicalists, noting Ekengren and Rüdiger by name, to do the same. They should only send articles in English to Wanchoo.

On Acharya's request, Wanchoo followed up on Acharya's letter to Souchy a few months later and provided information about himself: 'I am a journalist by profession and libertarian by views', he explained.[32] Optimistic about the new venture, Wanchoo wrote:

> I have been trying to bring out a libertarian monthly from here, but as you know well the financial fate of all such ventures, it has not been possible for me to bring it out so far, though a lot of ground has already been covered and if everything goes well, it will make its first appearance somewhere next month.[33]

He asked Souchy for business connections to help them get the publication off the ground. In February 1951, CRIA contacted Acharya for more information about *The Crucible*, having circulated their request for contributions in the *CRIA Bulletin*, which suggests that there was international interest in this new publication from India.[34]

War in Asia

While Acharya and Wanchoo struggled to get their new publication off the ground, Acharya remained in close contact with Yamaga and other Asian anarchists. He had sent a copy of *Whither India?* with his essay 'What is Anarchism?' to Li Pei Kan, who felt it would be good to translate it into Chinese and Japanese and asked Acharya to send a

ANARCHY

copy to Yamaga.[35] However, Acharya needed legal authorisation from the editors, Singh and Rao, to allow this and had asked a lawyer friend to help him.[36] Unfortunately, this proved more difficult than anticipated, and the process dragged on for years.

In the meantime, the civil war in China, leading to the foundation of the People's Republic of China and the ousting of Chiang Kai-shek in 1949, and the outbreak of the Korean War in June 1950 changed the political landscape in Asia. As Acharya put it to Yamaga: '[a]lthough the dethronement of Chiang-Kai shek should be welcomed, the successes of the Red Army are not enough'.[37] Acharya wanted to write more about the situation in China for Yamaga, which he could publish 'for the benefit of Chinese comrades'.[38] On his part, Yamaga wrote to Yelensky about the situation in China and Korea, passing on information from the Korean anarchist Yu Rim to Acharya in his letter and giving news of Lu Chien Bo's activities.[39] The correspondence between Acharya, Yamaga, Li Pei Kan, and Yu Rim as well as with Yelensky open a window onto the global entanglement of anarchist networks at the time of immense crisis.

The world seen from a libertarian point of view

Those global networks were also brought together in the booklet *The World Scene from the Libertarian Point of View* (1951). On 9 November 1948, to mark twenty-five years of 'spreading libertarian thought among the people', the Free Society Group of Chicago invited a select group of anarchists to contribute a 'booklet of collected articles under the title *Current Events in the Light of Libertarian Philosophy*'.[40] The publication committee, comprising Yelensky, Maximoff, and Irving S. Abrams, enclosed a list of topics and asked for short English-language articles by February 1949. In addition to Acharya, veteran figures such as Rocker, Souchy, Meltzer, Yamaga, and Li Pei Kan were also invited. Despite the tight deadline, Acharya sent his contribution to the committee a few weeks later.[41]

While aiming to 'present the libertarian view on the present world situation', the publication was delayed for several years, due to Maximoff's untimely death in March 1950, and appeared under a different title: *The World Scene from the Libertarian Point of View*. Despite

229

ANARCHY OR CHAOS

the delay, the editors noted that 'the articles contained herein generally have quite as much point as if they had been published at the intended time—for world conditions today, except for the greater tension caused by the war in Korea, are but little different from what they were then'.[42] For some such as Maximoff, the Cold War forced them to reconsider their anarchist principles and side with the United States against the USSR.[43] Maximoff's piece, as Andrew Cornell argues, represented a generational gap and the dull force of anarchism in the early Cold War period.[44]

By contrast, in his piece 'How Long Can Capitalism Survive?', Acharya argued that capitalism was on the brink of collapse. Instead of siding with capitalism and the US, Acharya claimed that '[c]apitalism will collapse even without a general strike for social revolution. Otherwise, let us not think of Socialism at all'.[45] In his usual style, Acharya argued that 'Socialism and Anarchism are ahead of us, or chaos', and urged that, '[i]f the great collapse is to come, it is up to Socialists and Anarchists to prepare for it'.[46] Whereas Maximoff denounced theoretical debates and sided with the capitalist bourgeoisie against totalitarian communism, Acharya urged anarchists to prepare for anarchy after chaos.

In many ways, there was nothing new in Acharya's contribution. He advanced many of the same arguments as he had done since the 1920s. By the time of the booklet's publication, however, things had changed dramatically for Acharya. After many years of illness, Acharya had contracted tuberculosis in early 1948. As he explained to Steelink: 'I began to spit blood and the doctor advised me to keep to bed. He has stopped me spitting blood, but he thinks I have T.B. and must go to a sanatorium for some months'.[47] Though slowly recovering, Acharya and Nachman lived in deep poverty and relied financially on Nachman's income from her paintings. In December 1950, Acharya wrote to Souchy:

> I am still confined to home as I do not get breath when I walk. Our financial situation is worse than ever. My wife had no sales or orders since 5 months. Just now she made a portrait. We do not know from week to week where we will get money. But till now some luck happened. Two months ago, some friend told about my condition to Pandit Nehru and he sent me Rs. 500 from his pocket. Next month I

ANARCHY

got [a] present from some friends amounting to Rs. 200. No chance of earning. If everything goes well, my wife hopes to exhibit her pictures for the first time in New Delhi and if she has luck she may sell—for there are many embassies there. But till next March we have to live.[48]

In view of Acharya's dislike of Nehru's politics, Nehru's financial contribution to Acharya was remarkable. In fact, less than a year earlier, Acharya had complained about Nehru to Ekengren: '[h]e is a born fascist coming from a rich family .... Only hypocrites or idiots can please him—yes-men—to do stupid or useless things'.[49] Such was Acharya's animosity for Nehru, but desperate times meant that he accepted the money.

Tragedy strikes

In early 1951, on the way to the Bombay Art Society's annual exhibition, Nachman suffered a stroke and was hospitalised at St. George's Hospital in Bombay. To raise money for her treatment, friends organised an exhibition of her paintings at the Institute of Foreign Languages on 13 February.[50] However, tragedy struck and Nachman died the day before. As the *Times of India* reported: '[a] large gathering of artists and art lovers, thronging the hall of the Institute of Foreign Languages, Bombay, on Monday night to witness the opening of an exhibition of paintings of Magda Nachman became a memorial meeting for the artist. She had died four hours earlier'.[51] A notice announcing her death greeted the audience. At the funeral the next day, 'her husband and her friends stood in the cemetery broken-hearted to watch her being buried', Nachman's friend Irena Pohrille recounted.[52] The exhibition ran for ten days, and sales brought Acharya enough money to receive medical treatment for some time.

However, Acharya was heartbroken. For months, he could not write anything and felt lost. In mid-April, he wrote to Souchy about Nachman's death: 'Magda died of apoplexy after one month in hospital and I am alone after 30 years life with her and I am still ill'.[53] In his letters to Yamaga, he was more devastated, but explained that 'the doctors say that even if she had come back to life, she would have preferred to be

ANARCHY OR CHAOS

dead and would have committed suicide. So that catastrophe is spared to her by her death'.[54] In another letter to Yamaga shortly after, Acharya despaired:

> I feel terribly alone now as there is no one to take care of me in my illness. I really don't know what to eat and how much to eat as these have been attended to by my wife. If I become ill, I will die in hospital. So I am afraid of becoming ill, since no one will attend to me.[55]

It was with a similar tone that he wrote to the Belgian anarchist Hem Day (Marcel Dieu) in May: 'I have been ill for the last 3 years and postponed writing a large number of friends abroad. Recently my wife and breadwinner also died, and I feel like a baby without anyone to take care of me. I am now 65 years old'.[56]

After Nachman's death, Acharya's old friend K. S. Karanth invited Acharya to come and stay with him in Puttur. However, Acharya declined:

> I do not think it is necessary for me to do so at present. When I am down and out, I may come if there is no other way. I am going to keep our flat as long as possible. In Bombay I can always get good doctors free and even sometimes medicines free.[57]

Acharya and Karanth had corresponded since the late 1920s, Nachman had painted a picture of Karanth in 1938, and Karanth was a frequent guest to the couple's home in Bombay.[58] Acharya confessed to Karanth: '[t]hanks to her, people are now more friendly to me than before', and wrote that he wanted to keep their house 'as Magda's memorial gallery'.[59] He also explained to Karanth that he was trying to get 'a small collection of Magda's pictures, esp. of her Indian figures, exhibited in Europe'.[60] At the same time, as he wrote to Yamaga, he was trying to organise an exhibition in Delhi for October 1951.[61] The exhibition in Europe was in the hands of Meltzer in London but did not materialise for years.[62] However, Acharya made concerted efforts to promote Nachman's work in Japan through Yamaga. In April 1951, Acharya sent Yamaga a collection of photos of Nachman's paintings as well as a copy of the art periodical *Aesthetics* dedicated to Nachman, which Yamaga could translate or use for a photo album. He suggested to Yamaga that he should 'find a good bourgeois art publisher if possible'.[63] In May, Acharya contacted the

232

ANARCHY

Japanese art critic and artist Kunitaro Suda and asked him to 'write an article about her and her pictures in any of the magazines in Japan'.[64] He was also trying to persuade the British art historian and anarchist Herbert Read to do the same.

By then, *The World Scene from a Libertarian Point of View* had been published, and Acharya urged Yamaga to translate and publish his piece in Japan. He was also keen to have his essay 'What is Anarchism?' published but struggled to obtain permission from Singh and Rao. Wanchoo had moved in with Acharya when Nachman was hospitalised in January 1951.[65] As Acharya was ill and devastated after Nachman's death, he could not meet Rao in person. Rao had also gone to Paris, then to the US, but was back in Bombay by April. While Acharya told Yamaga that Padmaja Publishers had gone bankrupt and that he probably did not need permission anymore, he was still trying to talk to Rao about translation rights. In July, on behalf of Acharya, Wanchoo managed to meet Rao and obtain the necessary permission for Yamaga and his comrade Endo Sakan to translate and publish Acharya's essay in Japan.[66]

Acharya and Wanchoo soon had to abandon their plan for setting up a new anarchist publication in India as Wanchoo could not raise the required funds and had to leave Bombay: 'Wanchoo cannot live in Bombay and has to go away. He has no money nor can find work here. I hope he will still not give up his idea after the struggles here'.[67] While Wanchoo left Bombay and abandoned the plan for a new anarchist publication, he remained involved in the international anarchist movement and, with Acharya, represented India in CRIA.[68] Instead, Acharya informed Yamaga, he had heard from the Australian poet and anarchist Harry Hooton that students at Sydney University were trying to set up an anarchist journal which, Acharya hoped, could circulate in Asia.[69]

Cultural freedom, libertarianism, and non-violence

A few months after Nachman's death, Acharya wrote three articles on the anti-communist Congress for Cultural Freedom, an event later revealed to have been backed by the American CIA, held in late March 1951 in Bombay.[70] While other anarchists such as Rüdiger

233

ANARCHY OR CHAOS

were sympathetic towards the Congress for Cultural Freedom, Acharya was critical of the congress' basic understanding of freedom: '[m]any of the delegates spoke for individual freedom. But that is used as a slogan of individualists, egoists, dictators, and enslavers. No doubt, individuals are pioneers of thought. But left to them, there can be Fascism and Bolshevism'.[71] These adherents of state politics, Acharya argued, did not understand the true meaning of freedom for that would require denouncing everything they believed in. As he saw it, while many of the delegates denounced Bolshevism as fascism, their attachment to state philosophy made them fascists themselves.

Severing his ties with Lotvala, in May 1951 Acharya wrote a critical article in Lotvala's new paper *The Libertarian*. Lotvala had framed the future of Indian libertarian politics in the tradition of past glories: 'India must be strong and build her economico-social future on her perennial philosophy, on the cultural achievements of her past, and by abiding by the eternal maxim: "To thine own Self be true"'.[72] Acharya rejected Lotvala's affinity for libertarian nationalism and criticised the authoritarian tendencies: '[w]e are no better than any. We must have anti-authoritarian and anti-capitalist culture if we want to save ourselves and show the way to others; no imitation, ancient or modern will do'.[73] Acharya decried the myth of national unity and argued that '[t]hey can cry as much as they like but Islamic and even Pakistan unity is as much a myth as Hindu unity'.[74] Acharya had no further contact with Lotvala after this.

The near-anarchists

Acharya's writings on non-violence in French papers signalled a gradual return to Gandhism and pacifism. However, when he wrote to Hem Day, he had noted that '[s]ince Gandhi was killed, pacifism is dead in India. Although J. Nehru, Indian Premier, tries to be neutral, he cannot be as a man of state'.[75] But Gandhi's legacy carried on through *Harijan* and disciples such as Kishorlal G. Mashruwala, Vinoba Bhave (often referred to as Acharya, meaning 'teacher' in Sanskrit), and Maganbhai P. Desai in the *Bhoodan* (land-gift) movement. Initiated by Bhave in 1951, the *Bhoodan* movement sought to reform India's land problem through redistribution of land and decen-

234

ANARCHY

tralised ownership and positioned itself against Nehru's statist, post-colonial economic policies.[76]

Seen by many as the direct heir to Gandhi, Bhave and the *Bhoodan* movement attracted attention worldwide, including among anarchists.[77] As it happened, though they had corresponded previously in *Les Nouvelles Pacifistes*, Louvet mistook Acharya for Bhave. Impressed by the *Bhoodan* movement, Louvet had written to Acharya, thinking he was Bhave, and asked him to contribute to *Contre-Courant*. Correcting Louvet, Acharya admitted that he had a lot of respect for Bhave 'because he is really the spiritual descendant of Gandhi whose teaching is respected as that of a Holy man. I can't be a saint like him!'.[78] Acharya passed Louvet's request on to Mashruwala, editor of *Harijan*, who, Acharya noted, had become attracted to anarchism, and would facilitate contact with Bhave. In fact, as Acharya explained to Yelensky: '[t]he only people who are nearest to anarchists are the Gandhians of the *Harijan* group. They are near-anarchists because they want decentralisation (independent village communes), production for use and direct action. They lay more importance on villages'.[79]

In 1950, Mashruwala published a series of articles entitled 'Gandhi and Marx' in *Harijan*, published in book form as *Gandhi and Marx* with an introduction by Bhave in 1951, in which he compared Gandhism and communism. In the article 'The Basis of Ethics', Mashruwala noted that 'the main question, namely, what is the true basis for the ethics of truth, non-violence etc., remains unsolved'.[80] In a letter to Mashruwala, Acharya criticised Mashruwala for not setting yardsticks for the ethics of non-violence and countered that

> [i]f the problem is unsolved, then it is a self-confession that we can have no truth, non-violence, etc., because the basis is not found or is not there. All discussions about them are speculation without any yardstick to measure by. It is then no use to ask people to act according to truth, non-violence, morality, humanity and ethics. For what is the yardstick by which these can be measured and judged?[81]

Society and humanity had collapsed, as diagnosed by Proudhon, Marx, Bakunin, Kropotkin and Malatesta in the nineteenth century, Acharya noted, and had to be reorganised without state, business, wages, and money for non-violence to succeed.

ANARCHY OR CHAOS

While Acharya still wrote for anarchist papers such as *Freedom*, *Contre-Courant*, and the Japanese anarchist papers *Heiminshinbun* and *Anakizumu*, he made a living from writing for smaller Indian papers, including mainstream papers such as *Times of India*, *Thought*, and *Economic Weekly*. Many of his articles for these focused on his experiences in Russia and condemning Bolshevik politics. In the early 1950s, however, it was *Harijan* that became his main sources of income. From 1951 to 1954, more than thirty articles by Acharya appeared in this periodical, covering a wide range of topics from an anarchist perspective.

However, Acharya was not afraid to take on Mashruwala and Bhave. In *Harijan*, Mashruwala, Bhave, and the veteran CPI leader S. A. Dange had engaged in a debate about communism and Gandhism.[82] As Acharya saw it, though, the entire debate was misplaced, as they all confused communism with Bolshevism: '[t]hey give the Bolsheviks the undeserved compliments of being Communists. They do not know that it is not Communism but Russian Bolshevism, which is a danger to the peace of the world'.[83] The Bolsheviks were no different from capitalists, and real communism, Acharya argued, 'cannot be established until the peasants take over all the land and instruments and run the lands collectively for their own benefit without any state to interfere with, or "protect" them'.[84] Though he took Mashruwala and Bhave to task, Mashruwala actually agreed with Acharya, adding an editorial note to Acharya's article: '[i]n *Gandhi and Marx*, I said that Communism as known in India is Marxism as prevailing in Russia, and it is State Capitalism. I thank Shri M. P. T. Acharya for making this very clear'.[85] According to Acharya, Mashruwala was starting to adopt anarchist ideas but died from an asthmatic attack on 9 September 1952. Only hours before his death, Mashruwala had written to Acharya and thanked him for their friendship and correspondence, which had helped Mashruwala articulate his own thoughts on Gandhi. Mashruwala's successor, Maganbhai P. Desai, was also sympathetic to Acharya's thoughts.[86] In fact, after Mashruwala's death, Desai travelled from Ahmedabad to visit Acharya in Bombay: '[i]t was a joy to see the old man quite fresh and alert in mind, though ailing and completely bed-ridden with none by his side. However, it was a painful experience to see a life-long worker of India's freedom in such dire difficulty'.[87]

236

ANARCHY

In his many writings for *Harijan*, Acharya merged anarchism and Gandhism into a unique articulation of decentralised, non-violent, and anti-statist politics. The logical conclusion for Acharya was to reconsider his thoughts on Gandhi himself. For twenty-five years, Acharya had engaged extensively with Gandhi's thoughts and actions, wavering between great admiration and fierce criticism, but now embraced Gandhi into the anarchist fold. As Acharya noted: 'his ideas of Socialism may be—are—different from that of Western Socialists and he may be nearer Socialism than Western Socialists—I mean more correct'.[88] In fact, he continued,

> Gandhiji understood Socialism as a Socialist while 'Socialists' understand Socialism like capitalists. If classes have to be abolished and a classless society has to be generated—we must start thinking in terms of classless society to produce a classless society—instead of thinking in terms of class conflict and class State as the starting point.[89]

For Acharya, this meant that 'Gandhiji did not believe any State will establish Socialism, i.e., classless society. He was right. In this matter, he was an anarchist, maybe a philosophical anarchist'.[90] Citing Gandhi's claim that '[t]he nearest approach to purest anarchy would be a democracy based on non-violence', Acharya argued that 'people can act only decentralistically and Gandhiji stood not for village autonomy under a State but complete and unfettered village independence'.[91] By finally embracing Gandhi as an anarchist, though with reservations, Acharya also asserted a longer tradition of anarchism in India that defied Eurocentric definitions of the concept.[92] Perhaps in response to the individualist turn by Lotvala and Wanchoo's failure to get the anarchist publication off the ground, as a self-reflexive reading of Gandhi, Acharya authoritatively asserted himself into and influenced this tradition.

The death of an Indian anarchist

Since the early 1920s, Acharya had often been ill and on the brink of starvation. Having contracted tuberculosis in 1948, by 1953 he was unable to speak and in May wrote a heartbreaking letter to Yelensky:

> I have been confined to bed all these five years and [especially] during the last year I have been worse off. You probably know that my

237

ANARCHY OR CHAOS

Russian wife died over two years ago. She was earning and I am not earning anything since 1939. I am ill, alone, and without any money and I find that I will die of malnutrition [very] gradually. I have let [out] two rooms—keeping a small one for myself—but that is not to give me food. I must have at least 20 dollars more a month if I must get enough food.[93]

Yelensky replied to Acharya a few months later: '[w]e took up your appeal for help, so enclosed you will find a check for $15 from the Alexander Berkman Aid Fund'.[94]

The money from the Alexander Berkman Aid Fund obviously did not support Acharya for long. Throughout the latter part of 1953 and into early 1954, Acharya wrote extensively for *Harijan*, by then his only source of income. However, in mid-April 1954, back issues of *Harijan* were returned to Desai with a notice that Acharya had died. In mid-March, Acharya had gone to the Bhatia Hospital where he died from cardiac arrest on the morning of 20 March 1954. After his death, his 'body was taken by a Municipal hearse to the cremation ground where the last rites were performed before a handful of friends and admirers'.[95]

With his death, India lost its most important anarchist. At a time when Acharya had found a venue for his anarchist thoughts, and anarchism had found its own Indian articulation in *Harijan*, his persistent efforts to bring anarchism into India's political landscape had finally found some currency. Though abandoning the idea of establishing a decidedly anarchist publication in India, Acharya's thoughts influenced the 'near-anarchists' such as Mashruwala and Desai. Ultimately, his prolific writings and international correspondence, right up until the time of his death, are testimony to a rich intellectual life promoting anarchy and freedom.

EPILOGUE

AFTERLIFE OF AN INDIAN REVOLUTIONARY

Memories of a revolutionary

An attempt to recover a life like Acharya's, and to think more broadly about its implications for wider political movements such as the Indian freedom struggle and the international anarchist movement, presupposes that aspects of his life have been lost, marginalised, or written out of history altogether. Indeed, while this biography has demonstrated that Acharya's life was far from marginal or inconsequential, it is instructive to look more closely at how and when such acts of silencing happened and what this means for our understanding of the struggles in which Acharya was involved.

After Acharya's death, two of his articles appeared posthumously in *Harijan*.[1] Perhaps unsurprisingly, it was also in *Harijan* that one of the first obituaries appeared. Having confirmed Acharya's death from the announcement in the *Sunday Chronicle*, Desai recounted his memories of Acharya in *Harijan*. According to Desai, Acharya had an estranged brother in Bombay who came to see him once, but 'his last days were a veritable battle between him and crushing poverty and benumbing illness'.[2] Despite this, Desai continued, 'Acharya had humour enough to bear and brave the ordeal'.[3] 'Acharya was a total believer in the doctrine of philosophical anarchism', Desai concluded, and 'he stood for a free and decentralized social order based on complete liberty, equality, and the dignity of true human personality'.[4] In

239

ANARCHY OR CHAOS

January 1955, Desai reprinted an expanded version of Acharya's article 'Capital and Unemployment' from the August 1953 issue of *Harijan* with a note clarifying: '[t]his is an epitome of some thoughts that late Shri M. P. T. Acharya used to send me as they came to him in his compulsory seclusion. This was lying with me since long. On reading it again, I feel it can well bear publication even now'.[5] Desai appended his own comments to Acharya's article, extending some of Acharya's arguments and indicating his agreement with Acharya. Desai's acknowledgement of Acharya's anarchist philosophies is significant, as it shows an understanding of Acharya's political project and his distinction from other philosophical ideas in India.

In June 1954, in the Gujarati periodical *Kumar*, J. Mazumdar provided a biographical account of Acharya's peripatetic travels:

> [h]e bravely fought for half a century for freedom of our Motherland in utter neglect and poverty, unattended by his countrymen .... None came to honour him and perform his obsequies. He left no European capital unvisited, for the propagation of the torch of freedom of his Motherland, and yet his passing away was so singularly record-breaking in its tragedy.[6]

Like Desai, Mazumdar commented on the desolation of Acharya's last years: '[a]fter the death of Mrs. Acharya, four years ago, Shri Acharya was reduced to abject poverty. Though India attained Independence, this veteran freedom fighter breathed his last in utter poverty, unsung, unwept, and unhonoured'.[7]

In the summer of 1954, Acharya's friend Vasant Paranjape had written to Coutinho and informed him of Acharya's death. Coutinho replied to Paranjape: 'I was very depressed with the news of our brother Shri Acharya. Poor Acharya! He was a very noble type of mankind. Intelligent, enthusiastic, and generous. Devoted to the limit'.[8] Coutinho recounted his many meetings with Acharya in London, Lisbon, New York, and Berlin with fondness and lamented: 'I feel really ashamed to learn that Shri Acharya was abandoned and died in great poverty. As a patriot who gave all his energy for the liberation of India, the Pandit Nehru should have done something for him, especially when he kept his connections with Mahatma Gandhi'.[9]

Paranjape also informed Aldred of Acharya's death. 'I saw him many times here in Bombay', Paranjape wrote to Aldred.[10] 'It is very

EPILOGUE

sad to think that such a great patriot died like a beggar in a charitable hospital'.[11] While Acharya contributed to Aldred's *The Word*, they were also at odds over the question of *Hindutva* as espoused by Savarkar. At the time, Aldred had defended Savarkar publicly in the Godse trial, a position that brought Aldred into disrepute with the Freedom Group in London (see Chapter 15). Initially, however, it was Aldred's defence of Dhingra and association with the Indian nationalists in London in 1909 that lingered in Aldred's mind (see Chapter 1). As he said about Acharya's association with Meltzer and the Freedom Group: '[t]he curious thing is that his Anarchism caused him to associate with the Freedom Group people who accused me of being a police agent, at the time of my imprisonment in 1909, and later, because I had championed the cause of Indian Freedom'.[12] This was unforgivable, Aldred felt, '[y]et Acharya associated himself with these enemies of the Indian struggle. I do not say he upheld them. He ought, however, to have rebuked them strongly and definitely'.[13]

Acharya never rebuked the Freedom Group and maintained a close friendship with Meltzer. The exhibition of Nachman's paintings that Meltzer had promised to arrange in London had dragged on for years, but by the summer of 1954, through various connections and office lettings, Meltzer had managed to find an art gallery willing to stage an exhibition. However, just as he had arranged this, news reached him that Acharya had died and that, at the request of Acharya's legal widow, the Indian authorities had blocked the shipment of Nachman's paintings to London for the exhibition.[14] In September 1954, Meltzer wrote to Wolfe that he had received a letter from a lawyer in India regarding Acharya's death. Meltzer informed Wolfe that copies of *Freedom* were accumulating in Acharya's mailbox, and the lawyer asked that Meltzer should stop sending *Freedom*. Meltzer also wrote that the lawyer might contact Wolfe, as Acharya had mentioned *Freedom* in his will, to ask for money. A doctor who had rented Acharya's apartment for two years, leaving one room for Acharya, owed rent for eighteen months and refused to pay, wrote Meltzer, but he suspected that nothing could be done to collect the owed rent money.[15] It is uncertain who this lawyer and the doctor lodging with Acharya were. Intriguingly, it appears that Acharya left a will. In his obituary, Meltzer commemorated Acharya's life as the most prominent advocate of anar-

ANARCHY OR CHAOS

chism in India, his many articles for *Kaiser-i-Hind* and *Harijan*, and his uncompromising anarchist ideals: '[d]espite the fact that there were a few other Anarchists over the whole of India, it was the great tragedy of Acharya's later years that he was in such isolation that headway was made almost impossible'.[16] In fact, Meltzer said,

> [i]t was impossible to comprehend the difficulty in standing out against the tide so completely as was necessary in a country like India. It was easy for former 'nationalist revolutionaries' to assert their claims to the positions left vacant by the old 'imperialist oppressors'. This Acharya would not do. He remained an uncompromising rebel, and when age prevented him from speaking, he continued writing right up to the time of his death.[17]

Meltzer's understanding of Acharya's difficulties in building an anarchist movement alone is telling of the death of anarchism in India.

After reading Meltzer's note in *Freedom*, Rüdiger wrote about Acharya's death in *Arbetaren* in August and informed Rocker about it as well.[18] 'He was an incredibly productive journalist', Rüdiger noted, 'and his manuscripts used to pile up on *Der Syndikalist*'s editorial desk'.[19] Acharya would 'send even more articles to the whole world without caring what the editors did with them'.[20] Commenting on Acharya's personality, Rüdiger recalled that he was '[a]lways friendly and laughing, [and] at meetings he would present his ideas that were a synthesis of anarchism and Gandhian perspectives with a strong hint of Proudhon'.[21] In a personal note, published a few days later, one of Acharya's correspondents—probably Ekengren—wrote movingly that the libertarian movement had lost one of its most unique figures. Acharya's thoughts extended well beyond India and had influenced many people in Europe, he noted. However, it was Acharya's connection to Sweden—his time in Sweden during the First World War, his ability to read and write Swedish—that struck Ekengren the most: 'in that way he became an interesting link between Indian and Swedish anarchism, a link that sadly was not explored'.[22]

Having not heard from Acharya for months, Armand also read about Acharya's death in *Freedom*. In his obituary, echoing some of Meltzer's sentiments, Armand characterised Acharya as an 'old school libertarian … whom neither isolation nor poverty could overpower'.[23] Commenting on Acharya's life and escape from Germany, his frequent

242

EPILOGUE

contributions to *L'En Dehors* and *L'Unique*, and his views on Gandhi, Armand called Acharya 'incorruptible' and noted that, 'wherever he wrote, he ensured that the ringing bell of anarchism, as he understood it, and as his declining strength permitted, was heard'.[24] Yamaga's note on Acharya's death appeared in *La Anarkismo: Inland Bulletin of the Japanese Anarchist Federation* in October 1954: '[h]e very often sent us articles. We profoundly regret his passing and commiserate his unhappy circumstances before his death in Bombay'.[25]

More than a year after his death, an obituary appeared in *Dielo Trouda-Probuzhdenie*, perhaps by Yelensky. Giving a brief account of Acharya's association with anarchists in Russia during the civil war years—with a few inaccuracies about his travels and age—the obituary noted:

> [t]he last years of his adult life, Acharya devoted to literary work and wrote a lot on socio-economic issues. His favorite topics were: the role of labour in the capitalist economy, the general strike and social revolution, the abolition of the monetary system, etc. .... His numerous articles have always attracted great interest and were often debated in anarchist circles.[26]

In the CNT organ *Cenit*, Vladimir Muñoz remarked upon Acharya's death in a footnote: 'Acharya accepted Gandhism with reservations, denouncing its clear nationalistic and political nuances, so emphasized by Nehru. Acharya, incorruptible, made his anarchist sentiments heard everywhere'.[27] These testimonials from across the world are evidence of Acharya's great reach and global network. An important thread ran through many of these obituaries: they connected Acharya's anticolonial revolutionary activities with his anarchist philosophy, interweaving anticolonialism and anarchism into an exceptional life, and highlighted Acharya's solitary struggle to establish an anarchist movement in India.

Forgotten legacies

However, aside from these initial testimonies to Acharya's life and activities in the Indian freedom struggle and the international anarchist movement, he was soon forgotten. It was only a few years later that his friends Victor Garcia and Hem Day eulogised Acharya. In a series of articles in *Tierra y Libertad* on the history of anarchism in

ANARCHY OR CHAOS

India, Garcia devoted a section to Acharya alongside Gandhi, Bhave, and M. N. Roy.[28] In *Contre-Courant*, giving a longer biography of Acharya's anticolonial activities, Garcia commemorated Acharya as:

> [t]he most prominent figure among Indian libertarians. He was above all a very informed connoisseur of the social theories of the West. Compared to most of the thinkers and men of action of India whom it is difficult to give a descriptive label, although they are all great humanists who fight for the abolition of the state and political and economic authority, one can clearly classify Acharya among the anarchists since he defined himself as such.[29]

In 1962, Hem Day summed up: 'he is not well known to all, even to our own people, for he has neither the fame of Gandhi, nor the fame of Nehru, nor the popularity of Vinoba, nor the notoriety of Kumarapa, nor the dignity of Tagore. He is Acharya, a revolutionary, an agitator, a writer'.[30] Both Garcia and Day spoke about Acharya alongside other libertarians and teased out a particular strand of anarchism in India championed by Acharya.

In December 1969, a colloquium of anarchist scholars in Italy compiled a bibliography of anarchist literature and concluded that Acharya's activities were 'of irrelevant and exclusively editorial nature'.[31] However, following on from the colloquium, the Italian anarchist Michele Moramano discussed Acharya alongside Jiddu Krishnamurti and Bhave, noting that 'Indian anarchism's embryonic history is identified with the activities pursued by M. P. T. Acharya, a decidedly original, maverick and legendary figure', but Moramano also lamented that Acharya did not succeed in building an anarchist movement in India.[32] Meltzer also recalled his friendship and collaboration with Acharya in his memoirs *The Anarchists in London* (1976), dedicating the book to Acharya, among others:

> for years there was in the whole continent only one active militant ... my old friend M. P. T. Acharya plugged away on his own .... With a growing interest in anarchism among Indian students, a Bombay publishing house reprinted many classical Anarchist works, but Acharya did not succeed in building a movement before his death, nor do I think one exists yet.[33]

Thus, many years after Acharya's death, with the exception of Moramano and Meltzer, his activities were slowly forgotten and writ-

244

EPILOGUE

ten off as 'irrelevant' by scholars. After the initial obituaries and the memories that resurfaced about twenty years after his death, interest in Acharya and the history of anarchism in India virtually disappeared.

Questions unanswered

While this biography is most importantly an attempt to recover Acharya's life and political ideas from such silencing, his death also leaves many questions unanswered. For example, while Acharya's *Reminiscences* were published in 1937, these eight instalments only covered the period from 1907 until 1910. His articles on Savarkar, Chatto, and Madame Cama, as well as the accounts of his life in Stockholm from 1917 to 1918, provide more insight into his revolutionary activities, but ultimately leave a major gap in his life story. However, Acharya may have left us another more substantial record. In his letter to Karanth, written shortly after Nachman's death, Acharya mentioned that he was writing his autobiography and that Nachman had wanted him to cover his entire life.[34]

Perhaps most intriguingly, in a letter to Aldred from August 1954, Paranjape said that he had Acharya's memoirs, which covered his experiences in Europe, the United States, and Russia, and that he would send them to Aldred.[35] A few years later, Paranjape wrote even further to Aldred: 'I got articles back written by the late M. P. T. Acharya on revolutionaries including Dhingra, Shyamaji Krishnavarma, Guy Aldred, Sir Walter Strickland, De Valera, and also his secret activities. I want to get those typed for *The Word*. That would be valuable information'.[36] These articles never appeared in *The Word*, and my search in the Guy Aldred Collection at the Mitchell Library in Glasgow, Scotland has yielded no results.

According to Garcia, Acharya was also working on 'his most important work' entitled *Mutualism*, which was also mentioned in Acharya's brief biography in his contribution to *World Scene from a Libertarian Point of View* and by Moramano. In fact, Moramano refers to the French anarchist Guy Malouvier, who appeared to have read the work and noted that *Mutualism* 'limited itself to rehearsing the key concepts of Proudhonian anarchism'.[37] Nothing has been found in Garcia's estate.

245

ANARCHY OR CHAOS

Despite being forgotten a few years after his death, only to be dismissed by scholars in the late 1960s, Acharya's legacy can be felt decades later. As historians of South Asia and colonialism have begun to take the history of anarchism seriously, Acharya's contribution to transnational, anticolonial thought is undeniable. His activities and extensive writings open new ways of thinking about emancipatory politics from below—a politics of resistance to several forms of oppression simultaneously. In doing so, Acharya articulated new ways of organising and obtaining true freedom. At the same time, the last fifteen years have seen a growing interest in non-Western, global, and anticolonial histories of anarchism that bring anarchists such as Acharya into broader conversations around anarchism's impetus for freedom. Examining Acharya's life and activities through such lenses bring together histories that illuminate the necessity of thinking about resistance to colonialism, nationalism, militarism, and totalitarianism in conjunction and conversation with each other. However, there is still more to uncover and, in turn, to build upon. If anything, this biography is a starting point for exploring the deep entanglements of the radical worlds of anticolonialism and anarchism that uproot conventional narratives of resistance to oppression in all its forms. As nationalism, fascism, and the defence of colonialism is rearing its head again across the world, Acharya's life and extensive body of writings contain lessons for us to learn. As Acharya would have put it, the choice is between anarchy or chaos.

pp. [2–10]

NOTES

INTRODUCTION

1. Acharya to Reisner, 18 December 1922, 495/68/64/36, RGASPI. I am grateful to Lina Bernstein for sharing this document with me.
2. Tim Harper, *Underground Asia: Global Revolutionaries and the Assault on Empire* (Cambridge: Harvard University Press, 2021), pp. 50–1.
3. Andrew Davies, *Geographies of Anticolonialism: Political Networks Across and Beyond South India, c. 1900–1930* (Hoboken, NJ: Wiley, 2020), pp. 137–60. I am indebted to Kama Maclean and Daniel Elam's engaging debate on the nature of 'revolutionaries' in my description of Acharya as a revolutionary. Kama Maclean and J. Daniel Elam, 'Reading Revolutionaries: Texts, Acts, and Afterlives of Political Action in Late Colonial South Asia', *Postcolonial Studies*, 16:2 (2013), pp. 113–23.
4. Leela Gandhi, *Affective Communities: Anticolonial Thought, Fin-De-Siècle Radicalism, and the Politics of Friendship* (Durham: Duke University Press, 2006), p. 9.
5. Priyamvada Gopal, *Insurgent Empire: Anticolonial Resistance and British Dissent* (London: Verso, 2019), p. 22.
6. Kris Manjapra, *Age of Entanglement: German and Indian Intellectuals across Empire* (Cambridge: Harvard University Press, 2014)
7. Manu Goswami, 'Imaginary Futures and Colonial Internationalisms', *American Historical Review*, 117:5 (December 2012), p. 1463.
8. Acharya to Aiyar, 16 November 1911, History of the Freedom Movement Papers, GO 1014, Judicial Department, Tamil Nadu Archives, Chennai (TNA). I am grateful to Andrew Davies for sharing this material with me.
9. Priyamvada Gopal, 'On Decolonisation and the University', *Textual Practice*, 35:6 (2021), p. 886.
10. C. S. Subramanyam, *M. P. T. Acharya: His Life and Times: Revolutionary Trends in the Early Anti-Imperialist Movements in South India and Abroad* (Madras: Institute of South Indian Studies, 1995), p. 189.
11. M. P. T. Acharya, Bishamber Dayal Yadav (ed.), *M. P. T. Acharya: Reminiscences of an Indian Revolutionary* (New Delhi: Anmol Publications, 1991).

247

pp. [10–12] NOTES

12. Maia Ramnath, *Decolonizing Anarchism: An Antiauthoritarian History of India's Liberation Struggle* (Edinburgh: AK Press, 2011).

13. Davies, *Geographies of Anticolonialism*.

14. Lina Bernstein, *Magda Nachman: An Artist in Exile* (Boston: Academic Studies Press, 2020).

15. M. P. T. Acharya, Ole Birk Laursen (ed.), *We Are Anarchists: Essays on Anarchism, Pacifism, and the Indian Independence Movement, 1923–1953* (Chico, California: AK Press, 2019).

16. Dinyar Patel, *Naoroji: Pioneer of Indian Nationalism* (Cambridge: Harvard University Press 2020); Harald Fischer-Tiné, *Shyamji Krishnavarma: Sanskrit, Sociology, and Anti-Imperialism* (New Delhi: Routledge, 2014); Vinayak Chaturvedi, *Hindutva and Violence: V. D. Savarkar and the Politics of History* (Albany: State University of New York Press, 2022); Vineet Thakur, *India's First Diplomat: V. S. Srinivasa Sastri and the Making of Liberal Internationalism* (Bristol: Bristol University Press, 2021); Michele Louro, *Comrades against Imperialism: Nehru, India, and Interwar Internationalism* (Cambridge; New York: Cambridge University Press, 2018); Kris Manjapra, *M. N. Roy: Marxism and Colonial Cosmopolitanism* (London: Routledge, 2010). Of slightly older date, Nirode K. Barooah's, *Chatto: The Life and Times of an Indian Anti-Imperialist in Europe* (Oxford: Oxford University Press, 2004), still stands as the best biography of Chatto to date.

17. Alongside these biographies, recent studies have contributed greatly to interrogating the intellectual history of India's independence struggle: Durba Ghosh, *Gentlemanly Terrorists: Political Violence and the Colonial State in India, 1919–1947* (Cambridge: Cambridge University Press, 2017); Shruti Kapila, *Violent Fraternity: Indian Political Thought in the Global Age* (Princeton: Princeton University Press, 2021); Kama Maclean, *A Revolutionary History of Interwar India: Violence, Image, Voice and Text* (London: Hurst & Company, 2015); Vikram Visana, *Uncivil Liberalism: Labour, Capital and Commercial Society in Dadabhai Naoroji's Political Thought* (Cambridge: Cambridge University Press, 2022).

18. Mike Finn, *Debating Anarchism: A History of Action, Ideas and Movements* (London: Bloomsbury, 2021), p. 141.

19. Geoffrey Ostergaard, 'Indian Anarchism: The Sarvodaya Movement', in David E. Apter and James Joll (eds), *Anarchism Today: Studies in Comparative Politics* (London: Palgrave Macmillan, 1971), pp. 145–63; Geoffrey Ostergaard and Melville Currell, *The Gentle Anarchists: A Study of the Leaders of the Sarvodaya Movement for Nonviolent Revolution in India* (Oxford: Clarendon Press, 1991).

20. Benedict Anderson, *Under Three Flags: Anarchism and the Anti-Colonial Imagination* (London: Verso, 2005); Steven Hirsch and Lucien van der Walt (eds), *Anarchism and Syndicalism in the Colonial and Postcolonial World, 1870–1940: The Praxis of National Liberation, Internationalism, and Social Revolution* (Leiden; Boston: Brill, 2010); Ilham Khuri-Makdisi, *The Eastern Mediterranean and the Making of Global Radicalism, 1860–1914* (Berkeley; London: University of California Press, 2010); Kenyon Zimmer, *Immigrants against the State: Yiddish and Italian Anarchism in America* (Urbana: University of Illinois Press, 2015).

NOTES   pp. [12–27]

21. Carl Levy, 'Social Histories of Anarchism', *Journal for the Study of Radicalism*, 4:2 (2010), pp. 1–44.

22. Laura Galián, *Colonialism, Transnationalism, and Anarchism in the South of the Mediterranean* (Cham: Palgrave Macmillan, 2020), pp. 2–3.

23. Acharya, 'Max Nettlau como biógrafo y como historiador', *La Revista Blanca*, 13:328 (3 May 1935), pp. 410–12.

24. Neilesh Bose, 'Taraknath Das: A Global Biography', in Neilesh Bose (ed.), *South Asian Migrations in Global History: Labor, Law, and Wayward Lives* (London: Bloomsbury, 2020), p. 157.

25. Constance Bantman, 'Anarchist Transnationalism', in Marcel van der Linden (ed.), *Cambridge History of Socialism*, Vol. I (Cambridge: Cambridge University Press, 2022), p. 600.

26. Ruth Kinna, 'What is Anarchist Internationalism?', *Nations and Nationalism*, 27:4 (2020), p. 988.

27. Acharya to CRIA, 12 September 1949, Commission for International Anarchist Relations Archives, ARCH00318, International Institute of Social History, Amsterdam (IISH).

28. Nathan Jun, 'Anarchism without Archives', *American Periodicals: A Journal of History & Criticism*, 29:1 (2019), pp. 3–5.

29. Farina Mir, Introduction, AHR Roundtable: The Archives of Decolonization, *American Historical Review*, 120:3 (June 2015), pp. 844–51; Pragya Dhital, 'Archiving Insurgence', *History Workshop*, 23 March 2020 [https://www.historyworkshop. org.uk/archiving-insurgency/], accessed 14 June 2022.

30. Lok Sabha Debates, 22 August 1984, session XV, number 07 [https://eparlib.nic. in/handle/123456789/2048?], accessed 6 June 2022.

31. Razak Khan, 'Entangled Institutional and Affective Archives of South Asian Muslim Students in Germany', Modern India in German Archives (MIDA), online article, 14 February 2019 [https://www.projekt-mida.de/reflexicon/entangled-institutional-and-affective-archives-of-south-asian-muslim-students-in-germany/], accessed 8 June 2022.

32. Edward Said, *Culture and Imperialism* (London: Vintage, 1994), p. 59.

33. Souchy to Berkman, 10 February 1931, Alexander Berkman Papers, ARCH00040.140, IISH; Faruqui to de Jong, 13 September 1927, Archief IAMV, ARCH00662.83, IISH.

34. Adom Getachew, *Worldmaking after Empire: The Rise and Fall of Self-Determination* (Princeton: Princeton University Press, 2019), p. 1.

1. NATIONALISM IN THE BRITISH EMPIRE

1. H. M. Minister at Lisbon to Foreign Office, December 1909, 'Movements of M. P. Tirumalachari, formerly Proprietor, Publisher and Editor of a Tamil Newspaper called *India* and Sukhsagar Dutt', Home & Political, B, 1909, Dec 37, National Archives of India (NAI).

pp. [27–31]　　　　NOTES

2. C. S. Subramanyam, *M. P. T. Acharya: His Life and Times: Revolutionary Trends in the Early Anti-Imperialist Movements in South India and Abroad* (Madras: Institute of South Indian Studies, 1995), p. 7; Bishamber Dayal Yadav (ed.), *M. P. T. Acharya: Reminiscences of an Indian Revolutionary* (New Delhi: Anmol Publications, 1991), p. 3.

3. Acharya's high school diploma was found during a raid of Chandra Kanta Chakravarty's house in New York in 1917. M1085, Bureau of Investigation, Old German Files, Case 8000–1396, National Archives and Records Administration (NARA). I am grateful to Tim Harper for pointing me to these files.

4. In two separate letters, Acharya stated that V. S. Srinivasa Sastri was his headmaster at the Hindu High School: 'File 6303/22—Orientals in Berlin and Munich: S I S and D I B reports', India Office Records, L/PJ/12/102, British Library, London (IOR); 'Passports: grant of facilities for Mr Lakshman P Varma and his wife and to Mr M P Tirumal Acharya', IOR/L/PJ/6/1968, file 3981.

5. M. P. T. Acharya, 'Reminiscences of a Revolutionary', *Mahratta*, 36 (23 July 1937), p. 5.

6. Andrew Davies, 'Exile in the Homeland? Anti-Colonialism, Subaltern Geographies and the Politics of Friendship in Early Twentieth Century Pondicherry, India', *Environment and Planning D: Society and Space*, 35:3 (2017), pp. 457–74.

7. Acharya, 'Reminiscences of a Revolutionary', *Mahratta*, 36 (23 July 1937), p. 5.

8. For material on the Surat session, see *Source Material for a History of the Freedom Movement in India* (Bombay: Printed at the Govt. Central Press, 1957–).

9. V. S. Srinivasa Sastri, *Life and Times of Sir Pherozeshah Mehta* (Bombay: Bharatiya Vidya Bhavan, 1975), p. 126; *Source Material for a History of the Freedom Movement in India*, pp. 143–73.

10. Vineet Thakur, *India's First Diplomat: V. S. Srinivasa Sastri and the Making of Liberal Internationalism* (Bristol: Bristol University Press, 2021), p. 30.

11. Acharya, 'Reminiscences of a Revolutionary', *Mahratta*, 36 (23 July 1937), p. 5.

12. Andrew Davies, *Geographies of Anticolonialism: Political Networks Across and Beyond South India, c. 1900–1930* (Hoboken: Wiley, 2020), pp. 90–114.

13. Subramanyam, *M. P. T. Acharya*, p. 97; History Sheet of Jnanendra Nath Sharma, alias Jnanendra Nath Chatterji, alias J. N. Sharman, alias Jagat Singh, Home & Political, B, 1913, September 5, NAI.

14. Acharya, 'Reminiscences of a Revolutionary', *Mahratta*, 36 (30 July 1937), p. 2.

15. Ibid.

16. Alex Tickell, 'Scholarship Terrorists: The India House Hostel and the "Student Problem" in Edwardian London', in Rehana Ahmed and Sumita Mukherjee (eds), *South Asian Resistances in Britain, 1858–1947* (London: Continuum, 2012), pp. 3–18.

17. Harald Fischer-Tiné, *Shyamji Krishnavarma: Sanskrit, Sociology and Anti-Imperialism* (New Delhi: Routledge, 2014).

18. Acharya, 'Reminiscences of a Revolutionary', *Mahratta*, 36 (20 August 1937), p. 3.

19. For more on Savarkar and Mazzinian influences, see Vinayak Chaturvedi, *Hindutva and Violence: V. D. Savarkar and the Politics of History* (Albany: State University of New York Press, 2022)

NOTES

pp. [31–35]

20. T. S. S. Rajan quoted in: R. A. Padmanabhan, 'M. P. T. Acharya', *Indian Review*, 70:2 (May 1974), p. 29.

21. For a summary of the Kirtikar case, see Paul Schaffel, 'Empire and Assassination: Indian Students, "India House", and Information Gathering in Great Britain, 1898–1911', a thesis submitted to the faculty of Wesleyan University, April 2012, pp. 96–103.

22. Rajan quoted in: Padmanabhan, 'M. P. T. Acharya', p. 29.

23. Schaffel, 'Empire and Assassination', pp. 96–103; Janaki Bakhle, 'Savarkar (1883–1966), Sedition and Surveillance: The Rule of Law in a Colonial Situation', *Social History*, 35:1 (2010), p. 60.

24. Vasant Paranjape, 'Dr. Joachim De Sequeira Coutinho' *The Hindu (Weekly)* (10 May 1953), n.p.; Prabha Chopra and P. N. Chopra (eds), *Indian Freedom Fighters Abroad: Secret British Intelligence Report* (New Delhi: Criterion Publications, 1988), p. 44; Helen Coutinho, *Pleasant Recollections of Dr. Joaquim de Siqueira Coutinho* (New York: Saint Anthony Press, 1969), pp. 10–14.

25. Acharya, 'Reminiscences of a Revolutionary', *Mahratta*, 36 (27 August 1937), p. 5.

26. Acharya, 'Savarkar in London', *Mahratta*, 37 (27 May 1938), p. 5.

27. 24 April 1909, Weekly Report of the Director of Criminal Intelligence, IOR Neg 3095–3096 (WRDCI).

28. M. Asaf Ali, G. N. S Raghavan, Aruna Asaf Ali (eds.), *M. Asaf Ali's Memoirs: The Emergence of Modern India* (Delhi: Ajanta, 1994), p. 69.

29. Bakhle, 'Savarkar (1883–1966), Sedition and Surveillance', 54; Vinayak Chaturvedi, 'A Revolutionary's Biography: The Case of V. D. Savarkar', *Postcolonial Studies*, 16:2 (2013), pp. 124–39; Vikram Visana, 'Savarkar before Hindutva: Sovereignty, Republicanism and Populism in India, c. 1900–1920', *Modern Intellectual History* (2020), pp. 1–24.

30. 'The Original Publisher's Preface', Vinayak Damodar Savarkar, *The Indian War of Independence of 1857* (New Delhi: Rajdhani Granthagar, 1970), pp. xi–xii.

31. 'Information about the Revolutionary Movement in London; Statement of H. K. Koregaonkar', IOR/L/PJ/6/986, file 349.

32. 26 December 1908, WRDCI; 'Establishment of a miniature rifle range at India house, Highgate', IOR/L/PJ/6/920, file 384.

33. Acharya, 'Reminiscences of a Revolutionary', *Mahratta*, 36 (27 August 1937), p. 5.

34. Ole Birk Laursen, 'Anarchist Anti-Imperialism: Guy Aldred and the Indian Revolutionary Movement, 1909–14', *Journal of Imperial and Commonwealth History*, 46:2 (2018), pp. 286–303.

35. 17 July 1909, WRDCI.

36. Ibid.

37. 'Information about the Revolutionary Movement in London; Statement of H. K. Koregaonkar', IOR/L/PJ/6/986, file 349.

38. 31 July 1909, WRDCI.

39. Acharya, 'Reminiscences of a Revolutionary', *Mahratta*, 36 (3 September 1937), 3; 'Criminal: Dhingra, Madan Lal; Court: Central Criminal; Offence: Murder; Sentence: Death', HO 144/919/180952, National Archives, Kew (NA).

pp. [35–41]   NOTES

40. 31 July 1909, WRDCI.
41. 'The Murder of Sir Curzon Wyllie', *The Times* (6 July 1909), p. 10.
42. Acharya, 'Reminiscences of a Revolutionary', *Mahratta*, 36 (3 September 1937), p. 3.
43. 21 August 1909, WRDCI.
44. Laursen, 'Anarchist Anti-Imperialism', pp. 286–303.

2. EXILE IN EUROPE

1. Sukh Sagar Dutt to A. C. Bose, 30 March 1958, in A. C. Bose (ed.), *Indian Revolutionaries Abroad: 1905–1927* (New Delhi: Northern Book Centre, 2002), p. 39.
2. Acharya, 'Reminiscences of a Revolutionary', *Mahratta*, 36 (10 September 1937), p. 3
3. Outwards passenger lists: Port: Southampton (1909 August [part], September [part]), BT 27/640, NA. In the passenger list, Acharya and Dutt are listed as 'students' and the only two 'British Colonials'.
4. C. A. Souter, Under Secretary to the Government of Madras, to Secretary to the Government of India, 25 September 1909, 'Movements of M. P. Tirumalachari, formerly Proprietor, Publisher and Editor of a Tamil Newspaper called *India* and Sukhsagar Dutt', Home & Political, B, 1909, Dec 37, NAI.
5. Acharya, 'Reminiscences of a Revolutionary', *Mahratta*, 36 (17 September 1937), p. 3.
6. The story of Acharya's activities in Gibraltar, Tangier, and Lisbon is in 'Movements of M. P. Tirumalachari, formerly Proprietor, Publisher and Editor of a Tamil Newspaper called *India* and Sukhsagar Dutt', NAI.
7. 8 November 1910, WRDCI.
8. Ole Birk Laursen, '"I have only One Country, it is the World": Madame Cama, Anticolonialism, and Indian-Russian Revolutionary Networks in Paris, 1907–1917', *History Workshop Journal*, 90 (Autumn 2020), pp. 96–114.
9. 25 December 1909, WRDCI; Janaki Bakhle, 'Savarkar (1883–1966), Sedition and Surveillance: The Rule of Law in a Colonial Situation', *Social History*, 35:1 (2010), pp. 51–75.
10. Bakhle, 'Savarkar (1883–1966), Sedition and Surveillance', pp. 51–75; Nawaz B. Mody, 'Perin Captain: From Dadabhai to Mahatma Gandhi', in Nawaz B. Mody (ed.), *Women in India's Freedom Struggle* (Mumbai: Allied Publishers, 2000), pp. 205–18; Dinyar Patel, *Naoroji: Pioneer of Indian Nationalism* (Cambridge: Harvard University Press, 2020), p. 147.
11. 'Statement of Chanjeri Rao convicted at Bombay of importing arms, ammunition and seditious books', IOR/L/PJ/6/993, file 860.
12. Arrest and Return of Savarkar (France/Great Britain), Award of the Tribunal, Permanent Court of Arbitration, The Hague, The Netherlands, [https://pca-cpa.org/en/cases/79/], accessed 21 May 2022.

NOTES
pp. [41–45]

13. 11 October 1910, WRDCI.

14. Noor-Aiman I. Khan, *Egyptian–Indian Nationalist Collaboration and the British Empire* (New York: Palgrave Macmillan, 2011), pp. 48–50; Daniel Brückenhaus, *Policing Transnational Protest: Liberal Imperialism and the Surveillance of Anticolonialists in Europe, 1905–1945* (New York: Oxford University Press, 2017), pp. 23–4, 34–5; 5 October 1910, WRDCI.

15. 5 October 1910, WRDCI; see also, Kate Marsh, '"The only safe haven of refuge in all the world": Paris, Indian "Revolutionaries" and Imperial Rivalry, c. 1905–40', *French Cultural Studies*, 30:3 (2019), pp. 196–219.

16. 18 October 1910, WRDCI.

17. *Œuvres du Congres National Egyptien tenu a Bruxelles le 22, 23, 24 Septembre 1910* (Bruges: The St. Catherine Press, 1911).

18. 25 October 1910, WRDCI.

19. Acharya to Aiyar, 8 November 1911, TNA. See also, Acharya to P. Parthasarathy, 4 September 1923, quoted in: 'Orientals in Berlin and Munich: S I S and D I B reports', IOR/L/PJ/12/102, file 6303/22.

20. 25 October 1910, WRDCI.

21. 17 May 1910, WRDCI.

22. 12 July 1910, WRDCI; 13 September 1910, WRDCI.

23. 'The Right of Asylum', Second International Archives, ARCH01299.473, IISH.

24. 24 January 1911, WRDCI.

25. 24 January 1911, WRDCI; 20 September 1910, WRDCI; 5 October 1910, WRDCI; 11 October 1910, WRDCI; 1 November 1910, WRDCI.

26. Letter of recommendation from Allgemeine Teeimport-Gesellschaft, 31 December 1910. Several letters of recommendation from Acharya's employers were found in M1085, Bureau of Investigation, Old German Files, Case 8000–1396, NARA.

27. 19 September 1911, WRDCI. For more on Strickland, see Harald Fischer-Tiné, *Shyamji Krishnavarma: Sanskrit, Sociology and Anti-Imperialism* (New Delhi: Routledge, 2014), pp. 76–7.

28. Acharya to Aiyar, undated but from Munich, written prior to subsequent dated correspondence, TNA; see also, 12 May 1914, WRDCI.

29. Bakhle, 'Savarkar (1883–1966), Sedition and Surveillance', pp. 51–75. Primary source material on the Savarkar affair is included in *Source Material for a History of the Freedom Movement in India* (Bombay: Printed at the Govt. Central Press, 1957–).

30. Acharya to Aiyar, quoted in: History Sheet of Jnanendra Nath Sharma, alias Jnanendra Nath Chatterji, alias J. N. Sharman, alias Jagat Singh, Home & Political, B, 1913, September 5, NAI.

31. Quoted in: 10 October 1911, WRDCI.

32. Ibid.

33. Ibid.

34. Acharya to Aiyar, undated but from Munich, written prior to subsequent dated correspondence, TNA.

pp. [45–48]   NOTES

35. Acharya to Aiyar, 4 October 1911, TNA.
36. Ajit Singh, Pardaman Singh, Joginder Singh Dhanki (eds), *Buried Alive: Autobiography, Speeches and Writings of an Indian Revolutionary* (New Delhi: Gitanjali, 1984), pp. 60–3; 'Sirdar Ajit Singh', *Bande Mataram* 3:1 (September 1911), p. 4; 'Ajit Singh, "Indian anarchist": possible deportation from Switzerland', FO 1093/35, NA.
37. 14 November 1911, WRDCI.
38. 21 November 1911, WRDCI; see also, Bose (ed.), *Indian Revolutionaries Abroad, 1905–1927*, pp. 119–20.
39. 21 November 1911, WRDCI.
40. Cemil Aydin, *The Politics of Anti-Westernism in Asia: Visions of World Order in Pan-Islamic and Pan-Asian Thought* (New York: Columbia University Press, 2007), pp. 10–11.
41. Acharya to Aiyar, 8 November 1911, TNA.
42. Ibid.
43. Ibid.
44. Ibid.
45. Ibid.
46. Ibid.
47. Ibid.
48. Acharya to Aiyar, 16 November 1911, TNA.
49. Ibid.
50. Ibid.
51. Ibid.
52. Ibid.
53. Ibid.
54. Acharya to Chatto, quoted in: 16 December 1911, WRDCI.
55. 19 January 1912, WRDCI.
56. Letter of recommendation from S. R. Rana, after 10 January 1912, M1085, Bureau of Investigation, Old German Files, Case 8000–1396, NARA.
57. Letter of recommendation from Tewfik Beg, after 10 January 1912, M1085, Bureau of Investigation, Old German Files, Case 8000–1396, NARA.
58. WRDCI, 23 April 1912.
59. WRDCI, 12 July 1912.
60. WRDCI, 20 August 1912.
61. In late August 1912, Govind Amin stole a large number of pearls from Rana and some other Indian pearl merchants in Paris to pay off gambling debt. Rana and the others reported him to the police, but Amin committed suicide on 17 September 1912 before he was caught. See Ole Birk Laursen, 'Spaces of Indian Anti-Colonialism in Early Twentieth-Century London and Paris', *South Asia: Journal of South Asian Studies*, 44:4 (2021), pp. 634–50.
62. M1085, Bureau of Investigation, Old German Files, 1909–1921, Case 8000–1396, NARA, p. 54; 'The San Francisco Conspiracy Case: trial of 1917–18; sentencing of the accused; newspaper cuttings; photograph of Sekunna and C. K. Chakravarty,

NOTES

pp. [51–53]

taken after their arrest in New York', IOR/L/PJ/6/1559, file 5784; Chopra and Chopra (eds), *Indian Freedom Fighters Abroad*, pp. 32–4.

3. THE GHADAR PERIOD

1. William Williams, US Commissioner of Immigration, to H. M. Consul General, New York, 31 March 1913, R194–64–6-E, Volume 1003, Folder 5, Department of External Affairs. Asiatic Immigration. Prints 1 to 42 inclusive, 1884–1925. Set III. 1884–1925, Library and Archives of Canada.
2. Acharya to Rana, 14 October 1912, Horst Krüger Papers, Box 7, 48–1, Leibniz-Zentrum Moderner Orient, Berlin (ZMO).
3. Ibid.
4. Ibid.
5. Hopkinson to W. W. Cory, 16 November 1912, 'Activities of Indian political agitators in Canada (and on the Pacific Coast of America)', IOR/L/PJ/6/1137, file 276.
6. Hopkinson to Cory, 27 November 1912, IOR/L/PJ/6/1137, file 276.
7. Emily C. Brown, *Har Dayal: Hindu Revolutionary and Rationalist* (Tucson: University of Arizona Press, 1975), pp. 85, 246; Maia Ramnath, *Haj to Utopia: How the Ghadar Movement Charted Global Radicalism and Attempted to Overthrow the British Empire* (Berkeley: University of California Press, 2011), pp. 20–33.
8. Brown, *Har Dayal*, p. 138.
9. For more on Indian nationalist periodicals, see Ole Birk Laursen, 'The Indian Nationalist Press in London, 1865–1914', in Constance Bantman and Ana Cláudia Suriani da Silva (eds), *The Foreign Political Press in Nineteenth-Century London: Politics from a Distance* (London: Bloomsbury, 2017), pp. 175–91; Neilesh Bose, 'Taraknath Das: A Global Biography', in Neilesh Bose (ed.), *South Asian Migrations in Global History: Labor, Law, and Wayward Lives* (London: Bloomsbury, 2020), pp. 157–77; Harald Fischer-Tiné, 'Indian Nationalism and the "World Forces": Transnational and Diasporic Dimensions of the Indian Freedom Movement on the Eve of the First World War', *Journal of Global History*, 2:3 (2007), pp. 325–44.
10. 'The Society of Political Missionaries', *The Indian Sociologist*, 3:6 (June 1907), p. 23; Ramnath, *Haj to Utopia*, p. 37.
11. Maia Ramnath, *Decolonizing Anarchism: An Antiauthoritarian History of India's Liberation Struggle* (Edinburgh: AK Press, 2011), p. 91; Daniel Kent-Carrasco, 'Beyond the Reach of Empire: Pandurang Khankhoje's Transit from British Colonial Subject to Mexican "Naturalizado" (1924–1954)', in Neilesh Bose (ed.), *South Asian Migrations in Global History: Labor, Law, and Wayward Lives* (London: Bloomsbury, 2020), pp. 179–99.
12. Tariq Khan, 'Living Social Dynamite: Early Twentieth-Century IWW–South Asia Connections', in Peter Cole, David Struthers, Kenyon Zimmer (eds), *Wobblies of the World: A Global History of the IWW* (London: Pluto, 2017), pp. 59–72; Ramnath, *Decolonizing Anarchism*, pp. 80–109.

255

pp. [53–57]   NOTES

13. H. M. Consul General, New York, to Secretary of State for Foreign Affairs, 1 April 1913, R194–64–6-E Volume 1003, Folder 5, Department of External Affairs. Asiatic Immigration. Prints 1 to 42 inclusive, 1884–1925. Set III. 1884–1925, Library and Archives of Canada.

14. 'Shortens Name for Citizenship', *Boston Herald* (16 March 1913), p. 1; 'Alphabetical Student Desires Citizenship', *Rockford Morning Star* (16 March 1913), p. 1; 'Looks Like a Pied Line', *Richmond Times Dispatch* (17 March 1913), p. 1.

15. H. M. Consul General, New York, to Secretary of State for Foreign Affairs, 1 April 1913, R194–64–6-E Volume 1003, Folder 5, Department of External Affairs. Asiatic Immigration. Prints 1 to 42 inclusive, 1884–1925. Set III. 1884–1925, Library and Archives of Canada.

16. 12 May 1914, WRDCI.

17. 'Councillors', *The Hindusthanee Student: A Quarterly Review of Education* (January 1914), p. 2. I am grateful to Sara Legrandjacques for pointing me to this reference.

18. Ibid.

19. IOR/L/PJ/6/1559, file 5784.

20. Ibid.

21. Brown, *Har Dayal*, pp. 152–66.

22. 12 May 1914, WRDCI; Bhikaiji Rustom Cama, 'Le Nationaliste hindou Har Dyal arrête aux États-Unis', *L'Humanité*, 11:3638 (3 April 1914), p. 1; Margaret Ward, *Maud Gonne: Ireland's Joan of Arc* (London: Pandora, 1990), p. 91; Har Dayal, 'Why I Should be Freed', *La Patrie Egyptienne*, 5 (15 May 1914), p. 4.

23. Harald Fischer-Tiné, 'The Other Side of Internationalism: Switzerland as a Hub of Militant Anti-Colonialism, c. 1910–1920', in Patricia Purtschert and Harald Fischer-Tiné (eds), *Colonial Switzerland: Rethinking Colonialism from the Margins* (Houndmills, Basingstoke, Hampshire: Palgrave Macmillan, 2015), pp. 234–5.

24. 16 June 1914, WRDCI.

25. 10 November 1914, WRDCI; Brown, *Har Dayal*, pp. 142–3.

26. Acharya to Keell, 2 August 1928, Freedom Archives, ARCH00428.435, IISH; Acharya to Yelensky, 28 April 1947, Boris Yelensky Papers, ARCH01674.46, IISH; Acharya to Yelensky, 22 May 1947, Boris Yelensky Papers, ARCH01674.46, IISH.

27. Francisco Ferrer's execution in October 1909 had not escaped Har Dayal, see: 'Senor Ferrer', *Bande Mataram*, 1:3 (November 1909), p. 4.

28. Acharya to Ekengren, 23 October 1949, Berk Ekengren Papers, Arbetarrörelsens Arkiv och Bibliotek, Huddinge, Sweden (ARBARK).

29. M1085, Bureau of Investigation, Old German Files, Case 8000–1396, NARA.

4. WAR AGAINST THE BRITISH EMPIRE

1. Nirode K. Barooah, *Chatto: The Life and Times of an Indian Anti-Imperialist in Europe* (New Delhi; Oxford: Oxford University Press, 2004), pp. 39–52.

2. 'The Anglo-German War-Cloud: England's Peril, Hindusthan's Opportunity', *Talvar*, 1:3 (March 1910), pp. 1–2.

NOTES   pp. [57–60]

3. There is a growing body of historical scholarship on the Indian Independence Committee: Heike Liebau, 'The German Foreign Office, Indian Emigrants, and Propaganda Efforts Among the "Sepoys"', in Franziska Roy, Heike Liebau, and Ravi Ahuja (eds.), *'When the War Began we Heard of Several Kings': South Asian Prisoners in World War I Germany* (London: Routledge, 2017), pp. 96–129; Frank Oesterheld, '"Der Feind meines Feindes ist mein Freund"—Zur Tätigkeit des Indian Independence Committee (IIC) während des Ersten Weltkrieges in Berlin', Magisterarbeit zur Erlangung des akademischen Grades Magister Artium im Fach Neuere I Neueste Geschichte (2004); Kris K. Manjapra, 'The Illusions of Encounter: Muslim 'Minds' and Hindu Revolutionaries in First World War Germany and After', *Journal of Global History*, 1:3 (2006), pp. 363–82; Benjamin Zachariah, 'Indian political activities in Germany, 1914–1945', in J. Cho, E. Kurlander, and D. T. McGetchi (eds), *Transcultural Encounters between Germany and India: Kindred Spirits in the 19th and 20th Centuries* (London: Routledge, 2013), pp. 141–54.

4. Dr Mansur Ahmed is referred to as 'Dr Mansur' in all reports, so this is the name used here rather than his last name.

5. For a personal recollection of this early group, see Raja Mahendra Pratap, Vir Singh (ed.), *Reminiscences of a Revolutionary* (New Delhi: Books India International, 1999), p. 21.

6. Emily C. Brown, *Har Dayal: Hindu Revolutionary and Rationalist* (Tucson: University of Arizona Press, 1975), pp. 186–8.

7. Gerhard Höpp, 'Zwischen Entente und Mittelmächten: Arabische Nationalisten und Panislamisten in Deutschland (1914 bis 1918)', *Asien, Afrika, Lateinamerika*, 19:5 (1991), pp. 827–45; Jennifer Jenkins, Heike Liebau, and Larissa Schmid, 'Transnationalism and Insurrection: Independence Committees, Anti-Colonial Networks, and Germany's Global War', *Journal of Global History*, 15:1 (2020), pp. 61–79; Nathanael Kuck, 'Anti-colonialism in a Post-Imperial Environment—The Case of Berlin, 1914–33', *Journal of Contemporary History*, 49:1 (2014), pp. 134–59.

8. Graf von Bernstorff to AA, 6 November 1914, RZ 201/21074, PAAA; RZ 207/80564, PAAA.

9. Acharya to Lenort, 8 December 1914, RZ 201/21075, PAAA.

10. Berlin, Betr. Pässe der Inder, 22 December 1914, RZ 201/21075, PAAA.

11. 'Betrifft indische Gefangene im Zossener Lager', 7 January 1915, RZ 201/21244, PAAA. For more on Indian prisoners of war, see Franziska Roy, Heike Liebau and Ravi Ahuja (eds), *'When the War Began, We Heard of Several Kings': South Asian Prisoners in World War I Germany* (Bangalore: Orient Blackswan, 2011), pp. 42–3.

12. Nadolny to AA, 10 January 1915, RZ 201/21076, PAAA.

13. For an examination of these missions, see Maia Ramnath, *Haj to Utopia: How the Ghadar Movement Charted Global Radicalism and Attempted to Overthrow the British Empire* (Berkeley: University of California Press, 2011).

14. See Pratap's mission statement, 17 February 1915, RZ 201/21078, PAAA. See

257

pp. [60–63] NOTES

also Humayun Ansari, 'Maulana Barkatullah Bhopali's Transnationalism: Pan-Islamism, Colonialism, and Radical Politics', in Gotz Nordbruch and Umar Ryad (eds), *Transnational Islam in Interwar Europe: Muslim Activists and Thinkers* (London: Palgrave Macmillan, 2014), pp. 181–209.

15. IIC report, 17 February 1915, RZ 201/21078, PAAA.

16. Chatto to German Embassy, 25 February 1915, RZ 201/21079, PAAA. Das Gupta subsequently travelled under the name 'Mirza Ali Haidar'.

17. Thomas L. Hughes, 'The German Mission to Afghanistan, 1915–1916', *German Studies Review*, 25:3 (Oct 2002), pp. 447–76.

18. Bern Legation to AA, 8 March 1915, RZ 201/21080, PAAA.

19. AA report, 10 March 1915, RZ 201/21080, PAAA.

20. German Embassy, Constantinople to AA, 21 March 1915, RZ 201/21080, PAAA.

21. Telegram to Mr Kersasp (alias Hassan Ali Khan), Constantinople, 26 March 1915, RZ 201/21081, PAAA.

22. Telegram, Constantinople, to AA, 26 March 1915, RZ 201/21081, PAAA.

23. Wangenheim to Nadolny, 2 May 1915, RZ 201/21082, PAAA.

24. Har Dayal to IIC, 23 April 1915, RZ 201/21082, PAAA.

25. 19 March 1915, RZ 201/21080, PAAA.

26. Wangenheim to Hollweg, 22 May 1915, RZ 201/21082, PAAA.

27. Varma to Chatto, 14 May 1915, RZ 201/21083, PAAA.

28. Har Dayal to IIC, 5 June 1915, RZ 201/21083, PAAA.

29. Chatto to IIC, 23 June 1915, RZ 201/21084, PAAA.

30. Pratap to Wesendonk, 27 May 1915, RZ 201/21084, PAAA. See Hughes, 'The German Mission to Afghanistan, 1915–1916', pp. 447–76; Ansari, 'Maulana Barkatullah Bhopali's Transnationalism', pp. 181–209.

31. Kaiserliche Generalkonsul in Jerusalem to German Embassy in Pera, 21 June 1915, report written 17 June 1915, RZ 201/21084, PAAA.

32. Kaiserliche Generalkonsul in Jerusalem to German Embassy in Pera, 30 June 1915, RZ 201/21085, PAAA.

33. IIC to AA, 12 October 1915, RZ 201/21090, PAAA.

34. Ibid.; see also, Tapan K. Mukherjee (ed.), *Taraknath Das: Life and Letters of a Revolutionary in Exile* (Calcutta: National Council of Education, Bengal, Jadavpur University, 1998), p. 77.

35. Kaiserliche Generalkonsul in Jerusalem to German Embassy in Pera, 13 July 1915, RZ 201/21085, PAAA.

36. Kaiserliche Generalkonsul in Jerusalem to German Embassy in Pera, 24 July 1915, RZ 201/21086, PAAA.

37. Kaiserliche Generalkonsul in Jerusalem to IIC, 25 August 1915, RZ 201/21088, PAAA.

38. Kaiserliche Generalkonsul in Jerusalem to IIC, 28 August 1915, RZ 201/21088, PAAA.

39. IIC to AA, 3 September 1915, RZ 201/21088, PAAA.

40. Hohenlohn to German Embassy in Pera, 14 September 1915, RZ 201/21089, PAAA.

NOTES   pp. [63–67]

41. IIC to AA, 6 October 1915, RZ 201/21089, PAAA.

42. Neurath to Nadolny, 4 November 1915, RZ 201/21091, PAAA.

43. Metternich to Nadolny, 18 November 1915, RZ 201/21091, PAAA; Har Dayal, *Forty-Four Months in Germany and Turkey*, pp. 73–4.

44. Ole Birk Laursen, '"A Dagger, a Revolver, a Bottle of Chloroform": Colonial Spy Fiction, Revolutionary Reminiscences and Indian Nationalist Terrorism in Europe', in Elleke Boehmer, Dominic Davies (eds), *Planned Violence: Post/Colonial Urban Infrastructure, Literature and Culture* (Basingstoke, Hampshire: Palgrave Macmillan, 2018), pp. 255–71.

45. For more on Abdul Jabbar Kheiri, see Heike Liebau, 'Navigating Knowledge, Negotiating Positions: The Kheiri Brothers on Nation and Islam', *Geschichte und Gesellschaft*, 45 (2019), pp. 341–61.

46. Taraknath Das to IIC, 12 November 1915, RZ 201/21091, PAAA.

47. IIC to Wesendonk, 5 March 1916, RZ 201/21095, PAAA.

48. Note that this was different from the Indian Volunteer Corps. For more on Prasad, see, 'Persia: Sufi Amba Parshad, Indian anarchist, at Shiraz', IOR/L/PS/11/106, P 2181/1916.

49. Metternich to AA, 14 January 1916, RZ 201/21093, PAAA; IIC to Wesendonk, 16 January 1916, RZ 201/21093, PAAA; IIC to Wesendonk, 5 February 1916, The Baghdad Work and the Indian National Corps, RZ 201/21094, PAAA.

50. Indian Committee, Constantinople to the Tashkilat-i-Makhsusa (Special Department of the Turkish War Office), report of the unlucky journey of the Baghdad Mission to Ismidt, and the return of Dr. Mansur and Mr. Maqbul Husain to Constantinople, 15 February 1916, RZ 201/21095, PAAA.

51. Ibid.

52. Ibid.

53. Dr Mansur to Young Hindusthan Association (YHA), 10 April 1916, RZ 201/21098, PAAA; IIC to AA, 13 April 1916, RZ 201/21098, PAAA.

54. Acharya to IIC, A Report on the Baghdad Mission, 23 October 1916, RZ 201/21104, PAAA.

55. Ibid,

56. Acharya to Chatto, 19 May 1916, RZ 201/21099, PAAA.

57. Hesse, German Consulate, Baghdad to AA, 20 June 1916, RZ 201/21099, PAAA; see also, 'Collection 425/1330 Punishment of Indian revolutionaries (Ghadar party) captured at Baghdad', IOR/L/MIL/7/18504.

58. Chatto and Datta to Hafis, 1 July 1916, RZ 201/21099, PAAA.

59. IIC to Dr Weber, Imperial German Embassy, Constantinople, 8 September 1916, RZ 201/21102, PAAA. For more on Abdur Rabb, see 'Collection 425/1330 Punishment of Indian revolutionaries (Ghadar party) captured at Baghdad', IOR/L/MIL/7/18504.

60. Pillai to Dr Weber, Imperial German Embassy, Constantinople, 12 October 1916, RZ 201/21103, PAAA; IIC to Wesendonk, AA, 26 November 1916, RZ 201/21104, PAAA.

259

pp. [67–75]   NOTES

61. IIC to Wesendonk, AA, Our Withdrawal from Turkey, 1 December 1916, RZ 201/21104, PAAA.
62. IIC to Wesendonk, AA, 19 December 1916, RZ 201/21104, PAAA.
63. IIC to Wesendonk, AA, Instructions to Constantinople, 22 December 1916, RZ 201/21104, PAAA.
64. Acharya to IIC, 10 February 1917, RZ 201/21106, PAAA.
65. Ibid.
66. IIC to Wesendonk, AA, 21 February 1917, RZ 201/21106, PAAA.
67. Constantinople report to IIC, 17 March 1917, RZ 201/21106, PAAA.
68. IIC to Wesendonk, AA, 7 April 1917, RZ 201/21107, PAAA; German legation to AA, 11 April 1917, RZ 201/21107, PAAA.

5. INTERNATIONAL SOCIALISM AND WORLD PEACE

1. R. Craig Nation, *War on War: Lenin, the Zimmerwald Left, and the Origins of Communist Internationalism* (Durham: Duke University Press, 1989), pp. 99–130, 177.
2. Fredrik Petersson, 'A Neutral Place? Anti-Colonialism, Peace, and Revolution in Stockholm, 1917', in Holger Weiss (ed.), *Locating the Global: Spaces, Networks and Interactions from the Seventeenth to the Twentieth Century* (Berlin, Boston: De Gruyter Oldenbourg, 2020), pp. 283–314.
3. Härbärgerarkort (poliseringskort), 1917, SE/RA/420367/E/6/24, Statens Polisbyrå, Swedish National Archives (SNA); Ansökninger om uppehållsböcker, huvudserie, 1918–1927, E8A: 15, Statens Polisbyrå, SNA; Chatto to M. von Sydow, 15 July 1921, FO 371/6954, Sweden, NA.
4. Chatto to IIC, 20 May 1917, RZ 201/21107, PAAA.
5. Ibid.
6. Ibid.
7. Ibid.
8. Ibid.
9. Ibid.
10. 'Indiens emancipationsplaner', *Dagens Nyheter* (20 May 1917), p. 13.
11. Ibid.
12. Chatto to IIC, 30 May 1917, RZ 201/21108, PAAA.
13. Chatto to IIC, 26 May 1917, GFM 6/41, NA.
14. Executive Committee of the Indian National Party (European Centre), *Speeches and Resolutions on India at the International Socialist Congresses* (Berlin: Julius Sittenfeld, 1917), p. 4.
15. 'Chattopadhyaya, Virendranath', Stockholm, F3:4, HII 125; F10 A:3, SNA; Stephen McQuillan, '"Revolutionaries, Renegades and Refugees": Anti-British Allegiances in the Context of World War I', in Enrico Dal Lago, Róisín Healy, and Gearóid Barry (eds), *1916 in a Global Context: An Anti-Imperial Moment* (London: Routledge, 2017), pp. 117–30.
16. 'The War: Stockholm Peace Congress; attitude of Oriental delegates', IOR/L/PS/11/126, P3449/1917.

260

NOTES pp. [75–82]

17. Arthur Holitscher, *Reisen* (Potsdam: Gustav Kiepenheuer Verlag, 1928), p. 55; Höpp, 'Zwischen Entente und Mittelmächten: Arabische Nationalisten und Panislamisten in Deutschland (1914 bis 1918)', pp. 827–45; documents from these meetings are available online at [https://www.socialhistoryportal.org/stockholm1917/documents], accessed 21 May 2022.

18. 'En intervju på indiska byrån i Stockholm', *Svenska Dagbladet* (12 July 1917), p. 12.

19. Acharya, 'Indian Propaganda During the Great War', *Mahratta*, 37 (21 October 1938), p. 3.

20. 'Sitzung des Holländisch-skandinavischen Komitees mit der Delegation aus Indien, 12 July 1917', P/55 [https://www.socialhistoryportal.org/stockholm1917/documents/111637], accessed 22 May 2022.

21. INK to IIC, 16 July 1917, GFM 6/41, NA.

22. The Stockholm Conference, CAB 23/3/59, NA.

23. Nation, *War on War*, pp. 188–90, 197.

24. Ibid.

25. INK to IIC, 1 November 1917, RZ 201/21110, PAAA.

26. 'Entwurf zu einem Friedensprogramm des Holländisch-skandinavischen Komitees, 10. Oktober 1917', [https://www.socialhistoryportal.org/stockholm1917/documents/111665], accessed 22 May 2022.

27. Indiska Nationalkommittén to the Dutch-Scandinavian Committee, 16 November 1917, Carl Lindhagen Papers, B5 9, Stockholm City Archive. See also, Indiska Nationalkommittén, *Indien und der Weltfrieden: Ein Protest gegen das Friedensprogramm des Holländisch-Skandinavischen Sozial-Demokratischen Komitees von Europäischen Zentralkomitee der Indischen Nationalisten. Mit einem Anhang* (Stockholm: Indiska Nationalkommittén, 1918).

28. Ibid.

29. Ibid.

30. 'Indiska frågan berörd i Brest Litowsk', *Stockholms Dagblad* (24 January 1918), p. 1.

31. 'Reports on Finnish and Russian works', 4 February 1918, RZ 201/21111, PAAA.

32. Ibid.

33. Ibid.

34. INK to IIC, 12 February 1918, RZ 201/21111, PAAA.

35. Har Dayal to Bhupendranath Datta, 18 March 1918, RZ 201/21112, PAAA.

36. Ibid.

37. INK to IIC, 26 March 1918, RZ 201/21113, PAAA.

38. IIC to AA, 11 December 1917, RZ 201/21110, PAAA.

39. Annie Åkerhielm, *En Bok om England och dess Undertryckta Folk* (Stockholm: Nationalförlaget, 1918)

40. 'Englands kulturgärning i Indien', *Social-Demokraten* (12 June 1918), p. 3.

41. 'Englands största kulturbragd', *Aftonbladet* (22 June 1918), p. 5.

42. 'Det indiska problemet', *Folkets Dagblad Politiken* (20 August 1918), pp. 4–5.

43. Erez Manela, *The Wilsonian Moment: Self-Determination and the International Origins of Anticolonial Nationalism* (Oxford: Oxford University Press, 2007), p. 4.

pp. [82–87] NOTES

44. 'Det engelska väldet i Indien', *Nya Dagligt Allehanda* (22 June 1918), p. 8.

45. 'Våldet och förtrycket mot Indien', *Aftonbladet* (2 June 1918), p. 3.

46. 'Indien och Wilson', *Folkets Dagblad Politiken* (24 October 1918), p. 5.

47. Glasenapp, 'Bericht über meine amtliche Reise nach Stockholm', 7 December 1918, RZ 201/21116, PAAA.

48. IIC to AA, 6 December 1918, RZ 201/21117, PAAA.

49. IIC to Wesendonk, 13 November 1918, RZ 201/21116, PAAA; IIC to Romberg, 4 December 1918, RZ 201/21117, PAAA.

50. Ibid.

51. Acharya to Romberg, 22 December 1918, RZ 201/21117, PAAA.

52. Pierre Broué, *The German Revolution, 1917–1923* (London; Boston: Brill, 2005).

53. 9 June 1919, WRDCI.

54. Acharya, 'Viren Chattopadhyaya: Revolutionary Fighter for India's Freedom', *Bombay Chronicle* (2 November 1947), p. 6.

55. 17 January 1919, RZ 201/21117, PAAA.

56. Mrs Philip [Ethel] Snowden, *A Political Pilgrim in Europe* (London; New York: Cassell, 1921), pp. 3, 14, 38.

57. Acharya, 'Viren Chattopadhyaya', p. 6.

58. 'Britische Delegation Indien. Die britische Delegation berichtet, dass an der Jahreskonferenz der Arbeiterpartei', Second International Archives, ARCH01299.282, IISH; Ramsay MacDonald, 'Territorial Questions', *Official Bulletin of the International Labour and Socialist Conference*, 1:8 (21 February 1919), p. 2; 'La tormenta degli scioperi nell'impere britannico', *Avanti!*, 23:31 (31 January 1919), p. 1.

59. Geheimrat Romberg report, 22 February 1919, RZ 201/21117, PAAA; Acharya to AA, 3 April 1919, RZ 201/21117, PAAA.

6. REVOLUTION IN RUSSIA

1. Wesendonk to AA, 6 May 1919, RZ 201/21117, PAAA.

2. Glasenapp to von Grundherr, 12 May 1919, RZ 201/21117, PAAA; 'Die indische kolonie in Deutschland', *Berliner Börsen-Zeitung, Abend-Ausgabe* (12 May 1919), p. 2.

3. 25 August 1919, WRDCI.

4. Maia Ramnath, *Haj to Utopia: How the Ghadar Movement Charted Global Radicalism and Attempted to Overthrow the British Empire* (Berkeley: University of California Press, 2011), pp. 226–8; Ansari, 'Maulana Barkatullah Bhopali's Transnationalism', pp. 181–209; Samee Siddiqui, 'Coupled Internationalisms: Charting Muhammad Barkatullah's Anti-colonialism and Pan-Islamism', *ReOrient*, 5:1 (2019), pp. 25–46.

5. '"A few words written in the interest of The Soviet Russia and India". Handwritten text by Raja Mahendra Pratap dated December, 1921', in Purabi Roy, Sobhanlal Datta Gupta, and Hari Vasudevan (eds), *Indo-Russian Relations, 1917–1947: Select Documents from the Archives of the Russian Federation* (Calcutta: Asiatic Society, 1999), p. 150.

NOTES pp. [88–91]

6. 'Dalip Singh Gill: activities in Europe and USA', IOR/L/PJ/12/, file 4991/21; 'Dalip Singh Gill: branded a Communist by the German Intelligence Authorities', IOR/L/PS/11/213, P 1436/1922.

7. Wilkin von Glasenapp to Helmuth von Glasenapp, 19 June 1919, RZ 201/21118, PAAA.

8. 15 September 1919, WRDCI.

9. Intelligence briefing, Mitau, to AA, 28 June 1919, RZ 201/21118, PAAA.

10. 'Indian Emissaries to the Bolshevists', *Evening Mail* (28 July 1919), p. 3; 'Indian Emissaries to the Bolshevists', *Times* (28 July 1919), p. 3; 'Berlin's Luck', *Leicester Daily Post* (29 July 1919), p. 1; report by Deutsche Orient-Institut, 13 August 1919, RZ 201/21118, PAAA.

11. 'Mahendra Pratap on Interview with Lenin', in Adhikari (ed.), *Documents of the History of the Communist Party of India*, p. 112. Moisej Aronovič Persic, *Revolutionaries of India in Soviet Russia: Mainsprings of the Communist Movement in the East* (Moscow: Progress Publishers, 1983), p. 40, notes that Pratap's group probably arrived in Moscow in early July 1919, but that the exact date is unknown. Dalip Singh Gill in a letter to the AA stated that he was in Moscow from 6 July 1919 to 6 August 1919, and that he had met Lenin on 26 July 1919, RZ 201/21118, PAAA.

12. Alif Khan to AA, 5 November 1919, RZ 201/21118, PAAA.

13. M. Acharya, statement, 27 July 1920, F. 5, OP. 3, D. 79, Secretariat V.I. Lenin (1917–1924), RGASPI.

14. Shaukat Usmani, *Peshawar to Moscow: Leaves from an Indian Muhajireen's Diary* (Benares: Swarajy Publishing House, 1927), pp. 132–3.

15. Bhupendra Nath Datta, *Dialectics of Land-Economics of India* (Calcutta: Mohendra Publishing Committee, 1952), pp. iii–iv.

16. Raja Mahendra Pratap, Vir Singh (ed.), *Reminiscences of a Revolutionary* (New Delhi: Books India International, 1999), pp. 38–9.

17. Ansari, 'Pan-Islam and the Making of the Early Indian Muslim Socialists', pp. 509–37.

18. 'Central Asia, Persia, and Afghanistan. Bolshevik and Pan-Islamic Movements and connected Information', IOR/L/PS/18/A184.

19. Quoted in: A. Raikov, 'October Revolution and Indian Immigrants in Germany', in Ilasai Manian and V. Rajesh (eds), *The Russian Revolution and India* (London: Routledge, 2020), p. 104.

20. Frederick M. Bailey, *Mission to Tashkent* (London: Jonathan Cape, 1946), p. 228.

21. 20 March 1920, WRDCI; '"A few words written in the interest of The Soviet Russia and India". Handwritten text by Raja Mahendra Pratap dated December, 1921', in Roy *et al.* (eds), *Indo-Russian Relations*, p. 150.

22. Ansari, 'Pan-Islam and the Making of the Early Indian Muslim Socialists', pp. 519–21; see also, M. A. Faruqui to Mahendra Pratap, 1 August 1928, IOR/Mss Eur F265/13.

23. 'Russia. Code 38 File 123 (to paper 10625)', FO 371/8170, NA.

24. Ibid.

263

pp. [91–95] NOTES

25. Ibid.
26. Ibid.
27. Ibid.
28. Ibid.
29. Ibid.
30. Indian Revolutionary Association, 'Revolutionary India', *Pravda* (20 May 1920), p. 1. See also V. I. Lenin, 'To the Indian Revolutionary Association', 13 May 1920 [https://www.marxists.org/archive/lenin/works/1920/may/13b.htm], accessed 21 May 2022.
31. Ibid; see also, 'Wireless message of greetings dated 14.5.1920 from V. I. Lenin to Abdur Rabb Barq, Chairman, Indian Revolutionary Association', in Roy *et al.* (eds), *Indo-Russian Relations*, p. 6.
32. Ansari, 'Pan-Islam and the Making of the Early Indian Muslim Socialists', pp. 519–21.
33. Kris Manjapra, *M. N. Roy: Marxism and Colonial Cosmopolitanism* (London: Routledge, 2010), pp. 37–8; Isabel Huacuja Alonso, 'M. N. Roy and the Mexican Revolution: How a Militant Indian Nationalist Became an International Communist', *South Asia: Journal of South Asian Studies*, 40:3 (2017), pp. 517–30.
34. M. N. Roy, *M. N. Roy's Memoirs* (Bombay: Allied Publishers Private Limited, 1964), pp. 290–7; Tim Harper, *Underground Asia: Global Revolutionaries and the Assault on Empire* (Cambridge: Harvard University Press, 2021), pp. 380–1.
35. C. S. Subramanyam, *M. P. T. Acharya: His Life and Times: Revolutionary Trends in the Early Anti-Imperialist Movements in South India and Abroad* (Madras: Institute of South Indian Studies, 1995), p. 156; Ansari, 'Pan-Islam and the Making of the Early Indian Muslim Socialists', pp. 520–2; Suchetana Chattopadhyay, 'Via Kabul: *Muhajirs* Turned Early Communists from India (1915–1923)', in Anne Garland Mahler and Paolo Capuzzo (eds), *The Comintern and the Global South: Global Designs/Local Encounters* (London: Routledge, 2022), pp. 125–46.
36. V. I. Lenin, 'Draft Theses on National and Colonial Questions for The Second Congress Of The Communist International', [https://www.marxists.org/archive/lenin/works/1920/jun/05.htm#fw01], accessed 21 May 2022.
37. M. N. Roy, 'Supplementary Theses on the National and Colonial Questions', in John Riddell (ed.), *Workers of the World, Unite!: Proceedings and Documents of the Second Congress, 1920* (New York: Pathfinder, 1991), pp. 218–22; J. P. Haithcox, 'The Roy–Lenin Debate on Colonial Policy: A New Interpretation', *The Journal of Asian Studies*, 23:1 (November 1963), pp. 93–101.
38. M. Acharya, 'M. N. Roy As I Knew Him', unpublished (February 1937), HD (Special)/1937, Maharashtra State Archives. I am grateful to Gautam Pemmaraju for sharing this document with me.
39. M. Acharya, statement, 27 July 1920, F. 5, OP. 3, D. 79, Lenin's Secretariat (1917–1924), RGASPI.
40. Ibid.
41. Acharya, 'M. N. Roy As I Knew Him'; Persic, *Revolutionaries of India in Soviet Russia*, p. 125, n. 1.

264

NOTES

pp. [95–99]

42. Riddell (ed.), *Workers of the World and Oppressed Peoples, Unite!*, p. 835; 'Letter from the Indian Delegation dated 9.8.20. at the Second Congress of Comintern to S. Saklatvala and R. Palme Dutt', in Roy *et al.* (eds), *Indo-Russian Relations*, pp. 22–5; see also, 'Abani Nath Mukherji, communist exile: application for an amnesty and passport to return to India', IOR/L/PJ/12/212, file 961/24.

43. To the members of the Presidium, India, 489/1/24/030, RGASPI. Sneevliet also signed the proposition, but his name is crossed out in the document. [http://sovdoc.rusarchives.ru/sections/organizations//cards/134542/images], accessed 22 May 2022.

44. Proposal, combination commission, national and colonial question, 489/1/24/032, RGASPI [http://sovdoc.rusarchives.ru/sections/organizations//cards/134542/images], accessed 22 May 2022.

45. André Liebich and Svetlana Yakimovich (eds), *From Communism to Anti-Communism: Photographs from the Boris Souvarine Collection at the Graduate Institute, Geneva* (Geneva: Graduate Institute Publications, 2016); 'Second Congress of the Comintern in Petrograd (1920)', [https://www.net-film.ru/en/], accessed 21 May 2022; 78884, Soviet Propaganda Film Communist International, 1919–1943', [https://stock.periscopefilm.com/78884-soviet-propaganda-film-communist-international-1919–1943/], accessed 21 May 2022.

46. Acharya to Lenin, 24 July 1920, 2/1/24686/012:014, RGASPI. I am grateful to Lina Bernstein for sharing this document with me.

47. Ibid.

48. Ibid.

49. Quoted in: 22 November 1920, WRDCI.

50. 'Resolution on the contract coolie and indentured labour systems in the colonies and subject countries', undated, 489/1/14/142, RGASPI.

51. Ibid.

52. Ibid.

53. Riddell (ed.), *Workers of the World and Oppressed Peoples, Unite!*, p. 828.

54. Ibid.

55. Roy *et al.* (eds), *Indo-Russian Relations*, p. 43, note.

56. 'Letter from (?) dated 30.12.20. to Shiva Prasad Gupta', in Roy *et al.* (eds), *Indo-Russian Relations*, pp. 44–50. In a footnote, the letter is attributed to Mukherji.

57. 'Program of the Provisional All-India Central Revolutionary Committee', Archief Henk Sneevliet, ARCH00984.340, IISH.

58. Ibid.

59. Ibid.

60. Quoted in Alastair Kocho-Williams, 'The Soviet Challenge to British India' in Oleksa Drachewych and Ian McKay (eds), *Left Transnationalism: The Communist International and the National, Colonial, and Racial Questions* (Montreal; Kingston; London; Chicago: McGill-Queen's University Press, 2019), p. 131; Roy, *Memoirs*, p. 391.

61. 'Manifesto of the Congress to the Peoples of the East', [https://www.marxists.

pp. [99–102]   NOTES

org/history/international/comintern/baku/manifesto.htm], accessed 21 May 2022.

62. 'Mohammad Abdur Rabb Barq's note dated 10.8.20. to the Comrades of the Third International, Second Congress, Baku', in Roy *et al.* (eds), *Indo-Russian Relations*, pp. 25–6.

63. 'Bolshevism: The Oriental Congress at Baku', P 6583/1920, IOR/L/PS/11/176.

64. Riddell (ed.), *To See the Dawn*, p. 61. However, see also Brian Pearce (ed.), *Congress of the Peoples of the East, Baku, September 1920, Stenographic Report* (London: New Park Publications, 1977), p. 190: 'Though there seems to be no evidence of [Acharya's] attendance at the congress' (190).

65. Riddell (ed.), *To See the Dawn*, pp. 208–9; Pearce (ed.), *Congress of the Peoples of the East*, pp. 151–2.

66. For more on Ragdaev's involvement with the CAPE and Indians in Tashkent and Bukhara, see 'Memorandum on preparations in Bukhara by N. Rogdaev', 1 April 1921, RGASPI, f. 544, op. 4, d. 26, l.77–81, *Russian Perspectives on Islam*, [https://islamperspectives.org/rpi/items/show/11389], accessed 23 May 2022.

67. Ali Raza, *Revolutionary Pasts: Communist Internationalism in Colonial India* (Cambridge: Cambridge University Press, 2020), pp. 73–4.

68. See also, Drachewych, *Left Transnationalism*, pp. 130–1.

7. THE INDIAN COMMUNIST PARTY

1. Acharya, 'Revolutionary Party of India', *Izvestiia* (19 September 1920), p. 1. I am grateful to Lina Bernstein for translating this article.

2. See Shafique's statement in 'Judgement by the Sessions Judge, Peshawar, convicting Mohammad Shafiq to 3 years imprisonment for Bolshevik activities', IOR/L/PJ/6/1884, file 3110; see also Minutes of the ICP meeting, 28 December 1920, 495/68/4, RGASPI.

3. M. N. Roy, *M. N. Roy's Memoirs* (Bombay: Allied Publishers Private Limited, 1964), p. 465.

4. Roy to Suritz, 4 October 1920, 495/68/2–17, RGASPI. I am grateful to Natalia Mikaberidze for sharing these files with me.

5. Roy to Suritz, 4 October 1920, 495/68/2–17, RGASPI.

6. Ibid.

7. 495/68/4–12, RGASPI. See also, 'Handwritten Minutes of meetings concerning the formation of the Indian Communist Party at Tashkent between 18.10.20. and 26.12.20', in Purabi Roy, Sobhanlal Datta Gupta, and Hari Vasudevan (eds), *Indo-Russian Relations, 1917–1947: Select Documents from the Archives of the Russian Federation* (Calcutta: Asiatic Society, 1999), pp. 38–9; see also, 'Minutes of the Meeting held on 17 October 1920', in Gangadhar Adhikari (ed.), *Documents of the History of the Communist Party of India, Vol. 1, 1917–1922* (New Delhi: People's Publishing House, 1971), p. 231.

8. Moisej Aronovič Persic, *Revolutionaries of India in Soviet Russia: Mainsprings of the Communist Movement in the East* (Moscow: Progress Publishers, 1983), pp. 197–8.

NOTES
pp. [102–107]

9. K. H. Ansari, 'Pan-Islam and the Making of the Early Indian Muslim Socialists', *Modern Asian Studies*, 20:3 (1986), pp. 528–31; Roy, *Memoirs*, p. 469.

10. Shaukat Usmani, 'Russian Revolution and India—III', *Mainstream Weekly*, 55:48 (18 November 2017), [http://mainstreamweekly.net/article7591.html], accessed 21 May 2022; for more on Usmani, see Ali Raza, *Revolutionary Pasts: Communist Internationalism in Colonial India* (Cambridge: Cambridge University Press, 2020), pp. 52–9.

11. Ibid.

12. Acharya to Roy, 28 October 1920, 495/68/17–30, RGASPI.

13. Roy to Acharya, 1 November 1920, 495/68/17–1, RGASPI.

14. Acharya to Roy, 6 November 1920, 495/68/17–20, RGASPI.

15. Roy to Acharya, 11 November 1920, 495/68/17–21, RGASPI.

16. Acharya to Roy, 12 November 1920, 495/68/17–22, RGASPI.

17. Acharya to Roy, 17 November 1920, 495/68/17–39–40, RGASPI.

18. Acharya to Roy, 19 November 1920, 495/68/17–34, RGASPI.

19. Acharya to Roy, 30 November 1920, 495/68/17–41, RGASPI.

20. Shaukat Usmani, *Historic Trips of a Revolutionary: Sojourn in the Soviet Union* (New Delhi: Sterling Publishers, 1977), p. 49.

21. Usmani to Roy, December 1920, 495/68/17–33, RGASPI.

22. Ibid.

23. Typed scripts (regarding meetings of the P.A.I.C.R.C., jointly with the Indian Communist Party, held in the Headquarter of the Committee), Papers on the Communist Party of India, Horst Krüger Papers, Box 45, 337–1, ZMO; 'Virendranath Chattopadhyaya's Speech', in Adhikari (ed.), *Documents of the History of the Communist Party of India*, p. 86; Nirode K. Barooah, *Chatto: The Life and Times of an Indian Anti-Imperialist in Europe* (New Delhi; Oxford: Oxford University Press, 2004), pp. 158–9.

24. Acharya to Roy, 4 December 1920, 495/68/17–37, RGASPI.

25. Quoted in: Persic, *Revolutionaries of India in Soviet Russia*, p. 204.

26. Typed scripts (regarding meetings of the P.A.I.C.R.C., jointly with the Indian Communist Party, held in the Headquarter of the Committee), Papers on the Communist Party of India, Box 45, 337, 1, Horst Krüger Papers, ZMO.

27. Minutes of meeting in the ICP, 15 December 1920, 495/68/4, RGASPI.

28. Ibid.

29. Ibid.

30. Shaukat Usmani, 'Russian Revolution and India—V', *Mainstream Weekly*, 55:50 (2 December 2017), [http://mainstreamweekly.net/article7626.html], accessed 21 May 2022.

31. Typed scripts (regarding meetings of the P.A.I.C.R.C., jointly with the Indian Communist Party, held in the Headquarter of the Committee), Papers on the Communist Party of India, Box 45, 337, 1, Horst Kruger Papers, ZMO.

32. Minutes of the ICP meeting, 18 December 1920, 495/68/4, RGASPI.

33. Ibid.

pp. [107–110] NOTES

34. Ibid.
35. Ibid.
36. Ibid.
37. Minutes of the ICP meeting, 26 December 1920, 495/68/4, RGASPI.
38. Minutes of the ICP meeting, 28 December 1920, 495/68/4, RGASPI.
39. Ibid.
40. Ibid.
41. Ibid.
42. Ibid.
43. Ibid.
44. Ibid.
45. Roy, *Memoirs*, pp. 464–5.
46. 'Copy of letter dated 30.1.21. from Secretary, Indian Communist Party, to M.P.B.T. Acharya criticising his activities and informing him of his removal from the Chairmanship of the Central Committee', in Roy *et. al* (eds), *Indo-Russian Relations*, pp. 58–9.
47. Persic, *Revolutionaries of India in Soviet Russia*, p. 205.
48. Ibid.
49. Cecil Kaye (ed.), *Communism in India: Unpublished Documents from National Archives of India (1919–1924)* (Calcutta: Editions Indian, 1971), p. 165.
50. 'Copy of letter of Provisional All India Central Revolutionary Committee dated 24.1.21. to M.P.B.T. Acharya removing him from membership of the Committee' in Roy *et. al* (eds), *Indo-Russian Relations*, pp. 57–8.
51. Ibid.
52. 'Copy of letter dated 30.1.21. from Secretary, Indian Communist Party, to M.P.B.T. Acharya criticising his activities and informing him of his removal from the Chairmanship of the Central Committee', in Roy *et. al* (eds), *Indo-Russian Relations*, pp. 58–9.
53. Acharya to ECCI, 30 January 1921, quoted in: C. S. Subramanyam, *M. P. T. Acharya: His Life and Times: Revolutionary Trends in the Early Anti-Imperialist Movements in South India and Abroad* (Madras: Institute of South Indian Studies, 1995), p. 162.
54. Acharya to Lenin, 1 February 1921, F. 5, OP. 3, D. 79, Secretariat V.I. Lenin (1917–1924), RGASPI.
55. 495/68/1, RGASPI; see also, 'Copy of Telegram dated 14.3.21. sent by Carl Steinhardt and D. Zetkin to the Small Bureau of Comintern (with copies to V. I. Lenin and G. Zinoviev) regarding discord between the IRA, Tashkent and the Communist Group of M. N. Roy and Abani Mukherji', in Roy *et. al* (eds), *Indo-Russian Relations*, pp. 59–60.
56. Acharya to ECCI, 23 March 1921, 495/68/17, RGASPI.
57. Ibid.
58. 'Minutes of a Meeting of Indian revolutionaries dated 3.4.21. at Tashkent', in Roy *et. al* (eds), *Indo-Russian Relations*, p. 64.
59. Ibid.

NOTES pp. [111–118]

60. Kaye (ed.), *Communism in India*, p. 169; Jyoti Basu (ed.), *Documents of the Communist Movement in India, Vol. 1, 1917–1928* (Calcutta: National Book Agency, 1997), p. 99.
61. Barooah, *Chatto*, pp. 159–60.
62. Persic, *Revolutionaries of India in Soviet Russia*, pp. 111–12.
63. Acharya to Keell, 2 August 1925, Freedom Archives, ARCH00428.435, IISH; 'Third Congress of the Comintern (1921)', [2:05–2:09], Russian Archives of Documentary Films and Newsreels, [https://www.net-film.ru/en/film-79466/], accessed 8 November 2020.
64. Barooah, *Chatto*, pp. 163–9; 'Thesis on India and the World Revolution. Presented to the ECCI and the Congress Commission on Oriental Questions by V. Chattopadhyaya, G.A.K. Luhani and P. Khankhoje on the occasion of Comintern's Third Congress', in Roy *et. al* (eds), *Indo-Russian Relations*, pp. 116–25.
65. Janice Mackinnon and Stephen Mackinnon, *Agnes Smedley: The Life and Times of an American Radical* (Berkeley: University of California Press, 1988), p. 74.
66. Emma Goldman, *Living My Life* (Garden City: Garden City Publishers, 1934), p. 771.
67. Acharya to ECCI, 22 July 1921, 495/68/45, 16–19, RGASPI.
68. Acharya to ECCI, 3 August 1921, 495/68/45, RGASPI.
69. Ibid.
70. Ibid.

8. ANTI-COMMUNIST ACTIVITIES

1. Acharya, 'Memories of a Revolutionary', *People* (4 August 1927), pp. 90–1.
2. Ibid.
3. Ibid.
4. Acharya, 'Madame Kollontai', *Thought*, 4:14 (5 April 1952), p. 6.
5. Acharya to Yelensky, 22 May 1947, Boris Yelensky Papers, ARCH01675.46, IISH.
6. Acharya, 'Lenin after the NEP', *Thought*, 4:3 (19 January 1952), p. 6. For more on Balabanoff, Kollontai, and the Workers' Opposition, see Cathy Porter, *Alexandra Kollontai. A Biography* (London: Virago, 1980), pp. 365–98.
7. Lina Bernstein, *Magda Nachman: An Artist in Exile* (Brookline: Academic Studies Press, 2020), pp. 167–9.
8. Acharya, 'Lenin after the NEP', p. 6.
9. Bertrand Patenaude, *The Big Show in Bololand: The American Relief Expedition to Soviet Russia in the Famine of 1921* (Stanford: Stanford University Press, 2002), p. 413.
10. Kedleston to British Commercial Mission, Moscow, 4 September 1922, FO 371/8170, NA; Muzaffar Ahmad, *Myself and the Communist Party of India, 1920–1927* (Calcutta: National Book Agency, 1970), pp. 55–6.
11. John J. Mangan, letter of reference, 8 September 1922, RZ 207/80564, PAAA.
12. Alexander Berkman, *The Bolshevik Myth* (London: Hutchinson & Co., 1925), p. 54.
13. Alexander Berkman, 9 March 1920, 'Russian diary', 20 December 1919–22 January 1922, Alexander Berkman Papers, ARCH00040.2, IISH.

pp. [118–126]   NOTES

14. Goldman, *Living My Life*, p. 751.

15. Alexander Berkman, 8 March 1920, 'Russian diary', 20 December 1919–22 January 1922, Alexander Berkman Papers, ARCH00040.2, IISH; Applebaum quoted in: Grigori P. Maximoff, *The Guillotine at Work: Twenty Years of Terror in Russia (Data and Documents), Vol. 2* (Chicago: Chicago Section of the Alexander Berkman Fund, 1940), pp. 577–8, 617–18. 'Applebaum' might be Naum Aaronovich Epplebaum. I am grateful to Kenyon Zimmer for this suggestion.

16. Acharya to Yelensky, 23 June 1947, Boris Yelensky Papers, ARCH01675.46, IISH.

17. Avrich, *The Russian Anarchists*, p. 244; for more on Ragdaev, see 'Memorandum on preparations in Bukhara by N. Rogdaev', 1 April 1921, RGASPI, f. 544, op. 4, d. 26, l.77–81, *Russian Perspectives on Islam*, [https://islamperspectives.org/rpi/items/show/11389], accessed 23 May 2022.

18. Acharya to Yelensky, 28 April 1947, Boris Yelensky Papers, ARCH01675.46, IISH; Shaukat Usmani, 'Russian Revolution and India—IV', *Mainstream Weekly*, 55:49 (25 November 2017), [http://www.mainstreamweekly.net/article7609.html], accessed 21 May 2022; Usmani, *Historic Trips of a Revolutionary*, p. 54.

19. Avrich, *The Russian Anarchists*, pp. 228–31.

20. Acharya, 'Lenin after the NEP', p. 6.

21. Bernstein, *Magda Nachman*, pp. 161–72.

22. Bernstein, *Magda Nachman*, pp. 142, 159–62.

23. 'Russia. Code 38 File 123 (to paper 10625)', FO 371/8170, NA.

24. Bernstein, *Magda Nachman*, p. 169.

25. Gill had been imprisoned in the Butyrka Prison in March 1921 at the request of the Berlin Indians, who suspected him of being a spy: 2 May 1921, WRDCI; 5 June 1921 WRDCI.

26. 'Dalip Singh Gill: activities in Europe and USA', IOR/L/PJ/12/65, file 4991/21; see also 'Russian communist influence in India: agents, recruitment, training and propaganda', IOR/L/PJ/12/117, file 6533/22.

27. Acharya to Reisner, 18 December 1922, 495/68/64, RGASPI. On Gill's imprisonment, see Cecil Kaye (ed.), *Communism in India: Unpublished Documents from National Archives of India (1919–1924)* (Calcutta: Editions Indian, 1971), pp. 167–8.

28. Ibid.

9. ANTICOLONIALISM AND ANARCHISM IN WEIMAR BERLIN

1. Polizeipräsidium, Passstelle fur Ausländer, 24 November 1922, RZ 207/80558, PAAA.

2. Acharya to Reisner, 18 December 1922, 495/68/64/36, RGASPI. I am grateful to Lina Bernstein for sharing this document with me.

3. Acharya to Parthasarathy, 4 September 1923, quoted in: 'Orientals in Berlin and Munich: S I S and D I B reports', IOR/L/PJ/12/102, file 6303/22.

4. See, Gerdien Jonker, *On the Margins: Jews and Muslims in Interwar Berlin* (Leiden;

NOTES pp. [127–130]

Boston: Brill, 2020); Weijia Li, 'Otherness in Solidarity: Collaboration between Chinese and German Left-Wing Activists in the Weimar Republic', in Qinna Shen and Martin Rosenstock (eds), *Beyond Alterity: German Encounters with Modern East Asia* (New York; Oxford: Berghahn Books, 2014), pp. 73–93.

5. Acharya to Parthasarathy, 4 September 1923, IOR/L/PJ/12/102, file 6303/22.

6. Acharya to Reisner, 18 December 1922, 495/68/64/36, RGASPI.

7. Nirode K. Barooah, *Chatto: The Life and Times of an Indian Anti-Imperialist in Europe* (Oxford: Oxford University Press, 2004), p. 179.

8. For more on Suhasini Chattopadhyaya, see Ania Loomba, *Revolutionary Desires: Women, Communism, and Feminism in India* (Milton: Routledge, 2018), pp. 244–7.

9. A. C. N. Nambiar, Industrial and Trade Review for India, 23 September 1925, RZ 207/80564, PAAA.

10. IOR/L/PJ/12/102, file 6303/22.

11. B. Rosenthal, Zonophon A.G., letter of recommendation, 31 July 1925, RZ 207/80564, PAAA.

12. Acharya to Parthasarathy, 4 September 1923, IOR/L/PJ/12/102, file 6303/22.

13. 'Mandayam P Tirumal Acharya, anarchist: activities and passport application', IOR/L/PJ/12/174, file 7997/23.

14. Polizeiprasidium, Abteilung I A, Fremdenamt, 15 June 1923, RZ 207/80558, PAAA.

15. Rudolf Rocker, *Revolución y Regresión (1918–1951)* (Buenos Aires: Editorial Tupac, [1952]), pp. 194–5.

16. Ibid.

17. Barooah, *Chatto*, pp. 231, 267; Ole Birk Laursen, 'Anti-Colonialism, Terrorism, and the "Politics of Friendship": Virendranath Chattopadhyaya and the European Anarchist Movement', *Anarchist Studies*, 27:1 (2019), pp. 47–62.

18. Wayne Thorpe, *The Workers Themselves: Revolutionary Syndicalism and International Labour, 1913–1923* (Dordrecht; Boston: Kluwer Academic and International Institute of Social History, 1989), pp. 244–68.

19. Internationalen Arbeiter-Assoziation, *Resolutionen, angenommen auf dem Internationalen Kongress der Revolutionären Syndikalisten zu Berlin, vom 25. Dezember 1922 bis 2. Januar 1923* (Berlin: Internationalen Arbeiter-Assoziation, 1923), p. 12

20. 'Die Propaganda des revolutionaren Syndikalismus in Indien', *Der Syndikalist*, 5:4 (1923), Beilage, n.p.

21. Souchy to Berkman, 10 February 1931, Alexander Berkman Papers, ARCH00040.140, IISH.

22. 'Die Lage in Indien', *IAA Pressedienst*, 12 (17 July 1923), n.p.

23. 'Bericht des Sekretariats der I.A.A. über 1923–1924', IWMA Archives, ARCH00658.17, IISH.

24. 'Prohibition of the bringing by sea or by land into British India of any copy of any publication issued by the International Working Men's Association, Berlin', Home & Political, 1923, file 115, NAI.

25. Mr Bhayankar, 'The "Communist" Programme: A Critical Review', *The Hindu*

pp. [130–134]   NOTES

(14 February 1923), n.p. I am grateful to Lina Bernstein and Vadim Damier for sharing this article with me.

26. Ibid.

27. 'Mandayam P Tirumal Acharya, anarchist; activities and passport application', IOR/L/PJ/12/174, file 7997/23. There are several reports on affairs in India in *Workers' Dreadnought* from that period but mostly anonymous and none under Acharya's name.

28. Acharya to Labour Kisan Party of Hindustan, June 1923, quoted in: 'Mandayam P Tirumal Acharya, anarchist; activities and passport application', IOR/L/PJ/12/174, file 7997/23.

29. Acharya to Velayudham, July 1923, quoted in: C. S. Subramanyam, *M. P. T. Acharya: His Life and Times: Revolutionary Trends in the Early Anti-Imperialist Movements in South India and Abroad* (Madras: Institute of South Indian Studies, 1995), p. 176; M. P. S. Velayudham—A Life Sketch, 1925/139, P. C. Joshi Collection, Archives on Contemporary History, Jawaharlal Nehru University, Delhi. I am grateful to Maria Framke for sharing this file with me.

30. Joshi to Acharya, no date, Horst Krüger Papers, Box 2, 6–1, ZMO.

31. Acharya to Das, July 1923, quoted in: 'Mandayam P Tirumal Acharya, anarchist; activities and passport application', IOR/L/PJ/12/174, file 7997/23.

32. Kw file 139, 1925, Home & Political, NAI.

33. Nirode K. Barooah, *Germany and the Indians between the Wars* (Norderstedt: Books on Demand, 2018), pp. 24–37.

34. Chatto and Pillai to Foreign Minister of the Reich, 21 July 1924, 'Indian political activity in Germany; deportation requests', IOR/L/PJ/12/223, file 1387(a)/24.

35. 'Treatment of Indians in Berlin', Home & Political, 1924, file 384, NAI.

36. Kw file 139, 1925, Home & Political, NAI.

37. 'Proposed deportation of certain Indian seditionists from Germany', Home & Political, 1925, file 139, NAI.

38. Ibid.; 'Application of Mr M P T Acharya for a British passport', IOR/L/E/7/1439, file 721; Polizeiprasidium, Abteilung I A, Fremdenamt, Jan 1925, RZ 207/80558, PAAA.

39. Barooah, *Germany and the Indians between the Wars*, pp. 12–24.

40. Acharya to British Consul, Berlin, 15 February 1926, IOR/L/E/7/1439, file 721.

41. H. Roger Grant, 'Portrait of a Workers' Utopia: The Labor Exchange and the Freedom, Kan., Colony', *Kansas Historical Quarterly*, 43:1 (Spring 1977), pp. 56–66.

42. W. H. G. Armytage, *Heavens Below: Utopian Experiments in England, 1560–1960* (London: Routledge & Kegan Paul, 1961), pp. 413–15.

43. Antony Taylor, 'The Whiteway Anarchists in the Twentieth Century: A Transnational Community in the Cotswolds', *History*, 101:1 (2016), pp. 62–83.

44. Acharya to Keell, 26 July 1926, Freedom Archives, ARCH00428.435, IISH.

45. 'Slog Slog Slog', *British Llano Circle Bulletin*, 9 (November 1926), p. 1.

46. Ibid.

47. 'Payment of interest', *Llano Colonist*, 8:823 (29 September 1928), p. 16.

NOTES

pp. [134–137]

48. Ibid.
49. Ibid.
50. 'Correspondence', *Llano Colonist*, 10:1017 (16 August 1930), p. 9.
51. Acharya to Keell, 2 August 1925, Freedom Archives, ARCH00428.435, IISH.
52. Keell to Berkman, 7 August 1925, Alexander Berkman Papers, ARCH00040.2, IISH; Berkman to Keell, 26 August 1925, Emma Goldman Papers, David M. Rubinstein Rare Book and Manuscript Library, Duke University.
53. Acharya to Keell, 3 September 1925, Freedom Archives, ARCH00428.435, IISH. Keell's notebooks shows that he continued to send copies of *Freedom* to Acharya throughout the 1920s to 1930s, Freedom Archives, ARCH00428.479, ARCH00428.488, ARCH00428.493, IISH.
54. Acharya to Keell, 24 September 1925, Freedom Archives, ARCH00428.435, IISH.
55. Jose C. Moya, 'Anarchism', in Akira Iriye and Pierre-Yves Saunier (eds), *Palgrave Dictionary of Transnational History* (New York: Palgrave Macmillan, 2009), p. 40.
56. M. N. Roy, 'What Is a Communist Party?', *Masses of India*, 2:1 (January 1926), pp. 9–14.
57. Acharya, 'Hinter den Kulissen der sowjetrussischen Diplomatie', *Der Syndikalist*, Beilage, 8:8 (20 February 1926), p. 1; 'Die Niederlage Moskaus', *IAA Pressedienst*, 4:25 (67) (12 June 1926), n.p; 'The Communist "Revelations"', *Freedom*, 40:435 (June–July 1926), p. 1; '"Communism", Toryism, and Spies', *The Commune* (May 1926), pp. 128–32; 'Indien', *Der Syndikalist*, Beilage, 8:34 (21 August 1926), n.p.
58. Acharya to Keell, 24 July 1926, Freedom Archives, ARCH00428.435–438, IISH.
59. Acharya, 'Communism in Its True Form', *Mahratta*, 25 (13 June 1926), pp. 306–7.
60. Ibid. Italics in original.
61. 'National Communism: Beware of False Friends', *Masses of India*, 2:9 (September 1926), p. 7.
62. Ibid.
63. Ibid.
64. Acharya, 'Anarchist Manifesto', *Road to Freedom*, 3:1 (1 September 1926), pp. 5–6.
65. Ibid.
66. 'Proscription Under the Sea Custom Act, 1878 of the *Industrial and Trade Review for Asia* and Subsequent Withdrawal of This Proscription in Regards to Future Loans of the Paper', Home & Political, 1926, F-135-II, NAI.
67. A. C. Berman, Deutsche Film Union, letter of recommendation, 27 March 1928, RZ 207/80564, PAAA.
68. 'Indians in Berlin: A National Evening', *Bombay Chronicle* (1 March 1926), p. 9; 'Our Berlin Letter', *Bombay Chronicle* (3 August 1926), p. 10; 'Our Berlin Letter', *Bombay Chronicle* (19 January 1927), p. 10.
69. Eric Ames, *Carl Hagenbeck's Empire of Entertainments* (Seattle: University of Washington Press, 2008).
70. The Indians in Berlin had already protested against Jürgen Johansen's, one of Carl Hagenbeck's former associates, exhibition of Indians in the Zoo Stellingen in Hamburg in May 1925; see 'Animals and Indians at the Hamburg Zoo', *Industrial and Trade Review for India*, 12 (15 June 1925), p. 195.

pp. [137–144] NOTES

71. Acharya, 'Poor Indians Abroad: Jugglers at a Berlin Zoo', *Bombay Chronicle* (20 July 1926), p. 6.
72. Ibid.
73. Barooah, *Germany and the Indians between the Wars*, pp. 37–43.
74. Ibid., p. 44.
75. Acharya, 'The Hagenbeck Show', *People* (10 April 1927), p. 289.
76. Ibid.
77. Acharya to de Jong, 3 April 1928, Archief IAMV, ARCH00662.455, IISH.
78. Acharya, 'Usury', *People* (21 November 1926), p. 410. Italics in original.
79. Ibid.
80. Acharya, 'Wages and Politics', *People* (6 February 1927), p. 109.
81. Benjamin Zachariah, *Nehru* (London: Routledge, 2004), pp. 57–60; Michele Louro, *Comrades against Imperialism: Nehru, India, and Interwar Internationalism* (Cambridge; New York: Cambridge University Press, 2018), pp. 27–33.
82. Letter from Jawaharlal Nehru to Vijaya Lakshmi Pandit, 10–12 November 1927, reprinted in: 'Comrades All in Resurgent Russia', *Bombay Chronicle* (10 December 1927), p. 4.
83. Ibid.
84. Ibid.
85. Acharya, 'Bolshevik Prisons—A Protest', *People* (23 February 1928), pp. 120–1.
86. Ibid.
87. Ibid.
88. Jawaharlal Nehru, 'Bolshevik Prisons', *People* (29 March 1928), p. 204.
89. Ibid.
90. Ibid.
91. Acharya, 'Russian Prisons', *People* (24 May 1928), p. 326.
92. Acharya, 'Dear "Comrade" (?) Nehru', *People* (24 May 1928), p. 326.
93. Agnes Smedley, 31.5.28, KV 2/2207, NA; IOR/L/PJ/12/174, file 7997/23.

10. ANTI-IMPERIALISM AND ANTI-MILITARISM

1. For a list of attendees at the Rathauskeller conference, see 542/1/4, RGASPI.
2. Fredrik Petersson, *"We are Neither Visionaries nor Utopian Dreamers": Willi Münzenberg, the League Against Imperialism, and the Comintern, 1925–1933* (Lewiston: Queenston Press, 2013); 'Oppression in Colonies: League formed in Berlin', *Bombay Chronicle* (1 February 1927), p. 3.
3. ECCI to Willi Münzenberg, 29 May 1926, 542/1/3, RGASPI.
4. Ibid.
5. Ibid.; see also Petersson, *"We are Neither Visionaries nor Utopian Dreamers"*, pp. 107–8.
6. Purabi Roy, Sobhanlal Datta Gupta, and Hari Vasudevan (eds), *Indo-Russian Relations, 1917–1947: Select Documents from the Archives of the Russian Federation* (Calcutta: Asiatic Society, 1999), p. 373.
7. 'Reports on League against Cruelties and Oppression in the Colonies, International

NOTES pp. [144–147]

Committee for the Liberation of Native People in the Colonies', IOR/L/PJ/12/265, file 1309/25.

8. Michele Louro, *Comrades against Imperialism: Nehru, India, and Interwar Internationalism* (Cambridge; New York: Cambridge University Press, 2018), pp. 22–4.

9. Michele Louro, Carolien Stolte, Heather Streets-Salter, Sana Tannoury-Karam, 'The League Against Imperialism: Lives and Afterlives', in Michele Louro, Carolien Stolte, Heather Streets-Salter, and Sana Tannoury-Karam (eds), *The League Against Imperialism: Lives and Afterlives* (Leiden: Leiden University Press, 2020), pp. 17–52.

10. 'A Berlin Letter: Brussels Congress Criticized', *Bombay Chronicle* (9 April 1927), p. 15.

11. Ibid.

12. Ibid.

13. Ibid.

14. Ibid.

15. Ibid.

16. For Acharya's talks at the Berlin Quakers, see Acharya to Albert de Jong, 23 February 1931, Archief IAMV ARCH00662.458, and Acharya to Albert de Jong, 25 June 1930, Archief IAMV, ARCH00662.458; Acharya, 'A Pacifist Meeting', 20 June 1927, unpublished article, Horst Krüger Papers, Box 2, 6–1, ZMO.

17. 'Notes of the Day: Practical Anti-War Propaganda', *Bombay Chronicle* (11 April 1928), p. 6; M. A., 'Der Antimilitarismus in Indien', *Die Internationale*, 1:7 (1928), pp. 14–17; 'Items of Note', *The Llano Colonist*, 8:824 (6 October 1928), p. 4.

18. 'Principles and Tasks of I.A.M.B', Archief IAMV, ARCH00662.505, IISH.

19. Ole Birk Laursen, Introduction, *Lay Down Your Arms: Anti-Militarism, Anti-Imperialism, and the Global Radical Left in the 1930s* (Atlanta: On Our Own Authority! Publishing, 2019), pp. 16–17.

20. 'Comments', *Road to Freedom: A Periodical of Anarchist Thought, Work, and Literature*, 2:11 (1 August 1926), p. 4; Laursen, Introduction, *Lay Down Your Arms*, p. 18.

21. A. M. Faruqui, *Verslag van het internationale Congres voor Dienstweigering, gehouden te Amsterdam, 25 en 26 mei 1927* (1927), pp. 22–7. Note that Faruqui's initials are incorrectly inversed in this publication.

22. Acharya, 'India's Man Power and the Next Imperialist War', *Forward* (21 August 1927), pp. 4, 12; Acharya, 'Mother India', *Road to Freedom*, 4:9 (April 1928), pp. 6–7; M. A., 'Der Antimilitarismus in Indien', pp. 14–17.

23. De Jong to Faruqui, 9 September 1927, Archief IAMV, ARCH00662.421, IISH.

24. Faruqui to the Secretary of the International Anti-Militarist Committee, 13 September 1927, Archief IAMV, ARCH00662.497, IISH.

25. Ibid.

26. Souchy to de Jong, 21 September 1927, Archief IAMV, ARCH00662.83, IISH.

27. Faruqui to de Jong, 24 November 1927, Archief IAMV, ARCH00662.455; M. A. Faruqui, 'Anti-Militarisme en "Brits"-Indie', *Internationaal Antimilitaristisch Jaarboek* (Amsterdam: I.A.M.V. Sectie Holland, 1928), pp. 47–9; Letter to German General Consulate in Calcutta, 14 December 1933, RZ 207/77416, PAAA.

pp. [148–152]   NOTES

28. International Antimilitaristische Kommission, Tatigkeitsbericht Januar 1927–Mai 1928, Archief Albert de Jong, ARCH00684.5, IISH.
29. Text of the declaration of the International Antimilitarist Commission (IAMC, which consist of the IWA and IAMB) read by A. Müller-Lehning, 1927, League against Imperialism Archives, ARCH00804.60, IISH; also as 'Die IAK tegen de Koloniale Onderdrukking', *IAK Persdient*, 1 (March 1927), p. 1; Arthur Müller-Lehning, 'Der anti-koloniale Kongreß von Brüssel', *Der Syndikalist*, 9:10 (5 March 1927), Beilage, n.p.
30. Ibid.
31. Ibid.
32. de Jong to Faruqui, 19 October 1927, Archief IAMV, ARCH00662.421, IISH.
33. Acharya to de Jong, 21 September 1927, Archief IAMV, ARCH00662.455, IISH.
34. Acharya to the AITUC, 29 April 1928, box 2, 6.1.25, Horst Krüger Papers, ZMO.
35. Ibid.
36. Ibid.
37. Berkman to Goldman, 27 April 1928, Alexander Berkman Papers, ARCH00040.26, IISH.
38. Ibid.
39. 'Passports: grant of facilities for Mr Lakshman P Varma and his wife and to Mr M P Tirumal Acharya', IOR/L/PJ/1968, file 3981.
40. Ibid; 'Death Penalties in Indonesia', *IAC Press Service*, 11 (March 1928), p. 5.
41. Acharya to de Jong, 30 April 1932, Archief IAMV, ARCH00662.462, IISH.
42. Correspondence with de Jong, Archief IAMV, ARCH00662.455 and ARCH0 0662.458, IISH.
43. Acharya to de Jong, 3 April 1928, Archief IAMV, ARCH00662.455, IISH.
44. 'International Anti-Militaristic Bureau (IAMB): Report of the Secretariat for the Year 1929', *IAC Press Service*, 39 (28 March 1930), pp. 2–3.
45. Text of the speech of A. Müller-Lehning, representative of the International Anti-Military Bureau (IAMB) on the conflict between China and the Soviet-Union, League against Imperialism Archives, ARCH00804.83, IISH; 'The IAMB at the Anticolonial World Congress', *IAC Press Service*, 31 (1 August 1929), pp. 1–3; see also, 'Het Revolutionnaire Anti-Militarisme en de Anti-Imperialistische Taktiek', *IAK Persdienst* (13 August 1929), p. 1.
46. Müller-Lehning to Acharya, 15 August 1929, Archief IAMV, ARCH00662.455, IISH.
47. Ibid.
48. Fredrik Petersson, '"We will fight with our lives for the equal rights of all peoples": Willi Münzenberg, the League Against Imperialism, and the Comintern', in Louro *et al.* (eds), *League Against Imperialism*, pp. 159–86.
49. Bart de Ligt, 'Gandhi en de Oorlog', *IAK Persdient* (28 November 1928), pp. 1–3.
50. Acharya, 'Mother India', *Road to Freedom*, 4:9 (April 1928), pp. 6–7.
51. For more on Gandhi's antistatism, see Karuna Mantena, 'On Gandhi's Critique of the State: Sources, Contexts, Conjunctures', *Modern Intellectual History*, 9:3 (November 2012), pp. 535–63.

NOTES

pp. [152–158]

52. Ibid.
53. Acharya, 'De la India: El congreso nacional hindú', *La Protesta*, 6532 (26 March 1930), p. 2.
54. See, 'Die zivile Gerhorsamsverweigerung', *IAA Pressedienst*, 8:2 (117) (17 March 1930), p. 14.
55. Acharya, 'Gandhi and Non-Violence', *Road to Freedom*, 7:1 (September 1930), p. 1.
56. Acharya, 'Why Gandhi Attacks Salt-Tax', *IAC Press Service*, 45 (25 April 1930), p. 3.
57. Ibid.
58. Ibid.
59. Acharya, 'Nationalism in India', *Man!* (July 1933), p. 3.
60. 'Inderkundgebund in Berlin', *Badische Presse* (7 May 1930), p. 1; 'Der Indische Boycott', *Berliner Börsen-Zeitung* (7 May 1930), p. 2; 'Die Lage in Indien', *Jeversches Wochenblatt* (7 May 1930), p. 1.
61. Berlin, Humboldthaus. Protestveranstaltung von Indern gegen die Verhaftung von Mahatma Gandhi, Bild 102–09732, Bundesarchiv, Germany.
62. Acharya, 'Der Militarismus in Asien', *Der Syndikalist*, 12:31 (2 August 1930), n.p. I am grateful to Smaran Dayal for translating this article. 'Militarism in Asia: The Obligations of European Workers', *Barricade: A Journal of Antifascism and Translation*, 4 (Fall 2021) [http://barricadejournal.org/issue-4/militarism-in-asia/].
63. Ibid.
64. Ibid.
65. 'Does Europe Want to Know Truth about India? Servile and Subsidized Press Shuts Our Indian News', *Bombay Chronicle* (16 December 1930), p. 5.
66. Souchy to Jensen, 29 September 1932, Albert Jensen International Correspondence, 1931–1932, E 6:7, SAC Archives, ARBARK.

11. ULTRA-LEFTISTS AND OUTSIDERS

1. Magnus Schwantje is listed as a referee for Acharya in a list of references from 1931, RZ 207/80564, PAAA.
2. Karl Korsch to Irving B. Canter, 18 October 1950, in: Karl Korsch, Michael Buckmiller (ed.), *Gesamtausgabe: Briefe, 1940–1958*, (Europäische Verlagsanstalt, 2001), pp. 1281–2; see also Mario Kessler, *Ruth Fischer: Ein Leben mit und gegen Kommunisten (1895–1961)* (Köln: Böhlau Verlag, 2013), p. 286.
3. Augustin Souchy, *Beware! Anarchist! A Life for Freedom: The Autobiography of Augustin Souchy* (Chicago: Charles H. Kerr, 1992 [1977]), pp. 59–60; Henry Pachter, *Weimar études* (New York: Columbia University Press, 1982), p. 54.
4. Acharya to de Jong, 20 October 1929, Archief IAMV, ARCH00662.455, IISH.
5. Acharya, 'Vad är Marxism?', *Arbetaren* (2 January 1951), p. 3.
6. Korsch to Canter, 18 October 1950, in: Korsch, *Gesamtausgabe*, pp. 1281–2.
7. Ibid.
8. KAI afz. KAI (Steckbrief, betr. Friedländer und Raminoff), 1926, Collectie Henk Canne Meijer, ARCH00252.241, IISH.

pp. [158–162] NOTES

9. Pachter, *Weimar études*, p. 55.

10. Acharya to Yelensky, 22 May 1947, Boris Yelensky Papers, ARCH01675.46, IISH.

11. Acharya to Yelensky, 22 May 1947, Boris Yelensky Papers, ARCH01675.46, IISH; Acharya to Yelensky, 23 June 1947, Boris Yelensky Papers, ARCH01675.46, IISH.

12. Paul Avrich, 'Bolshevik Opposition to Lenin: G. T. Miasnikov and the Workers' Group', *Russian Review*, 43:1 (Jan 1984), pp. 1–29.

13. Leon Trotsky, 'Who Is Leading The Comintern Today?', [https://www.marxists.org/archive/trotsky/1928/03/comintern.htm], accessed 21 May 2022.

14. Acharya to Trotsky, 7 January 1932, Leon Trotsky Exile Papers, MS Russ 13.1, (95), Houghton Library, Harvard College Library.

15. Ibid.

16. Alexander Berkman, 'An Anarchist on India', *People* (23 May 1929), pp. 273–4.

17. Ibid.

18. Ibid.

19. Acharya, 'Vom Klassenkampf in Indien', *Der Syndikalist*, Beilage, 9:6 (5 February 1927), n.p.; Acharya, 'Arbeitervertreter in der gesetzgebenden Körperschaft', *IAA Pressedienst*, 5:4 (10 March 1927), pp. 2–3; Acharya, 'Dans l'Inde', *La Voix du Travail*, 2:9 (April 1927), p. 16; Acharya, 'Moderne Sklaverei in Indien', *IAA Pressedienst*, 6:5, 95 (21 April 1928), p. 4; Acharya, 'La huelga de los obreros textile', *Acción Social Obrera* (8 September 1928), p. 4.

20. Acharya, 'Indien', *IAA Pressedienst*, 7:8 (111) (28 September 1929), pp. 5–6; Acharya, 'La cuestión social en la India', *La Revista Blanca* (1 December 1929), supplemento, p. 12; Acharya, 'De la India', *La Protesta*, 6438 (5 December 1929), p. 2; Acharya, 'India', *Acción Social Obrera* (7 December 1929), p. 4; Acharya, 'Dans l'Inde', *Le Libertaire* (7 December 1929), p. 3.

21. Acharya, 'Unity—What For?', *Road to Freedom* (September 1928), p. 6; Acharya, 'Why This Judicial Murder?', *Road to Freedom* (August 1929), p. 8.

22. Acharya, 'Les Trusts et la Démocratie', *L'En Dehors*, 133–134, 135 (April–May 1928), pp. 4, 5. An anonymous response to Acharya appeared soon after: 'Réflexions suscitées par la lecture de *L'En Dehors*', *L'En Dehors*, 138–139 (end-July 1928), p. 6.

23. Acharya, 'Les Trusts et la Démocratie', pp. 4, 5.

24. Ibid.

25. Ibid.

26. Acharya, 'The Mystery Behind the Chinese Trouble', *Road to Freedom*, 3:4 (1 November 1926), pp. 2–3.

27. Acharya, 'Die Ereignisse in China und die freiheitliche Bewegung', *Der Syndikalist*, Beilage, 9:10 (5 March 1927), n.p.

28. Acharya, 'De gebeurtenissen in China', *De Syndicalist*, 4:200 (23 April 1927), p. 1.

29. Acharya, 'Dr Sun Yat Sen's Principles', *Forward* (21 July 1927), p. 7.

30. Ibid.

31. Ibid.

32. Acharya, 'Die proletarierin in Indien', *Der Frauen-Bund*, Monatsbeilage *Der Syndikalist* (November 1926), p. 5.

NOTES pp. [162–165]

33. 'Association de Combat Contre la Jalousie et l'Exclusivisme en Amour', *L'En Dehors* (August 1926), p. 5; Cécilia Varela, 'Au-delà des normes? "L'amour libre" et la famille antiautoritaire (1880–1930)', *Mouvements*, 82:2 (2015), pp. 123–31. Armand would sometimes insert a note in *L'En Dehors* asking Acharya to be patient and notifying him that all letters and articles had been received; see *L'En Dehors* (end-September 1928), p. 8; *L'En Dehors* (mid-May 1929), p. 8.

34. Acharya, 'Pourquoi faire de la Sexologie', *L'En Dehors* (February 1930), p. 6.

35. Acharya, 'De l'influence de la toilette sur la mentalité', *L'En Dehors* (mid-March 1929), p. 1; Acharya, 'La "barbarisation" de la beauté', *L'En Dehors* (mid-November 1931), p. 2.

36. Acharya, 'Les éléments de la prostitution dans le mariage', *L'En Dehors* (mid-March 1931), pp. 12–13.

37. Acharya, 'les "cabarets nudistes"', *L'En Dehors* (April 1935), p. 268.

38. Ibid.

39. Acharya, 'La nature est mon aphrodisiaque', *L'En Dehors* (mid-March 1932), pp. 73–4.

40. Acharya, 'De la jalousie', *L'En Dehors* (November 1929), p. 6; Acharya, 'Les tragédies de l'adultéré', *L'En Dehors* (March 1934), pp. 6–7.

41. Acharya, 'Ou la chasteté n'a pas de raison d'être', *L'En Dehors* (15 May 1932), p. 101; Acharya, 'Le Combat contre la jalousie', *L'En Dehors* (15 June 1932), p. 114.

42. Acharya, 'A propos de la libération du sentiment en Russie', *L'En Dehors* (15 July 1932), p. 142.

43. Acharya, 'Étude sur le matriarcat', *L'En Dehors* (November 1933), pp. 4–6; Acharya, 'A propos d'une enquête sur le féminisme', *L'En Dehors* (June 1935), pp. 311–12.

44. Acharya, 'A propos de la Saint-Barthélemy Hitlerienne', *L'En Dehors* (mid-August–mid-September 1934), pp. 164–5.

45. Ibid.

46. Ibid.

47. Acharya, 'Shittoshin no mondai ni tsuite', *Fujin Sensen*, 2:2 (February 1931), pp. 14–17.

48. Takamure Itsue quoted in: Andrea Germer, 'Continuity and Change in Japanese Feminist Magazines: *Fujin Sensen* (1930–31) and *Onna Erosu* (1973–82)', in Ulrike Wöhr, Barbara Hamill Sato, and Suzuki Sadamo (eds), *Gender and Modernity: Rereading Japanese Women's Magazines* (Kyoto: International Research Center for Japanese Studies, 2000), p. 125.

49. Acharya to Armand, 1 April 1931, Fonds Armand, Correspondence, 14AS/211, Institut Français d'Histoire Sociale (IFHS), Archives Nationales (AN).

50. Acharya to Armand, undated but after April 1931, Fonds Armand, Correspondence, 14AS/211, IFHS, AN.

51. Harold Coward, *Indian Critiques of Gandhi* (Albany: State University of New York Press, 2003), 41–66; Ankur Barua, 'Revisiting the Gandhi–Ambedkar Debates

pp. [165–172] NOTES

over "Caste": The Multiple Resonances of Varna', *Journal of Human Values*, 25:1 (January 2019), pp. 25–40.

52. Acharya, 'Indiens frihetsrörelser under andra världskriget', *Arbetaren* (10 June 1947), p. 4.

53. Acharya to the INC, 15 April 1928, Horst Krüger Papers, Box 2, 6–1, ZMO.

54. Acharya, 'Geistiges Leben, Duldsamkeit und Gegensätze in Indien', *Der Syndikalist*, Beilage, 10:28 (14 July 1928), n.p.

55. Albert Bruhl, 'Indien', *Contra: Anarchistische Monatsschrift*, 1:2 (25 May 1930), pp. 1–5.

56. Acharya, 'Die indische Erhebung als freiheitliche Revolution', *Der Syndikalist*, 12:25 (21 June 1930), n.p.

57. Acharya, 'Sur la question de race', *L'En Dehors* (September 1933), pp. 174–5; see also, Camilo Berneri, *El Delirio Racista* (Buenos Aires: Editions Iman, February 1935).

58. Indulal Yagnik, *The Autobiography of Indulal Yagnik* (New Delhi: Manohar Publishers and Distributors, 2011), pp. 439–40.

59. Ibid., p. 440.

60. Indulal Yagnik, *Life of Ranchoddas Bhavan Lotvala* (Bombay: Writers' Emporium, 1952), p. 76.

61. Maia Ramnath, *Decolonizing Anarchism: An Antiauthoritarian History of India's Liberation Struggle* (Oakland: AK Press, 2011), p. 132.

62. 'Mandayam P Tirumal Acharya, anarchist; activities and passport application', IOR/L/PJ/12/174, file 7997/23.

63. Yagnik, *The Autobiography of Indulal Yagnik*, pp. 440–1.

64. Ibid.

65. *Indian Press Service*, 7 (14 February 1931), p. 7; Yagnik, *The Autobiography of Indulal Yagnik*, pp. 437, 441.

66. 'Ranchoodas Bhavan Lotwalla and son Narottam R Lotwalla: communist activities; passport facilities', IOR/L/PJ/12/167, file 7475/23; Ahmad, *Myself and the Communist Party of India*, p. xi.

67. Yagnik, *Life of Ranchoddas Bhavan Lotvala*, 75–6; 'Mandayam P Tirumal Acharya, anarchist; activities and passport application', IOR/L/PJ/12/174, file 7997/23; for Nitisen Lotvala, see, 'Duplicate Passport', IOR/L/PJ/11/1/728: 1932.

12. ESCAPE FROM EUROPE

1. Acharya, 'Lettre d'Allemagne', *L'En Dehors* (15 August 1932), p. vi.

2. Ibid.

3. Acharya to Armand, 28 November 1932, Fonds Armand, Correspondence, 14AS/211, IFHS, AN.

4. Acharya to Armand, Christmas 1932, Fonds Armand, Correspondence, 14AS/211, IFHS, AN.

5. 'Der Presse-Dienst der IAA Verboten', *IAA Presse-Dienst*, 2:158 (3 March 1933), p. 6.

NOTES pp. [172–177]

6. Augustin Souchy, *Beware! Anarchist! A Life for Freedom: The Autobiography of Augustin Souchy* (Chicago: Charles H. Kerr, 1992 [1977]), pp. 60–1.

7. 'Two documents on the loss of the archives of the IMWA by A. Souchy. [1933]', IWMA Archives, ARCH00658.81, IISH.

8. A. C. N. Nambiar, 'Nambiar's Story of His Arrest in Berlin', *Bombay Chronicle* (8 May 1933), p. 7.

9. Nirode K. Barooah, *Germany and the Indians between the Wars* (Norderstedt: Books on Demand, 2018), pp. 89–94; Vappala Balachandran, *A Life in Shadow: The Secret Story of A. C. N. Nambiar: A Forgotten Anti-Colonial Warrior* (New Delhi: Lotus Collection, Roli Books, 2016), pp. 72–3; Gautam Pemmaraju, 'The Dark Foreigner with the Great Dog: Jayasurya Naidu in Germany, 1922–1934', *Nidan: International Journal for Indian Studies*, 7:1 (July 2022), pp. 115–31; Daniel Brückenhaus, *Policing Transnational Protest: Liberal Imperialism and the Surveillance of Anticolonialists in Europe, 1905–1945* (New York: Oxford University Press, 2017), pp. 169–71.

10. Politische Beziehungen Indiens zu Deutschland, RZ 207/77416, PAAA.

11. For more on Bose's sojourn in Berlin, see Leonard A. Gordon, *Brothers against the Raj: A Biography of Indian Nationalists Sarat and Subhas Chandra Bose* (New York: Columbia University Press, 1990), pp. 274–5; Sugata Bose, *His Majesty's Opponent: Subhas Chandra Bose and India's Struggle against Empire* (Cambridge: Harvard University Press, 2011), pp. 91–2.

12. Acharya to AA, September 1933, RZ 207/77455, PAAA.

13. Ibid.

14. Ibid.

15. Acharya, 'Indian Exiles Abroad: An Appeal', *Forward* (18 August 1927), 4.

16. Acharya, 'Passport Refused to Mr. Acharyya', *Forward* (21 January 1928), 3.

17. Brockway to Dalton, 3 July 1931, IOR/L/PJ/6/1968, file 3981.

18. Brockway to Hoare, 21 September 1931, IOR/L/PJ/6/1968, file 3981.

19. Hoare to Brockway, 25 September 1931, IOR/L/PJ/6/1968, file 3981.

20. Acharya to Gandhi, 12 September 1931, Correspondence: 1931, 000018200, Sabarmati Ashram Preservation and Memorial Trust, Ahmedabad. I am grateful to Kinnari Bhatt for sharing this material with me.

21. Acharya to Gandhi, 29 October 1931, Correspondence: 1931, 000018200, Sabarmati Ashram Preservation and Memorial Trust, Ahmedabad.

22. Acharya to AA, 29 April 1932, RZ 207/80564, PAAA; Brockway to Acharya, 23 August 1932, RZ 207/80564, PAAA.

23. 'Passports: grant of facilities for Mr Lakshman P Varma and his wife and to Mr M P Tirumal Acharya', IOR/L/PJ/6/1968, file 3981.

24. Schmidt-Rolke to Acharya, 3 March 1934, RZ 207/78314, PAAA; Lina Bernstein, *Magda Nachman: An Artist in Exile* (Boston: Academic Studies Press, 2020), p. 199.

25. AA to German Ministry of the Interior, 17 February 1934, RZ 207/78316, PAAA.

26. Acharya to Armand, 18 February 1934, Fonds Armand, Correspondence, 14AS/211, IFHS, AN.

27. Ibid.

pp. [177–181] NOTES

28. Ibid.

29. Ibid.

30. Ibid.; Acharya to Armand, 24 April 1934, Fonds Armand, Correspondence, 14AS/211, IFHS, AN; Qiang Lei, 'Bibliotheque Sino-Internationale Geneve and the *Orient et Occident*', *Journal of Library and Information Studies*, 13:1 (June 2015), pp. 135–61.

31. Acharya to Armand, 18 February 1934, Fonds Armand, Correspondence, 14AS/211, IFHS, AN.

32. 'Hindou', *L'En Dehors* (mid-April 1934), p. 4.

33. Acharya to Armand, 18 February 1934, Fonds Armand, Correspondence, 14AS/211, IFHS, AN.

34. Acharya to Armand, 24 April 1934, Fonds Armand, Correspondence, 14AS/211, IFHS, AN.

35. 'Notes', *The British Llano Circle Bulletin*, 72 (June/July/August 1934), p. 4.

36. Ibid.

37. Acharya, 'An American Experiment Worth Trying in India', *Bombay Chronicle* (17 March 1936), p. 3.

38. Acharya, 'Madame Cama: A Rebel Throughout Her Life', *Mahratta* (12 August 1938), p. 5.

39. 'Grant of permission to Madame Cama, a notorious revolutionary, to return to India from Europe', Home & Political, 1935, file 28–38, NAI.

40. Acharya, 'Madame Cama', p. 5.

41. 'Grant of permission to Madame Cama, a notorious revolutionary, to return to India from Europe', Home & Political, 1935, file 28–38, NAI.

42. See also, Hillary Lazar, '*Man!* and the International Group: Anti-Radicalism, Immigrant Solidarity and Depression-Era Transnational Anarchism', in Frank Jacob and Mario Kessler (eds), *Transatlantic Radicalism: Socialist and Anarchist Exchanges in the 19th and 20th Centuries* (Liverpool: Liverpool University Press, 2021), pp. 109–27.

43. Acharya, 'A Belated Forecast for the Year 1934', *Man!* (March 1934), p. 99.

44. Acharya, 'Anarchy or Chaos?', *Man!*, 2: 9–10 (September–October 1934), p. 4.

45. Acharya to Armand, 1 December 1934, Fonds Armand, Correspondence, 14AS/211, IFHS, AN.

46. Acharya to Armand, 18 December 1934, Fonds Armand, Correspondence, 14AS/211, IFHS, AN.

47. Ibid.

48. Acharya to Armand, 7 February 1935, Fonds Armand, Correspondence, 14AS/211, IFHS, AN.

49. Ibid.

50. Acharya to Armand, 14 February 1935, Fonds Armand, Correspondence, 14AS/211, IFHS, AN.

51. Acharya to Armand, 1 March 1935, Fonds Armand, Correspondence, 14AS/211, IFHS, AN.

52. Ibid.

NOTES pp. [181–187]

53. Acharya to Armand, 5 March 1935, Fonds Armand, Correspondence, 14AS/211, IFHS, AN.
54. Kuijsten to Roland Holst, 12 February 1935, Archief IAMV, ARCH00662.524, IISH.
55. Beyer to IAMB, 4 March 1935, Archief IAMV, ARCH00658.524, IISH. In a letter to Armand, 18 December 1934, Acharya stated that he and Nachman were friends of Henriette Roland Holst.
56. Acharya to Armand, 18 February 1934, Fonds Armand, Correspondence, 14AS/211, IFHS, AN.
57. Acharya to AA, 25 September 1933, RZ 207/455, PAAA.
58. Acharya to Armand, 5 March 1935, Fonds Armand, Correspondence, 14AS/211, IFHS, AN.
59. Ibid.

13. RETURN TO INDIA

1. 'Passports: grant of facilities for Mr Lakshman P Varma and his wife and to Mr M P Tirumal Acharya', IOR/L/PJ/6/1968, file 3981.
2. Acharya, 'Armament Race in Europe', *Bombay Chronicle* (10 April 1935), p. 5.
3. Ibid.
4. Ibid.
5. Ibid.
6. Acharya to Armand, 17 May 1935, Fonds Armand, Correspondence, 14AS/211, IFHS, AN. See also, C. S. Subramanyam, *M. P. T. Acharya: His Life and Times: Revolutionary Trends in the Early Anti-Imperialist Movements in South India and Abroad* (Madras: Institute of South Indian Studies, 1995), p. 189.
7. Acharya to Armand, 14 June 1935, Fonds Armand, Correspondence, 14AS/211, IFHS, AN.
8. Ibid.
9. Acharya to Armand, 17 May 1935, Fonds Armand, Correspondence, 14AS/211, IFHS, AN.
10. Acharya to Armand, 14 June 1935, Fonds Armand, Correspondence, 14AS/211, IFHS, AN.
11. 'Around Theatre and Film Land', *Bombay Chronicle* (1 December 1935), 15.
12. Lina Bernstein, *Magda Nachman: An Artist in Exile* (Boston: Academic Studies Press, 2020), pp. 202–3.
13. Acharya, 'De ineenstorting van de britse macht', *De Wapens Neder*, 31:11 (November 1935), p. 9.
14. Ibid.
15. Ibid.
16. For an insightful analysis of 'anarchy' as 'government of no one' rather than 'self-government', see Ruth Kinna, *The Government of No One: The Theory and Practice of Anarchism* (London: Pelican, 2019).

pp. [188–190] NOTES

17. 'Discontinuance of the International Antimilitarist Commission', *IAMB Press Service* (3 September 1937), n.p.

18. Acharya, 'A Letter from India', *Man!* (November 1937), p. 3. Acharya is listed as an editor of the *Bombay Chronicle* in a list of recipients in the CNT (España) Archives. *Notas y direcciones en España y en el extranjero para enviar periódicos, los boletines de información y otros materiales de propaganda*, CNT (España) Archives, ARCH00293.103D.1, IISH. I am grateful to Julia Lange for sharing this file with me.

19. Ibid.

20. Ibid.

21. Ibid.

22. Lina Bernstein, 'The Great Little Lady of the Bombay Art World', in Christoph Flamm, Roland Marti, Ada Raev (eds), *Transcending the Borders of Countries, Languages, and Disciplines in Russian émigré Culture* (Newcastle: Cambridge Scholars Publishing, 2018), p. 145.

23. Acharya to Armand, 7 February 1935, Fonds Armand, Correspondence, 14AS/211, IFHS, AN; Acharya, 'Reminiscences of a Revolutionary', *Mahratta* (23 July; 30 July; 20 August; 27 August; 3 September; 10 September; 17 September; 3 October 1937)

24. Acharya to Armand, 16 September 1938, Fonds Armand, Correspondence, 14AS/211, IFHS, AN.

25. M. P. T. Acharya, Bishamber Dayal Yadav (ed.), *Reminiscences of an Indian Revolutionary* (New Delhi: Anmol Publications, 1991).

26. Acharya, 'Madame Cama: A Rebel Throughout Her Life', *Mahratta* (12 August 1938), pp. 3, 5; Acharya, 'The Most Anti-British Englishman: Sir Walter Strickland', *Mahratta* (9 September 1938), p. 3.

27. 'The 18th of August 1938', *Mahratta* (19 August 1939), p. 1.

28. Nirode K. Barooah, *Chatto: The Life and Times of an Indian Anti-Imperialist in Europe* (Oxford: Oxford University Press, 2004), pp. 285–6; Michele Louro, *Comrades against Imperialism: Nehru, India, and Interwar Internationalism* (Cambridge; New York: Cambridge University Press, 2018), p. 260; Fredrik Petersson, 'Hub of the Anti-Imperialist Movement', *Interventions: International Journal of Postcolonial Studies*, 16:1 (2014), pp. 49–71.

29. 'Whereabouts of Virendranath Chattopadhyaya', IOR/L/PJ/7/12100, file 6471.

30. Acharya, 'What is the Fact? Fate of Viren Chattopadhyay', *Mahratta* (3 June 1938), p. 3; Acharya, 'Viren Chattopadhyaya: A Chequered Career', *Mahratta* (10 June 1938), p. 7; Acharya, 'Viren Chattopadhyaya Trapped by a British Spy', *Mahratta* (17 June 1938), p. 3; Acharya, 'Swiss Attempts to Trap Chatto', *Mahratta* (24 June 1938), p. 3; see also Ole Birk Laursen, '"A Dagger, a Revolver, a Bottle of Chloroform": Colonial Spy Fiction, Revolutionary Reminiscences and Indian Nationalist Terrorism in Europe', in Elleke Boehmer and Dominic Davies (eds), *Planned Violence: Post/Colonial Urban Infrastructure, Literature and Culture* (Palgrave Macmillan, 2018), pp. 255–71.

31. 'Viren Chattopadhyaya', *Oriental Review*, 2:6 (June 1938), pp. 266–7.

NOTES   pp. [190–195]

32. 'Whereabouts of Virendranath Chattopadhyaya', IOR/L/PJ/7/12100, file 6471.

33. Barooah, *Chatto*, pp. 314–27; Petersson, 'Hub of the Anti-Imperialist Movement', pp. 63–4.

34. For more on Savarkar and the Hindu Mahasabha, see Dhirendra K. Jha, *Gandhi's Assassin: The Making of Nathuram Godse and His Idea of India* (Gurugram: Vintage by Penguin Random House India, 2021), p. 32.

35. Indulal Yagnik, *Life of Ranchoddas Bhavan Lotvala* (Bombay: Writers' Emporium, 1952), p. 75.

36. Lotvala to Frank Chodorov, 15 May 1950, quoted in: Yagnik, *Life of Ranchoddas Bhavan Lotvala*, p. v; see also, D. M. Kulkarni, 'Shri R. B. Lotwala: The Prophet of Human Freedom—A Life-Sketch', *Selections from The Indian Libertarian Part 2: 1971–1981* (1981), p. 1; 'Some Important years and events in Shri R. B. Lotwala's Life & Career', *Selections from The Indian Libertarian Part 2: 1971–1981* (1981), p. 8.

37. Acharya to Yelensky, 27 May 1953, Boris Yelensky Papers, ARCH01675.87, IISH. Acharya stated that it was him who facilitated the contact to Rocker.

38. Lotvala to Rocker, 1 June 1938, Rudolf Rocker Papers, ARCH01194.58, IISH.

39. Ibid.

40. Ibid.

41. For Rocker's position on nationalism, see Ruth Kinna, 'What is Anarchist Internationalism?', *Nations and Nationalism*, 27:4 (2020), pp. 976–91.

42. Rocker to Souchy, 23 April 1946, Augustin Souchy Papers, ARCH01364.17, IISH.

43. 'Editor of *Man!* Jailed Again', *Oriental Review*, 2:6 (June 1938), pp. 280–2, 288.

44. 'A Co-Operative Organisation in India', *Community Life: Monthly Journal of Movement for Communal Living*, 1:4 (June 1939), p. 8.

45. Acharya to Armand, 12 September 1946, Fonds Armand, Correspondence, 14AS/211, IFHS, AN.

46. Acharya to Armand, 14 June 1935, Fonds Armand, Correspondence, 14AS/211, IFHS, AN.

47. Acharya, 'Latin Script for India', *Mahratta* (2 and 9 July 1937), pp. 8, 9.

48. Paul Jauzin, 'A Propos de l'alphabet Latin', *L'En Dehors* (August–September 1938), p. 93.

49. Acharya to Armand, 16 September 1938, Fonds Armand, Correspondence, 14AS/211, IFHS, AN.

50. Acharya, 'Distribution of Colonial Products: Will It Help Economic Recovery?', September 1937, unknown publication, Joseph A. Labadie Collection, Special Collections Library, University of Michigan, Ann Arbor, United States.

51. Acharya, 'Is War Inevitable?', *Mahratta* (15 April 1938), p. 5.

52. Ibid.

53. Acharya, 'Failure of Democracy and Rise of Fascism', *Mahratta* (8–15 December 1939), p. 7.

54. Marco Polo [Acharya], 'That Jigsaw Puzzle Remains Unsolved: Can Sir Cripps Solve It?', *Kaiser-i-Hind* (5 April 1942), n.p; private correspondence with Barry Pateman, 6 March 2020.

pp. [195–202]   NOTES

55. Yasmin Khan, *India at War: The Subcontinent and the Second World War* (New York: Oxford University Press, 2015), pp. 41–2.
56. 'List of Books Published in England and Withheld in India Under the General Communist Notification of the 10th Sept 1932', May 1938, Home & Political, 1937, file 41–10, NAI.
57. 'Annual Report of the Year Indian and Anglo-Indian Newspapers Published in the Bombay Province for the Year 1940', Home & Political, I 1941, F-53 1 41 KW PART 3, NAI; 'Fortnightly reports on the political situation in India for the Month of May 1940', Home & Political, File No. 18/5/40, NAI.

14. TOWARDS FREEDOM

1. 'Magda Nachman Paintings', *Times of India* (9 November 1940), p. 13; 'Famous Landmarks Absent', *Times of India* (22 November 1941), p. 11; 'Three Enchanting Ballets', *Times of India* (24 February 1943), p. 2.
2. Acharya to Armand, 2 July 1945, Fonds Armand, Correspondence, 14AS/211, IFHS, AN; Acharya, 'Request from India', *The Word* (March 1946), p. 95; Acharya to Yelensky, 22 May 1947, Boris Yelensky Papers, ARCH01675.46, IISH.
3. Lama Anagarika Govinda, 'A Visit to Magda Nachman's Studio', *Aesthetics* (Jan–March 1951), p. 7. I am grateful to Lina Bernstein for sharing this article with me.
4. Ibid., p. 8.
5. Acharya to Armand, 2 July 1945, Fonds Armand, Correspondence, 14AS/211, IFHS, AN.
6. Ibid.
7. Ibid.
8. Acharya to Armand, 18 March 1946, Fonds Armand, Correspondence, 14AS/211, IFHS, AN.
9. 'Trois mots aux amis', *L'Unique*, 1:10 (May 1946), p. 140.
10. Acharya, 'Request from India', *The Word* (March 1946), p. 95.
11. Souchy to Rocker, 13 July 1946, Rudolf Rocker Papers, ARCH01194.199, IISH.
12. Ibid.
13. Rocker to Souchy, 17 August 1946, Augustin Souchy Papers, ARCH01364.17, IISH.
14. Rocker to Souchy, 13 February 1947, Augustin Souchy Papers, ARCH01364.17, IISH.
15. Souchy to Rocker, 25 January 1947, Augustin Souchy Papers, ARCH01364.17, IISH.
16. de Santillan to Rocker, 20 December 1946, Rudolf Rocker Papers, ARCH0 1194.192, IISH.
17. Mario Kessler, *Ruth Fischer: Ein Leben mit und gegen Kommunisten (1895–1961)* (Köln: Böhlau Verlag, 2013), pp. 393–405.
18. Acharya to Yelensky, 22 May 1947, Boris Yelensky Papers, ARCH01675.46, IISH.
19. K. R. [Kate Ruminov] to Acharya, 22 January 1947, Ruth Fischer Papers, Box 20,

NOTES pp. [202–207]

MS Ger 204, 1024, Houghton Library, Harvard University; Acharya, 'The Indian Struggle', *The Word* (August 1946), p. 11.

20. Basil Ruminov, 'Communist Workers' Opposition', *The Word* (November 1946), p. 35.

21. Acharya to Steelink, 7 March 1948, Nicolaas Steelink Papers, Walter P. Reuther Library, Archives of Labor and Urban Affairs, Wayne State University, Detroit.

22. Korsch to Fischer, 6 October 1951, in: Karl Korsch, Michael Buckmiller (ed.), *Gesamtausgabe: Briefe, 1940–1958* (Europäische Verlagsanstalt, 2001), p. 1388.

23. Lotvala to Rocker, 14 February 1946, Rudolf Rocker Papers, ARCH01194.58, IISH.

24. Lotvala to Rocker, 11 March 1946, Rudolf Rocker Papers, ARCH01194.58, IISH.

25. Ibid.

26. Lotvala to Rocker, 26 November 1946, Rudolf Rocker Papers, ARCH01194.58, IISH; Rudolf Rocker, *Socialism and the State* (Indore City: Modern Publishers, 1946).

27. Lotvala to Rocker, 9 May 1947, Rudolf Rocker Papers, ARCH01194.58, IISH.

28. Lotvala to Rocker, 24 July 1947, Rudolf Rocker Papers, ARCH01194.58, IISH; Nicolas Walter, Introduction, Rudolf Rocker, *Anarcho-Syndicalism* (London: Pluto Press, 1989), p. xvi.

29. 'What is Libertarian Socialism?', *The Indian Sociologist*, 6:3 (June–July–August 1947), pp. 45–48.

30. Indulal Yagnik, *Life of Ranchoddas Bhavan Lotvala* (Bombay: Writers' Emporium, 1952), p. 83.

31. Acharya to Armand, 18 March 1946, Fonds Armand, Correspondence, 14AS/211, IFHS, AN.

32. Acharya to Yelensky, 28 April 1947, Boris Yelensky Papers, ARCH01675.46, IISH.

33. Ibid.

34. Acharya to Yelensky, 28 April 1947, Boris Yelensky Papers, ARCH01675.46, IISH.

35. Acharya to Yelensky, 22 May 1947, Boris Yelensky Papers, ARCH01675.46, IISH.

36. Ibid; Acharya to Yelensky, 23 June 1947, Boris Yelensky Papers, ARCH01675.46, IISH.

37. Acharya to Yelensky, 24 July 1947, Boris Yelensky Papers, ARCH01675.46, IISH; Yelensky to Acharya, 21 August 1947, Boris Yelensky Papers, ARCH01675.46, IISH.

38. 'Today's Engagements', *Bombay Chronicle* (11 January 1947), p. 3.

39. D. M. Kulkarni, 'Shri R. B. Lotvala: The Prophet of Human Freedom—A Life-Sketch', *Selections from The Indian Libertarian Part 2: 1971–1981* (1981), p. 1.

40. Lotvala to Rocker, 24 July 1947, Rudolf Rocker Papers, ARCH01194.58, IISH.

41. 'Important Announcement', *The Indian Sociologist*, 6:3 (June–July–August 1947), p. 58.

42. 'Libertarian Socialist Institute: Principal Aims and Objects', *The Libertarian Socialist*, 1:1 (Jan–Feb–March 1950), inside cover page.

43. Acharya to Rodriguez, 10 March 1948, Fonds de la Commission des relations internationales anarchistes, A 002 CRIA, Centre International de Recherches sur

287

pp. [207–209] NOTES

l'Anarchisme, Lausanne (CIRA). I am grateful to Marianne Enckell for sharing these documents with me.

44. Ibid.

45. Ibid.

46. Ibid.

47. Ibid.

48. Ibid.

49. Ibid.

50. Ibid.

51. Ibid.

52. Ibid.

53. Ibid.

54. 'Memorandum on the Bases, Structures and Function of the Commission for International Anarchist Relations (CRIA)', Commission for International Anarchist Relations Archives, ARCH00318, IISH.

55. Ibid.

56. Ibid.

57. Acharya, 'India: Vientos de fronda', *C.N.T.* (13 August 1948), p. 2.

58. Acharya to Yamaga, 21 November 1948, Yamaga Collection, Center for International Research on Anarchism, Japan (CIRA Japan). Acharya refers to Ba Jin's pen name Li Pei Kan in his letters, hence this variant is used here. I am grateful to Hikaru Tanaka for sharing this material with me.

59. Steven Wright, 'Left Communism in Australia: J. A. Dawson and the *Southern Advocate for Workers' Councils*', *Thesis Eleven*, 1:1 (1980), pp. 43–77.

60. Acharya to Yamaga, 26 December 1948, Yamaga Collection, CIRA Japan.

61. Acharya to Yamaga, 21 November 1948, Yamaga Collection, CIRA Japan. See also, Acharya, 'Les Japonais et les mœurs', *L'Unique*, 43 (November–December 1949), pp. 46–7.

62. Acharya to Baldwin, 1 December 1948, India—Indian Civil Liberties Union. 1940–1948. MS Years of Expansion, 1950–1990: Series 3: Subject Files: International Civil Liberties, 1942–1982 Box 1149, Folder 13, Item 2. American Jurisprudence Collections at the Mudd Manuscript Library: American Civil Liberties Union, Princeton University.

63. Baldwin to Acharya, 9 December 1948, India—Indian Civil Liberties Union. 1940–1948. MS Years of Expansion, 1950–1990: Series 3: Subject Files: International Civil Liberties, 1942–1982 Box 1149, Folder 13, Item 2. American Jurisprudence Collections at the Mudd Manuscript Library: American Civil Liberties Union, Princeton University.

64. Baldwin to Mehra, 8 December 1948, India—Indian Civil Liberties Union. 1940–1948. MS Years of Expansion, 1950–1990: Series 3: Subject Files: International Civil Liberties, 1942–1982 Box 1149, Folder 13, Item 2. American Jurisprudence Collections at the Mudd Manuscript Library: American Civil Liberties Union, Princeton University.

NOTES pp. [210–215]

65. For a list of these questions, see Yu Rim to CRIA, Our Opinion on the Bill of International Anarchist Meeting, 9 September 1949, Commission for International Anarchist Relations Archives, ARCH00318, IISH.
66. Acharya to CRIA, 12 September 1949, Commission for International Anarchist Relations Archives, ARCH00318, IISH.
67. Ibid.
68. Ibid.
69. Ibid.
70. Ibid.
71. Ibid.
72. Ibid.
73. Ibid.
74. For more on Esperanto and anarchism, see Sho Konishi, 'Translingual World Order: Language without Culture in Post-Russo-Japanese War Japan', *Journal of Asian Studies*, 72:1 (2013), pp. 91–114.
75. Yu Rim to CRIA, Our Opinion on the Bill of International Anarchist Meeting, 9 September 1949, Commission for International Anarchist Relations Archives, ARCH00318, IISH.
76. Acharya to CRIA, 12 September 1949, Commission for International Anarchist Relations Archives, ARCH00318, IISH.
77. Ibid.
78. Ibid.
79. Ibid.
80. 'Memorandum on the Bases, Structures and Function of the Commission for International Anarchist Relations (CRIA)', Commission for International Anarchist Relations Archives, ARCH00318, IISH.

15. VIOLENT INDEPENDENCE

1. Marco Polo [Acharya], 'How Can Self Government Be Real?', *Freedom*, 7:15 (18 May 1946), p. 3.
2. Ibid.
3. Acharya, 'De la Filosofia a la Economia ... Anarquia', *Tierra y Libertad*, 3:56 (November 1946), p. 2.
4. 'Social Oro i Indien', *IAA Presstjänst* (5 July 1947), pp. 14–16.
5. Acharya, 'Labour Splits in India', *Freedom: Anarchist Fortnightly* (31 May 1947), p. 5.
6. Ibid.
7. Acharya, 'In Defence of Foreign Rule!', *Mahratta* (22 October 1937), p. 1.
8. Acharya, 'Libertarianism versus Dictatorship', *The Libertarian* (July–August–September 1951), pp. 42–3.
9. Marco Polo [Acharya], 'World Government & All That', *Kaiser-i-Hind* (3 July 1949), p. 19.
10. Ibid.

289

pp. [215–220] NOTES

11. Acharya to Armand, 2 July 1945, Fonds Armand, Correspondence, 14AS/211, IFHS, AN.

12. Acharya to Armand, 18 March 1946, Fonds Armand, Correspondence, 14AS/211, IFHS, AN.

13. For more on Kalidas Nag, see Carolien Stolte and Harald Fischer-Tiné, 'Imagining Asia in India: Nationalism and Internationalism (ca. 1905–1940)', *Comparative Studies in Society and History*, 54:1 (2012), pp. 65–92.

14. Kalidas Nag, Introduction, M. P. T. Acharya, *Principles of Non-Violent Economics* (Calcutta: International University of Non-Violence, 1947), p. 1.

15. Ibid.

16. Ibid.

17. Acharya to Relgis, 31 March 1950, Victor Garcia Papers, Biblioteca y Archivo de Sociología y Economía, Montady, Spain (BASE). I am grateful to Danny Evans for sharing these documents with me.

18. Iqbal Singh and Raja Rao, Introduction, *Whither India? (Socio-Politico Analyses)* (Baroda: Padmaja Publications, 1949), p. ix.

19. Ibid.

20. Ibid.

21. Acharya, 'What is Anarchism?', in Iqbal Singh and Raja Rao (eds), *Whither India?*, p. 119.

22. Ibid.

23. Ibid., p. 118.

24. Ibid., p. 120.

25. Acharya, 'Lettre de l'Inde', *L'Unique*, 11 (June 1946), p. 13.

26. Ibid.

27. Ibid.

28. Ibid., p. 14.

29. Ibid., p. 14.

30. Dhirendra K. Jha, *Gandhi's Assassin: The Making of Nathuram Godse and His Idea of India* (Gurugram: Vintage by Penguin Random House India, 2021), p. 114.

31. Shruti Kapila, *Violent Fraternity: Indian Political Thought in the Global Age* (Princeton: Princeton University Press, 2021), p. 95.

32. Jha, *Gandhi's Assassin*, p. 15.

33. Ibid, p. 118.

34. Ibid, p. 127; Kapila, *Violent Fraternity*, p. 126.

35. Guy Aldred, 'Gandhi and India', *The Word* (October 1950), p. 134.

36. Om. P. Kahol, 'Remember, Remember!', *The Word* (November 1950), pp. 6–7.

37. LSI [Lotvala] to Guy Aldred, 10 September 1950, Guy Aldred Collection, 39, non-British correspondence, Mitchell Library, Glasgow, Scotland.

38. Acharya, 'Savarkar: A Criticism', *The Word* (December 1950), pp. 23–4.

39. Ibid.

40. Ibid.

41. Ole Birk Laursen, 'Anarchist Anti-Imperialism: Guy Aldred and the Indian

NOTES pp. [221–225]

Revolutionary Movement, 1909–14', *Journal of Imperial and Commonwealth History*, 46:2 (2018), pp. 286–303.

42. Acharya to Souchy, 12 December 1950, Augustin Souchy Papers, ARCH01364.17, IISH.

43. Daniel Kent-Carrasco, 'From British Colonial Subject to Mexican "Naturalizado": Pandurang Khankhoje's Life Beyond the Reach of Imperial Power (1924–1954)', in Neilesh Bose (ed.), *South Asian Migrations in Global History: Labor, Law, and Wayward Lives* (London: Bloomsbury Academic, 2020), pp. 191–2.

44. Acharya to Souchy, 12 December 1950, Augustin Souchy Papers, ARCH01364.17, IISH. For Gupta's death, see 'Herambalal Gupta', *Modern Review*, 88 (July–December 1950), p. 20.

45. 'Indian Revolutionaries Abroad', *Modern Review* (September 1950), pp. 183–4.

46. Ibid.

47. Sundaram to Rana, 16 April 1951, S. R. Rana Private Papers, online [http://www.sardarsinhrana.com/correspondence] accessed 9 November 2019.

48. 'Exiles' Contribution to Freedom Fight', *Times of India* (15 August 1950), p. 5; 'Exploits of Indian Revolutionaries Abroad', *Indian Daily Mail* (2 December 1954), p. 2.

16. ANARCHY

1. Sandipto Dasgupta, 'Gandhi's Failure: Anticolonial Movements and Postcolonial Futures', *Perspectives on Politics*, 15:3 (September 2017), pp. 647–62.

2. Acharya, 'Indian Opinion', *Southern Advocate for Workers' Council*, 47 (November 1948), p. 6.

3. Jake Hodder, 'Conferencing the international at the World Pacifist Meeting, 1949', *Political Geography*, 49 (November 2015), pp. 40–50.

4. Political Correspondent [Acharya], 'Pacifism: Hypocrisy', *Kaiser-i-Hind* (27 November 1949), p. 1.

5. Ibid.

6. Acharya, 'Voix de l'Inde', *Les Nouvelles Pacifistes*, 2:7 (1 March 1950), p. 3.

7. Ibid.

8. Acharya to Rüdiger, 1 May 1950, Helmut Rüdiger Papers, ARCH01220.49, IISH.

9. Acharya, 'L'exemple Japonais', *Le Libertaire* (23 March 1951), p. 3; Acharya, 'Les Japonais et les mœurs', *L'Unique*, 43 (November–December 1949), pp. 46–7; Acharya, 'Les Japonais et les mœurs', *La Vie au Soleil*, 6 (February 1950), p. 19; Acharya, 'La Vie des Travailleurs aux Indes', *Etudes Anarchistes* (December 1949), pp. 5–6.

10. Acharya, 'Voz Libertaria en la India', *Inquietud*, 2:42 (April 1948), p. 1; Acharya, 'El Pensamiento Libertario en la India', *Inquietud*, 2:43 (May 1948), p. 3; Eugen Relgis, *Los Principios Humanitaristas*. Edición definitiva. (Traducida por Eloy Muñiz del francés y por el autor del rumano) (Montevideo: Ediciones "Humanidad", [1922] 1950).

291

pp. [225–229]   NOTES

11. Acharya to Relgis, 31 March 1950, Victor Garcia Papers, BASE.
12. Wolfe to Ekengren, 19 September 1949, Bert Ekengren Papers, ARBARK.
13. Acharya to Ekengren, 23 October 1949, Bert Ekengren Papers, ARBARK.
14. Acharya to Ekengren, 1 January 1950, Bert Ekengren Papers, ARBARK.
15. Ibid.
16. Ibid.
17. Ibid.
18. Ibid.
19. Ibid.
20. Ibid.
21. A. W. Smith, review of James Joll, *The Anarchists*, *East London Papers*, 8:2 (1972), p. 126; Albert Meltzer, *I Couldn't Paint Golden Angels: Sixty Years of Commonplace Life and Anarchist Agitation* (Edinburgh; San Francisco: AK Press, 1996), p. 127.
22. Internationalist [Meltzer], 'M. P. T. Acharya', *Freedom: The Anarchist Weekly*, 15:33 (14 August 1954), p. 3. Given that Acharya did not leave India after he returned in 1935, I surmise that Meltzer visited him in Bombay. However, Meltzer never explained when and where they had met and has not left any personal papers behind.
23. Minutes of first meeting between V. Richards and A. Meltzer, 2 February 1950, Vernon Richards Papers, ARCH01182.46, IISH.
24. Acharya to Ekengren, 1 January 1950, Bert Ekengren Papers, ARBARK; Acharya to Rüdiger, 1 May 1950, Helmut Rüdiger Papers, ARCH01220.49, IISH.
25. 'Project for an Indian Libertarian Review', *Freedom*, 11:16 (5 August 1950), p. 4; see also 'India', *Freedom*, 11:21 (14 October 1950), p. 3.
26. Ibid.
27. Canter to Korsch, 2 October 1950, Karl Korsch Papers, ARCH00750.5, IISH.
28. Korsch to Canter, 18 October 1950, Karl Korsch Papers, ARCH00750.5, IISH.
29. Ibid.
30. Ibid.
31. Acharya to Souchy, 12 December 1950, Augustin Souchy Papers, ARCH01364.17, IISH.
32. Wanchoo to Souchy, 16 April 1951, Augustin Souchy Papers, ARCH01364.17, IISH.
33. Ibid.
34. CRIA to Acharya, 26 February 1951, CIRA.
35. Acharya to Yamaga, 21 November 1948, Yamaga Collection, CIRA Japan.
36. Acharya to Yamaga, 22 July 1949, Yamaga Collection, CIRA Japan.
37. Ibid.
38. Ibid.
39. Yamaga and S. Ishida to Yelensky, 10 November 1950, Boris Yelensky Papers, ARCH01674.51, IISH.
40. Free Society Group, Chicago, 9 November 1949, Boris Yelensky Papers, ARCH01674.87, IISH.
41. Acharya to Yelensky, 30 November 1948, Boris Yelensky Papers, ARCH01675.46, IISH. Li Pei Kan had to withdraw.

NOTES pp. [230–233]

42. Foreword, *The World Scene from the Libertarian Point of View* (Chicago: Free Society Group, 1951), p. 3.
43. G. P. Maximoff, 'The State of the World', in Free Society Group (ed.), *The World Scene from the Libertarian Point of View* (Chicago: Free Society Group, 1951), p. 5.
44. Andrew Cornell, *Unruly Equality: U.S. Anarchism in the Twentieth Century* (Oakland: University of California Press 2016), p. 199.
45. Acharya, 'How Long Can Capitalism Survive?', in Free Society Group (ed.), *The World Scene from the Libertarian Point of View* (Chicago: Free Society Group, 1951), p. 52.
46. Ibid., p. 54.
47. Acharya to Steelink, 7 March 1948, Nicolaas Steelink Papers, Walter P. Reuther Library, Archives of Labor and Urban Affairs, Wayne State University, Detroit.
48. Acharya to Souchy, 12 December 1950, Augustin Souchy Papers, ARCH01364.17, IISH.
49. Acharya to Ekengren, 1 January 1950, Bert Ekengren Papers, ARBARK.
50. Lina Bernstein, *Magda Nachman: An Artist in Exile* (Boston: Academic Studies Press, 2020), pp. 1–2.
51. 'Artist Dies 4 Hours Before Opening of Exhibition', *Times of India* (13 February 1951), p. 7.
52. Irena Pohrille, *Aesthetics*, 5:1 (January–March 1951), 18, quoted in: Bernstein, *Magda Nachman*, p. 248.
53. Acharya to Souchy, 16 April 1951, Augustin Souchy Papers, ARCH01364.17, IISH.
54. Acharya to Yamaga, 19 April 1951, Yamaga Collection, CIRA Japan.
55. Acharya to Yamaga, 29 April 1951, Yamaga Collection, CIRA Japan.
56. Acharya to Hem Day, 15 May 1951, Mandyam ACHARYA, révolutionnaire agitateur indou; Cote de Rangement: ANAR 3F 01 30, Hem Day Personal Papers, Mundaneum Archives, Mons, Belgium.
57. Acharya to Karanth, undated but probably shortly after Nachman's death, quoted in: C. S. Subramanyam, *M. P. T. Acharya: His Life and Times: Revolutionary Trends in the Early Anti-Imperialist Movements in South India and Abroad* (Madras: Institute of South Indian Studies, 1995), p. 146.
58. K. S. Karanth, *Ten Faces of a Crazy Mind* (Bombay: Bharatiya Vidya Bhavan, 1993), pp. 54, 106, 157; personal correspondence with Dr Ullas Karanth, 18 January 2020.
59. Karanth, *Ten Faces of a Crazy Mind*, p. 157.
60. Acharya to Karanth, quoted in: Subramanyam, *M. P. T. Acharya*, p. 146.
61. Acharya to Yamaga, 19 April 1951, Yamaga Collection, CIRA Japan.
62. Meltzer, *I Couldn't Paint Golden Angels*, p. 130.
63. Acharya to Yamaga, 19 April 1951, Yamaga Collection, CIRA Japan.
64. Acharya to Kunitaro Suda, 22 May 1951, Yamaga Collection, CIRA Japan.
65. Acharya to Karanth, quoted in: Subramanyam, *M. P. T. Acharya*, p. 146.
66. Acharya to Yamaga, 19 April 1951, Yamaga Collection, CIRA Japan; Acharya to Yamaga, 1 August 1951, Yamaga Collection, CIRA Japan.

pp. [233–237]   NOTES

67. Acharya to Yamaga, 1 August 1951, Yamaga Collection, CIRA Japan.

68. 'Informations Internationales', *CRIA Bulletin*, 10:2 (April 1952), n.p.

69. Acharya to Yamaga, 1 August 1951, Yamaga Collection, CIRA Japan.

70. Sarah Miller Harris, *The CIA and the Congress for Cultural Freedom in the Early Cold War: The Limits of Making Common Cause* (Milton: Taylor and Francis, 2016), p. 179; Thomas William Shillam, 'Shattering the "looking-glass world": The Congress for Cultural Freedom in South Asia, 1951–55', *Cold War History*, 20:4 (2020), pp. 441–59.

71. Acharya, 'Freedom and Individualism', *Kaiser-i-Hind* (22 April 1951), p. 20; see also, Acharya, 'State is not Society', *Kaiser-i-Hind* (29 April 1951), p. 24.

72. 'Indian Periscope', *The Libertarian*, 1:1 (April–May–June 1951), p. 15.

73. Acharya, 'Libertarianism versus Dictatorship', *The Libertarian*, 1:2 (July–August–September 1951), p. 43.

74. Ibid.

75. Acharya to Day, 15 May 1951, Hem Day Personal Papers, Mundaneum Archives.

76. Taylor Sherman, 'A Gandhian Answer to the Threat of Communism? Sarvodaya and Postcolonial Nationalism in India', *The Indian Economic & Social History Review*, 53:2 (2016), pp. 249–70.

77. Geoffrey Ostergaard and Melville Currell, *The Gentle Anarchists: A Study of the Leaders of the Sarvodaya Movement for Nonviolent Revolution in India* (Oxford: Clarendon Press, 1991); Geoffrey Ostergaard, 'Indian Anarchism: The Sarvodaya Movement', in D. E. Apter and J. Joll (eds), *Anarchism Today: Studies in Comparative Politics* (London: Palgrave Macmillan, 1971), pp. 145–63.

78. Acharya, 'Une Voix de l'Inde', *Contre-Courant* (July 1952), p. 91.

79. Acharya to Yelensky, 27 May 1953, Boris Yelensky Papers, ARCH01674.46, IISH.

80. Mashruwala, *Gandhi and Marx*, p. 56.

81. Acharya to Mashruwala, 1950, Victor Garcia Papers, BASE.

82. 'Dange–Vinoba Correspondence', *Harijan* (18 August 1951), pp. 210–11; Kishorlal Mashruwala, 'In Regard to Communism', *Harijan*, (August 18, 1951), p. 212.

83. Acharya, 'Confusion Between Communism and State Capitalism', *Harijan* (27 October 1951), p. 298.

84. Ibid.

85. K. G. Mashruwala, Note, *Harijan* (27 October 1951), p. 299.

86. Acharya, 'Lettre de Bombay', *L'Unique*, 73–74 (June–July 1953), p. 8. See, Maganbhai P. Desai, 'We Require a New Economic Policy', *Harijan* (30 May 1953), p. 100.

87. M. P. Desai, 'M. P. T. Acharya', *Harijan* (1 May 1954), pp. 73–4.

88. Acharya, 'Gandhiji and Socialism', *Harijan* (27 June 1953), p. 134.

89. Ibid.

90. Ibid.

91. Ibid.

92. See also, Karuna Mantena, 'On Gandhi's Critique of the State: Sources, Contexts, Conjunctures', *Modern Intellectual History*, 9:3 (November 2012), pp. 535–63.

NOTES   pp. [238–243]

93. Acharya to Yelensky, 27 May 1953, Boris Yelensky Papers, ARCH01674.46, IISH.
94. Yelensky to Acharya, 18 July 1953, Boris Yelensky Papers, ARCH01674.46, IISH.
95. 'This Revolutionary Carried Flag of India's Freedom Abroad', *Sunday Chronicle* (18 April 1954), p. 6.

EPILOGUE: AFTERLIFE OF AN INDIAN REVOLUTIONARY

1. Acharya, 'The Spiral of Prices', *Harijan* (17 April 1954), pp. 73–4; Acharya, 'Capital and Unemployment', *Harijan* (15 January 1955), pp. 371–2.
2. M. P. Desai, 'M. P. T. Acharya', *Harijan* (1 May 1954), pp. 73–4.
3. Ibid.
4. Ibid.
5. Acharya, 'Capital and Unemployment', *Harijan* (15 January 1955), p. 371.
6. J. Mazumdar, 'A Story of a Neglected Freedom Fighter of India', *Kumar*, 355 (June 1954), n.p., in Victor Garcia Papers, BASE; reprinted as J. Mazumdar, 'A Story of a Neglected Freedom Fighter of India', *The Indian Libertarian* (15 February 1958), p. 13.
7. Ibid.
8. Coutinho to Paranjape, 15 August 1954, quoted in: C. S. Subramaniam, *M. P. T. Acharya: His Life and Times: Revolutionary Trends in the Early Anti-Imperialist Movements in South India and Abroad* (Madras: Institute of South Indian Studies, 1995), p. 147.
9. Ibid.
10. Vasant Paranjape, 'M. P. T. Acharya', *The Word* (October 1954), p. 143. The letter to Aldred is dated 15 August 1954.
11. Ibid.
12. Guy Aldred, 'The Hindu Struggle', *The Word* (February 1955), p. 45.
13. Ibid.
14. Albert Meltzer, *I Couldn't Paint Golden Angels: Sixty Years of Commonplace Life and Anarchist Agitation* (Edinburgh: AK Press, 1996), p. 130.
15. Meltzer to Wolfe, 16 September 1954, Freedom Archives, ARCH00428.378, IISH.
16. Internationalist [Albert Meltzer], 'M. P. T. Acharya', *Freedom: The Anarchist Weekly*, 15:33 (14 August 1954), p. 3.
17. Ibid.
18. 'M. P. T. Acharya död', *Arbetaren* (18 August 1954), p. 2; Rüdiger to Rocker, 9 December 1954, Rudolf Rocker Papers, ARCH01194.188, IISH.
19. 'M. P. T. Acharya död'.
20. Ibid.
21. Ibid.
22. En av hans brevvänner, 'MPT Ascharya', *Arbetaren* (24 August 1954), p. 3.
23. E. Armand, 'M. P. T. Acharya', *L'Unique* (September 1954), p. 171.
24. Ibid.

295

pp. [243–245]   NOTES

25. *La Anarkismo: Inland Bulletin of the Japanese Anarchist Federation*, 18 (October 1954), WRI Archives, ARCH01537.336, IISH.

26. 'Morray Acharya', *Dielo Trouda-Probuzhdenie*, 48 (May–July 1955), pp. 19–20. I am grateful to Anatol Dubovik for sharing and translating this obituary.

27. Vladimir Muñoz, 'Filosofemas la Masculinocracia', *Cenit: Revista de Sociologia, Ciencia y Literatura*, 5:58 (October 1955), p. 1678.

28. Victor Garcia, 'El anarquismo en la India', *Tierra y Libertad* (Nov 1959–Feb 1960); also published as Victor Garcia, 'Le radici libertarie in India', *Volontà*, 13:8–9 (August 1960), pp. 525–49.

29. Victor Garcia, 'Mandyam Acharya', *Contre-Courant*, 9:9 (Nov–Dec 1960), pp. 219–24.

30. Hem Day, 'Voici un agitateur Indou: M. P. Acharya', *Inde: Social-Philosophie, Impressions, Essais* (Paris; Bruxelles: Pensee et Action, 1962), p. 106.

31. 'Bibliografia Essenziale', *Anarchici e Anarchia nel Mondo Contemporaneo: Atti del Convegno Promosso dalla Fondazione Luigi Einaudi (Torino, 5, 6 e 7 dicembre 1969)* (Torino: Fondazione Luigi Einaudi, 1971), pp. 196–7.

32. Michele Moramano, 'L'Anarchismo nella storia e nel pensiero dell'India', *Volontà*, 26:4 (July–August 1973), pp. 265–9.

33. Albert Meltzer, *The Anarchists in London, 1935–1955: A Personal Memoir* (Sanday Box A, Over the Water, Sanday, Orkney: Cienfuegos Press, 1976), pp. 29–30.

34. Acharya to Karanth, undated 1951, quoted in: Subramanyam, *M. P. T. Acharya*, p. 146.

35. Vasant Paranjape, 'M. P. T. Acharya', *The Word* (October 1954), p. 143.

36. A Nationalist Hindu, 'Indian Letter', *The Word* (April 1960), p. 43.

37. Moramano, 'L'Anarchismo nella storia e nel pensiero dell'India', p. 265; 'Notes on the Authors Herein', *World Scene from a Libertarian Point of View*, p. 95.

PUBLISHED WORKS BY M. P. T. ACHARYA

Original articles (chronological)

Acharya, 'Revolutionary Party of India', *Izvestia* (19 September 1920), p. 1.

Mr Bhayankar, 'The "Communist" Programme: A Critical Review', *The Hindu* (14 February 1923), n.p.

M. A., 'Hinter den Kulissen der sowjetrussischen Diplomatie', *Der Syndikalist*, 8:8, Beilage (20 February 1926), p. 1.

'Communism in Its True Form', *Mahratta* (13 June 1926), pp. 306–7.

M. Acharya, 'Poor Indians Abroad: Jugglers at a Berlin Zoo', *Bombay Chronicle* (20 July 1926), p. 6.

M. Acharya, 'Bücherbesprechung', *Der Syndikalist*, 8:32 (7 August 1926), n.p.

M. Acharya, 'Anarchist Manifesto', *Road to Freedom*, 3:1 (1 September 1926), pp. 5–6.

Published Works by M. P. T. Acharya

Reprinted as:

M. Acharya, 'Un manifiesto anarquista en la India', *La Protesta*, 5473 (28 October 1926), p. 2.

M. Acharya, 'The Mystery Behind the Chinese Trouble', *Road to Freedom*, 3:4 (1 November 1926), pp. 2–3.

Reprinted as:

M. Acharya, 'El misterio oculto tras la perturbación china', *La Protesta*, 5502 (1 December 1926), p. 3.

M. Acharya, 'L'imbroglio chinois', *L'En Dehors* (early-December 1926), p. 3.

M. Acharya, 'L'Imbroglio Cinese', *L'Adunata dei Refrattari* (22 January 1927), p. 2.

M. Acharya, 'Die proletarierin in Indien', *Der Frauen-Bund*, Monatsbeilage *Der Syndikalist*, 5 (November 1926), n.p.

PUBLISHED WORKS BY M. P. T. ACHARYA

Reprinted as:

M. Acharya, 'De la India: la mujer obrera', *La Protesta*, 5516 (17 December 1926), p. 2.

M. Acharya, 'Die proletarierin in Indien', *New Yorker Volkszeitung* (26 December 1926), p. 10.

M. Acharya, 'De arbeidersvrouw in Indië', *De Syndicalist*, 4:185 (8 January 1927), p. 2.

M. Acharya, 'Usury', *The People* (21 November 1926), p. 410.

M. A., 'Mrs Dryhurst on Russia', *The People* (5 December 1926), p. 444.

M. Acharya, 'Vom Klassenkampf in Indien', *Der Syndikalist*, Beilage, 9:6 (5 February 1927), n.p.

Reprinted as:

M. Acharya, 'Vom Klassenkampf in Indien', *IAA Pressedienst*, 5:2 (12 February 1927), p. 3.

M. Acharya, 'Klassenstrijd in Indië', *De Syndicalist*, 4:192 (26 February 1927), pp. 2–3.

M. Acharya, 'Wages and Politics', *The People* (6 February 1927), p. 109.

M. Acharya, 'More About the Hagenbeck Show', *The People* (6 February 1927), p. 108.

M. Acharya, 'Die Ereignisse in China und die freiheitliche Bewegung', *Der Syndikalist*, Beilage, 9:10 (5 March 1927), n.p.

Reprinted as:

M. Acharya, 'Frihetsrörelsen i Kina', *Arbetaren* (17 March 1927), p. 3.

M. Acharya, 'Die elende Lage der Arbeiterschaft', *IAA Pressedienst*, 5:3 (5 March 1927), p. 4.

M. Acharya, 'Political Sufferers' Conference and Socialism', *The People* (6 March 1927), pp. 184–5.

M. Acharya, 'Arbeitervertreter in der gesetzgebenden Körperschaft', *IAA Pressedienst*, 5:4 (10 March 1927), pp. 2–3.

Reprinted as:

M. Acharya, 'Arbeitervertreter in der gesetzgebenden Körperschaft, Internationale Arbeiterbewegung, Indien', *Der Syndikalist*, Beilage, 10:23 (4 June 1927), n.p.

M. Acharya, 'Die Schliche der Unternehmer', *IAA Pressedienst*, 5:5 (27 March 1927), pp. 3–4.

M. Acharya, 'Dans l'Inde', *La Voix du Travail*, 2:9 (April 1927), p. 16.

Berlin Correspondent, 'A Berlin Letter: Brussels Congress Criticized', *Bombay Chronicle* (9 April 1927), p. 15.

298

PUBLISHED WORKS BY M. P. T. ACHARYA

M. Acharya, 'The Hagenbeck Show', *The People* (10 April 1927), p. 289.

M. Acharya, 'De gebeurtenissen in China', *De Syndicalist*, 4:200 (23 April 1927), p. 1.

M. Acharya, 'Libel Charge against Agnes Smedley', *Bombay Chronicle* (28 April 1927), p. 10.

M. A. Acharya, 'L'imbroglio chinois', *L'En Dehors*, 6:109 (May 1927), p. 7.

M. Acharya, 'Disruption of Marxism', *The People* (12 June 1927), pp. 465–7.

Reprinted as:

M. Acharya, 'Disruption of Marxism', *Road to Freedom*, 3:12 (July 1927), pp. 6–7.

M. Acharya, 'Dirompimento del Marxismo', *L'Adunata dei Refrattari* (20 July 1927), p. 3.

M. Acharya, 'Labour in India: A German View', *The People* (26 June 1927), pp. 506–7.

M. Acharya, 'Dr Sun Yat Sen's Principles', *Forward* (21 July 1927), p. 7.

M. Acharya, 'Memories of a Revolutionary', *The People* (4 August 1927), pp. 90–1.

Reprinted as:

M. Acharya, 'From a Bolshevik', *Road to Freedom*, 4:6 (January 1928), p. 3.

M. Acharya, 'Indian Exiles Abroad: An Appeal', *Forward* (18 August 1927), p. 4.

M. Acharya, 'India's Man Power and the Next Imperialist War', *Forward* (21 August 1927), pp. 4, 12.

Reprinted as:

M. Acharya, 'Mother India', *Road to Freedom*, 4:9 (April 1928), pp. 6–7.

M. A., 'Der Antimilitarismus in Indien', *Die Internationale*, 1:7 (May 1928), pp. 14–17.

M. Acharya, 'The Coming War', *Forward* (8 September 1927), p. 4.

M. Acharya, 'Die Zustände der Indischen Arbeiter', *IAA Pressedienst*, 5:13 (29 September 1927), pp. 2–3.

M. Acharya, 'Politics and Democracy', *The People* (20 October 1927), p. 200.

M. Acharya, 'The Limitations of Birth Control', *Forward* (10 January 1928), pp. 14–15.

M. Acharya, 'Passport Refused to Mr. Acharyya', *Forward* (21 January 1928), p. 3.

M. Acharya, 'The Inconsistency of Talk', *The People* (9 February 1928), pp. 89–90.

PUBLISHED WORKS BY M. P. T. ACHARYA

M. Acharya, 'Bolshevik Prisons—A Protest', *The People* (23 February 1928), pp. 120–1.

M. Acharya, 'Commerce and Nationalism', *Bombay Chronicle* (17 March 1928), p. 8.

M. Acharya, 'Moderne Sklaverei in Indien', *IAA Pressedienst*, 6:5, 95 (21 April 1928), p. 4.

M. Acharya, 'Les Trusts et la Démocratie', *L'En Dehors*, 133–134, 135 (April–May 1928), pp. 4, 5.

Reprinted as:

M. Acharya, 'Trusts und Demokratie', *Die Internationale* (March–April 1930), pp. 110–3, 134–8.

M. Acharya, 'Trust y Democracia', *La Protesta: Suplemento Quincenal*, 9:313 (March 1930), pp. 243–7.

Second part reprinted as:

M. P. T. Acharya, *Principles of Non-Violent Economics* (Calcutta: International University of Non-Violence, 1947)

M. P. T. Acharya, 'Las comunas libertarias', *Tierra y Libertad*, 20:244 (1963), pp. 44–6.

M. Acharya, 'Zum Streik der Textilarbeiter', *IAA Pressedienst*, 6:6, 96 (12 May 1928), p. 4.

Reprinted as:

M. Acharya, 'La huelga de los obreros textile', *Acción Social Obrera* (8 September 1928), p. 4.

M. Acharya, 'Russian Prisons', *The People* (24 May 1928), p. 326.

M. Acharya, 'Dear "Comrade" (?) Nehru', *The People* (24 May 1928), p. 326.

M. Acharya, 'What is Socialism?', *The People* (7 June 1928), p. 356.

M. Acharya, 'Shiraz', *Bombay Chronicle* (22 June 1928), p. 6.

M. Acharya, 'Geistiges Leben, Duldsamkeit und Gegensätze in Indien', *Der Syndikalist*, Beilage, 10:28 (14 July 1928), n.p.

M. Acharya, 'Art et "Art"', *L'En Dehors* (end August 1928), p. 6.

M. Acharya, 'Unity—What For?', *Road to Freedom* (September 1928), p. 6.

M. Acharya, 'Items of Note', *Llano Colonist*, 8:824 (6 October 1928), p. 4.

M. Acharya, 'Der Kommunismus in Indien', *IAA Pressedienst*, 6:12 (12 October 1928), p. 8.

M. Acharya, 'De la Pudeur et de la Nudité', *L'En Dehors* (mid-October–mid-November 1928), pp. 3, 3.

M. Acharya, 'The Days of Authority are Numbered', *The People* (31 January 1929), pp. 58–9.

M. Acharya, 'De l'influence de la toilette sur la mentalité', *L'En Dehors* (mid-March 1929), p. 1.

PUBLISHED WORKS BY M. P. T. ACHARYA

M. A. Acharya, 'Modern Acquisitive Society', *Bombay Chronicle* (11 April 1929), pp. 6, 10.

M. Acharya, 'Why This Judicial Murder?', *Road to Freedom* (August 1929), p. 8.

M. Acharya, 'Art et "Art"', *L'En Dehors* (fin August 1929), p. 6.

M. Acharya, 'La conscience physiologique de l'espèce', *L'En Dehors* (September 1929), pp. 1–2.

M. Acharya, 'Indien', *IAA Pressedienst*, 7:8 (111) (28 September 1929), pp. 5–6.

Reprinted as:

M. Acharya, 'La cuestión social en la India', *La Revista Blanca*, supplemento (1 December 1929), p. 12.

Acharya, 'De la India', *La Protesta*, 6438 (5 December 1929), p. 2.

M. Acharya, 'India', *Acción Social Obrera* (7 December 1929), p. 4.

Acharya, 'Dans l'Inde', *Le Libertaire* (7 December 1929), p. 3.

M. Acharya, 'De la Jalousie', *L'En Dehors* (November 1929), p. 6.

M. Acharya, 'Pourquoi faire de la Sexologie', *L'En Dehors* (February 1930), p. 6.

M. Acharya, 'Die zivile Gerhorsamsverweigerung', *IAA Pressedienst*, 8:2 (1 March 1930), p. 14.

M. Acharya, 'Discutamos sobre socialismo', *La Protesta*, 6529 (22 March 1930), p. 4.

M. Acharya, 'De la India: El congreso nacional hindú', *La Protesta*, 6532 (26 March 1930), p. 2.

M. Acharya, 'Projet: destine à arracher les petites industries aux griffes du capitalisme', *L'En Dehors* (April 1930), pp. 5–6.

M. Acharya, 'Waarom Gandhi de Zoutbelasting Tracht te Breken', *IAK Persdienst*, 45:3 (19 April 1930), n.p.

Reprinted as:

M. Acharya, 'Why Gandhi Attacks Salt-Tax', *IAC Press Service*, 45 (25 April 1930), p. 3.

M. Acharya, 'Pourquoi Gandhi s'efforce de detruire l'impot sur le sel', *L'En Dehors* (early May 1930), p. 6.

M. Acharya, 'Pourquoi Gandhi s'efforce de detruire l'impot sur le sel', *Cahiers de la Réconciliation: bulletin mensuel de la Section française du mouvement international de réconciliation* (May 1930), p. 18.

M. Acharya, 'Weshalb Gandhi die Salzteuer zu brechen versucht', *Der Freie Arbeiter*, 19 (10 May 1930), p. 4.

'Chronik der Zeit', *Die Chronik der Menschheit*, 7 (17 May 1930), pp. 145–8.

'La Rebelion de la India', *La Protesta*, 6581 (23 May 1930), p. 1.

PUBLISHED WORKS BY M. P. T. ACHARYA

M. Acharya, 'Why Gandhi Attacks Salt-Tax', *The Equitist*, 608 (23 May 1930), p. 2.

M. Acharya, 'Waarom Gandhi de Zoutbelasting Tracht te Breken', *De Syndicalist* (24 May 1930), p. 3.

'Porque Gandhi se esforça por destruir o imposto sobre o sal', *Vanguarda Operária: porta-voz da Organização Operária Portuguêsa*, 39 (22 June 1930), p. 3.

M. Acharya, 'Die indische Erhebung als freiheitliche Revolution', *Der Syndikalist*, 12:25 (21 June 1930), n.p.

M. Acharya, 'Gandhi en de Geweldloosheid', *IAK Persdienst*, 52 (15 July 1930), p. 1.

Reprinted as:

M. Acharya, 'Gandhi et la Non-Violence', *La Voix Libertaire* (26 July 1930), p. 1.

M. Acharya, 'Gandhi und die Gewaltlosigkeit', *Der Freie Arbeiter*, 30 (26 July 1930), p. 4.

M. Acharya, 'Gandhi en de Geweldloosheid', *De Vrije Socialist*, 33 (30 July 1930), pp. 1–2.

M. Acharya, 'Gandhi en de Geweldloosheid', *De Arbeider*, 40: 31 (2 August 1930), p. 1.

M. Acharya, 'Gandhi und die Gewaltlosigkeit', *Erkenntnis und Befreiung*, 31 (3 August 1930), pp. 1–2.

M. Acharya, 'Gandhi und seine Taktik', *Der Syndikalist*, Beilage, 12:32 (9 August 1930), n.p.

M. Acharya, 'Gandhi and Non-Violence', *Llano Colonist*, 10:1017 (16 August 1930), p. 3.

M. Acharya, 'Gandhi and Non-Violence', *Road to Freedom*, 7:1 (September 1930), p. 1.

From a Correspondent, 'Astonishing Attitude of the German Press', *Bombay Chronicle* (21–25 July 1930), pp. 7, 10.

M. Acharya, 'L'anarchisme et les associations volontaires', *L'En Dehors*, (end-July 1930), p. 6.

M. Acharya, 'Der Militarismus in Asien', *Der Syndikalist*, 12:31 (2 August 1930), n.p.

M. Acharya, 'Correspondence', *Llano Colonist*, 10:1017 (16 August 1930), p. 9.

M. Acharya, 'Das indische Problem', *Der Syndikalist*, Beilage, 12:36 (6 September 1930), n.p.

From Our Correspondent, 'Does Europe Want to Know Truth about India?', *Bombay Chronicle* (16 December 1930), p. 5.

M. Acharya, 'Shittoshin no mondai ni tsuite', *Fujin Sensen* (February 1931), pp. 14–17.

302

PUBLISHED WORKS BY M. P. T. ACHARYA

M. Acharya, 'War and "Civil" War', *Bombay Chronicle* (7 February 1931), p. 13.

M. Acharya, 'Les éléments de la prostitution dans le mariage', *L'En Dehors* (15 March 1931), pp. 12–13.

M. Acharya, 'Das Problem der Ausbeutung und ihrer Beseitigung', *Die Internationale* (April 1931), pp. 131–4.

M. Acharya, 'De Strijd in India Moet Worden Voortgezet', *IAK Persdienst*, 71 (10 April 1931), n.p.

M. Acharya, 'Purna Swaraj—But What Next?', *The People* (12 April 1931), pp. 238–9.

M. Acharya, 'De huidige toestand in India', *IAK Persdienst*, 72 (17 April 1931), p. 1.

Reprinted as:

M. Acharya, 'De huidige toestand in India', *De Vrije Socialist*, 34 (6 May 1931), p. 2.

M. Acharya, 'Wie ist die Lage in Indien?', *Der Syndikalist*, 13:20 (16 May 1931), n.p.

Reprinted as:

M. Acharya, 'La situación actual en la India', *Acción Social Obrera* (30 May 1931), p. 2.

M. Acharya, '"Vasant-Sena" Creates Mixed Feelings and Impressions', *Bombay Chronicle* (25 June 1931), p. 4.

M. Acharya, 'De quelques confusions parmi les ouvriers', *L'En Dehors* (15 September 1931), pp. 6–7.

Reprinted as:

M. Acharya, 'Some Confusion Among Workers', *Road to Freedom*, 8:3 (November 1931), p. 1.

M. Acharya, 'La defensa de la Revolución', *Acción Social Obrera* (31 October 1931), p. 3.

Reprinted as:

M. Acharya, 'Het Standpunt van Acharya', *De Wapens Neder*, 27:11 (November 1931), p. 3.

M. Acharya, 'Economic Confusion Follows Political Confusion', *The People* (3 November 1931), pp. 274–6.

M. Acharya, 'La "barbarisation" de la beauté', *L'En Dehors* (15 November 1931), p. 2.

M. Acharya, 'The Logical Consequences of Business', *The People* (1 December 1931), p. 347.

M. Acharya, 'La nature est mon aphrodisiaque', *L'En Dehors* (15 March 1932), pp. 73–4.

PUBLISHED WORKS BY M. P. T. ACHARYA

M. Acharya, 'Who Are Workers?', *Road to Freedom*, 8:9 (May 1932), pp. 1–2.

M. Acharya, 'Ou la chasteté n'a pas de raison d'être', *L'En Dehors* (15 May 1932), p. 101.

M. Acharya, '¿Es económico el intercambio entre la ciudad y el campo?', *Orto*, 1:5 (July 1932), p. 321.

Acharya, 'Whose Triumph?', *Bombay Chronicle* (11 July 1932), p. 6.

M. Acharya, 'A propos de la libération du sentiment en Russie', *L'En Dehors* (15 July 1932), p. 142.

Acharya, 'In the Melting Pot', *Bombay Chronicle* (22 July 1932), p. 4.

M. Acharya, 'Lettre d'Allemagne', *L'En Dehors* (15 August 1932), p. 6.

M. Acharya, 'Die indischen Frauen', *Der Syndikalist*, Beilage, 14:37 (27 August 1932), n.p.

Reprinted as:

M. Acharya, 'Die indischen Frauen', *New Yorker Volkszeitung* (11 September 1932), p. 6.

M. Acharya, 'L'inceste devant les juges allemands', *L'En Dehors* (15 October 1932), p. 180.

From a Correspondent, 'German Economic Situation: Return of Confidence', *Bombay Chronicle* (17 October 1932), p. 8.

M. Acharya, 'Réponse a tout les "économistes"', *L'En Dehors* (February 1933), pp. 52–3.

M. Acharya, 'The End of the Money System', *Man! A Journal of the Anarchist Ideal and Movement*, 1:4 (April 1933), pp. 1, 8.

M. Acharya, 'Verfolgung und Quälereien in den indischen Gefängnissen', *IAA Pressedienst*, 2 (158) (3 April 1933), p. 9.

M. Acharya, 'Nationalism in India', *Man! A Journal of the Anarchist Ideal and Movement*, 1:7 (July 1933), p. 2.

M. Acharya, 'Sur la question de race', *L'En Dehors* (mid-September 1933), pp. 174–5.

Reprinted as:

M. Acharya, 'De rassenleer', *De Vrije Socialist*, 42 (9 August 1939), p. 2.

M. Acharya, 'Is the Present System Doomed?', *Man! A Journal of the Anarchist Ideal and Movement*, 1:10 (October 1933), p. 5.

M. Acharya, 'Étude sur le matriarcat', *L'En Dehors* (November 1933), pp. 4–6.

M. Acharya, 'A Belated Forecast for the Year 1934', *Man! A Journal of the Anarchist Ideal and Movement*, 2:3 (March 1934), p. 99.

M. Acharya, 'Les tragédies de l'adultéré', *L'En Dehors* (March 1934), pp. 6–7.

PUBLISHED WORKS BY M. P. T. ACHARYA

'Hindou', *L'En Dehors* (mid-April 1934), p. 4.

M. Acharya, 'Parliamentarism on Trial', *Bombay Chronicle* (26 April 1934), p. 6.

M. Acharya, 'Fight for Bread', *Bombay Chronicle* (19 May 1934), p. 6.

M. Acharya, 'Spengler and his Critics', *Bombay Chronicle* (23 May 1934), p. 11.

M. A., 'A propos de la Saint-Barthélemy Hitlerienne', *L'En Dehors* (mid-August–mid-September 1934), pp. 164–5.

M. Acharya, 'Anarchy or Chaos?', *Man! A Journal of the Anarchist Ideal and Movement*, 2:9–10 (September–October 1934), p. 4.

M. Acharya, 'The Machine in a Free Society', *Man! A Journal of the Anarchist Ideal and Movement*, 3:1 (January 1935), p. 2.

M. Acharya, 'Le cas de Bouddhisme', *L'En Dehors* (mid-February 1935), pp. 236–8.

M. Ach., 'Les "cabarets nudistes"', *L'En Dehors* (April 1935), p. 268.

M. Acharya, 'La légende du Christ', *Le Fraterniste* (April 1935), p. 3.

M. P. T. Acharya, 'Armament Race in Europe', *Bombay Chronicle* (10 April 1935), p. 5.

M. Acharya, 'Max Nettlau como biógrafo y como historiador', *La Revista Blanca*, 13:328 (3 May 1935), pp. 410–12.

M. Acharya, 'A propos d'une enquête sur le féminisme', *L'En Dehors* (June 1935), pp. 311–12.

M. Acharya, 'De Ineenstorting van de Britse Macht', *De Wapens Neder*, 31:11 (November 1935), p. 9.

M. P. T. Acharya, 'Is Earth Overpopulated?', *Bombay Chronicle* (6 November 1935), p. 6.

M. Ach., 'Pourqoui la lachete, pourqoui la brutalite?', *L'En Dehors* (mid-November 1935), p. 72.

M. Acharya, 'An American Experiment Worth Trying in India', *Bombay Chronicle* (17 March 1936), p. 3.

M. A., 'Economics of the Constitution', *Mahratta* (4 June 1937), p. 14.

P. T. Acharya, 'Ethics and "Isms"', *Mahratta* (11 June 1937–18 June 1937), pp. 11, 3.

M. P. T. Acharya, 'Latin Script for India?', *Mahratta* (2 July 1937–9 July 1937), pp. 8, 9.

Reprinted as:

M. P. T. Acharya, 'L'alphabet latin convient-il a l'Inde?', *L'En Dehors* (May–June 1938), pp. 59–60.

M. P. T. Acharya, 'Reminiscences of a Revolutionary', *Mahratta* (17 September 1937), p. 3.

M. P. T. Acharya, 'Reminiscences of a Revolutionary', *Mahratta* (23 July 1937), p. 5.

PUBLISHED WORKS BY M. P. T. ACHARYA

M. P. T. Acharya, 'Reminiscences of a Revolutionary', *Mahratta* (30 July 1937), p. 2.

M. P. T. Acharya, 'Reminiscences of a Revolutionary', *Mahratta* (20 August 1937), p. 3.

M. P. T. Acharya, 'Reminiscences of a Revolutionary', *Mahratta* (27 August 1937), p. 5.

M. P. T. Acharya, 'Reminiscences of a Revolutionary', *Mahratta* (3 September 1937), p. 3.

M. P. T. Acharya, 'Reminiscences of a Revolutionary', *Mahratta* (10 September 1937), p. 3.

M. P. T. Acharya, 'Reminiscences of a Revolutionary', *Mahratta* (17 September 1937), p. 3.

M. P. T. Acharya, 'European Wrestlers' Challenge to India', *Bombay Chronicle* (19 September 1937), p. 3.

M. P. T. Acharya, 'Reminiscences of a Revolutionary', *Mahratta* (8 October 1937), p. 5.

M. P. T. Acharya, 'In Defence of Foreign Rule', *Mahratta* (22 October 1937), p. 1.

M. Acharya, 'A Letter from India', *Man! A Journal of the Anarchist Ideal and Movement!* (November 1937), p. 3.

M. P. T. Acharya, 'Constituent Assembly: Its Conditions and "Possibilities"', *Oriental Review*, 1:4 (November 1937), pp. 10–12.

M. P. T. Acharya, 'Germany Squaring the Circle!', *Bombay Chronicle* (20 February 1938), p. 62.

M. P. T. Acharya, 'Is War Inevitable?', *Mahratta* (15 April 1938), p. 5.

M. P. T. Acharya, 'Savarkar in London', *Mahratta* (27 May 1938), p. 3.

'Viren Chattopadhyaya', *Oriental Review*, 2:6 (June 1938), pp. 266–7.

M. P. T. Acharya, 'What is the Fact? Fate of Viren Chattopadhyay', *Mahratta* (3 June 1938), p. 3

M. P. T. Acharya, 'Viren Chattopadhyaya: A Chequered Career', *Mahratta* (10 June 1938), p. 7.

M. P. T. Acharya, 'Viren Chattopadhyaya Trapped by a British Spy', *Mahratta* (17 June 1938), p. 3.

M. P. T. Acharya, 'Swiss Attempts to Trap Chatto', *Mahratta* (24 June 1938), p. 3.

M. P. T. Acharya, 'Madame Cama: A Rebel Throughout Her Life', *Mahratta* (12 August 1938), p. 5.

'The Future of India', *IAMB Press Service*, 12 (29 August 1938), n.p.

M. P. T. Acharya, 'The Most Anti-British Englishman', *Mahratta* (9 September 1938), p. 3.

M. P. T. Acharya, 'Indian Propaganda During the Great War', *Mahratta* (21 October 1938), p. 3.

PUBLISHED WORKS BY M. P. T. ACHARYA

M. P. T. Acharya, 'Traitor Turned Out: Indian Propaganda in The Great War', *Mahratta* (4 November 1938), p. 2.

'A Co-Operative Organisation in India', *Community Life: Monthly Journal of Movement for Communal Living*, 1:4 (June 1939), p. 8.

M. A., 'Failure of Democracy and Rise of Fascism', *Mahratta* (8–15 December 1939), pp. 7, 5.

Marco Polo, 'That Jigsaw Puzzle Remains Unsolved: Can Sir Cripps Solve It?', *Kaiser-i-Hind* (5 April 1943), n.p.

M. P. T. Acharya, 'The Housewife's Work', *Indian Social Reformer*, 55:20 (13 January 1945), p. 88.

M. P. T. Acharya, 'Request from India', *The Word* (March 1946), p. 95.

Marco Polo, 'How Can Self Government Be Real?', *Freedom*, 7:15 (18 May 1946), p. 3.

M. P. T. Acharya, 'The Indian Struggle', *The Word* (August 1946), p. 11.

M. P. T. Acharya, 'Lettre de l'Inde', *L'Unique*, 11 (June 1946), pp. 13–14.

M. Acharya, 'Dorothy Hoog: *The Moral Challenge of Gandhi*—A Plea for Understanding India', *L'Unique* (15 November 1946), p. 3.

M. P. T. Acharya, 'Anarquia: De la Filosofia a la Economia', *Tierra y Libertad*, 3:56 (November 1946), p. 2.

M. P. T. Acharya, 'The Problem of Germany', *Bombay Chronicle* (5 January 1947), p. 4.

M. P. T. Acharya, 'Que Faut-il Penser de la Radio', *L'Unique*, 18 (March 1947), p. 119.

M. P. T. Acharya, 'Labour Splits in India', *Freedom: Anarchist Fortnightly* (31 May 1947), p. 5.

M. P. T. Acharya, 'Indiens frihetsrörelser under andra världskriget', *Arbetaren* (9 June 1947), pp. 1, 8.

M. P. T. Acharya, 'Indiens frihetsrörelser under andra världskriget', *Arbetaren* (10 June 1947), p. 4.

M. P. T. Acharya, 'Bedeuten Höhere Löhne Erhöung der Kaufkraft: Eine Stimme aus Indien', *Der Freiheitliche Sozialist*, 6 (October 1947), pp. 7–8

M. P. T. Acharya, 'Viren Chattopadhyaya: Revolutionary Fighter for India's Freedom', *Bombay Chronicle* (2 November 1947), p. 6.

M. P. T. Acharya, 'Too Much Gandhiana', *The Word* (March 1948), p. 62.

M. P. T. Acharya, 'Voz Libertaria en la India', *Inquietud*, 2:42 (April 1948), p. 1.

M. P. T. Acharya, 'El Pensamiento Libertario en la India', *Inquietud*, 2:43 (May 1948), p. 3.

Reprinted as:

M. P. T. Acharya, 'El Pensamiento Libertario en la India: Por Que el Problema Alimento no Puede ser Solventado', *Tierra y Libertad*, 5:91 (September 1948), p. 3.

PUBLISHED WORKS BY M. P. T. ACHARYA

M. P. T. Acharya, 'El Pueblo No Vive de Promesas', *C.N.T.: Portavoz de la CNT de España en el Exilio* (22 October 1948), p. 2.

T. Acharya, 'Indian Opinion', *Southern Advocate for Workers' Council: An International Digest*, 47 (November 1948), p. 6.

M. P. T. Acharya, 'Evolution of "Economic" Thought', *Southern Advocate for Workers' Council: An International Digest*, 47 (November 1948), p. 8.

Marco Polo, 'We Are No Longer Indians! What a Linguistic Province is Bound to Create?', *Kaiser-i-Hind* (28 November 1948), p. 19.

M. P. T. Acharya, 'Money & Moral Values', *Freedom: Anarchist Fortnightly*, 9:27 (24 December 1948–7 January 1949), pp. 4, 4.

M. P. T. Acharya, 'Artists are Forgotten', *Times of India* (15 January 1949), p. 6.

M. P. T. Acharya, 'Foreigners, Get Out!', *Bombay Chronicle* (8 April 1949), p. 5.

M. P. T. Acharya, 'Gandhi—Pacifist eller Realpolitiker?', *Arbetaren* (20 June 1949), p. 3.

Marco Polo, 'World Government & All That', *Kaiser-i-Hind* (3 July 1949), pp. 19, 22.

Reprinted as:

Marco Polo, 'World Government & All That', *Freedom* (3 September 1949), p. 3.

From Our Political Correspondent, 'Pacifism: Hypocrisy', *Kaiser-i-Hind* (27 November 1949), pp. 19, 26.

Reprinted as:

M. P. T. Acharya, 'Pacifism—Fake or Real', *Freedom: Anarchist Fortnightly* (10 December 1949), p. 3.

M. P. T. Acharya, 'Les Japonais et les mœurs', *L'Unique*, 43 (November–December 1949), pp. 46–7.

Reprinted as:

M. P. T. Acharya, 'Les Japonais et les mœurs', *La Vie au soleil*, 6 (February 1950), p. 19.

M. P. T. Acharya, 'La Vie des Travailleurs aux Indes', *Etudes Anarchistes* (December 1949), pp. 5–6.

M. P. T. Acharya, 'Gandhi et les contrôles de naissances', *L'Unique*, 46 (February–March 1950), pp. 93–4.

M. P. T. Acharya, 'Voix de l'Inde', *Les Nouvelles Pacifistes*, 2:7 (1 March 1950), p. 3.

M. P. T. Acharya, 'Communal Rule', *Times of India* (20 June 1950), p. 6.

M. P. T. Acharya, 'El Fin de Una Era: Ecos Libres de la India', *Tierra y Libertad*, 8:113 (July 1950), p. 2.

PUBLISHED WORKS BY M. P. T. ACHARYA

M. P. T. Acharya, 'Jugglery of Words', *Times of India* (18 July 1950), p. 6.

M. P. T. Acharya, 'Co-Operatives', *Thought*, 2:30 (4 August 1950), p. 5.

M. P. T. Acharya, 'Baba Nand Singh', *Times of India* (13 September 1950), p. 6.

M. P. T. Acharya, 'Trade Unions in India—Pillars of Capitalism', *Freedom: Anarchist Fortnightly*, (16 September 1950), p. 3.

M. P. T. Acharya, 'An Indian Looks at "Independence"', *Freedom: The Anarchist Weekly*, (28 October 1950), p. 3.

M. P. T. Acharya, 'Savarkar: A Criticism', *The Word* (December 1950), pp. 23–4.

M. P. T. Acharya, 'Vad är Marxism?', *Arbetaren* (2 January 1951), p. 4.

M. P. T. Acharya, 'L'exemple Japonais', *Le Libertaire* (23 March 1951), p. 3.

M. P. T. Acharya, 'Freedom and Individualism', *Kaiser-i-Hind* (22 April 1951), p. 20.

M. P. T. Acharya, 'State Is Not Society: Beauties of Individual Freedom Analysed', *Kaiser-i-Hind* (29 April 1951), p. 24.

M. P. T. Acharya, 'Gandhi and War', *The Word*, 12:8 (June 1951), p. 91.

Marco Polo, 'Our Indian Correspondent on the Stuffed Dove of Peace at the Indian Peace Convention', *Freedom: The Anarchist Weekly*, 12:18 (30 June 1951), p. 3.

M. P. T. Acharya, 'Protection of Women', *Harijan* (7 July 1951), pp. 165–6.

M. P. T. Acharya, 'Russia and Its People', *Thought*, 3:36 (14 September 1951), pp. 6, 20.

M. P. T. Acharya, 'Libertarianism versus Dictatorship', *The Libertarian*, 1:2 (July–August–September 1951), pp. 42–3.

M. P. T. Acharya, 'Confusion Between Communism and State Capitalism', *Harijan* (27 October 1951), pp. 298–9.

M. P. T. Acharya, 'Anarchism and Pacifism', *Freedom: The Anarchist Weekly* (3 November 1951), p. 4.

M. P. T. Acharya, 'Ballot Box Will Not Solve Problems', *Kaiser-i-Hind* (16 December 1951), p. 1.

M. P. T. Acharya, 'Non-Violence', *Freedom: The Anarchist Weekly* (5 January 1952), p. 4.

M. P. T. Acharya, 'Bogey of Revolution', *Thought*, 4:2 (12 January 1952), p. 6.

M. P. T. Acharya, 'Travellers' Tales about Russia', *Freedom: The Anarchist Weekly* (12 January 1952), pp. 2–3.

M. P. T. Acharya, 'Lenin after the NEP', *Thought*, 4:3 (19 January 1952), p. 6.

M. P. T. Acharya, 'Pravda's Circulation', *Thought*, 4:9 (1 March 1952), p. 6.

PUBLISHED WORKS BY M. P. T. ACHARYA

M. P. T. Acharya, 'Madame Kollontai', *Thought*, 4:14 (5 April 1952), p. 6.

M. P. T. Acharya, 'Production in Russia', *Thought*, 4:15 (12 April 1952), p. 6.

M. P. T. Acharya, 'The Moscow Conference', *Thought*, 4:18 (3 May 1952), p. 6.

M. P. T. Acharya, 'Russia's Communism is National Capitalism', *Heimin shinbun* (3 May 1952), p. 3.

M. P. T. Acharya, 'Ein indischer Leser bittet ums Wort', *Die Freie Gesellschaft*, 3 (June 1952), p. 12.

M. P. T. Acharya, 'Une Voix de l'Inde', *Contre-Courant* (July 1952), p. 91.

M. P. T. Acharya, 'Wages and Prices in Russia', *Economic Weekly* (19 July 1952), p. 731.

M. P. T. Acharya, 'Common Man's Welfare in Russia', *Harijan* (23 August 1952), pp. 221–2.

M. P. T. Acharya, 'Nehru and Korea', *Freedom: The Anarchist Weekly* (13 September 1952), p. 3.

M. P. T. Acharya, 'Conditions for Economic Equality', *Harijan* (27 September 1952), p. 270.

M. P. T. Acharya, 'Funny Story', *Times of India* (21 October 1952), p. 6.

M. P. T. Acharya, 'Salaries in Russia', *Harijan* (8 November 1952), p. 319.

M. P. T. Acharya, 'For A Balanced Diet', *Harijan* (29 November 1952), p. 343.

M. P. T. Acharya, 'Is World Government an Idling Carousel Horse? Peaceful Comment on the Simpleton of the Bonvivant Class', *Anakizumu*, 1 (1 Dec 1952), p. 3.

M. P. T. Acharya, 'From Pillar to Post', *Harijan* (13 December 1952), pp. 359–60.

M. P. T. Acharya, 'Illusion of Averages & Food and Money', *Harijan* (3 January 1953), p. 379.

M. P. T. Acharya, 'Money is Rationing', *Harijan* (10 January 1953), p. 390.

M. P. T. Acharya, 'Abolition of Profit Economy', *Harijan* (21 February 1953), p. 434.

M. P. T. Acharya, 'Notes on Several Myths', *Harijan* (21 March 1953), pp. 23–4.

M. P. T. Acharya, 'Profit v. Purchasing Power', *Harijan* (28 March 1953), pp. 27–8.

M. P. T. Acharya, 'Preventive Medicine', *Harijan* (4 April 1953), p. 40.

M. P. T. Acharya, 'Les missionaries du gouvernement mondial en Inde', *Contre-Courant* (7 April 1953), pp. 95–6.

M. P. T. Acharya, 'Gouvernement mondial et pacifisme', *Contre-Courant* (12 May 1953), p. 133.

M. P. T. Acharya, 'In Defence of the Common Man', *Harijan* (16 May 1953), p. 83.

PUBLISHED WORKS BY M. P. T. ACHARYA

M. P. T. Acharya, 'Antisocialismo socialista', *L'Adunata dei Refrattari* (23 May 1953), pp. 4–5.

M. P. T. Acharya, 'Social Insurance Analysed', *Harijan* (30 May 1953), pp. 102–3.

M. P. T. Acharya, 'Capitalism and Trade Unionism', *Harijan* (13 June 1953), p. 117.

M. P. T. Acharya, 'Money—The Mechanism of Exploitation', *Harijan* (20 June 1953), pp. 126–7.

M. P. T. Acharya, 'Gandhiji and Socialism', *Harijan* (27 June 1953), p. 134.

M. P. T. Acharya, 'McCarthyism', *Times of India* (4 July 1953), p. 6.

M. P. T. Acharya, 'How to Abolish Poverty', *Harijan* (11 July 1953), p. 152.

M. P. T. Acharya, 'A Vicious Circle', *Harijan* (25 July 1953), p. 163.

M. P. T. Acharya, 'Indians in British Colonies', *Economic Weekly*, 5:30 (25 July 1953), pp. 821–2.

M. P. T. Acharya, 'Lettre de Bombay', *L'Unique*, 73–74 (June–July 1953), p. 8.

M. P. T. Acharya, 'Capital and Unemployment', *Harijan* (1 August 1953), p. 176.

M. P. T. Acharya, 'Modern Business', *Harijan* (29 August 1953), p. 207.

M. T. Acharya, 'Le mariage dans l'inde', *L'Unique*, 75–76 (August–September 1953), p. 8.

M. P. T. Acharya, 'The Profit Motive', *Harijan* (5 September 1953), p. 215.

M. P. T. Acharya, 'Capital and Labour', *Harijan* (12 September 1953), p. 223.

M. P. T. Acharya, 'Social Self-Help is the Only Solution', *Harijan* (19 September 1953), p. 231.

M. P. T. Acharya, 'The Language of the Capitalist "Producer" (Investor)', *Harijan* (31 October 1953), p. 274.

M. P. T. Acharya, 'Les illusions du Gandhisme', *L'Unique*, 77–78 (October–November 1953), pp. 59–60.

M. P. T. Acharya, 'Do Machines Make Jobs?', *Harijan* (7 November 1953), p. 286.

M. P. T. Acharya, 'Illusion Created by Words', *Harijan* (14 November 1953), p. 296.

M. P. T. Acharya, 'Government and Big Business', *Harijan* (9 January 1954), p. 354.

M. P. T. Acharya, 'The Crux of the Problem', *Harijan* (16 January 1954), p. 363.

M. P. T. Acharya, 'The Spiral of Prices', *Harijan* (17 April 1954), pp. 56–7.

M. P. T. Acharya, 'Capital and Unemployment', *Harijan* (15 January 1955), pp. 371–2.

PUBLISHED WORKS BY M. P. T. ACHARYA

Pamphlets

M. P. T. Acharya, *Principles of Non-Violent Economics* (Calcutta: International University of Non-Violence, 1947)

Book chapters

M. P. T. Acharya, 'What is Anarchism?', in Iqbal Singh and Raja Rao (eds), *Whither India? Socio-Politico Analyses* (Baroda: Padmaja Publications, 1948), pp. 117–40.

M. P. T. Acharya, 'How Long Can Capitalism Survive?', in Free Society Group of Chicago (ed.), *World Scene from the Libertarian Point of View* (Chicago: Free Society Group, 1951), pp. 52–6.

BIBLIOGRAPHY

Unpublished archival sources

Arbetarrörelsens Arkiv och Bibliotek, Huddinge, Sweden (ARBARK)
Bert Ekengren Papers
SAC Archives

Biblioteca y Archivo de Sociología y Economía, Montady, Spain (BASE)
Victor Garcia Papers

British Library, London, United Kingdom
India Office Records (IOR)
Newspaper collection
Weekly Report of the Director of Criminal Intelligence (WRDCI), IOR
   Neg 3095–3096

Cambridge South Asian Archive, Cambridge, United Kingdom
Newspaper collection

Center for International Research on Anarchism, Fujinomiya, Japan
(CIRA Japan)
Yamaga Collection

Centre International de Recherches sur l'Anarchisme, Lausanne, Switzerland
(CIRA)
Fonds de la Commission des relations internationales anarchistes

BIBLIOGRAPHY

David M. Rubenstein Rare Book & Manuscript Library, Duke University, Durham, NC, United States

Emma Goldman Papers

Houghton Library, Harvard University, Cambridge, United States

Leon Trotsky Exile Papers
Ruth Fischer Papers

Institut Français d'Histoire Sociale (IFHS), Archives nationales, Paris, France (AN)

Fonds Ernest Juin, dit Armand

International Institute of Social History, Amsterdam, Netherlands (IISH)

Alexander Berkman Papers
Archief Henk Sneevliet
Archief IAMV
Augustin Souchy Papers
Boris Yelensky Papers
Freedom Archives
Helmut Rüdiger Papers
IWMA Archives
Karl Korsch Papers
League against Imperialism Archives
Rudolf Rocker Papers
Second International Archives
Vernon Richards Papers

Leibniz-Zentrum Moderner Orient, Berlin, Germany (ZMO)

Horst Krüger Papers

Library and Archives of Canada, Ottawa, Canada

Department of External Affairs, Asiatic Immigration to Canada

Library of Congress, Washington D.C., United States

Asian Division

Maharashtra State Archives, Mumbai, India

HD (Special)/1937

Mitchell Library, Glasgow, Scotland

Guy Aldred Collection

314

BIBLIOGRAPHY

American Jurisprudence Collections at the Mudd Manuscript Library, Princeton University, United States

American Civil Liberties Union Papers

Mundaneum Archives, Mons, Belgium

Hem Day Personal Papers

National Archives, Kew, United Kingdom (NA)

Foreign Office (FO) Files

National Archives of India, New Delhi, India (NAI)

Home and Political

National Archives and Records Administration, College Park, Maryland, United States (NARA)

Bureau of Investigation, Old German Files

Politisches Archiv des Auswärtigen Amts, Berlin, Germany (PAAA)

Indien Politik 15: Agenten- und Spionagewesen.
Unternehmungen und Aufwiegelungen gegen unsere Feinde—in Indien
Unternehmungen und Aufwiegelungen gegen unsere Feinde—Tätigkeit in den Gefangenenlagern Deutschland

Russian State Archive for Social and Political History, Moscow, Russia (RGASPI)

Communist International Archives
Lenin's Secretariat

Sabarmati Ashram Preservation and Memorial Trust, Ahmedabad, India

Gandhi Correspondence

Special Collections Library, University of Michigan, Ann Arbor, United States

Joseph A. Labadie Collection

Swedish National Archives, Stockholm, Sweden (SNA)

Statens polisbyrå för övervakande av utlänningar i riket

Tamil Nadu Archives, Chennai, India (TNA)

Judicial Department, GO 1014

Walter P. Reuther Archive, Archives of Labor and Urban Affairs, Wayne State University, Detroit, United States

Nicolaas Steelink Papers

BIBLIOGRAPHY

Online archival sources

Arbetarrörelsens arkiv och bibliotek, Huddinge, Sweden (ARBARK)
https://socialhistoryportal.org/stockholm1917

S. R. Rana Private Papers
http://www.sardarsinhrana.com

Secondary sources

Acharya, M. P. T., Bishamber Dayal Yadav (ed.), *Reminiscences of an Indian Revolutionary* (New Delhi: Anmol Publications, 1991).

Acharya, M. P. T., Ole Birk Laursen (ed.), *We Are Anarchists: Essays on Anarchism, Pacifism, and the Indian Independence Movement, 1923–1953* (Chico: AK Press, 2019).

Adhikari, Gangadhar (ed.), *Documents of the History of the Communist Party of India, Vol. 1, 1917–1922* (New Delhi: People's Publishing House, 1971).

Œuvres du Congres National Egyptien tenu a Bruxelles le 22, 23, 24 Septembre 1910 (Bruges: St. Catherine Press, 1911).

Ahmad, Muzaffar, *Myself and the Communist Party of India, 1920–1927* (Calcutta: National Book Agency, 1970).

Ali, M. Asaf, G. N. S Raghavan, Aruna Asaf Ali (eds.) *M. Asaf Ali's Memoirs: The Emergence of Modern India* (Delhi: Ajanta, 1994).

Alonso, Isabel Huacuja, 'M. N. Roy and the Mexican Revolution: How a Militant Indian Nationalist Became an International Communist', *South Asia: Journal of South Asian Studies*, 40:3 (2017), pp. 517–30.

Ames, Eric, *Carl Hagenbeck's Empire of Entertainments* (Seattle: University of Washington Press, 2008).

Anderson, Benedict, *Under Three Flags: Anarchism and the Anti-Colonial Imagination* (London: Verso, 2005).

Ansari, Humayun, 'Maulana Barkatullah Bhopali's Transnationalism: Pan-Islamism, Colonialism, and Radical Politics', in Gotz Nordbruch and Umar Ryad (eds), *Transnational Islam in Interwar Europe: Muslim Activists and Thinkers* (London: Palgrave Macmillan, 2014), pp. 181–209.

Ansari, K. H., 'Pan-Islam and the Making of the Early Indian Muslim Socialists', *Modern Asian Studies*, 20:3 (1986), pp. 509–37.

Armytage, W. H. G., *Heavens Below: Utopian Experiments in England, 1560–1960* (London: Routledge & Kegan Paul 1961).

Avrich, Paul, 'Bolshevik Opposition to Lenin: G. T. Miasnikov and the Workers' Group', *Russian Review*, 43:1 (Jan 1984), pp. 1–29.

———, *The Russian Anarchists* (Edinburgh: AK Press, 2005).

Aydin, Cemil, *The Politics of Anti-Westernism in Asia: Visions of World Order in Pan-Islamic and Pan-Asian Thought* (New York: Columbia University Press, 2007).

BIBLIOGRAPHY

Åkerhielm, Annie, *En Bok om England och dess Undertryckta Folk* (Stockholm: Nationalförlaget, 1918).

Bailey, Frederick M., *Mission to Tashkent* (London: Jonathan Cape, 1946).

Bakhle, Janaki, 'Savarkar (1883–1966), Sedition and Surveillance: The Rule of Law in a Colonial Situation', *Social History*, 35:1 (2010), pp. 51–75.

Balachandran, Vappala, *A Life in Shadow: The Secret Story of ACN Nambiar: A Forgotten Anti-Colonial Warrior* (New Delhi: Lotus Collection, Roli Books, 2016).

Bantman, Constance, 'Anarchist Transnationalism', in Marcel van der Linden (ed.), *Cambridge History of Socialism*, Vol. I (Cambridge: Cambridge University Press, 2022), pp. 599–620.

Barooah, Nirode K., *Chatto: The Life and Times of an Indian Anti-Imperialist in Europe* (Oxford: Oxford University Press, 2004).

———, *Germany and the Indians between the Wars* (Norderstedt: Books on Demand, 2018)

Barua, Ankur, 'Revisiting the Gandhi–Ambedkar Debates over "Caste": The Multiple Resonances of Varna', *Journal of Human Values*, 25:1 (January 2019), pp. 25–40.

Basu, Jyoti (ed.), *Documents of the Communist Movement in India, Vol. 1, 1917–1928* (Calcutta: National Book Agency, 1997).

Berkman, Alexander, *The Bolshevik Myth* (London: Hutchinson & Co., 1925).

Berneri, Camillo, *El Delirio Racista* (Buenos Aires: Editions Iman, February 1935).

Bernstein, Lina, *Magda Nachman: An Artist in Exile* (Boston: Academic Studies Press, 2020).

———, 'The Great Little Lady of the Bombay Art World', in Christoph Flamm, Roland Marti, and Ada Raev (eds), *Transcending the Borders of Countries, Languages, and Disciplines in Russian émigré Culture* (Newcastle: Cambridge Scholars Publishing, 2018), pp 143–58.

'Bibliografia Essenziale', *Anarchici e Anarchia nel Mondo Contemporaneo: Atti del Convegno Promosso dalla Fondazione Luigi Einaudi (Torino, 5, 6 e 7 dicembre 1969)* (Torino: Fondazione Luigi Einaudi, 1971), pp. 196–7.

Bose, A. C. (ed.), *Indian Revolutionaries Abroad: 1905–1927* (New Delhi: Northern Book Centre, 2002).

Bose, Neilesh, 'Taraknath Das: A Global Biography', in Neilesh Bose (ed.), *South Asian Migrations in Global History: Labor, Law, and Wayward Lives* (London: Bloomsbury, 2020), pp. 157–77.

Bose, Sugata, *His Majesty's Opponent: Subhas Chandra Bose and India's Struggle against Empire* (Cambridge: Harvard University Press, 2011).

British Llano Circle, *The Comradeship of Economic Equality* (Farnham: Committee of the British Llano Circle, 1926),

BIBLIOGRAPHY

Broué, Pierre, *The German Revolution, 1917–1923* (London; Boston: Brill, 2005).

Brown, Emily C., *Har Dayal: Hindu Revolutionary and Rationalist* (Tucson: University of Arizona Press, 1975).

Brückenhaus, Daniel, *Policing Transnational Protest: Liberal Imperialism and the Surveillance of Anticolonialists in Europe, 1905–1945* (New York: Oxford University Press, 2017).

Brunton, Paul, *A Search in Secret India* (London: Rider & Co., 1934).

Chattopadhyay, Suchetana, 'Via Kabul: *Muhajirs* Turned Early Communists from India (1915–1923)', in Anne Garland Mahler and Paolo Capuzzo (eds), *The Comintern and the Global South: Global Designs/Local Encounters* (London: Routledge, 2022), pp. 125–46.

Chaturvedi, Vinayak, *Hindutva and Violence: V. D. Savarkar and the Politics of History* (Albany: State University of New York Press, 2022).

———, 'A Revolutionary's Biography: The Case of V. D. Savarkar', *Postcolonial Studies*, 16:2 (2013), pp. 124–39.

Chopra, Prabha, and P. N. Chopra (eds), *Indian Freedom Fighters Abroad: Secret British Intelligence Report* (New Delhi: Criterion Publications, 1988).

Cornell, Andrew, *Unruly Equality: U.S. Anarchism in the Twentieth Century* (Oakland: University of California Press, 2016).

Coutinho, Helen, *Pleasant Recollections of Dr Joaquim de Siqueira Coutinho* (New York: Saint Anthony Press, 1969).

Coward, Harold, *Indian Critiques of Gandhi* (Albany: State University of New York Press, 2003).

Dasgupta, Sandipto, 'Gandhi's Failure: Anticolonial Movements and Postcolonial Futures', *Perspectives on Politics*, 15:3 (September 2017), pp. 647–62.

Datta, Bhupendra Nath, *Dialectics of Land-Economics of India* (Calcutta: Mohendra Publishing Committee, 1952).

Davies, Andrew, 'Exile in the Homeland? Anti-Colonialism, Subaltern Geographies and the Politics of Friendship in Early Twentieth Century Pondicherry, India', *Environment and Planning D: Society and Space*, 35:3 (2017), pp. 457–74.

———, *Geographies of Anticolonialism: Political Networks Across and Beyond South India, c. 1900–1930* (London: Wiley, 2019).

Day, Hem, 'Voici un agitateur Indou: M. P. Acharya', *Inde: Social-Philosophie, Impressions, Essais* (Paris: Bruxelles: Pensee et Action, 1962), pp. 106–17.

Dhital, Pragya, 'Archiving Insurgence', *History Workshop*, 23 March 2020 [https://www.historyworkshop.org.uk/archiving-insurgency/], accessed 14 June 2022.

Drachewych, Oleksa, *The Communist International, Anti-Imperialism and Racial Equality in British Dominions* (London: Routledge, 2018).

BIBLIOGRAPHY

Executive Committee of the Indian National Party (European Centre), *Speeches and Resolutions on India at the International Socialist Congresses* (Berlin: Julius Sittenfeld, 1917).

Faruqui, M. A., 'A. M. Faruqui', *Verslag van het internationale Congres voor Dienstweigering, gehouden te Amsterdam, 25 en 26 mei 1927* (1927), pp. 22–7.

———, 'Anti-Militarisme en "Brits"-Indie', *Internationaal Antimilitaristisch Jaarboek* (Amsterdam: I.A.M.V. Sectie Holland, 1928), pp. 47–9.

Finn, Mike, *Debating Anarchism: A History of Action, Ideas and Movements* (London: Bloomsbury, 2021).

Fischer-Tiné, Harald, 'Indian Nationalism and the "World Forces": Transnational and Diasporic Dimensions of the Indian Freedom Movement on the Eve of the First World War', *Journal of Global History*, 2:3 (2007), pp. 325–44.

———, *Shyamji Krishnavarma: Sanskrit, Sociology, and Anti-Imperialism* (New Delhi: Routledge, 2014).

———, 'The Other Side of Internationalism: Switzerland as a Hub of Militant Anti-Colonialism, c. 1910–1920', in Patricia Purtschert and Harald Fischer-Tiné (eds), *Colonial Switzerland: Rethinking Colonialism from the Margins* (Houndmills, Basingstoke, Hampshire: Palgrave Macmillan, 2015), pp. 221–58.

Galián, Laura, *Colonialism, Transnationalism, and Anarchism in the South of the Mediterranean* (Cham: Palgrave Macmillan, 2020).

Gandhi, Leela, *Affective Communities: Anticolonial Thought, Fin-De-Siècle Radicalism, and the Politics of Friendship* (Durham: Duke University Press, 2006).

Germer, Andrea, 'Continuity and Change in Japanese Feminist Magazines: *Fujin Sensen* (1930–31) and *Onna Erosu* (1973–82)', in Ulrike Wöhr, Barbara Hamill Sato, and Suzuki Sadamo (eds), *Gender and Modernity: Rereading Japanese Women's Magazines* (Kyoto: International Research Center for Japanese Studies, 2000), pp. 101–30.

Getachew, Adom, *Worldmaking after Empire: The Rise and Fall of Self Determination* (Princeton: Princeton University Press, 2019).

Ghosh, Durba, *Gentlemanly Terrorists: Political Violence and the Colonial State in India, 1919–1947* (Cambridge: Cambridge University Press, 2017).

Goldman, Emma, *Living My Life* (Garden City, NY: Garden City Publishers, 1934).

Gopal, Priyamvada, *Insurgent Empire: Anticolonial Resistance and British Dissent* (London: Verso, 2019).

———, 'On Decolonisation and the University', *Textual Practice*, 35:6 (2021), pp. 873–99.

Gordon, Leonard A., *Brothers against the Raj: A Biography of Indian Nationalists Sarat and Subhas Chandra Bose* (New York: Columbia University Press, 1990).

BIBLIOGRAPHY

Goswami, Manu, 'Imaginary Futures and Colonial Internationalisms', *American Historical Review*, 117:5 (December 2012), pp. 1461–85.

Grant, H. Roger, 'Portrait of a Workers' Utopia: The Labor Exchange and the Freedom, Kan., Colony', *Kansas Historical Quarterly*, 43:1 (Spring 1977), pp. 56–66.

Haithcox, J. P., 'The Roy-Lenin Debate on Colonial Policy: A New Interpretation', *The Journal of Asian Studies*, 23:1 (November 1963), pp. 93–101.

Har Dayal, Lala, *Forty-Four Months in Germany and Turkey* (London: P. S. King & Son, 1920).

Harper, Tim, *Underground Asia: Global Revolutionaries and the Assault on Empire* (Cambridge: Harvard University Press, 2021).

Harris, Sarah Miller, *The CIA and the Congress for Cultural Freedom in the Early Cold War: The Limits of Making Common Cause* (Milton: Taylor and Francis, 2016).

Hirsch, Steven, and Lucien van der Walt (eds), *Anarchism and Syndicalism in the Colonial and Postcolonial World, 1870–1940: The Praxis of National Liberation, Internationalism, and Social Revolution* (Leiden; Boston: Brill, 2010).

Hodder, Jake, 'Conferencing the international at the World Pacifist Meeting, 1949', *Political Geography*, 49 (November 2015), pp. 40–50.

Holitscher, Arthur, *Reisen* (Potsdam: Gustav Kiepenheuer Verlag, 1928).

Höpp, Gerhard, 'Zwischen Entente und Mittelmächten: Arabische Nationalisten und Panislamisten in Deutschland (1914 bis 1918)', *Asien, Afrika, Lateinamerika*, 19:5 (1991), pp. 827–45.

Hughes, Thomas L., 'The German Mission to Afghanistan, 1915–1916', *German Studies Review*, 25:3 (Oct 2002), pp. 447–76.

Indiska Nationalkommittén, *Indien und der Weltfrieden: Ein Protest gegen das Friedensprogramm des Holländisch-Skandinavischen Sozial-Demokratischen Komitees von Europäischen Zentralkomitee der Indischen Nationalisten. Mit einem Anhang* (Stockholm: Indiska Nationalkommittén, 1918).

Internationalen Arbeiter-Assoziation, *Resolutionen, angenommen auf dem Internationalen Kongress der Revolutionären Syndikalisten zu Berlin, vom 25. Dezember 1922 bis 2. Januar 1923* (Berlin: Internationalen Arbeiter-Assoziation, 1923).

Jenkins, Jennifer, Heike Liebau, and Larissa Schmid, 'Transnationalism and Insurrection: Independence Committees, Anti-Colonial Networks, and Germany's Global War', *Journal of Global History*, 15:1 (2020), pp. 61–79.

Jha, Dhirendra K., *Gandhi's Assassin: The Making of Nathuram Godse and His Idea of India* (Gurugram: Vintage by Penguin Random House India, 2021).

Jonker, Gerdien, *On the Margins: Jews and Muslims in Interwar Berlin* (Leiden; Boston: Brill, 2020).

BIBLIOGRAPHY

Jun, Nathan, 'Anarchism without Archives', *American Periodicals: A Journal of History & Criticism*, 29:1 (2019), pp. 3–5.

Kapila, Shruti, *Violent Fraternity: Indian Political Thought in the Global Age* (Princeton: Princeton University Press, 2021).

Karanth, K. S., *Ten Faces of a Crazy Mind* (Bombay: Bharatiya Vidya Bhavan, 1993).

Kaye, Cecil (ed.), *Communism in India: Unpublished Documents from National Archives of India (1919–1924)* (Calcutta: Editions Indian, 1971).

Kent-Carrasco, Daniel, 'Beyond the Reach of Empire: Pandurang Khankhoje's Transit from British Colonial Subject to Mexican "Naturalizado" (1924–1954)', in Neilesh Bose (ed.), *South Asian Migrations in Global History: Labor, Law, and Wayward Lives* (London: Bloomsbury, 2020), pp. 179–99.

Ker, James Campbell, *Political Trouble in India, 1907–1917* (Calcutta: Superintendent Government Printing, 1917).

Kessler, Mario, *Ruth Fischer: Ein Leben mit und gegen Kommunisten (1895–1961)* (Köln: Böhlau Verlag, 2013).

Khan, Noor-Aiman I., *Egyptian-Indian Nationalist Collaboration and the British Empire* (New York: Palgrave Macmillan, 2011).

Khan, Razak, 'Entangled Institutional and Affective Archives of South Asian Muslim Students in Germany', Modern India in German Archives (MIDA), online article, 14 February 2019 [https://www.projekt-mida.de/reflexicon/entangled-institutional-and-affective-archives-of-south-asian-muslim-students-in-germany/], accessed 8 June 2022.

Khan, Tariq, 'Living Social Dynamite: Early Twentieth-Century IWW-South Asia Connections', in Peter Cole, David Struthers, Kenyon Zimmer (eds), *Wobblies of the World: A Global History of the IWW* (London: Pluto, 2017), pp. 59–72.

Khan, Yasmin, *India at War: The Subcontinent and the Second World War* (New York: Oxford University Press, 2015).

Khuri-Makdisi, Ilham, *The Eastern Mediterranean and the Making of Global Radicalism, 1860–1914* (Berkeley; London: University of California Press, 2010).

Kinna, Ruth, *The Government of No One: The Theory and Practice of Anarchism* (London: Pelican, 2019).

———, 'What is Anarchist Internationalism?', *Nations and Nationalism*, 27:4 (2020), pp. 976–91.

Kocho-Williams, Alastair, 'The Soviet Challenge to British India' in Oleksa Drachewych and Ian McKay (eds), *Left Transnationalism: The Communist International and the National, Colonial, and Racial Questions* (Montreal; Kingston; London; Chicago: McGill-Queen's University Press 2019), pp. 125–51.

BIBLIOGRAPHY

Korsch, Karl, Michael Buckmiller (ed.), *Gesamtausgabe: Briefe, 1940–1958* (Europäische Verlagsanstalt, 2001).

Kuck, Nathanael, 'Anti-Colonialism in a Post-Imperial Environment—The Case of Berlin, 1914–33', *Journal of Contemporary History*, 49:1 (2014), pp. 134–59.

Kulkarni, D. M., 'Shri R. B. Lotvala: The Prophet of Human Freedom—A Life-Sketch', *Selections from The Indian Libertarian Part 2: 1971–1981* (1981), pp. 1–2.

Laursen, Ole Birk, 'The Indian Nationalist Press in London, 1865–1914', in Constance Bantman and Ana Claudia Suriani da Silva (eds), *The Foreign Political Press in Nineteenth-Century London: Politics from a Distance* (London: Bloomsbury, 2017), pp. 175–91.

————, '"A Dagger, a Revolver, a Bottle of Chloroform": Colonial Spy Fiction, Revolutionary Reminiscences and Indian Nationalist Terrorism in Europe', in Elleke Boehmer and Dominic Davies (eds), *Planned Violence: Post/Colonial Urban Infrastructure, Literature and Culture* (Palgrave Macmillan, 2018), pp. 255–71.

————, 'Anarchist Anti-Imperialism: Guy Aldred and the Indian Revolutionary Movement, 1909–14', *Journal of Imperial and Commonwealth History*, 46:2 (2018), pp. 286–303.

————, 'Anti-Colonialism, Terrorism, and the "Politics of Friendship": Virendranath Chattopadhyaya and the European Anarchist Movement', *Anarchist Studies*, 27:1 (2019), pp. 47–62.

————, '"I have only One Country, it is the World": Madame Cama, Anticolonialism, and Indian-Russian Revolutionary Networks in Paris, 1907–1917', *History Workshop Journal*, 90 (Autumn 2020), pp. 96–114.

————(ed.), *Lay Down Your Arms: Anti-Imperialism, Anti-Militarism, and the Global Radical Left in the 1930s* (Atlanta: On Our Own Authority! Publishing, 2019).

————, 'Spaces of Indian Anticolonialism in Early Twentieth Century London and Paris', *South Asia: Journal of South Asian Studies*, 44:4 (2021), pp. 634–50.

Lazar, Hillary, '*Man!* and the International Group: Anti-Radicalism, Immigrant Solidarity and Depression-Era Transnational Anarchism', in Frank Jacob and Mario Kessler (eds), *Transatlantic Radicalism: Socialist and Anarchist Exchanges in the 19th and 20th Centuries* (Liverpool: Liverpool University Press, 2021), pp. 109–27.

Levy, Carl, 'Social Histories of Anarchism', *Journal for the Study of Radicalism*, 4:2 (2010), pp. 1–44

Liebau, Heike, 'The German Foreign Office, Indian Emigrants, and Propaganda Efforts Among the "Sepoys"', in Franziska Roy, Heike Liebau, and Ravi Ahuja (eds), *'When the War Began, we Heard of Several Kings': South*

BIBLIOGRAPHY

Asian Prisoners in World War I Germany (London: Routledge, 2017), pp. 96–129.

———, 'Navigating Knowledge, Negotiating Positions: The Kheiri Brothers on Nation and Islam', *Geschichte und Gesellschaft*, 45 (2019), pp. 341–61.

Liebich, André, and Svetlana Yakimovich (eds), *From Communism to Anti-Communism: Photographs from the Boris Souvarine Collection at the Graduate Institute, Geneva* (Geneva: Graduate Institute Publications, 2016).

Loomba, Ania, *Revolutionary Desires: Women, Communism, and Feminism in India* (Milton: Routledge, 2018).

Louro, Michele, *Comrades against Imperialism: Nehru, India, and Interwar Internationalism* (Cambridge; New York: Cambridge University Press, 2018).

Louro, Michele, Carolien Stolte, Heather Streets-Salter, Sana Tannoury-Karam, 'The League Against Imperialism: Lives and Afterlives', in Michele Louro, Carolien Stolte, Heather Streets-Salter, and Sana Tannoury-Karam (eds), *The League Against Imperialism: Lives and Afterlives* (Leiden: Leiden University Press, 2020), pp. 17–52.

Mackinnon, Janice, and Stephen Mackinnon, *Agnes Smedley: The Life and Times of an American Radical* (Berkeley: University of California Press, 1988).

Maclean, Kama, *A Revolutionary History of Interwar India: Violence, Image, Voice and Text* (London: Hurst & Company, 2015).

Maclean, Kama, and J. Daniel Elam, 'Reading Revolutionaries: Texts, Acts, and Afterlives of Political Action in Late Colonial South Asia', *Postcolonial Studies*, 16:2 (2013), pp. 113–23.

Manela, Erez, *The Wilsonian Moment: Self-Determination and the International Origins of Anticolonial Nationalism* (Oxford: Oxford University Press, 2007).

Manjapra, Kris, 'The Illusions of Encounter: Muslim 'Minds' and Hindu Revolutionaries in First World War Germany and After', *Journal of Global History*, 1:3 (2006), pp. 363–82.

———, *Age of Entanglement: German and Indian Intellectuals across Empire* (Cambridge: Harvard University Press, 2014).

———, *M. N. Roy: Marxism and Colonial Cosmopolitanism* (London: Routledge, 2010).

Mantena, Karuna, 'On Gandhi's Critique of the State: Sources, Contexts, Conjunctures', *Modern Intellectual History*, 9:3 (November 2012), pp. 535–63.

Marsh, Kate, '"The only safe haven of refuge in all the world": Paris, Indian "Revolutionaries" and Imperial Rivalry, c. 1905–40', *French Cultural Studies*, 30:3 (2019), pp. 196–219.

BIBLIOGRAPHY

Mashruwala, K. G., *Gandhi and Marx* (Ahmedabad: Navajivan Publishing House, 1951).

Maximoff, Grigori P., *The Guillotine at Work: Twenty Years of Terror in Russia (Data and Documents)*, Vol. 2 (Chicago: Chicago Section of the Alexander Berkman Fund, 1940).

———, 'The State of the World', in Free Society Group (ed.), *The World Scene from the Libertarian Point of View* (Chicago: Free Society Group, 1951), pp. 5–9.

McQuillan, Stephen, '"Revolutionaries, Renegades and Refugees": Anti-British Allegiances in the Context of World War I', in Enrico Dal Lago, Róisín Healy, and Gearóid Barry (eds), *1916 in a Global Context: An Anti-Imperial Moment* (London: Routledge, 2017), pp. 117–30.

Meltzer, Albert, *The Anarchists in London, 1935–1955: A Personal Memoir* (Sanday Box A, Over the Water, Sanday, Orkney: Cienfuegos Press, 1976).

———, *I Couldn't Paint Golden Angels: Sixty Years of Commonplace Life and Anarchist Agitation* (Edinburgh: AK Press, 1996).

Mir, Farina, Introduction, AHR Roundtable: The Archives of Decolonization, *American Historical Review*, 120:3 (June 2015), pp. 844–51.

Mody, Nawaz B., 'Perin Captain: From Dadabhai to Mahatma Gandhi', in Nawaz B. Mody (ed.), *Women in India's Freedom Struggle* (Mumbai: Allied Publishers, 2000), pp. 205–18.

Moya, Jose C., 'Anarchism', in Akira Iriye and Pierre-Yves Saunier (eds), *Palgrave Dictionary of Transnational History* (New York: Palgrave Macmillan, 2009), pp. 39–41.

Mukherjee, Tapan K. (ed.), *Taraknath Das: Life and Letters of a Revolutionary in Exile* (Calcutta: National Council of Education, Bengal, Jadavpur University, 1998).

Nag, Kalidas, Introduction, M. P. T. Acharya, *Principles of Non-Violent Economics* (Calcutta: International University of Non-Violence, 1947), p. 1.

Nation, R. Craig, *War on War: Lenin, the Zimmerwald Left, and the Origins of Communist Internationalism* (Durham: Duke University Press, 1989).

Oesterheld, Frank, '"Der Feind meines Feindes ist mein Freund"–Zur Tätigkeit des Indian Independence Committee (IIC) während des Ersten Weltkrieges in Berlin', Magisterarbeit zur Erlangung des akademischen Grades Magister Artium im Fach Neuere I Neueste Geschichte (2004).

Ostergaard, Geoffrey, 'Indian Anarchism: The Sarvodaya Movement', in David E. Apter and James Joll (eds), *Anarchism Today: Studies in Comparative Politics* (London: Palgrave Macmillan, 1971), pp. 145–63.

Ostergaard Geoffrey, and Melville Currell, *The Gentle Anarchists: A Study of*

BIBLIOGRAPHY

the Leaders of the Sarvodaya Movement for Nonviolent Revolution in India (Oxford: Clarendon Press, 1991).

Pachter, Henry, *Weimar études* (New York: Columbia University Press, 1982).

Padmanabhan, R. A., 'M. P. T. Acharya', *Indian Review*, 70:2 (May 1974), p. 29.

Patel, Dinyar, *Naoroji: Pioneer of Indian Nationalism* (Cambridge: Harvard University Press, 2020).

Patenaude, Bertrand, *The Big Show in Bololand: The American Relief Expedition to Soviet Russia in the Famine of 1921* (Stanford: Stanford University Press, 2002).

Pearce, Brian (ed.), *Congress of the Peoples of the East, Baku, September 1920, Stenographic Report* (London: New Park Publications, 1977).

Pemmaraju, Gautam, 'The Dark Foreigner with the Great Dog: Jayasurya Naidu in Germany, 1922–1934', *Nidan: International Journal for Indian Studies*, 7:1 (July 2022), pp. 115–31.

Persic, Moisej Aronovič, *Revolutionaries of India in Soviet Russia: Mainsprings of the Communist Movement in the East* (Moscow: Progress Publishers, 1983).

Petersson, Fredrik, *"We are Neither Visionaries nor Utopian Dreamers": Willi Münzenberg, the League Against Imperialism, and the Comintern, 1925–1933* (Lewiston: Queenston Press, 2013).

———, 'Hub of the Anti-Imperialist Movement', *Interventions: International Journal of Postcolonial Studies*, 16:1 (2014), pp. 49–71.

———, 'Imperialism and the Communist International', *Journal of Labor and Society*, 20:1 (March 2017), pp. 23–42.

———, 'A Neutral Place? Anti-Colonialism, Peace, and Revolution in Stockholm, 1917', in Holger Weiss (ed.), *Locating the Global: Spaces, Networks and Interactions from the Seventeenth to the Twentieth Century* (Berlin; Boston: De Gruyter Oldenbourg, 2020), pp. 283–314.

———, '"We will fight with our lives for the equal rights of all peoples": Willi Münzenberg, the League Against Imperialism, and the Comintern', in Michele Louro, Carolien Stolte, Heather Streets-Salter, and Sana Tannoury-Karam (eds), *The League Against Imperialism: Lives and Afterlives* (Leiden: Leiden University Press, 2020), pp. 159–86.

Petrie, David, and Mahadevaprasad Saha (eds), *Communism in India, 1924–1927* (Calcutta: Editions Indian, 1972).

Porter, Cathy, *Alexandra Kollontai: A Biography* (London: Virago, 1980).

Pratap, Raja Mahendra, Vir Singh (ed.), *Reminiscences of a Revolutionary* (New Delhi: Books India International, 1999).

Qiang Lei, 'Bibliotheque Sino-Internationale Geneve and the *Orient et Occident*', *Journal of Library and Information Studies*, 13:1 (June 2015), pp. 135–61.

BIBLIOGRAPHY

Raikov, A., 'October Revolution and Indian Immigrants in Germany', in Ilasai Manian and V. Rajesh (eds), *The Russian Revolution and India* (London: Routledge, 2020), pp. 101–5.

Ramnath, Maia, *Decolonizing Anarchism: An Antiauthoritarian History of India's Liberation Struggle* (Oakland: AK Press, 2011).

———, *Haj to Utopia: How the Ghadar Movement Charted Global Radicalism and Attempted to Overthrow the British Empire* (Berkeley: University of California Press. 2011).

Raza, Ali, *Revolutionary Pasts: Communist Internationalism in Colonial India* (Cambridge: Cambridge University Press, 2020).

Relgis, Eugen, *Los Principios Humanitaristas*. Edición definitiva. (Traducida por Eloy Muñiz del francés y por el autor del rumano) (Montevideo: Ediciones "Humanidad", [1922] 1950).

Riddell, John (ed.), *Workers of the World and Oppressed Peoples, Unite!: Proceedings and Documents of the Second Congress, 1920* (London: Pathfinder, 1991).

Rocker, Rudolf, *Revolución y Regresión (1918–1951)* (Buenos Aires: Editorial Tupac, 1952).

———, *Socialism and the State* (Indore City: Modern Publishers, 1946).

Roy, Franziska, Heike Liebau, and Ravi Ahuja, *'When the War Began, We Heard of Several Kings': South Asian Prisoners in World War I Germany* (Bangalore: Orient Blackswan, 2011).

Roy, M. N., *M. N. Roy's Memoirs* (Bombay: Allied Publishers, 1964).

Roy, Purabi, Sobhanlal Datta Gupta, Hari S. Vasudevan (eds), *Indo-Russian Relations, 1917–1947: Select Documents from the Archives of the Russian Federation* (Calcutta: Asiatic Society, 1999).

Said, Edward, *Culture and Imperialism* (London: Vintage, 1994).

Sastri, V. S. Srinivasa, *Life and Times of Sir Pherozeshah Mehta* (Bombay: Bharatiya Vidya Bhavan, 1975).

Savarkar, Vinayak Damodar, *The Indian War of Independence of 1857* (New Delhi: Rajdhani Granthagar, 1970 [1909]).

Sawhney, Savitri (ed.), Pandurang Khankhoje, *I Shall Never Ask for Pardon: A Memoir of Pandurang Khankhoje* (New Delhi: Penguin Books India, 2008).

Schaffel, Paul, 'Empire and Assassination: Indian Students, "India House", and Information Gathering in Great Britain, 1898–1911', a thesis submitted to the faculty of Wesleyan University, April 2012.

Sherman, Taylor, 'A Gandhian Answer to the Threat of Communism? Sarvodaya and Postcolonial Nationalism in India', *The Indian Economic & Social History Review*, 53:2 (2016), pp. 249–70.

Shillam, Thomas William, 'Shattering the "looking-glass world": The Congress for Cultural Freedom in South Asia, 1951–55', *Cold War History*, 20:4 (2020), pp. 441–59.

BIBLIOGRAPHY

Sho Konishi, 'Translingual World Order: Language without Culture in Post-Russo-Japanese War Japan', *Journal of Asian Studies*, 72:1 (2013), pp. 91–114.

Siddiqui, Samee, 'Coupled Internationalisms: Charting Muhammad Barkatullah's Anti-colonialism and Pan-Islamism', *ReOrient*, 5:1 (2019), pp. 25–46.

Singh, Ajit, Pardaman Singh, Joginder Singh Dhanki (eds), *Buried Alive: Autobiography, Speeches and Writings of an Indian Revolutionary* (New Delhi: Gitanjali, 1984).

Singh, Iqbal, and Raja Rao (eds), *Whither India? (Socio-Politico Analyses)* (Baroda: Padmaja Publications, 1949).

Smith, A. W., review of James Joll, *The Anarchists*, *East London Papers*, 8:2 (1972), pp. 124–8.

Snowden, Mrs Philip [Ethel], *A Political Pilgrim in Europe* (London; New York: Cassell, 1921).

Sohi, Seema, *Echoes of Mutiny: Race, Surveillance, and Indian Anticolonialism in North America* (Oxford: Oxford University Press, 2014).

Souchy, Augustin, *Beware! Anarchist! A Life for Freedom: The Autobiography of Augustin Souchy* (Chicago: Charles H. Kerr, 1992 [1977]).

Source Material for a History of the Freedom Movement in India (Bombay: Printed at the Govt. Central Press, 1957–).

Stolte, Carolien, and Harald Fischer-Tiné, 'Imagining Asia in India: Nationalism and Internationalism (ca. 1905–1940)', *Comparative Studies in Society and History*, 54:1 (2012), pp. 65–92.

Subramanyam, C. S., *M. P. T. Acharya: His Life and Times: Revolutionary Trends in the Early Anti-Imperialist Movements in South India and Abroad* (Madras: Institute of South Indian Studies, 1995).

Taylor, Antony, 'The Whiteway Anarchists in the Twentieth Century: A Transnational Community in the Cotswolds', *History*, 101:1 (2016), pp. 62–83.

Thakur, Vineet, *India's First Diplomat: V. S. Srinivasa Sastri and the Making of Liberal Internationalism* (Bristol: Bristol University Press, 2021).

Thorpe, Wayne, *The Workers Themselves: Revolutionary Syndicalism and International Labour, 1913–1923* (Dordrecht; Boston: Kluwer Academic and International Institute of Social History, 1989).

Tickell, Alex, 'Scholarship Terrorists: The India House Hostel and the "Student Problem" in Edwardian London', in Rehana Ahmed and Sumita Mukherjee (eds), *South Asian Resistances in Britain, 1858–1947* (London: Continuum, 2012), pp. 3–18.

Trotsky, Leon, 'Who Is Leading the Comintern Today?', [https://www.marxists.org/archive/trotsky/1928/03/comintern.htm], accessed 21 May 2022.

BIBLIOGRAPHY

Usmani, Shaukat, *Peshawar to Moscow: Leaves from an Indian Muhajireen's Diary* (Benares: Swarajy Publishing House, 1927).

———, 'Russian Revolution and India, III–V', *Mainstream Weekly*, 55:48 (18 November 2017–2 December 2017) [http://mainstreamweekly.net/article7591.html], accessed 21 May 2022.

Varela, Cécilia, 'Au-delà des normes? "L'amour libre" et la famille antiautoritaire (1880–1930)', *Mouvements*, 82:2 (2015), pp. 123–31.

Visana, Vikram, 'Savarkar before Hindutva: Sovereignty, Republicanism and Populism in India, c. 1900–1920', *Modern Intellectual History* (2020), pp. 1–24.

———, *Uncivil Liberalism: Labour, Capital and Commercial Society in Dadabhai Naoroji's Political Thought* (Cambridge: Cambridge University Press, 2022).

Walter, Nicolas, Introduction, Rudolf Rocker, *Anarcho-Syndicalism* (London: Pluto Press, 1989).

Ward, Margaret, *Maud Gonne: Ireland's Joan of Arc* (London: Pandora, 1990).

Weijia Li, 'Otherness in Solidarity: Collaboration between Chinese and German Left-Wing Activists in the Weimar Republic', in Qinna Shen and Martin Rosenstock (eds), *Beyond Alterity: German Encounters with Modern East Asia* (New York; Oxford: Berghahn Books, 2014), pp. 73–93.

Wright, Steven, 'Left Communism in Australia: J. A. Dawson and the *Southern Advocate for Workers' Councils*', *Thesis Eleven*, 1:1 (1980), pp. 43–77.

Yagnik, Indulal, *The Autobiography of Indulal Yagnik* (New Delhi: Manohar Publishers and Distributors, 2011).

———, *Life of Ranchoddas Bhavan Lotvala* (Bombay: Writers' Emporium, 1952).

Zachariah, Benjamin, *Nehru* (London: Routledge, 2004).

———, 'Indian Political Activities in Germany, 1914–1945', in J. Cho, E. Kurlander, and D. T. McGetchin (eds), *Transcultural Encounters between Germany and India: Kindred Spirits in the 19th and 20th Centuries* (London: Routledge, 2013), pp. 141–54.

Zimmer, Kenyon, *Immigrants against the State: Yiddish and Italian Anarchism in America* (Urbana: University of Illinois Press, 2015).

INDEX

Abrams, Irving S., 229
Abyssinia, 186, 194
Acción Social Obrera, 160
Acharya and Nachman
  in Berlin, 1–2, 125–8
  in Charlottenburg, 125–8, 136–7
  escaped to Zürich, 20
  marriage, 19, 120–21
Acharya, M. P. T.
  among the anarchists in Russia, 117–19
  among the ultra-leftists, 157–9
  analysis on rise of fascism, 194–5
  anti-British work in Constantinople, 46–9
  applied for US citizenship, 53–4
  arrest warrant for, 38
  arrival to Bombay, 185–6
  arrived in Zürich, 179
  Asian anarchism, 208–9
  associated with Bolshevik dissenters and critics, 115–16
  background, 27
  Berlin arrival (Nov 1914), 57, 58
  Berlin visit, first, 3

  biography, 12–13
  Bombay visit, 28
  as chairman of the Executive Committee of the ICP, 106
  conditions for the Comintern, 112–13
  death of, 8, 22, 237–8
  early life and career, 2–3, 27–9
  education, 27
  escape to the United States, 51–2
  exile in Europe, 37–49
  exile, 29–30
  fled Russia, 1
  illness, 47–8
  Latvia border crossing, 88–9
  letter to Armand, 172, 176–7
  letter to Gandhi, 175
  letter to Keell, 134
  letter to Lenin, 109
  letter to Reisner, 127
  letter to Romberg, 83
  letter to the CRIA, 13–15
  letter to Yelensky, 116
  in Lisbon, 38
  London and India House, 30–6
  marriage and escape from Russia, 29, 119–21

329

INDEX

meeting with Bose, 173–4
meeting with Lenin, 18, 89–90, 109–10
Morocco visit, 37–8
in New York City, 17
in Paris, 39–41, 177–8
Poona visit, 28
reconnection with international anarchist movement, 200–3
requested for IAMB's help, 181–2
to Rotterdam, 42
Russia visit (Jun 1919), 4–5
smuggling weapons and seditious literature, 40
sojourn in Germany, 42–6
split from the ICP, 111
Weimar era Berlin years, 6–7, 19
world anarchism, 209–12
Afghan Foreign Ministry, 94
Afghan-British War (1919), 87
Afghanistan
IRA in, 5, 90–4
Aftonbladet, 75, 81, 82
Ahmed, Mansur, 57, 59, 63, 65, 66, 67, 88
Aiyar, N. P. Narasimha, 27
Aiyar, V. V. S., 3, 8–9, 14, 16, 30, 31, 32, 34, 35, 41, 42, 43
Acharya's letter to, 38, 45, 46, 47
Albarda, Willem, 71
Aldred, Guy A., 36, 41, 219–20
Alexander Berkman Aid Fund, 238
Algeria, 187
Ali, Asaf, 31, 42
Ali, Inayat, 66, 68
Ali, Muhammad Rajab, 60, 64, 66, 68, 102
Allgemeine Teeimport-Gesellschaft, 43, 44

All-India Trade Union Congress (AITUC), 131, 139
Altendorf, Wright & Darf, 48
Ambedkar, B. R., 165
American Civil Liberties Union, 209
American Relief Administration (ARA), 18, 117, 120
Amin, Govind, 31, 38, 40, 42, 48, 51
anarchism
and archives, 13–15
and autonomous communes, 159–62
definition of, 216–18
end of, 8
as socialism, 138–9
anarchist internationalism, 13
'Anarchist Manifesto', 136
Andijan, 103, 104, 105
Anglo-Americans, 215
Anti-Bolshevik dissenters, 20, 115–16
anti-Bolshevism, 109, 142
anticolonial solidarity, 37–8
anticolonialism, 5, 7, 9–10, 16, 72–5
anti-imperialism, 4, 17, 18, 19, 22, 36
anti-militarism, 7, 19, 76–8
and anti-imperialism, 148–51
and pacifism, 146–7
antisemitism, 131–2
Arbetaren, 154
Argentina (steamship), 51
Armand, E., 6, 162, 164–5
Acharya's letter to, 172, 176–7
Arya Bhavan, 204
Ashur, Mohammed, 90, 91
Asian Prisoners Aid Group, 226
Atelierhaus, 174
Atlantic Charter, 213

INDEX

Atyyeh, Salim, 38
Australia, 8, 209
Auswärtiges Amt (German Foreign Office, AA), 57, 58, 59, 60, 64, 66, 73, 79, 80, 81, 82–3, 84, 132, 138
Avanti! (journal), 84
Azad Hindustan Akhbar (periodical), 94
Azef, Evno, 158
Azerbaijan, 98, 145
Aziz, Abdul, 117

Baghdad mission, 64–9
Bairstow, Ernest, 133, 178
Baku Congress (Sep 1920), 98
Bakunin, Mikhail, 12, 207
Bala Bharat (journal), 28
Balabanoff, Angelica, 77, 79, 115–16
Baldwin, Roger Nash, 209
Baltic Sea, 88
Bande Mataram (periodical), 39, 54
Bantman, Constance, 13
Barkatullah, Muhammed, 58, 59, 61–2, 87, 89, 93
Bedouins, 62
Begerhotta, J. P., 135
Berkman, Alexander, 6, 17, 53, 111–12, 117–18, 125, 129, 134, 135, 149, 159–60
  Acharya's meeting with, 55
  meeting with Karakhan, 118
Berlin
  anticolonialism and anarchism in, 125–42
  Berlin Indians in Moscow, 110–13
  cooperative living, 133–4
  deportation of Indians, 131–3
  as hub for international anarchists, 128

IIC in, 57–60, 61, 82–3
  Indians among the anarchists, 128–31
  struggles of Indians in, 172–3
  ultra-leftists, 20
Bernstein, Lina, 11
Bertoni, Luigi, 205
Bey, Abdullah Cevdet, 60, 67
Bey, Djelal Nuri, 47
Bey, Fuad, 68
Bey, Muhammad Farid, 41, 42, 47
Beyer, Hendrik Jan Mispelblom, 181–2
Bhakta, Satya, 135
Bharati, C. Subramania, 27, 28
Bhave, Vinoba, 22, 234–5, 236
Bhoodan movement, 12, 234–5
Bolshevik communism, 5
Bolshevik Myth, The (Berkman), 134
Bolshevik regime, 1, 2, 18, 19, 116, 117
Bolsheviks, 88, 90, 94, 99, 125
Bolshevism, 6, 9, 126, 141, 188, 234
Bombay Chronicle (newspaper), 137, 138, 140, 146, 185, 186
Bombay, 13, 20, 21
  Acharya's arrival to, 185–6
  library in, 21
Bonnier (publisher), 72
Borghi, Armando, 129
Borodin, Mikhail, 93
Bose, Neilesh, 12–13
Bose, Subhas Chandra, 7, 173–4
Bot, Lambertus Johannes, Jr., 150
'Brahmin landlords', 220
Branting, Hjalmar, 71, 75
Brest-Litovsk peace negotiations, 79–81
British imperialism, 111, 135, 137, 141, 186

331

INDEX

British Independent Labour Party, 145

British Llano Circle (BLC), 133

Brockway, Fenner, 174–5, 176

Brokaw, Warren, 133

Bruhl, Albert, 166

Brussels conference (Sep 1910), 41–2

Brussels congress (Feb 1927), 144–5, 148

Brussels, anticolonial alliances in, 41–2

Butyrka Prison, 140

Cama, Bhikhaiji Rustom (Madame Cama), 3, 20, 31, 39, 41, 42, 43–4, 54

Canter, Irving S., 227–8

capitalism, 96, 157, 163

caste, 165–6

Caxton Hall meeting (5 Jul 1909), 35

Cellular Jail (Andamans), 219

Central Revolutionary Committee, 102

Chakravarty, Chandra Kanta, 31, 48, 51, 54

Chandra, Harish, 59

Chandra, Ram, 53

Chatterji, Jnanendra Nath, 29, 44

Chattopadhyaya, Virendranath, 2, 3, 4, 16, 17, 18, 19, 20, 31, 35, 41, 42, 43–4, 45, 47, 61, 63–4, 68, 71–2, 73, 74–6, 79, 80, 82, 84, 96, 105, 109, 110, 111–12, 126, 127, 132, 142, 143–4, 149

Acharya's letter to, 66

Auswärtiges Amt and, 57

letter to the IIC, 72, 80–1

Nehru visited, 139

on Rocker, 128–9

Zimmerwald conference (1917), 76–8

Chettiar, Malaypuram Singaravelu, 130–1

Chiang Kai-shek, 161, 229

Chicago (French steamer), 58

Chinese activists, 177

Chinese civil war, 150–1

Chinese News Agency, 161–2

Chinese revolution, 161–2

Chitnis, Gajanan Yashwant, 190

CIA, 233

class, 165–6

Cold War, 8, 21, 223, 230

Comfort, Alex, 227

Commission for International Anarchist Relations (CRIA), 8, 21, 208, 209–10, 211–12

Commission on the National and Colonial Question, 95

Committee of Independent Georgia, 72

Committee of Union and Progress (CUP), 3, 47

communism, 9, 87–121, 134–6

Communist Party of Mexico, 95

Community Life, 192

Comradeship of Economic Equality, The, 133

Congress for Cultural Freedom, 233–4

Constantinople, 4, 57–8

IIC in, 67–8

Indian mission to, 59–62

cooperative living, 6–7, 133–4

Council for Action and Propaganda in the East (CAPE), 99

Coutinho, Joaquim de Siqueira, 31, 32

CRIA. *See* Commission for International Anarchist Relations (CRIA)

332

INDEX

Cripps Mission (1942), 195
Curzon-Wyllie, assassination of, 34, 35, 36, 39

Dagens Nyheter (newspaper), 73
Dalton, Hugh, 175
Damascus mission, 61
Dandi march, 152–3, 154
Dange, S. A., 135, 236
Das, Chittaranjan, 131
Das, Taraknath, 4, 58, 60, 62–3, 64, 221
Das, Thakur, 53
Datta, Bhupendranath, 58, 66, 76, 90, 93, 111, 127
Davies, Andrew, 10–11
Dawson, James, 202
Dayal, Lala Har, 3, 4, 14, 16, 31, 32, 51, 52–3, 55, 57, 59, 60, 61, 63, 80, 81, 82
  arrest of, 54
  Constantinople visit, 57–8
  Varma on, 61
Dayalbagh, 192
de Bernardi, Giuseppe B., 133
de Jong, Albert, 138, 146, 147, 148, 150, 151
de Ligt, Bart, 150, 151
de Santillan, Diego Abad, 201
De Syndicalist (Netherlands), 135, 161
De Wapens Neder (newspaper), 186
Delalsl, Francis, 160
Department of Criminal Intelligence (DCI), 31, 32, 33, 34, 37, 39, 43, 48, 52, 54–5, 87, 88
Der Frauen-Bund, 162
Der Freiheitliche Sozialist (Germany), 206
Der Syndikalist (Germany), 15, 135, 160, 162, 166

Desai, Maganbhai P., 22, 234, 236, 239–40
Deutsche Film Union, 137
Dhingra, Madan Lal, 31, 34–5, 36
Die Ahmadia-Sekte, 128
Die Internationale, 147, 161
Dielo Truda-Probuzhdenie (Maximoff), 204–5
Doubinsky, Jacques, 205
Dutch-Scandinavian Committee (DSC), 71, 75, 76, 78–9
Dutt, Sukh Sagar, 37–8

Ebert, Friedrich, 83
Economic Weekly (newspaper), 236
Efron, Elizabeth, 119
Egyptian nationalists, 41–2
Eisner, Kurt, 83
Ekengren, Bert, 55, 225–6
En Bok om England och dess Undertryckta Folk, 81
Encyclopedie Anarchiste (Faure), 204
English (language), 211
Equitist, The, 133
Ernst, E. Z., 133
Essentials of Hindutva (Acharya), 219
European Anarchist Congress, 207
European colonialism, 137
European languages, 193
European press, 154
European socialists, 4, 42, 78, 84, 96, 190
Executive Committee of the Communist International (ECCI), 101, 109–10, 111, 112, 144

Faruqui, Mohammed Amin, 18, 91, 111, 117, 126–7, 146–7
fascism, 7, 8
Felder, Adele, 176

333

INDEX

Ferrer, Francisco, 55
Fikret, Tevfik, 47
Finn, Mike, 11–12
Fischer, Ruth, 157, 202–3
Fitingov, Rosa, 102
Forward (Indian newspaper), 19, 138, 147, 150, 162
Frankfurt congress, 150–1
Free India Society (London), 31, 32, 53
Freedom (anarchist paper), 34, 133, 134
Freeman, George, 51, 53, 57
Freikorps, 83
French (language), 211
Friedländer, Käthe, 157, 158 *See also*, Kate Ruminov
Fugitive Offenders Act, 39
Fujin Sensen, 164–5

Gaelic American, 51
Galián, Laura, 12
Gandhi, Mahatma, 16, 151–5, 165, 166
  Acharya interacted with, 175
  assassination of, 21–2, 219
  Satyagraha campaign, 7
Gandhian anarchism, 12
Gandhian principles, 224
Gandhism, 7, 8, 9, 19, 151–5, 216
Garcia, Victor, 243–4
Geneva, 57, 58
Genoa, 180
German (language), 211
German Communist Party (KPD), 147, 157
German parliament, 171
German Revolution, 82–3
Getachew, Adom, 22
Ghadar ('Mutiny'), 53, 55
Ghadar Party, 17, 52–5
Ghadarites, 3, 53, 55, 59

Gibel Dersa, 37
Gill, Dalip Singh, 59, 88, 89, 120
Gloss, George, 227–8
God and the State (Bakunin), 204
Godse, Nathuram, 21, 218–19
Goldman, Emma, 53, 111–12, 129, 149
Gonne, Maud, 54
Gopal, Priyamvada, 6, 10
Gordin, Abba, 18, 117, 205
Goswami, Manu, 8
Govinda, Anagarika, 199–200
Govinda, Li Gotami, 199
Grossbeerenstrasse (56C), 174–5
guerrilla warfare, 37–8
Gullick, Donald, 63–4
Gupta, Birendra Nath Das, 57, 64, 67, 84
Gupta, Heramba Lal, 58, 60, 221
Gupta, Nalini Das, 105

Hafis, Abdul, 58, 63, 66, 67, 105, 111
Hagenbeck affair, 136–8
Hagenbeck, John, 137, 138
Hal, Hassan Syed, 48
Halbmondlager (Half Moon Camp), 59
Hamba, Ali Bach, 64, 68
'Hardayalism', 52
Hardie, Keir, 41, 43
Hardikar, N. S., 150
Harijan group, 22
Harijan, 8, 165, 235–6
Havel, Hippolyte, 17, 55
Hesse, W. G., 66
Hindenburg, Paul von, 172
Hindu Mahasabha, 218–19
Hindu nationalism, 21
Hindu, The, 138
Hindusthan Association of America (HAA), 17, 54

334

INDEX

Hindusthan Association of Central Europe (HACE), 52–3, 127, 137, 138, 144, 153

Hindutva ideology, 21, 22

Hitler, Adolf, 171–2

Hoare, Samuel, 175

Holger, Hilde, 199

homosexuality, 164

Hooton, Harry, 233

Hoover, Herbert, 117

Hopkinson, William C., 52, 54

Horsley, Arthur Fletcher, 34, 36

Husain, Maqbul, 64, 65, 66, 67, 68

Huxley, Aldous, 225

Huysmans, Camille, 71, 72, 73–4, 75–6

IAA Pressedienst, 160

IAC Press Service, 152, 153

IAMB Press Service, 146, 147

IIS. *See* Indian Institute of Sociology (IIS)

India (journal), 2, 16, 27, 28, 29, 30, 38

India House (hostel), 3, 30–6

India Office Records (IOR), 14

Indian Civil Liberties Union, 209

Indian Communist Party (ICP), 1, 5, 9, 18, 99, 101–13, 135
  Acharya's membership, 107
  Berlin Indians in Moscow, 110–13
  formation of, 101–2
  Indian revolutionaries in Russia, divisions between, 109–10
  Tashkent meeting, 102, 103

Indian Home Rule Society (IHRS), 30

Indian independence and Partition, 21

Indian Independence Committee (IIC), 4, 17, 57–60, 61, 63, 64, 67, 74, 76, 80, 82–3

Indian independence, 21, 79, 82, 83, 99
  ICP and, 106

Indian Institute of Sociology (IIS), 21, 190, 204, 206

Indian *Muhajirs*, 102

Indian Muslims, 46, 47

Indian National Congress (INC), 28, 79, 152, 165
  Surat meeting (Dec 1907), 28–9

Indian National Corps, 64

Indian News Service and Information Bureau (INSIB), 127

Indian parliament, 14

Indian Press (Emergency powers) Act (1931), 195

Indian Press Service, 166–7

Indian prisoners of war, in Germany, 58–9

Indian propaganda, 80, 81

Indian Revolt (1857), 87

Indian Revolutionaries Abroad Commemoration Committee (IRACC), 221

Indian Revolutionary Association (IRA), 1, 5, 18, 90–4, 99, 105, 106, 107, 112, 117
  message for Lenin, 92–3

Indian Sociologist, The (journal), 30, 34, 36

Indian soldiers, 213

Indian Volunteer Corps, 60

Indian War of Independence of 1857, The (Savarkar), 32, 42

Indian-Persian committee, 64

Indiska Nationalkommittén (Indian National Committee, INK), 17, 73, 74, 75, 76, 77, 80, 81, 82
  Dutch-Scandinavian Committee, breaking with, 78–9

335

INDEX

Indonesia, 150

Industrial and Trade Review for Asia, 127, 136

Industrial Workers of the World (IWW), 52, 150

Inquietud (Uruguay), 206

Institute of Anthropology and Ethnography (Leningrad), 189

Institute of Foreign Languages (Bombay), 231

Internationaal Anti-Militaristisch Jaarboek, 147

International Anti-Militarist Bureau (IAMB), 7, 19, 146, 147, 148, 150, 151, 166

International Antimilitarist Commission (IAC), 15, 19, 146, 148, 150, 151

International Federation of Trade Unions (Amsterdam International), 129

International Pro-India Committee, 54

international socialism, 4, 5, 17, 71–84

International Socialist Congress (Bern, Feb 1919), 83–4

International Socialist Congress (Copenhagen, Aug 1910), 41, 42–3

International Socialist Congress (Stockholm, May 1917), 4, 17, 71–5

International University of Non-Violence, 215

International Working Men's Association (IWMA), 6, 129–30, 131, 140, 146

Internationale Arbeiterhilfe, 158

Internationale der Kriegsdienstgegner, 146

Internationalism, 4, 10, 13, 92, 95, 96, 129, 142, 195, 221, 223, 224

Italo-Turkish war (1911), 16, 46–7

Italy, 44

IWMA Press Service, 129–30, 135, 172, 188, 225

Iyengar, S. Srinivasa, 150

Iyengar, Yogi Parthasarathy, 27

Izvestia, 101

Jabbar Kheiri, Abdul, 64

Jackson, A. M. T., 39

Jahan-i-Islam (periodical), 67

Japanese Anarchist Federation (JAF), 208

Japanese imperialism, 186–7

Jaurès, Jean, 39, 42–3

Jauzin, Paul, 192

Jensen, Albert, 201

Jerusalem, 62, 63

Jinnah, Muhammad Ali, 213–14

Joseph A. Labadie Collection, 210–11

Joshi, N. M., 131, 139, 143, 148–9

Jun, Nathan, 14

Kabul mission, 18, 61–2, 65, 90

Kadir, Fazl, 91, 117

Kahol, Om P., 220

Kaiser-i-Hind, 8, 205, 206

Kaiserplatz (17), 174

Kamala (wife of Nehru), 139

Kanhere, Anant Laxman, 39

Kapila, Shruti, 219

Karakhan, Lev, 95, 105, 112, 118, 120, 161

Karanth, K. S., 150, 232

Karl Frederick, 227–8

Karve, R. D., 164

Kashgar mission, 103–4

Keell, Thomas H., 6, 34, 111, 133, 134–5

INDEX

Kenafick, Kenneth Joseph, 209
Kennard, Coleridge, 75
Kersasp, Hormaz, 60
Khan, Alif, 87, 88
Khan, Amanullah, 91
Khan, Daud, 91
Khan, Razak, 14–15
Khankhoje, Pandurang, 52, 53, 111
Khaparde, G. S., 28
Kinna, Ruth, 13
'Kirtikar' (Indian spy), 31
Klindworth-Scharwenka Conservatory meeting, 87
Kobetsky, Mikhail, 112
Kollontai, Alexandra, 115, 116
Kommunistische Arbeiter-Partei Deutschlands (KAPD), 157, 158
Koning Willem III (Dutch steamer), 38
Korean anarchists, 211
Korean War (1950), 229
Koregaonkar, H. K., 31, 32, 34, 35
Korsch, Karl, 157–8, 227–8
Kraske, Erich, 58
Krishnamurti, Jiddu, 244
Krishnavarma, Shyamaji, 30, 34, 36, 40, 42
Kritischer Marxismus reading group, 20, 157, 158
Kronprinzendamm (19), 176
Kronstadt Rebellion (March 1921), 116, 119, 188
Kropotkin, Peter, 118–19, 207
Krylenko, Elena, 205
Kuijsten, Han, 181
Kushnarev, Theodore, 117

L'Adunata dei Refrattari (USA), 135, 161
L'En Dehors, 20, 160, 162, 164

L'Unique (journal), 200–1, 204
La Chaux-de-Fonds, 180
La Patrie Egyptienne, 54
La Protesta (Argentina), 135, 160, 161
La Revista Blanca (Spain), 160
La Voix du Travail (France), 135, 160
Labour Kisan Party of Hindustan, 130–1
Lakshmi, Vijaya, 140
Landgrafenstrasse (3a), 174
Latvia, 88–9
Le Libertaire (France), 160
League Against Colonial Oppression (LACO), 143, 144
League Against Imperialism (LAI), 19, 143–5, 148, 149, 150, 151, 155
League of Nations, 82, 145
Lenin, Vladimir, 5, 87, 89–90, 94, 97, 116–17, 119
  Acharya's letter to, 95–6
Les Nouvelles Pacifistes, 224–5
Les Plus Belles Pages (Bretonne), 182
'Les Trusts et la Démocratie' (article), 21
Li Pei Kan, 208, 228–9
Libertarian Book Depot, 204
Libertarian Publishing House, 203
Libertarian Socialist, The (Acharya), 206
Libya, 44
Liebknecht, Karl, 83, 88
Lindhagen, Carl, 74, 77
Llano colonies, 133–4
London County Council School of Photo-Engraving and Lithography, 32
Longuet, Jean, 39, 42–3
Lorenzo, José Tato, 225
Los Principios Humanitaristas (Relgis), 225

337

INDEX

Lotvala, Ranchoddas Bhavan, 21, 22, 167
Louvet, Louis, 224–5
LSI. *See* Libertarian Socialist Institute (LSI)
Ludendorff, General, 88
Luhani, Ghulam Ambia Khan, 111
Lützow (German steamer), 37
Luxemburg, Rosa, 83

MacDonald, Ramsay, 84
Mahabharata (epic), 164
Mahajan, Jodh Singh, 43
Mahratta, 135, 189, 194
Malabar Hill, 189
Man! (Graham), 160, 179, 188
Mangan, John J., 117
marriage, 163–4
Marseille, 29, 30
Marx, Karl, 157–8
Marxism, 102, 111, 158, 236
Mashruwala, Kishorlal G., 22, 234
Matchabelli, Georges, 72
Maximoff, Grigori, 130, 204–5, 229–30
Mazumdar, J., 240
Mehra, Kailash Nath, 209
Melillan campaign, 2nd (Aug 1909), 37
Meltzer, Albert, 226–7, 241–2
Menon, K. B., 209
Mexican Communist Party, 93
Mirza, Bahman, 46
Modern Publishers (Indore), 204
Modern School movement, 55
Mohamed, Sher, 64, 65, 66
Moor, Karl, 120
Moramano, Michele, 244–5
Morley, Lord, 40
Muhajirs, 18, 93
Mukherji, Abani, 18, 93, 95, 98, 101, 102, 105, 106, 110, 127, 132

Müller-Lehning, Arthur, 146, 148, 150, 151
Muñoz, Vladimir, 243
Münzenberg, Wilhelm, 143, 144
Mutual Banking (Greene), 204
My Disillusionment in Russia (Goldman), 134
Myasnikov, Gavril, 157, 158–9

Nachman, Magda (wife of Acharya), 1, 7, 11, 20, 167, 176–7
    background, 119
    death of, 8, 22, 231
Nachrichtenstelle für den Orient (Intelligence Bureau for the East, NfO), 57, 58, 88
Nag, Kalidas, 215–16
Naidu, Jaya Surya, 153, 172–3
Naidu, Sarojini, 150, 153, 176
Nambiar, A. C. N., 127, 136–7, 138, 143
Narayan, Jayaprakash, 217
National Indian Association, 34
Nationalism and Culture (Rocker), 191
Nationalsozialistische Deutsche Arbeiterpartei (Nazi Party), 171
Nayik, Kandubhai, 60, 67, 68, 87
Nazism, 7, 8, 20, 171–2, 173
Nehru, Jawaharlal, 19, 139–42, 143, 153, 213
Nehru, Motilal, 139–40, 141
Nettlau, Max, 12
New Delhi, 219
New Economic Policy (NEP), 116–17
Newspapers (Incitement to Offences) Act, 29
nirajya (no-government), 7, 187–8
Nobushima, E. K., 209
non-governed society, 217
non-violence, 16

INDEX

non-violent movement, 187
North America, 209, 215
North East London Anarchist
  Group, 226

Oblast Revolutionary Committee,
  104
October revolution, 77, 116
Oriental Review, 190–1
Ottoman Empire, 57, 59

Pachter, Henry, 158
pacifism, 6–7, 16, 22, 146–7,
  151–2
Padmaja Publishers, 233
Padmore, George, 227
Pakistan, 213
Pal, Bipin Chandra, 35
Pal, Niranjan, 35
Palmer, Edward, 35
pan-Islamic propaganda, 96
Pankhurst, Sylvia, 130
Paranjape, Vasant, 240–1
Paris conference (Sep 1910), 41
Paris Indian Society, 39–41, 43–4
Paris Peace Conference, 83
Paris, 16, 30, 39, 208, 210
  anticolonial alliances in, 41–2
Parthasarathy, P., 126–7, 128
Pasha, Enver, 58, 60, 64
Pasha, Halil, 65–6
Pasha, Mehmed Said, 47
Patel, Vallabhbhai J., 175, 213
Pathik, B. S., 150
People (Indian paper), 19, 136,
  138, 139, 141, 147, 150, 159
People's Commissariat for Foreign
  Affairs (NKID), 89, 106, 112,
  120
Père Lachaise Cemetery, 178
Perumal, Alasinga, 27
Peters, Yakov, 109

Petrograd Soviet, 71, 76, 79
Pillai, Chempakaraman, 4, 54, 57,
  67, 87, 127, 132
Pillai, Padmanabha, 43, 45
Pohrille, Irena, 231
Politisches Archiv des Auswärtigen
  Amts (German Foreign Office
  Political Archives, PAAA), 14
Pondicherry, 2, 16, 29, 30, 38,
  43, 44
Prabhakar, Moreshwar, 57, 76
Prasad, Rajendra, 213, 224
Prasad, Sufi Amba, 45, 64
Pratap, Mahendra, 18, 57, 58, 59,
  60, 84, 87, 88–90, 130
  Kabul mission, 61–2, 65
Pravda (publication), 116
Prevention of Seditious Meetings
  Act, 29
Priestley, J. B., 225
Principles of Non-Violent Economics
  (pamphlet), 21, 215–16
Proudhon, 207
Provisional All-India Central
  Revolutionary Committee
  (PAICRC), 98, 105, 106, 109
Provisional Government of India,
  87, 93–4
Purna Swaraj, 152–3

Rabb, Abdur, 5, 18, 87, 88, 89–
  90, 91, 98, 99, 101, 102, 106,
  107, 108, 109, 117
Rabochii Put (Maximoff), 130
racism, 132
Ragdaev, Nicolai, 18, 99, 118, 205
Rai, Lala Lajpat, 30
Rajan, T. S. S, 31–2
Ramnath, Maia, 10, 11
Rana, Sardarsinhji Ravaji, 3, 31,
  39, 42, 48, 51, 221
Rao, Chanjeri, 40

339

INDEX

Rao, Raja, 216, 229, 233
Rashtriya Swayamsevak Sangh, 219
Ratnagiri, 218
Raza, Haidar, 31, 32, 34
Read, Herbert, 227, 233
Reichstag, 172
Reisner, Igor, 90, 120, 125
    Acharya's letter to, 1–2
Relgis, Eugen, 216, 225
religion, 165–6
Reminiscences of a Revolutionary
    (Acharya), 10, 27–28, 29, 35,
    38, 189
Revolución y Regresión (Rocker),
    128–9
Reynolds, Reginald, 227
Richards, Vernon, 226
Rifat, Mansour, 42, 54, 128
Rifs, 16, 37, 38
Ringbahnstrasse (4), 174
Road to Freedom (USA), 135, 136,
    160
Rocker, Rudolf, 125, 128–9, 191,
    201, 203–4
Rodriguez, Araceli, 207
Röhm, Ernst, 164
Roland Holst, Henriette, 181
Rosenthal, B., 127–8
Rotterdamsche Boek- en
    Kunstdrukkerij, 33, 42
Roy, M. N. (Manabendra Nath
    Bhattacharya), 1, 2, 18, 93, 94,
    95, 96, 97, 98–9, 101, 102–4,
    105, 106, 107, 109–10, 111,
    126, 127, 130, 132, 136, 143,
    144, 157, 159
    Acharya's letter to, 103
    Kabul visit, 108
    'A Programme for the Indian
        National Congress', 130
Roy, Tarachand, 176
Royal Asiatic Society, 202

Rüdiger, Helmut, 224, 233–4, 242
Rue de Ponthieu, 178
Ruminov, Basil, 157, 158, 202
Ruminov, Kate, 202 *See also,*
    Käthe Friedländer
Russell, Bertrand, 225
Russian Revolution (Feb 1917),
    4–5, 71, 84, 87–100, 119
Russian State Political Directorate
    (GPU), 2, 120, 125
Rutgers, Sebald Justinus, 93

Sacco, Nicola, 160
Said, Edward, 15
Saklatvala, Shapurji, 144, 148–9
salt march, 152–3, 154
Sandhurst Road (Bombay), 204
Santiniketan, 223
Sastri, V. S. Srinivasa, 27, 28–9
'Savarkar affair', 41, 42–3
Savarkar Release Committee, 41
Savarkar, Ganesh D., 34, 39
Savarkar, Vinayak Damodar, 3, 16,
    20, 31, 35
    Acharya's views on, 32–3
    anti-Muslim sentiments, 32–3
    fled London for Paris, 39
    Fugitive Offenders Act, 39
    trial for sedition, 39, 40–1
Schapiro, Alexander, 129, 205
Schwantje, Magnus, 157
Scotland Yard, 31, 33, 35
Second Congress of the
    Comintern (1920), 1, 18, 93,
    94–7, 108, 158
Secrétariat Provisoire aux
    Relations Internationales
    (SPRI), 206–7
Section Française de
    l'Internationale Ouvrière, 39
sedition, 28, 29, 30, 36, 38, 41
self-determination, 19, 82, 84, 94,
    97, 152

INDEX

sex and gender relations, 162–5

Shafique, Mohamed, 18, 93, 95, 98, 101, 102, 106

Shkolnikoff, Izya, 118, 205

Shulman, Sam, 205

Siddiq, Nazir, 91, 117

Simon Commission, 152

Singammal (Acharya's mother), 27

Singh, Ajit, 30, 45, 46, 48

Singh, Iqbal, 21, 216, 229, 233

Sino-International Library (Geneva), 177

Smedley, Agnes, 111–12, 129, 138, 141, 143, 149

Smith, C. A., 204

Sneevliet, Henk 'Maring', 93, 96, 97

Snowden, Ethel, 84

Social-Demokraten, 81

Socialism and the State (pamphlet), 203

Socialist, The, 167

Society of Political Missionaries, 53

Souchy, Augustin, 6, 146, 147, 154

Southern Advocate for Workers' Council (Dawson), 202, 209

Soviet International Propaganda (Sovinterprop), 87, 96

Soviet Revolutionary Military Council, 104

Spain, 188

Spanish (language), 211

Spanish Civil War (1936), 20, 188

Spanish colonisers, 37

Special Branch of the Metropolitan Police, 31

SPRI. *See* Secrétariat Provisoire aux Relations Internationales (SPRI)

Srinivasacharya, C., 27, 28, 29

SS *Drottning Victoria*, 72

SS Morea (commercial vessel), 40

SS *Victoria* (ship), 180, 182

Stalin and German Communism (Fischer), 202

State and Revolution, The (Lenin), 94–5

Steelink, Nicolaas, 202

Steinhardt, Karl, 109

Stockholm, 194–5

a hub of anticolonialism, 17, 72–5, 76–8

Stockholms Dagblad, 79

Strickland, Walter, 43, 44, 46, 189

Stuttgart Congress (1907), 189

Subramanyam, C. S., 10

Suda, Kunitaro, 233

Suez Canal mission, 17, 60–1, 62–4

Suhasini (Chatto's sister), 127

Sun Yat-sen, 161

Svenska Dagbladet, 75

swarajya (self-government), 147, 187–8

Sweden, 190

Swedish Social Democratic Left Party, 74, 77, 81

Swedish Social Democrats, 81

Swedish socialism, 81

Swiss Government, 177

Switzerland, 63–4

Sydney University, 233

Tagore, Saumyendranath, 153, 173

Taiji Yamaga, 208–9, 229

Takamure Itsue, 164–5, 209

Talvar (journal), 57

Tangier, 37–8

Tanin (journal), 47, 48

Tawfik, Saiyid Muhammad, 46

Taylor, W. J., 204

Thalheimer, August, 93

The Hague, 41, 44

341

INDEX

Third Congress of the Comintern, 111, 112, 158
Thought (newspaper), 236
Three Principles of the People, 161–2
Tierra y Libertad (Mexico), 206
Tilak Mandir, 189
Tilak, Bal Gangadhar, 28
Times of India (newspaper), 231, 236
Times, The, 35
Tirumalacharya, S. N., 27
Tolstoyans, 218
Trent, Evelyn, 18, 93, 101, 102, 106–7
Troelstra, Pieter Jelles, 71, 75, 76
Trotsky, Leon, 79, 159
Troyanovsky, Konstantin, 77–8, 80
Tsvetaeva, Marina, 119
Turkestan Bureau of the Comintern, 93–4
Twentieth Century Press, 34

ultra-leftists, 157–9
University of Berlin, 59
University of Michigan, 210
US government, 202
Usmani, Shaukat, 102–3, 104–5, 106, 119

Vámbéry, Ármin, 44, 47
van Kol, Henri, 71, 72
Vanzetti, Bartolomeo, 160
Varma, G. C., 35
Varma, L. P., 4, 58, 60, 61, 62–3, 64, 66, 68, 174
Vasantha, 150
Velayudham, M. P. S., 131
Verslag van het Internationale Congres voor Dienstweigering, 146–7
Vestnik NKID (publication), 116
Vinson, Julien, 30

von der Goltz, Wilhelm, 64
von Glasenapp, Helmuth, 82, 88
von Humboldt-Haus, Alexander, 144, 153
Vorosky, Vatslav, 79
Vrienden van India, 182

Wafar, Ghulam Habib, 91
wage-price system, 210
Wahid, Abdul, 66
Wanchoo, D. N., 8, 22, 227–8, 233
War Commentary, 195
War Resister, 167
War Resisters' International (WRI), 146
Weekly Reports of the Director of Criminal Intelligence (WRDCI), 14
Wellock, Wilfred, 138–9
Weltjugendliga, 146
Weltjugendliga: Blätter der Weltjugendliga, 146
Western Socialists, 237
Whiteway Colony, 133–4
Whither India? (Rao), 21
Williams, William, 54
Wilson, Woodrow, 82
Witkop, Rose, 111
Wolfe, Lilian, 133, 225
Woodcock, George, 227
Word, The (Aldred), 204, 219
Workers' Dreadnought, 130, 131
World Congress of Anarchists (1949), 210, 212
World Pacifist Meeting (1949), 223, 224
World War I, 3, 4, 8, 17, 56, 68, 82, 93, 96, 145, 190, 194–5
World War II, 7, 8, 13, 21, 194–5, 213

Yadav, Bishamber Dayal, 10

INDEX

Yagnik, Indulal, 166–7
Yelensky, Boris, 116, 199, 204–5, 237–8
Yoshi Aso, 209
Young Hindusthan Association (YHA), 64
Young India, 147
Young Turks, 16

Zadah, Agha Rahim, 46
Zamindar (periodical), 94
Zetkin, Konstantin, 109
Zimmerwald conference (1917), 76–8
Zinoviev, Grigori, 98, 117, 120
Zürich, 20, 54, 58, 63, 128, 179, 180, 181, 182, 189